trial manual 5 for the defense of criminal cases

Volume 2: Proceedings Between Arraignment and Trial

American Law Institute American Bar Association Committee on Continuing Professional Education

As of April 24, 1989

trial manual 5 for the defense of criminal cases

Volume 2: Proceedings Between Arraignment and Trial

ANTHONY G. AMSTERDAM
of New York University School of Law
Reporter

A JOINT PROJECT OF THE

American College of Trial Lawyers

National Defender Project of the
National Legal Aid and Defender Association

ALI-ABA Committee on
Continuing Professional Education

AMERICAN LAW INSTITUTE-AMERICAN BAR ASSOCIATION
COMMITTEE ON CONTINUING PROFESSIONAL EDUCATION
4025 CHESTNUT STREET • PHILADELPHIA • PENNSYLVANIA 19104

Library of Congress Catalog Number: 88-71176

© 1989 by The American Law Institute. All rights reserved

First Edition 1967. Fifth Edition 1989

Printed in the United States of America

ISBN: 0-8318-0613-3

James D. Maugans of the ALI-ABA staff
supervised the production of this book

FOREWORD

Twenty-five years ago, the American College of Trial Lawyers and the ALI-ABA Joint Committee on Continuing Legal Education, known as ALI-ABA, undertook the preparation of publications and the conduct of courses for lawyers in elementary and advanced civil and criminal trial practice.

The President at the time of the American College of Trial Lawyers, Bernard G. Segal of Philadelphia, appointed a Committee on Professional Education in Trial and Appellate Practice, with the late Hicks Epton of Wewoka, Oklahoma, as Chairman, to oversee the project on behalf of the College.

Because of the urgent national need for lawyers to defend criminal cases, the project was initially oriented to the trial of a criminal case. The National Defender Project of the Legal Aid and Defender Association, the American College of Trial Lawyers, and ALI-ABA furnished the financing.

The sponsors were fortunate to obtain for the preparation of the *Trial Manual for the Defense of Criminal Cases* the brilliant and inspired services of Professor Anthony G. Amsterdam, then a member of the faculty of the Law School of the University of Pennsylvania, as Chief Reporter for the project. They were fortunate, too, in the fact that Professor Amsterdam engaged as Associate Reporters for the *Manual* Messrs. Bernard L. Segal, formerly the First Assistant Defender, Defender Association of Philadelphia, and Martin K. Miller, of the Philadelphia bar, whose zeal and expert contributions added immeasurably to the final product.

In addition to the Committees of the sponsors, the Reporters were assisted in their original endeavor by an able advisory committee[1] and by a national panel of consultants.[2]

---

[1]Lawrence A. Aschenbrenner, *Public Defender for the State of Oregon,* Portland, Oregon; John J. Cleary, *Deputy Director of the National Defender Project,* Chicago, Illinois; Edward Cleary, *University of Illinois College of Law,* Champaign, Illinois; Daniel Freed, *Acting Director, Office of Criminal Justice of the Department of Justice,* Washington, D.C.; Gerald S. Gold, Cleveland, Ohio; Richard A. Green, *Project Director, American Bar Association Project on Minimum Standards for Criminal Justice,* New York, New York; David Hall, *County Attorney,* Tulsa, Oklahoma; Thomas S. Jackson, Washington, D.C.; C. Paul Jones, *Public Defender, State of Minnesota,*

The first edition of the *Trial Manual for the Defense of Criminal Cases* appeared in 1967, and a second edition followed in 1971. In 1972, Professor Amsterdam undertook continuing responsibility for keeping the *Manual* current and produced the third edition, published in 1974 and supplemented in 1975, 1977, and 1978; and the fourth edition, published in 1984, which grew to two volumes.

Although there is no empirical data to measure the degree to which the *Trial Manual for the Defense of Criminal Cases* has advanced the competence of lawyers to defend criminal cases, the pervasive influence of this work is evidenced by the more than 27,000 copies of the various editions that have been purchased since the work first appeared. Without a doubt it has contributed immeasurably to advancing the cause of criminal trial advocacy in the United States.

This new edition, the fifth, has been divided into three volumes, each of which can stand alone, for those attorneys looking for coverage of particular portions of criminal defense process;

Minneapolis, Minnesota; Joseph Sloane, *President Judge, Court of Common Pleas No. 7,* Philadelphia, Pennsylvania; Roszel C. Thomsen, *Chief Judge, United States District Court,* Baltimore, Maryland; William F. Walsh, Houston, Texas.
Ex officio: The President and the Committee on Professional Education in Trial and Appellate Practice of the American College of Trial Lawyers; The ALI-ABA Joint Committee on Continuing Legal Education and Its Director; Association of Continuing Legal Education Administrators represented by: Eli Jarmel, *Administrator, Institute for Continuing Legal Education, Rutgers School of Law,* Newark, New Jersey; Douglas Lanford, *Director, Continuing Legal Education, University of Alabama, Extension Division,* University, Alabama; Peter C. Manson, *Director, J.C.C.L.E., Virginia State Bar and Virginia Bar Association,* Charlottesville, Virginia; Justin Reid, *Director, Pennsylvania Bar Institute,* Harrisburg, Pennsylvania.

[2]Lawrence A. Aschenbrenner, *Public Defender for the State of Oregon,* Portland, Oregon; James J. Doherty, *Chief Assistant to the Public for Cook County,* Chicago, Illinois; Donald Chapman, *Public Defender for Santa Clara County,* San Jose, California; Sam D. Johnson, Director, Houston Legal Foundation, Houston, Texas; Robert Nicco, *Chief Deputy Public Defender of the City and County of San Francisco,* San Francisco, California; Sam Robertson, *Chief, Criminal Division Houston Legal Foundation,* Houston, Texas; William J. Shaw, *Public Defender of St. Louis County,* Clayton, Missouri; Hugh Stanton, *Public Defender of Shelby County,* Memphis, Tennessee; William F. Walsh, Houston, Texas.

as a set, the three volumes will provide a complete manual for all phases of the criminal defense.

The first volume deals with all proceedings from initial client contact through arraignment. This second volume deals with pretrial motions, preparation, and proceedings. Volume three covers all proceedings from the election or waiver of a jury trial through appeal and post-conviction proceedings. Each volume has its own table of cases and subject index. The size of these individual volumes makes them more manageable and, therefore, more easily transported than the large binders used in the previous edition.

This fifth edition incorporates the numerous changes in the law and developments in trial tactics since the publication of the previous editions. A field as fluid and as essential to society as the criminal justice process requires periodic updating through new editions. ALI-ABA is most fortunate that Professor Amsterdam has remained at the helm of this project, thus assuring completeness of coverage and timeliness of the contents.

PAUL A. WOLKIN
Executive Director
American Law Institute-
American Bar Association Committee
on Continuing Professional Education

May 12, 1989

PREFACE

Bernard L. Segal and Martin K. Miller collaborated with me in the first edition of this book. Much of what remains useful in the present edition is the product of their insights and their efforts. My debt to Bernie and Marty continues undiminished. I have so frequently and thoroughly revised the text since 1967, however, that they cannot justly be held responsible for its errors.

Morton S. Freeman was the editor of the early editions and updates; James D. Maugans has edited the more recent ones. To both Mort and Jim, I owe all that any writer can owe to fine, intelligent, sensitive editing. That is a great deal.

Without the encouragement, understanding, and support of Paul A. Wolkin, neither the *Trial Manual* nor the project that produced it would have been possible. Thanks again, Paul.

My other debts would wear upon the reader unjustifiably. I feel them deeply but honor them in silence.

ANTHONY G. AMSTERDAM

CONTENTS

Foreword — **vii**

Preface — **xi**

Chapter 14 — **Defensive Procedures and Considerations Between Arraignment and Trial** **1**

§220   Checklist **1**

§221   Pretrial motions generally **3**

§222   Same **3**

Chapter 15 — **Motions To Suppress Illegally Obtained Evidence** **11**

§223   Illegally obtained evidence **11**

§224   Methods of objection **14**

§225   Issues **17**

§226   Introduction — bibliographical note **19**

§227   The relevant constitutional restraints **20**

§228   The Due Process Clause **22**

§229   The Fourth Amendment — the "warrant theory" and the "general reasonableness theory" **24**

§230   Summary of Fourth Amendment doctrine **29**

§231   Same **35**

§232   The Fifth Amendment privilege **45**

§233   The Sixth and Fifth Amendments rights to counsel **53**

§234   Has anything happened that may give rise to an issue under the constitutional doctrines relating to illegally obtained evidence? **64**

§235   Defendant stopped, accosted, arrested, or taken into custody **66**

§236   The stopping, accosting, or arrest **66**

§237   Postarrest custodial treatment **80**

§238   Body searches, physical examinations, extractions of body fluids, hair, and so forth **83**

§239   Defendant subpoenaed **87**

§240   Entry into premises with which the defendant has more than transitory connections **87**

§240-A   Grounds for exclusion of evidence seized pursuant to an invalid warrant **105**

§241   The concept of "probable cause" **108**

§242   Entry into premises where the defendant is, but with which s/he has only temporary connections . **118**

§243   Police surveillance **121**

§244   Yards, grounds, and outbuildings **129**

§245   Telephone wiretapping **131**

§246   Automobile stoppings, searches, and inspections . 132
§247   Taking of papers or objects from the
        defendant — the "dropsie" problem 145
§248   Search and seizure of objects belonging to the
        defendant, not in the defendant's possession 150
§249   Informers and police spies 156
§250   Investigative activity by private individuals 158
§251   Derivative evidence 160
§252   The motion for suppression 168
§253   Conduct of the hearing on the motion
        to suppress 168
§253-A Presenting defensive evidence at trial to rebut
        prosecution evidence that has been admitted
        over the objection that it was illegally obtained . . . 172

Chapter 16   **Motions for a Change of Venue and
              for Disqualification of a Judge** 173
§254   Initial venue and change of venue 173
§255   Grounds for a defensive motion for change of
        venue 173
§256   The motion for change of venue on the ground
        that a fair trial cannot be had 175
§257   Same 178
§258   Motion for disqualification of a judge 179

Chapter 17   **Motions for Severance or for Consolidation** 181
§259   Joinder; dismissal or severance for misjoinder . . . 181
§260   Severance by reason of prejudicial joinder 182
§261   Consolidation 183
§262   Joinder or consolidation of jury-tried and
        bench-tried cases 184
§263   Considerations favoring and disfavoring joint
        trial of multiple charges against one defendant . . . 184
§264   Considerations favoring and disfavoring joint
        trial of several defendants 186

Chapter 18   **Discovery Proceedings; Pretrial Conference** 191
§265   Traditional limitations of criminal discovery 191
§266   Checklist of self-help discovery devices 192
§267   Formal discovery devices — the bill of particulars
        and the list of witnesses 194
§268   Other formal discovery devices — in general 194
§269   Same — the general position of the defense on
        discovery 199
§270   Same — the constitutional concerns 202

§271 Specific discovery procedures: formal discovery and informal discovery **216**

§272 Defensive discovery at trial **227**

§273 Disclosure of the identity of government informers **227**

§273-A Work product **230**

§273-B Other claims of governmental privilege **231**

§274 Discovery by the prosecution against the defense.. **231**

§275 The pretrial conference **239**

§276 Memorializing the pretrial conference **241**

Chapter 19 **Defense Trial Preparation** **243**

§277 Preparation and organization **243**

§278 Selection of witnesses **243**

§279 Preparing witnesses to testify **244**

§280 Preparing the defendant **249**

§281 Defendant's dress for trial **251**

§282 Codefendants and accomplices **252**

§283 Expert witnesses **252**

§284 Keeping in touch with witnesses for trial; depositions **254**

§285 Compulsory process—subpoenas for witnesses; habeas corpus ad testificandum **255**

§286 Rights to compulsory process **255**

§287 Persons subject to subpoena **257**

§288 Subpoenas to avoid a missing-witness instruction against the defense **257**

§289 Laying a foundation for the missing-witness instruction against the prosecution **259**

§290 Procedure for obtaining subpoenas **259**

§291 Subpoenas duces tecum **260**

§292 Enforcing subpoenas **261**

§293 Review of decisions relating to compulsory process **261**

§294 Preparing real evidence **262**

§295 Tests on physical objects **263**

§296 Photographs and other visual aids **263**

§297 Preparation of a trial folder or "trial brief" and an exhibit file **264**

Chapter 20 **State-Paid Assistance for the Defense** **265**

§298 Availability of state-paid assistance under local practice **265**

§299 Rights under the Equal Protection Clause **266**

§300 Rights under the Due Process Clause 269
§301 Procedures 270

Chapter 21 **The Timing of Pretrial and Trial Proceedings** 273
§302 Terms of court 273
§303 Calendar control 273
§304 Continuances 274
§305 Speeding up the proceeding by waivers 276
§306 Speedy trial rights — generally 276
§307 Sources of speedy trial rights 278
§308 The court's docket control; dismissal for want of
prosecution 278
§309 Statutes delimiting time periods in the pretrial
stages 279
§310 Statutes requiring that prisoners be brought to
trial on demand; the Interstate Agreement 281
§311 State and federal guarantees of speedy trial; the
federal Due Process guarantee 282

Chapter 22 **Interlocutory Review and Prerogative Writs** 289
§312 Obtaining interlocutory review of pretrial orders
by prerogative writ and similar proceedings 289
§313 Mandamus and prohibition 289
§314 The advantages of interlocutory review 292

Table of Cases and Authorities 295

Index of Subjects 321

XIV. DEFENSIVE PROCEDURES AND CONSIDERATIONS BETWEEN ARRAIGNMENT AND TRIAL

[220] Checklist. After arraignment and before trial, counsel will want to consider:

(A) *Matters looking backward to arraignment and prearraignment proceedings: motions for leave to withdraw the plea entered at arraignment:*

(1) Motion for leave to withdraw a plea of not guilty and enter a guilty plea. (Leave is ordinarily freely given. See paragraphs [194], [218] *supra.*)

(2) Motion for leave to withdraw a not guilty plea in order to plead specially or to make prearraignment motions ordinarily waived by the plea. (This motion should be used when counsel wishes to make the special pleas described in paragraphs [192]-[193] *supra* or to raise the prearraignment points noted in paragraph [169] *supra.* Good cause must be shown. If the defendant was unrepresented by counsel at the arraignment, the Sixth Amendment doubtless requires that leave be granted. *See Hamilton v. Alabama,* 368 U.S. 52 (1961); *cf. Stevens v. Marks,* 383 U.S. 234, 243-44 (1966).)

(3) Motion for leave to withdraw a guilty plea or motion to vacate a guilty plea in order to plead specially, raise prearraignment matters, or plead not guilty. (A valid guilty plea may be withdrawn only by leave of court, in the court's discretion, usually for good cause shown. For obvious reasons leave is granted more freely prior to sentencing than after sentencing, whether or not the applicable rules explicitly so provide. (In federal practice a 1983 amendment to Federal Rule of Criminal Procedure 32(d) effectively eliminates the court's discretion to permit the withdrawal of a valid guilty plea after sentencing but liberalizes the standard for permitting withdrawal before sentencing.) Judges differ considerably in their willingness to permit guilty pleas to be withdrawn; and in multijudge courts where the judges rotate assignments from time to time, defense counsel should inquire of experienced criminal lawyers concerning the respective judges' attitudes, obtain the assignment schedule, and time the motion accordingly. The argument that a defendant

1

ought to be routinely permitted to withdraw a guilty plea before sentence, at least when neither the prosecutor nor the court has relied upon it to their disadvantage, has so far failed to command a majority of the Supreme Court of the United States, *see Neely v. Pennsylvania,* 411 U.S. 954 (1973) (opinion of Justice Douglas, dissenting from denial of *certiorari*); *cf. Dukes v. Warden,* 406 U.S. 250 (1972); but it is worth making in any reasonably enlightened state appellate court, as a matter of sound procedure if not of constitutional right, in any case in which there is no other ground on which to challenge as an abuse of discretion a trial judge's refusal to allow withdraw of a guilty plea before sentence. Of course, instead of (or in addition to) invoking judicial discretion to permit withdrawal of the plea, counsel may attack the validity of the plea by a motion to vacate, on such grounds as involuntariness, lack of understanding, or denial or inadequacy of counsel at the time the plea was made. The available grounds are listed in paragraph [195] *supra.* Conviction following denial of a motion to withdraw or to vacate a guilty plea may ordinarily be appealed. If the guilty plea is vacated or withdrawn by leave of the court, it may not be used against the defendant as evidence of guilt at a subsequent trial upon a plea of not guilty. This proposition was settled in federal practice by *Kercheval v. United States,* 274 U.S. 220 (1927); *see also* FED. R. CRIM. P. 11(e)(6); FED. R. EVID. 410; and the *Kercheval* rule appears to have been constitutionalized by dictum in *Hutto v. Ross,* 429 U.S. 28, 30 n.3 (1976) (per curiam).)

(B) *Matters looking forward to trial:*

(1) Required notices. (Occasionally the defendant is required to file, within a designated period prior to trial, specified notices relating to matters s/he intends to raise at trial. The most commonly required are notices of intention to present evidence of alibi or of insanity. See paragraph [193] (G), (H) *supra.* Failure to file the notice precludes the presentation of the defense except in the discretion of the court. But see paragraph [193] (H). Local practice should be consulted regarding the time and form of required notices.)

(2) Motions to suppress illegally obtained evidence. [Paragraphs [223]-[253-A] *infra*]

(3) Motions for a change of venue. [Paragraphs [254]-[257] *infra*]

(4) Motions for disqualification of a judge. [Paragraph [258] *infra*]

(5) Motions for severance or consolidation. [Paragraphs [259]-[264] *infra*]

(6) Motions for production, depositions, and other discovery proceedings. [Paragraph [265]-[273] *infra*]

(7) Pretrial conference. [Paragraphs [275]-[276] *infra*]

(8) Election of jury trial. [Paragraphs [316]-[318] *infra*]

(9) Challenge to the venire of petit jurors. [Paragraphs [319]-[324] *infra*]

(10) Investigation of prospective jurors. [Paragraph [325] *infra*]

(C) The matter of delay. [Paragraphs [302]-[311] *infra*]

[221] Pretrial motions generally. The various sorts of pretrial motions discussed in the following sections are ordinarily required to be made in writing. Written motions are filed with the clerk of court and copies served on the prosecutor. If the disposition of a motion requires argument or hearing, it is often customary to file a notice of motion and to serve a copy of the notice on the prosecutor. The notice states the date and time when counsel will present the motion in open court and proceed to argument or evidentiary hearing. Counsel should arrange the notice date in advance with the clerk of court, court administrator, or judge. Motions may be required by court rules to conform to specified forms. Local practice should be consulted.

[222] Same. (A) When local practice gives a defendant the option to make pretrial motions orally or in writing, it is ordinarily better to make them in writing. Written motions assure that both the relief sought by the defense and the grounds upon which it is sought are preserved in the record, whereas oral motions entail the risk that counsel may omit to make (or the court reporter may fail to hear) significant points. Many state appellate courts will not entertain claims of error unless the record shows that the specific legal contention sought to be raised on appeal was presented to the trial court; and federal constitutional contentions must ordinarily be made in state trial courts with explicit reference to the provision of the Constitution on which counsel relies, in order to support subsequent Supreme Court review (paragraph [472](B) *infra*) and to avoid the danger that the federal claim will be held to have been waived for purposes of postconviction federal habaeas corpus (paragraph [472](D) *infra*). *See Hill v. California,* 401 U.S. 797, 805-6 (1971); *Wainwright v. Sykes,* 433 U.S. 72 (1977). If, for any reason, a motion *is* made orally, counsel should be sure that a stenographer or reporter is present. Similarly, a stenographer or reporter should be present when the judge rules orally on any matter.

(B) When counsel's position on a motion depends upon the establishment of facts that are not already in the record, counsel should decide whether to request an evidentiary hearing of the motion or to file supporting factual affidavits with the motion. Local practice may, of course, compel one of these procedures or the other. If it leaves the option to the movant, counsel will want to consider a number of factors in making the choice:

(1) The relative persuasiveness of the factual showings that can be made, respectively, by affidavit and by live testimony;

(2) The opportunities that an evidentiary hearing may give the defense for pretrial discovery of the prosecution's case (see paragraph [266] *infra*);

(3) The opportunities that an evidentiary hearing may give the prosecution for pretrial discovery of the defendant's case and for locking defense witnesses into impeachable positions by cross-examination;

(4) The delay of the trial that may be necessitated by a pretrial evidentiary hearing; and

(5) In courts in which "long" or evidentiary pretrial motions are heard by a different judge from "short" or on-the-papers motions, the judge who will be most favorable to the defense.

In some jurisdictions, on some motions, factual affidavits are required to be filed in support of the request for an evidentiary hearing itself. These kinds of affidavits should be kept as brief and undetailed as local practice allows, in order to avoid giving the prosecution a preview of the affiant's testimony at the up-coming hearing.

(C) Similarly, in the drafting of written motions that will have to be presented at an evidentiary hearing, the best practice generally is (within the confines of applicable local rules) (1) to state the relief wanted with great clarity; (2) to state the source of law relied on (statute, constitutional provision, and so forth) specifically; but (3) to disclose as little as is possible of the legal theory and the factual matter that will be presented in support of the motion. It makes no sense to give the prosecution unnecessary advance notice of counsel's evidence, which the prosecutor can then arrange at leisure to rebut, or to give the prosecutor advance notice of counsel's legal theories, to which the prosecutor can then adjust the prosecution's proof. If counsel thinks it is desirable to clarify the defendant's factual and legal contentions for the court, this can be done by a brief, filed and served *at the close* of the evidentiary hearing.

(D) Local practice may also give the defendant the option of raising certain defenses and contentions either by pretrial motion or at trial. Choice between these options implicates a number of considerations:

(1) Election of the pretrial motion forum ordinarily results in an earlier adjudication of the issues raised. This may be important not only when success on the issues will require dismissal of the entire prosecution, so that termination of the case in the defendant's favor is expedited, but also when success on the issues will weaken the prosecution's litigating posture or morale and so increase the defendant's leverage in plea bargaining. (Conversely, when there is substantial likelihood that the defense will lose the issues no matter when they are presented, they may be more effective bargaining counters if mentioned to the prosecutor during plea negotiations as contentions that the defendant intends to raise at trial rather than being raised and definitively lost prior to the negotiation.) Presentation of matters on pretrial motion may have other advantages: *inter alia,* the allowance of ample time for the defense to seek pretrial appellate review of adverse rulings to the extent that review is legally available (see paragraphs [312]-[314] *infra*); the provision of defensive discovery opportunities

(see paragraphs [265]-[266] *infra*); the chance to draw a favorable judge on a pretrial motions listing (see subparagraph (B)
supra; see also paragraph [218] *supra*); and the avoidance of
the risks that lengthy sidebar proceedings or proceedings in
the jury's absence on defense motion at trial (see paragraphs
[358]-[359], [413]-[414] *infra*) will bore or irritate the jurors or
that prejudicial material exposed in these proceedings will be
leaked to the jury. In addition, when close questions of law or
fact or issues committed to trial court discretion are presented
by defense requests for relief that does not terminate the prosecution but only affects the time or manner of trial proceedings, judges understandably tend to be more sympathetic to
the position of the defense on pretrial motion than after the
parties have prepared and appeared for trial. If these considerations preponderate, counsel will want to employ any applicable pretrial motions procedure provided by statute or
court rule for raising issues alternatively raisable by motion or
objection at trial (for example, in federal practice, FED. R.
CRIM. P. 12(d)(2)); and if neither statues nor rules authorize
such procedures, counsel will want to be resourceful in in-
venting them. In a number of jurisdictions, for example,
courts will entertain common-law motions *in limine* seeking
pretrial rulings on:

   (a) Issues of law whose disposition importantly affects de-
       fense trial strategy (such as the admissibility of evi-
       dence that the prosecution is expected to offer to im-
       peach the defendant if the defendant elects to testify),
       e.g., New Jersey v. Portash, 440 U.S. 450 (1979);

   (b) The admissibility of prosecution evidence that if men-
       tioned in the prosecutor's opening statement or prof-
       fered at trial may prejudice the defendant despite an
       eventual ruling by the trial judge sustaining a defense
       objection to the evidence, *e.g., Gasaway v. State,* 249
       Ind. 241, 231 N.E.2d 513 (1967); *State v. Latham,* 30
       Wash. App. 776, 638 P.2d 592, 594-95 (1982), *aff'd,*
       100 Wash. 2d 59, 667 P.2d 56 (1983);

   (c) The admissibility of defense evidence, *cf. United States v.
       Helstoski,* 442 U.S. 477 (1979) (prosecution motion for

ruling *in limine* on the admissibility of prosecution evidence); or

(d) Issues of law whose disposition renders the presentation of certain defense evidence unnecessary or irrelevant, *e.g., Lewis v. United States,* 445 U.S. 55 (1980).

See Peskin, Innovative Pre-Trial Motions in Criminal Defense, 1 AM. J. TRIAL ADVOCACY 35, 64-73 (1977), and authorities collected; *Luce v. United States,* 469 U.S. 38, 41 n.4 (1984) (dictum). (The latter two kinds of motions *in limine* are particularly useful when defense counsel expects to lose the motion at the trial level but wishes to preserve the legal issue for appeal and when the defense evidence in question is difficult or costly to gather or present or is inconsistent with alternative defense trial strategies or may be less persuasive factually than is the legal claim for its admissibility.)

(2) On the other hand, there may be considerable advantages to postponing the presentation of certain defenses and contentions until after trial has begun. Some defense contentions will be more compelling in the context of the case as it develops at trial than in isolation as they appear on pretrial motion. Local practice may permit prosecutorial appeals (or petitions for prerogative writs) following pretrial rulings but not following rulings made in the course of trial. And the beginning of trial marks the point at which jeopardy attaches for purposes of the federal constitutional guarantee against double jeopardy. See paragraph [177] *supra.* Rulings in favor of the defendant prior to that point may be appealed by the prosecution (to the extent permitted by local practice), *Serfass v. United States,* 420 U.S. 377 (1975); *United States v. Sanford,* 429 U.S. 14 (1976) (per curiam); *United States v. Helstoski, supra,* 442 U.S. at 487 n.6; whereas rulings in favor of the defendant after that point may not be appealed (a) if they are tantamount to an acquittal (as defined in paragraph [177] *supra*), *United States v. Martin Linen Supply Co.,* 430 U.S. 564 (1977); *Sanabria v. United States,* 437 U.S. 54 (1978); *Smalis v. Pennsylvania,* 106 S. Ct. 1745 (1986); *United States v. Wilson,* 420 U.S. 332, 351-52 (1975) (dictum); *Arizona v. Manypenny,* 451 U.S. 232, 246 (1981) (dictum); *see also United States v.*

DiFrancesco, 449 U.S. 117, 129-30 (1980) (dictum), or (b) if they result in an acquittal, *Sanabria v. United States, supra* (ruling excluding certain prosecution evidence). Rulings in favor of the defendant after jeopardy attaches probably also cannot be appealed if they result in the termination of the trial prior to a general verdict or finding of guilty, other than upon the defendant's own motion, *compare United States v. Scott,* 437 U.S. 82 (1978), *with United States v. Jenkins,* 420 U.S. 358 (1975) (explicitly overruled by *United States v. Scott, supra,* but on reasoning that applies only "where the defendant himself seeks to have the trial terminated without any submission to either judge or jury as to his guilt or innocence," *id.,* 437 U.S. at 101), *and Finch v. United States,* 433 U.S. 676 (1977) (per curiam) — as, for example, when the charges are dismissed by the court *sua sponte* or at the instance of the prosecution following a trial ruling in favor of the defendant upon a motion or objection that does not affirmatively request dismissal or a mistrial, *cf. Crist v. Bretz,* 437 U.S. 28 (1978) — at least in the absence of "a manifest necessity" for terminating the trial (see paragraph [177] *supra;* paragraph [422] *infra*). (Prosecutorial appeals from rulings dismissing the charges or sustaining a motion in arrest of judgement *after* a general verdict or finding of guilty are permitted if they do not contemplate further trial proceedings on factual issues going to guilt. *United States v. Wilson, supra: United States v. Morrison,* 429 U.S. 1 (1976) (per curiam); *United States v. Kopp,* 429 U.S. 121 (1976) (per curiam); *United States v. Ceccolini,* 435 U.S. 268, 270-71 (1978); *United States v. Scott, supra,* 437 U.S. at 100 n.13; *and see United States v. DiFrancesco, supra* 449 U.S. at 130.) Although the law in this area is tortuous and badly confused, the bottom line is that serious, often insurmountable practical, statutory, and constitutional difficulties impede appeals by the prosecution from midtrial rulings in the defendant's favor, whereas pretrial (or postrial) rulings of identical purport can be readily appealed. Similarly, a pretrial ruling sustaining a defense or a defensive contention and dismissing the charging paper will ordinarily not preclude the prosecutor from filing new charges that avoid the defects of the old, *see*

Collins v. Loisel, 262 U.S. 426, 429 (1923); whereas an acquittal at trial will bar refiling, *cf. Fong Foo v. United States,* 369 U.S. 141, 143 (1962) (per curiam); and other sorts of post-jeopardy rulings in the defendant's favor may also preclude reprosecution within the doctrines summarized in paragraph [422] *infra.*

XV. MOTIONS TO SUPPRESS
ILLEGALLY OBTAINED EVIDENCE

[223] Illegally obtained evidence. (A) Under federal constitutional doctrines that have undergone elaborate development in the years since *Mapp v. Ohio,* 367 U.S. 643 (1961), evidence obtained by law enforcement officers in violation of certain guarantees of the Constitution is inadmissible in state or federal criminal trials upon objection by a proper party. Evidence obtained in violation of some statutory and other subconstitutional regulations of police conduct is similarly excluded. (*See, e.g., United States v. Chavez,* 416 U.S. 562 (1974), and cases cited together with *Chavez* in paragraph [243](B) *infra* (construing 18 U.S.C. §2518(10)(a) so as to require the exclusion of evidence obtained in violation of some, but not all, federal statutory restrictions of electronic surveillance); *McNabb v. United States,* 318 U.S. 332 (1943), and *Mallory v. United States,* 354 U.S. 449 (1957), described in paragraph [127](C) *supra* (requiring the exclusion of confessions obtained from arrested persons during periods of delay in taking them before a magistrate in violation of Federal Rule of Criminal Procedure 5(a) and its predecessor statute); *United States v. Caceres,* 440 U.S. 741 (1979) (refusing to exclude evidence obtained in violation of Internal Revenue Service regulations governing electronic surveillance).)

(B) These exclusionary rules are important to defense counsel for several reasons. Frequently (particularly in possession crimes), the entire case against a defendant is based on challengeable police-seized evidence, and successful objection to that evidence terminates the prosecution. Even when the objection is overruled, the ruling my provide a fertile source of reversible error on an appeal, since the controlling federal constitutional doctrines are evolving and far from clear. The mere opportunity to litigate issues relating to asserted police illegality is often a matter of consequence. When those issues are litigated before trial on the issue of guilt, they may provide the defense valuable opportunities for discovery of the prosecution's case on the merits. (See paragraphs [265]-[266] *infra.*) In instances in which police conduct is particularly reprehensible, the unpleasant prospect of its exposure at a hearing may occasionally persuade the prosecutor to drop charges (see paragraph [100] *supra*), or it may give the defense considerable leverage in plea bargaining (see paragraph [212] *supra*).

(C) Exclusionary rules saw their broadest expansion under the Warren Court, following the seminal *Mapp* decision, subparagraph (A) *supra*. The Burger and Rehnquist Courts have been relatively hostile to them, saying with increasing stridency in various formulations that "[w]hile we believe the exclusionary rule serves a necessary purpose, it obviously does so at a considerable cost to society as a whole, because it excludes evidence probative of guilt." *Malley v. Briggs,* 106 S. Ct. 1092, 1098 (1986). Accordingly, the Court has "cautioned against expanding 'currently applicable exclusionary rules by erecting additional barriers to placing truthful and probative evidence before state juries. . . .'" *Colorado v. Connelly,* 107 S. Ct. 515, 521-22 (1986), quoting *Lego v. Twomey,* 404 U.S. 477, 488-89 (1972). Refusals to apply the rules in various settings have been justified by employing a "pragmatic analysis of the exclusionary rule's usefulness in a particular context," *Stone v. Powell,* 428 U.S. 465, 488 (1976), which begins from the premise that "'the rule is a judicially created remedy designed to safeguard [constitutional] . . . rights generally through its deterrent effect . . .,'" *id.,* at 486, quoting *United States v. Calandra,* 414 U.S. 338, 348 (1974), and proceeds through the logic that, "[a]s in the case of any remedial device, 'the application of the rule has been restricted to those areas where its remedial objectives are thought most efficaciously served.'" *Stone v. Powell, supra,* 428 U.S. at 486-87, quoting *United States v. Calandra, supra,* 414 U.S. at 348. *See also* the cases cited together with *Stone* in paragraph [253](E) *infra; and see Kimmelman v. Morrison,* 106 S. Ct. 2574, 2583-84 (1986) (dictum). It was upon this reasoning that *Stone* repudiated the enforcement of the Fourth Amendment exclusionary rule through postconviction remedies (with some exceptions), see paragraph [472](D) *infra,* and that *Calandra* refused to apply the exclusionary rule to grand jury proceedings, see paragraph [172](D) *supra*. Similar reasoning has been invoked to permit the impeachment of a defendant's testimony by evidence obtained in violation of the Fourth Amendment and by his or her pretrial statements obtained without *Miranda* warnings, see paragraph [390](H) *infra,* and to limit the scope of "taint" of

Fourth Amendment, Sixth Amendment, and *Miranda* violations, see paragraph [251] *infra; Segura v. United States,* 468 U.S. 796, 804-5 (1984) (refusing to exclude evidence derived from an "'independent source'" following an unconstitutional search); *Murray v. United States,* 108 S. Ct. 2529 (1988) (extending *Segura* to evidence observed during the unconstitutional search); *United States v. Ceccolini,* 435 U.S. 268, 273-79 (1978), paragraph [251](A)(1) *infra* (restricting the exclusion of the testimony of witnesses whose incriminatory information came to the attention of the authorities through an unconstitutional search); *Nix v. Williams,* 467 U.S. 431, 441-46 (1984) (adopting the "inevitable discovery exception to the [Sixth Amendment] exclusionary rule," *id.* at 441, so as to admit evidence obtained as a consequence of an uncounseled confession "[i]f the prosecution can establish by a preponderance of the evidence that the information ultimately or inevitably would have been discovered by lawful means" in any event, *id.* at 444); *Oregon v. Elstad,* 470 U.S. 298, 304-9 (1985) (rejecting the submission that a confession obtained in violation of *Miranda* necessarily taints a subsequent confession because "the 'cat is out of the bag,'" *id.* at 304). In *United States v. Leon,* 468 U.S. 897 (1984), the Court began to use the same reasoning to support the creation of even broader "exceptions" to the exclusionary rule. *Leon* holds that evidence obtained by police officers in the execution of a "search warrant issued by a detached and neutral magistrate but ultimately found to be unsupported by probable cause," *id.* at 900, should not be suppressed unless "the officers were dishonest or reckless in preparing their affidavit or could not have harbored an objectively reasonable belief in the existence of probable cause" for the warrant, *id.* at 926. (*See also Malley v. Briggs, supra,* 106 S. Ct. at 1098, describing an "analogous question [as] . . . whether a reasonably well-trained officer in [the same] . . . position would have known that his affidavit failed to establish probable cause and that he should not have applied for the warrant.") Whether *Leon* presages the emergence of a general "good-faith exception to the . . . exclusionary rule," 468 U.S. at 913, remains to be seen. *See Arizona v. Hicks,* 107 S. Ct. 1149, 1155 (1987); *California v. Greenwood,* 108 S. Ct. 1625, 1631 (1988). So far, the Supreme Court has extended *Leon* only so far as to sustain the admission of evidence obtained by a search under a warrant that was invalid because the issuing judge had made a technical error in writing up the description in the warrant of the items to be seized, *Massachusetts v. Sheppard*, 468 U.S. 981 (1984), and of evidence obtained by a search made "in objectively reasonable reliance upon a *statute* authorizing warrantless administrative searches, but where the statute is ultimately found to violate the Fourth Amendment," *Illinois v. Krull*, 107 S. Ct. 1160, 1163 (1987) (emphasis in original) — that is, where any constitutional "defect in the statute was not sufficiently obvious so as to render a police officer's reliance upon the statute objectively unreasonable," *id.* at 1172, as might have been the case if the statute had offended "clearly established . . . constitutional rights of which a reasonable person would have known," *id.* at 1170.

[224] **Methods of objection.** Illegally obtained evidence is generally challenged by one or more of four methods:

(A) *Proceedings to quash search warrants or for the return of items seized in searches.* These proceedings are commonly authorized by the statutes that govern the issuance of warrants, although in some jurisdictions they are entertained by courts of equity without express statutory authority. In states where the proceedings rest exclusively upon statute, they may be allowed by some warrant-authorizing statutes (for example, statutes authorizing warrants for the seizure of obscene books or films) but not others (for example, statutes authorizing warrants for the seizure of gambling paraphernalia), or they may be allowed in connection with all search warrants or (less frequently) with searches generally, including warrantless searches. Proceedings to quash search warrants or for the return of seized items can usually be instituted immediately following the execution of a warrant and for some designated period thereafter. These proceedings are independent of the criminal prosecution (that is, they have a separate docket number, style, and calendar and may even be heard in a different court), and upon their disposition an appeal is usually allowable without awaiting further proceedings in the related criminal matter. Counsel should ordinarily make early use of these procedures, with relation to the progress of the criminal case, (1) in order to take advantage of the discovery opportunities of the hearing provided by the procedures at an early stage in the investigation of the criminal case; (2) in order to obtain the return or suppression of seized evidence before it can be used in the initial stages of the prosecution — that is, at the preliminary hearing and before the grand jury — stages at which its use may not be effectively challengeable within the criminal proceeding itself (see paragraphs [159], [172](D) *supra*); and (3) in order to have the evidence declared illegal and returned or suppressed prior to the criminal trial date, since protracted litigation, including appeals, may be necessary in the collateral proceeding. Applications for continuances of the criminal case pending disposition of the warrant-quashing proceeding may be advised. Local practice must be consulted.

(B) *Pretrial motions to suppress or for the return of illegally seized evidence.* These motions, authorized by rule or statute, are made in the criminal proceeding itself. *See, e.g.,* FED. R. CRIM. P. 12(b)(3), 41(e), (f); *compare G.M. Leasing Corp. v. United States,* 429 U.S. 338, 359-60 (1977). The provisions authorizing them are often limited in terms of the sort of contentions that may be presented; for example, motions may lie to suppress the products of unconstitutional searches and seizures condemned by the Fourth Amendment, but not the products of unconstitutional self-incrimination condemned by the Fifth. They are not usually limited in terms of the sort of objects that are sought to be suppressed; they do not, as do the search-warrant-quashing provisions described in subparagraph (A) *supra,* apply only to narcotics case, obscenity cases, or gambling cases. The authorizing statutes or rules fix the stage of the criminal proceeding at which the motions can or must be made. This may be as early as preliminary arraignment; it may be at or before arraignment; or it may be any time before trial (or more than a specified number of days before trial). An increasing number of jurisdictions are coming to require that challenges to illegally obtained evidence be made by pretrial motion rather than by objection or motion at trial (procedure (D) *infra*). (Federal Rules of Criminal Procedure 12(b)(3) and 41(f) so require in federal prosecutions.) Timely filing of the pretrial motions within the deadlines specified by statute or court rule, or by order of the court in the particular case, is indispensable to preserve the defendant's constitutional rights. *See Wainwright v. Sykes,* 433 U.S. 72 (1977). In addition, when counsel has the option of filing a suppression motion earlier or later in the pretrial process, it is ordinarily best to make suppression motions before preliminary hearing or before the presentation of the case to the grand jury, in order to deprive the prosecution of the use of the challenged evidence at those stages. See paragraphs [159], [172](D) *supra.* Denial of the motions is ordinarily unappealable as interlocutory; it may be reviewed on appeal from conviction. Some courts will entertain pretrial motions of this sort without express authority of statute or court rule; these motions may be titled "motion *in limine*" (see paragraph [222](D)(1) *supra*) or simply "motion to suppress [and for the return of] illegally obtained evidence." Again, local practice should be checked.

(C) *Motions to quash the indictment on the ground that illegally obtained evidence was used before the grand jury or to quash the magistrate's transcript or the information on the ground that illegally obtained evidence was admitted at the preliminary hearing.* The allowability of these motions is debatable in most jurisdictions. See paragraphs [146], [171], [172](C), (D) *supra.*

(D) *Objections to admission of the evidence at trial or motions to exclude it at trial.* These are ordinarily heard by the court out of the presence of the jury. See paragraph [358] *infra.* Trial rulings are, of course, interlocutory, but claims of error in the rulings may be made on appeal from conviction. Some jurisdictions that require pretrial motions to suppress (see subparagraph (B) *supra*) give the trial judge discretion to hear (1) untimely motions, first filed at trial, and (2) renewed motions, following a pretrial denial (*see United States v. Raddatz,* 447 U.S. 667, 678 n.6 (1980) (dictum); *cf. Luce v. United States,* 469 U.S. 38, 41-42 (1984) (dictum)). The refusal of the trial judge to entertain a federal constitutional objection in the exercise of this discretion may open the objection to subsequent consideration by the federal courts under the principle of *Williams v. Georgia,* 349 U.S. 375, 382-89 (1955), paragraph [192] *supra,* despite *Stone v. Powell,* 428 U.S. 465 (1976), paragraph [472](D) *infra.* Federal review should certainly be available when the discretion allowed by state law "has [not] been consistently or regularly applied" by the state courts. *Johnson v. Mississippi,* 108 S. Ct. 1981, 1987 (1988). In any event, if the facts underlying a constitutional challenge to prosecution evidence become apparent to the defense for the first time at trial, the trial court is probably constitutionally required to hear the challenge. *Gouled v. United States,* 255 U.S. 298, 305 (1921). It is unquestionably required to do so if the failure of the defense to learn about those facts at an earlier time was the result of their concealment by the prosecutor. *Cf. Amadeo v. Zant,* 108 S. Ct. 1771 (1988). The trial court may also be required to exclude evidence if the facts appearing at trial clearly show that it was the product of a violation of the defendant's constitutional rights, even though a pretrial motion to suppress was denied on a less convincing record. *See Gouled v. United States, supra,* 255 U.S. at 312-13.

[225] **Issues.** The issues raised by an objection to evidence on the ground that it was illegally obtained are basically four:

(A) *Has there been a violation of the substantive rules prescribed by the Constitution or relevant laws to govern the conduct of law enforcement authorities?* The principal constitutional provisions enforced by exclusionary sanctions are identified in paragraph [227] *infra* and described in paragraphs [228]-[233] *infra.* The substantive rules that they impose on the conduct of law enforcement authorities are treated in paragraphs [236]-[249] *infra* — the heart of the present chapter — and also in paragraphs [363] and [374] *infra.* (The constitutional provisions and their exclusionary sanctions have only limited applicability to the conduct of private individuals; this is discussed in paragraph [250] *infra.*) As indicated in paragraph [226] *infra,* most of the following discussion is organized by types of law enforcement activity that counsel may have occasion to challenge — for example, arrests and detentions, interrogations, building searches, auto searches, electronic surveillance. When statutory and other subconstitutional rules are enforced by exclusionary sanctions (see paragraph [223](A) *supra*), they are also discussed in connection with the sorts of law enforcement activity that they govern. Paragraphs [234] and [235] serve as an index to the categories of law enforcement activity covered.

(B) *Is the evidence in question sufficiently connected with the substantive violation to be tainted by it? See, e.g., United States v. Karo,* 468 U.S. 705, 719-21 (1984). This subject is addressed primarily in paragraph [251] *infra,* but subspecies of the question applicable to particular law enforcement activities are also discussed in paragraphs [236](A), [237](B), [241](B)(8), and [363](N) *infra.*

(C) *Did the violation infringe the defendant's own interests, so that s/he may complain of it?* Prior to *Rakas v. Illinois,* 439 U.S. 128 (1978), this question was ordinarily put in terms of whether the defendant had "standing" to complain of the violation. *Rakas* changed the terminology — at least in Fourth Amendment search-and seizure cases — to "whether the disputed search and seizure has infringed an interest of the defendant which the Fourth Amendment was designed to protect." *Id.* at 140. *See also United States v. Payner,* 447 U.S. 727, 731-32 (1980); *United States v. Salvucci,* 448 U.S. 83, 95 (1980); *Rawlings v. Kentucky,* 448 U.S. 98 104-6 (1980). But *Rakas* also recognized that this terminological change would seldom affect either the nature of the inquiry or its result, 439 U.S. at 138-9, and it is likely that the term "standing" will continue to be used to some extent at least as a conclusionary label to designate the inquiry whether a particular defendant "is entitled to contest the legality of [the law enforcement conduct which s/he challenges as the basis for invoking the exclusionary rule]," *id.* at 140; *see United States v. Payner, supra,* 447 U.S. at 731; *United States v. Karo,* subparagraph (B) *supra,* 468 U.S. at 720-21; *United States v. Leon,* 468 U.S. 897, 910 (1984). This inquiry is discussed in the context of various specific law enforcement activities in paragraphs [240](A), [242](B), (C) and (E), [243](C), [245](C), [246](F), and [248](A) *infra.*

(D) *Does some exception to the exclusionary rule apply, making the evidence admissible?* See paragraph [223](C) *supra;* paragraphs [240-A], [253](E) *infra.* Although a trend toward retrenchment of the exclusionary rule is apparent, the Supreme Court still appears to conceive of the inadmissibility of unconstitutionally obtained evidence as being the general rule, with admissibility in specified circumstances being the exception. *See, e.g., Illinois v. Krull,* 107 S. Ct. 1160, 1165 (1987) ("[w]hen evidence is obtained in violation of the Fourth Amendment, the judicially developed exclusionary rule usually precludes its use in a criminal proceeding against the victim of the illegal search and seizure").

[226] Introduction — bibliographical note. (A) Each of the four issues just stated is the subject of an extensive jurisprudence. The subordinate problems and doctrines relating to each are multiple and complex, the law uncertain and in flux. Commentaries on these subjects abound. The best general treatment of Fourth Amendment law relating to search and seizure is Professor Wayne LaFave's multi-volume treatise, LAFAVE, SEARCH AND SEIZURE (1978). Also useful are COOK, CONSTITUTIONAL RIGHTS OF THE ACCUSED — PRETRIAL RIGHTS 175-461 (1972); HALL, SEARCH AND SEIZURE (1982); MARKLE, THE LAW OF ARREST AND SEARCH AND SEIZURE (1974); RINGEL, SEARCHES & SEIZURES, ARRESTS AND CONFESSIONS (2d ed. 1979/1980); VARON, SEARCHES, SEIZURES AND IMMUNITIES (2d ed. 1974). Regarding interrogation and confessions, *see* COOK, CONSTITUTIONAL RIGHTS OF THE ACCUSED — TRIAL RIGHTS 271-368 (1974); GEORGE, CONSITUTIONAL LIMITATIONS ON EVIDENCE IN CRIMINAL CASES 257-332 (1973 printing); KAMISAR, POLICE INTERROGATION AND CONFESSIONS: ESSAYS IN LAW AND POLICY (1980); RINGEL, *op. cit. supra;* ZAGEL, CONFESSIONS AND INTERROGATIONS AFTER MIRANDA: A COMPREHENSIVE OUTLINE OF THE LAW (1971); Young, *Confessions and Interrogations,* in PUBLIC DEFENDER SOURCEBOOK 327 (Singer, ed. 1976). Regarding lineups and other staged identifications, *see* COOK, CONSTITUTIONAL RIGHTS OF THE ACCUSED — TRIAL RIGHTS 179-223 (1974); LOFTUS, EYEWITNESS TESTIMONY (1979); LOFTUS & DOYLE, EYEWITNESS TESTIMONY: CIVIL AND CRIMINAL (1987); MARKLE, CRIMINAL INVESTIGATION AND PRESENTATION OF EVIDENCE 230-258 (1976); RINGEL, IDENTIFICATION AND POLICE LINEUPS (1968); SOBEL, EYEWITNESS IDENTIFICATION — LEGAL AND PRACTICAL PROBLEMS (2d ed. 1981); WALL, EYEWITNESS IDENTIFICATION IN CRIMINAL CASES (1965).

(B) Rather than attempt still another doctrinal discourse here, the following paragraphs approach these and related subjects from a different angle. After a brief description of the major constitutional guarantees that defense counsel may invoke to challenge the legality of law enforcement activities and thereby the admissibility of prosecution evidence produced by those activities (paragraphs [227]-[233] *infra*), the text sets out a checklist of questions that counsel can ask and answer — with minimal investigation — about the facts of any particular case s/he is handling (paragraph [234] *infra*). The references following each question will direct counsel to subsequent paragraphs ([235]-[250]) containing functional analyses of the law applicable to the basic factual situation targeted by the question. These analyses should assist counsel to identify particular aspects of law enforcement activity that may be assailable in each situation, together with the theoretical grounds and supporting authorities for assailing them. The chapter closes with a paragraph ([251]) on the scope of the exclusionary consequences that flow from various illegal law enforcement activities and with several paragraphs ([252]-[253-A]) on tactical approaches and practical problems in litigation seeking to exclude illegally obtained evidence. Additional tips on conducting suppression hearings in confession cases are found in paragraphs [364]-[367] *infra,* following the MANUAL's principal discussion of substantive confession doctrines in paragraph [363].

[227] **The relevant constitutional restraints.** (A) The most important sources of federal constitutional restrictions upon police investigative activity are the Fourth, Fifth, Sixth, and Fourteenth Amendments to the Constitution of the United States. The first three of these, as written, restrain only the federal government; they do not apply to law enforcement or criminal trials by the states. The Fourteenth Amendment, with its Due Process and Equal Protection Clauses, does expressly bind the states. Overruling its prior decisions on the point, the Supreme Court in the celebrated case of *Mapp v. Ohio,* 367 U.S 643 (1961), held that the Due Process Clause of the Fourteenth Amendment "incorporated" or "absorbed" the right against unreasonable searches and seizures contained in the Fourth Amendment, with the result that the Fourth Amendment came to govern state criminal procedure as it had previously governed federal. *Ker v. California,* 374 U.S. 23 (1963), established that this "incorporation" operated to impose identical search-and-seizure restrictions on state and federal police. In *Gideon v. Wainwright,* 372 U.S. 335 (1963), the Court similarly incorporated the right-to-counsel guarantee of the Sixth Amendment, subsequently enforcing it as a restriction on certain sorts of state

police investigative activity, *Escobedo v. Illinois,* 378 U.S. 478 (1964); *Gilbert v. California,* 388 U.S. 263, 269-274 (1967); *Michigan v. Jackson,* 106 S. Ct. 1404 (1986). The Fifth Amendment privilege against self-incrimination shortly followed the applications of the Fourth and Sixth Amendments to the states, *Malloy v. Hogan,* 378 U.S. 1 (1964), and thereby to state law enforcement officers, *Miranda v. Arizona,* 384 U.S. 436 (1966). See generally paragraph [57-A](B) *supra.*

(B) Parallel state constitutional provisions may also be construed as imposing significant restrictions upon police investigative activity. *See* Utter, *Freedom and Diversity in a Federal System: Perspectives on State Constitutions and the Washington Declaration of Rights,* 7 U. PUGET SOUND L. REV. 491, 500-3 (1984). Particularly at a time when the Rehnquist Court is retracting both the substantive protections of the federal Constitution and the reach of the federal exclusionary rule, it is important for counsel to consider casting the defendant's claims alternatively or instead under state constitutional guarantees. *See, e.g.,* Peters, *State Constitutional Law: Federalism in the Common Law Tradition,* 84 MICH. L. REV. 583 (1986), reviewing DEVELOPMENTS IN STATE CONSTITUTIONAL LAW (McGraw, ed. 1985); Linde, *First Things First: Rediscovering the States' Bills of Rights,* 9 U. BALT. L. REV. 379 (1980); Brennan, *State Constitutions and the Protection of Individual Rights,* 90 HARV. L. REV. 489 (1977); Falk, *Foreword, The State Constitution: A More than "Adequate" Nonfederal Ground,* 61 CALIF. L. REV. 273 (1973). The argument for reading a state guarantee of civil rights more expansively than its federal counterpart will obviously be strengthened if counsel can point to differences between the two in language or constitutional history. *See, e.g., State v. Glass,* 583 P.2d 872 (Alaska 1978); *State v. Simpson,* 95 Wash.2d 170, 622 P.2d 1199 (1980). A creative search for historical evidence that the right in question has been viewed with special solicitude by the policy-making organs of the state — the courts, legislature, constitutional conventions — can produce paydirt. *See, e.g., State v. Stoddard,* 206 Conn.157, 537 A.2d 446 (1988). However, even without these added supports, counsel should not hesitate to urge that considerations of "sound policy, justice and fundamental fairness" call for state constitutional interpretations that are more protective than those which the Supreme Court of the United States has given to the federal Constitution, *see, e.g., People v. P.J. Video, Inc.,* 68 N.Y.2d 296, 303, 501 N.E.2d 556, 560, 508 N.Y.S.2d 907, 911 (1986), particularly when the Supreme Court's most recent interpretations are inconsistent with its own earlier opinions and have been unfavorably reviewed by other state courts and commentators, *see, e.g., Commonwealth v. Upton,* 394 Mass. 363, 476 N.E.2d 548 (1985); *State v. Novembrino,* 105 N.J. 95, 152-156, 519 A.2d 820, 853-56 (1987), or by dissenting Supreme Court Justices, *see, e.g., People v. Houston,* 42 Cal.3d 595, 724 P.2d 1166, 230 Cal. Rptr. 141 (1986). "[T]he privacy rights of our citizens and the enforcement of our criminal laws [are] . . . matters of 'particular state interest' that afford an appropriate basis for resolving [an] . . . issue on independent state grounds." *State v. Novembrino, supra,* 105 N.J. at 146, 519 A.2d at 850. And counsel should keep in mind that a decision in the defendant's favor cannot be upset by the Supreme Court of the United States if it rests explicitly on state law grounds, whether exclusive or alternative. *Michigan v. Long,* 463 U.S. 1032, 1041 (1983) (dictum).

[228] The Due Process Clause. The Due Process Clause, of course, has contents of its own, apart from the Bill of Rights guarantees that it has incorporated. During the period prior to *Mapp,* when the Court had expressly held that neither the Fourth nor the Fifth Amendment applied through the Fourteenth Amendment to the States, the Court nevertheless found in the unassisted Due Process Clause some basis for an inhibition of improper state police activity, to be enforced by compelling the exclusion of its products from evidence in state criminal trials. Virtually the only consistent application of this principle lay in the long line of decisions reversing state convictions for the admission of coerced or forced confessions. *See Miller v. Fenton,* 106 S. Ct. 445, 449-50 (1985). The progression of coerced confession cases over the years showed not only an increasing willingness by the Court to find unconstitutional "coercion," *compare Brown v. Mississippi,* 297 U.S. 278 (1936), *with Haynes v. Washington,* 373 U.S. 503 (1963), but also an increasing tendency to admit that the Court's concern with the problem involved as much a disapprobation of overbearing police methods as a sensitivity to their effect upon the accused. For a time the Court's opinions had steadfastly resisted the notion that the Fourteenth Amendment exclusionary rule was a kind of sanction intended to deter state law enforcement officers from conduct which the Court deemed shocking or uncivilized, by depriving the officers of the evidentiary use of the results of this conduct. *See Lisenba v. California,* 314 U.S. 219 (1941). But by the late 1950's, this theme of federal judicial control of the state police had begun to be sounded in a few decisions, *Spano v. New York,* 360 U.S. 315, 320-21 (1959); *Blackburn v. Alabama,* 361 U.S. 199, 206-7 (1960); and thereafter it was expressed with increasing force and frequency, *e.g., Jackson v. Denno,* 378 U.S. 368, 385-86 (1964); *Beecher v. Alabama,* 389 U.S. 35 (1967) (per curiam); *Sims v. Georgia,* 389 U.S. 404 (1967) (per curiam); *Brooks v. Florida,* 389 U.S. 413 (1967) (per curiam); *Miller v. Fenton, supra,* 106 S. Ct. at 449, 453; *Colorado v. Connelly,* 107 S. Ct. 515, 519-20 (1986); *Crane v. Kentucky,* 106 S. Ct. 2142, 2145 (1986); *Schneckloth v. Bustamonte,* 412 U.S. 218, 225 (1973) (dictum); *but see Moran v. Burbine,* 106 S. Ct. 1135, 1143 (1986). One striking instance was *Rochin v. California,* 342 U.S. 165 (1952), requiring the exclusion of narcotics recovered from an accused's stomach by forcible administration of an emetic accompanied by other physically brutal treatment — the whole course of police behavior amounting to "conduct that shocks the conscience," *id.* at 172. *Rochin* is the Supreme Court's only case of exclusion of nonconfessional evidence on the explicit ground of police barbarism, *cf. United States v. Payner,* 447 U.S. 727, 737 n.9 (1980)), but a few lower court decisions reflect the principle. *Taglavore v. United States,* 291 F.2d 262 (9th Cir. 1961) (alternative ground); *United States v. Townsend,* 151 F. Supp. 378 (D. D.C. 1957). Although the subsequent incorporation of the Fourth, Fifth, and Sixth Amendments has tended to take this kind of straight Due Process Clause contention out of the limelight (*see, e.g., Winston v. Lee,* 470 U.S. 753 (1985) [holding that the state-ordered surgical removal of a bullet from a criminal defendant's chest for evidentiary use against him would constitute an unreasonable search and seizure violating the Fourth Amendment on the facts of the particular case]; *Tennessee v. Garner,* 471 U.S. 1 (1985) [holding that the use of deadly force to effect the arrest of a fleeing felon constitutes an unreasonable seizure violating the Fourth Amendment in the absence of probable cause to believe that the suspect poses a significant threat of death or serious physical harm to the arresting officer or other persons]; *but see City of Oklahoma City v. Tuttle,* 471 U.S. 808, 817 n.4 (1985) (plurality opinion) (dictum)), the Clause remains a potentially fertile source of authority for imaginative attack on police procedures, not otherwise condemnable but extremely abusive, degrading, or unfair. *See Foster v. California,* 394 U.S. 440 (1969) (striking down an unreliable police-staged identification procedure); *Palmer v. Peyton,* 359 F.2d 199 (4th Cir. 1966) (same), approved in *Stovall v. Denno,* 388 U.S. 293, 301-2 (1967) (dictum); *Manson v. Brathwaite,* 432 U.S. 98, 113-14 (1977) (dictum) (same); *Watkins v. Sowders,* 449 U.S. 341, 347 (1981) (dictum) (same); *cf. Baker v. McCollan,* 443 U.S. 137, 145 (1979) (dictum); *Moran v. Burbine, supra,* 106 S. Ct. at 1147-48 (dictum); *Doe v. United States,* 108 S. Ct. 2341, 2350-51 nn.13, 14 (1988) (dictum) ("the Due Process Clause imposes limitations on the Government's ability to coerce individuals into participating in criminal prosecutions . . . [e]ven if the Self-Incrimination Clause [is] . . . not implicated . . .").

[229] The Fourth Amendment — the "warrant theory" and the "general reasonableness theory." (A) The Fourth Amendment provides:

> The right of the people to be secure in their persons, houses, papers, and effects, against unreasonable searches and seizures, shall not be violated, and no Warrants shall issue, but upon probable cause, supported by Oath or affirmation, and particularly describing the place to be searched, and the persons or things to be seized.

Obviously, it is oddly constructed. It consists of two conjunctive clauses, one prohibiting "unreasonable" searches and seizures, the other prescribing the conditions for issuance of a warrant. But it does not connect the two clauses. It does not say, as one might suppose it would, that searches without a warrant issued in compliance with the conditions specified in the second clause are thereby unreasonable under the first. This ellipsis has been a fruitful source of controversy and confusion.

(B) The controversy is best exemplified by the debate be-tween the majority and dissenting opinions in *United States v. Rabinowitz,* 339 U.S. 56 (1950), which express two radically dif-ferent conceptions of the Amendment. Justice Frankfurter, in dissent, expounds what may be called the "warrant theory": that the word *unreasonable* in the first clause is a word of art, to be read together with the second clause as signifying that all searches made without a warrant when it is practicable to obtain a warrant are unconstitutional, except in a few narrow, histori-cally defined situations in which warrantless searches have tradi-tionally been allowed. The majority rejects this view and adopts the competing "general reasonableness theory": that the Amend-ment does not demand a search warrant in every case in which it is practicable to get one, that it condemns only *unreasonable* searches, and that the question whether a search is reasonable depends on "the facts and circumstances of each case." 339 U.S. at 63.

(C) The confusion sets in atop the controversy at this point. For, notwithstanding the unequivocal language of *Rabinowitz,* the Court has never, in fact, acted the way it talked in that case. The whole body of the Court's Fourth Amendment holdings plainly makes up a pattern that is far closer to the Frankfurter warrant-theory model than to the general reasonableness model. *See, e.g., United States v. Chadwick,* 433 U.S. 1, 6-16 (1977). In-deed, the Court has persistently spoken in search-and-seizure cases in the very language of the *Rabinowitz* dissent, describing the principle of the Fourth Amendment as a pervasive "rule that a search must rest upon a search warrant," *Rios v. United States,* 364 U.S. 253, 261 (1960), subject only to a few "jealously and carefully drawn" exceptions, *Jones v. United States,* 357 U.S. 493, 499 (1958). The typical formulation is that "searches conducted outside the judicial process, without prior approval by judge or magistrate, are *per se* unreasonable under the Fourth Amendment — subject only to a few specifically established and well-delineated exceptions." *Katz v. United States,* 389 U.S. 347, 357 (1967). *See also Agnello v. United States,* 269 U.S. 20, 32 (1925); *Johnson v. United States,* 333 U.S. 10, 13-15 (1948); *United States v. Jeffers,* 342 U.S. 48, 51 (1951); *Chapman v. United States,* 365 U.S. 610, 613-15 (1961); *Preston v. United States,* 376 U.S.

364, 367 (1964); *Stoner v. California,* 376 U.S. 483, 486 (1964); *Camara v. Municipal Court,* 387 U.S. 523, 528-29 (1967); *Mancusi v. DeForte,* 392 U.S. 364, 370 (1968); *Chimel v. California,* 395 U.S. 752, 762 (1969); *Vale v. Louisiana,* 399 U.S. 30, 34-35 (1970); *Coolidge v. New Hampshire,* 403 U.S. 443, 454-55, 474-82 (1971); *United States v. United States District Court for the Eastern District of Michigan,* 407 U.S. 297, 309-10, 315-18 (1972); *G.M. Leasing Corp v. United States,* 429 U.S. 338, 352-58 (1977); *Marshall v. Barlow's, Inc.,* 436 U.S. 307, 312-13 (1978); *Michigan v. Tyler,* 436 U.S. 499, 506, 508-9 (1978); *Mincey v. Arizona,* 437 U.S. 385, 390, 393-95 (1978); *Payton v. New York,* 445 U.S. 573, 586-90 & nn.25, 26 (1980); *Steagald v. United States,* 451 U.S. 204, 211-12, 213-14 (1981); *Michigan v. Clifford,* 464 U.S. 287, 291-92 (1984); *Welsh v. Wisconsin,* 466 U.S. 740, 748-50 (1984); *Thompson v. Louisiana,* 469 U.S. 17, 19-20 (1984) (per curiam); *Schneckloth v. Bustamonte,* 412 U.S. 218, 219 (1973) (dictum); *Colorado v. Bannister,* 449 U.S. 1, 2-3 (1980) (per curiam) (dictum); *United States v. Ross,* 456 U.S. 798, 824-25 (1982) (dictum); *United States v. Karo,* 468 U.S. 705, 714-15, 717 (1984) (dictum); *Massachusetts v. Sheppard,* 468 U.S. 981, 988 n.5 (1987) (dictum); *O'Connor v. Ortega,* 107 S. Ct. 1492, 1499 (1987) (plurality opinion) (dictum); *cf. Torres v. Puerto Rico,* 442 U.S. 465, 471 (1979); *Walter v. United States,* 447 U.S. 649, 654 (1980); *United States v. Place,* 462 U.S. 696, 701 (1983); *Gerstein v. Pugh,* 420 U.S. 103, 112-13 & n.12 (1975) (dictum); *Franks v. Delaware,* 438 U.S. 154, 164 (1978) (dictum); *New York v. Belton,* 453 U.S. 454, 457 (1981) (dictum); *United States v. Johnson,* 457 U.S. 537, 552-53 nn.13, 14 (1982) (dictum); *Skinner v. Railway Labor Executives' Ass'n,* 109 S. Ct. 1402, 1414 (1989) (dictum). The *Chimel* case, *supra,* overruled *Rabinowitz* on a related point (see paragraph [240](C)(3)(d) *infra*); and although *Chimel* did not explicitly reject the "general reasonableness" theory, its approving quotation of the critical portions of Justice Frankfurter's *Rabinowitz* dissent (*see* 395 U.S. at 760-61) appears to relegate "general reasonableness" to the ash heap. *See also* the *Eastern District* opinion, *supra,* 407 U.S. at 315-16.

(D) "General reasonableness" language, however, continues to be used, *e.g., Wyman v. James,* 400 U.S. 309, 318 (1971); *United States v. Ramsey,* 431 U.S. 606, 617-19 (1977); *Zurcher v. Stanford*

Daily, 436 U.S. 547, 559-60 (1978); *Bell v. Wolfish,* 441 U.S. 520, 558-60 (1979); *Brown v. Texas,* 443 U.S. 47, 50-51 (1979); *Donovan v. Dewey,* 452 U.S. 594, 599 (1981); *Michigan v. Summers,* 452 U.S. 692, 699-701 & nn.11, 12 (1981); *United States v. Villamonte-Marquez,* 462 U.S. 579, 588, 593 (1983); *Illinois v. La-Fayette,* 462 U.S. 640, 643, 647-48 (1983); *Michigan v. Long,* 463 U.S. 1032, 1051 (1983); *United States v. Hensley,* 469 U.S. 221, 228 (1985); *New Jersey v. T.L.O.,* 469 U.S. 325, 340-41 (1985); *United States v. Montoya de Hernandez,* 473 U.S. 531, 537 (1985); *Colorado v. Bertine,* 107 S. Ct. 738, 741 (1987); *Scott v. United States,* 436 U.S. 128, 137 (1978) (dictum); *Delaware v. Prouse,* 440 U.S. 648, 653-55 & n.6 (1979) (dictum); *compare Texas v. Brown,* 460 U.S. 730, 735-39 (1983) (plurality opinion), with *id.* at 744-46 (concurring opinion of Justice Powell), sometimes in confusing conjunction with warrant-theory language, *see Cady v. Dombrowski,* 413 U.S. 433, 439, 448 (1973); *United States v. Chadwick, supra,* 433 U.S. at 9-10; *Marshall v. Barlow's Inc, supra,* 436 U.S. at 315-16; *Payton v. New York, supra,* 445 U.S. at 583-86; *United States v. Place, supra,* 462 U.S. at 700-5. A "general reasonableness" approach is particularly likely to be employed in cases of police activities that are viewed as less intrusive than the traditional forms of search and seizure exemplified by physical entries into closed premises or containers or arrests of persons. For example, in dealing with "stop and frisk" practices—brief on-the-street investigative detentions less intrusive than arrests, and weapons "pat-downs" less intrusive than full-scale body searches (see paragraph [236] *infra*)—the Court in *Terry v. Ohio,* 392 U.S. 1 (1968), invoked the "Fourth Amendment's general proscription against unreasonable searches and seizures," *id.* at 20, and said that "there is 'no ready test for determining reasonableness other than by balancing the need to search [or seize] against the invasion which the search [or seizure] entails,'" *id.* at 21. This notion of balancing "the nature and quality of the intrusion on the individual's Fourth Amendment interests against the importance of the governmental interests alleged to justify the intrusion," *United States v. Place, supra,* 462 U.S. at 703, has since become a standard methodology of Fourth Amendment analysis in opinions passing upon "police conduct . . . which historically has not been, and as a practical matter could not be, subjected to the warrant procedure," *Terry v. Ohio, supra,* 392 U.S. at 20; *see, e.g., Delaware v. Prouse, supra,* 440 U.S. at 653-55; *Michigan v. Summers, supra,* 452 U.S. at 699-701; *United States v. Villamonte-Marquez, supra,* 462 U.S. at 588; *Illinois v. LaFayette, supra,* 462 U.S. at 644; *United States v. Place, supra,* 462 U.S. at 702-7; *Michigan v. Long, supra,* 463 U.S. at 1046-52; *United States v. Jacobsen,* 466 U.S. 109, 124-25 (1984); *United States v. Hensley, supra,* 469 U.S. at 228; *Tennessee v. Garner,* 471 U.S. 1, 7-8 (1985); *United States v. Montoya de Hernandez, supra,* 473 U.S. at 537; *New York v. Class,* 106 S. Ct. 960, 967-68 (1986), and in passing upon the conduct of other government officials "'in those exceptional circumstances in which special needs, beyond the normal need for law enforcement, make the warrant . . . requirement impractical,'" *O'Connor v. Ortega,* subparagraph (C) *supra,* 107 S. Ct. at 1499 (plurality opinion); *see, e.g., Griffin v. Wisconsin,* 107 S. Ct. 3164 (1987); *New Jersey v. T.L.O., supra; Skinner v. Railway Labor Executives' Ass'n,* subparagraph (C) *supra,* 109 S. Ct. at 1413-14. Even in the case of more intrusive searches and seizures, "general reasonableness" decisions crop up sporadically. Searches that are condemnable under the warrant theory have been sustained because, on all the facts and circumstances, they are found reasonable, *Cooper v. California,* 386 U.S. 58 (1967); *South Dakota v. Opperman,* 428 U.S. 364, 369-76 (1976); *New York v. Class, supra,* 106 S. Ct. at 967-69; and searches that are sustainable under the warrant theory have been condemned because, on all the facts and circumstances, they are found unreasonable, *McDonald v. United States,* 335 U.S. 451 (1948); *Winston v. Lee,* 470 U.S. 753 (1985); *cf. Roaden v. Kentucky,* 413 U.S. 496, 501-6 (1973).

(E) It is therefore fair to describe the state of Fourth Amendment law as a game professedly played under general reasonableness rules, actually played for the most part under warrant-theory rules, and subject, from time to time, to the wild card of general reasonableness turning up. From the point of view of advocacy, this gives counsel two inconsistent, equally authoritative principles from which to argue when one or the other or both can be made to support counsel's position.

[230] Summary of Fourth Amendment doctrine. Subject to the wild card of general reasonableness, it is possible to summarize the principal doctrines of Fourth Amendment case law as follows:

(A) With the exceptions noted in the following subparagraphs, a search of protected premises, persons, or objects is invalid unless made under authority of a search warrant issued by a judicial officer. *Chapman v. United States,* 365 U.S. 610 (1961), and cases cited together with *Chapman* in paragraph [229](C) *supra; United States v. Chadwick,* 433 U.S. 1 (1977). A search warrant may be issued only upon a showing of probable cause to believe that criminal objects described in the warrant are presently in the place whose search is authorized. *Aguilar v. Texas,* 378 U.S. 108 (1964); *Spinelli v. United States,* 393 U.S. 410 (1969); *Michigan v. Tyler,* 436 U.S. 499, 512 (1978); *Franks v. Delaware,* 438 U.S. 154, 165 (1978); *Steagald v. United States,* 451 U.S. 204, 213 (1981). The warrant must describe with specificity both the things to be seized and the place to be searched. *Stanford v. Texas,* 379 U.S. 476 (1965); *Lo-Ji Sales, Inc. v. New York,* 442 U.S. 319, 325 (1979); *Massachusetts v. Sheppard,* 468 U.S. 981, 988 n.5 (1984) (dictum); *see Berger v. New York,* 388 U.S. 41, 55-60 (1967); *compare Andresen v. Maryland,* 427 U.S. 463, 478-82 (1976); *Maryland v. Garrison,* 107 S. Ct. 1013, 1017 (1987). With rare exceptions (*see Rugendorf v. United States,* 376 U.S. 528 (1964) (sub silentio); *Alderman v. United States,* 394 U.S. 165, 177 n.10 (1969) (dictum); *cf. Coolidge v. New Hampshire,* 403 U.S. 443, 464-73 (1971) (plurality opinion); *United States v. Donovan,* 429 U.S. 413, 436-37 n.24 (1977) (dictum); *and see generally Texas v. Brown,* 460 U.S. 730 (1983)), an officer executing a warrant may seize nothing that is not described in it. *Marron v. United States,* 275 U.S. 192 (1927); *Lo-Ji Sales, Inc. v. New York, supra,* 442 U.S. at 325.

(B) Search without a warrant may be made upon valid consent of a person affected by the search. *Davis v. United States,* 328 U.S. 582 (1946); *Frazier v. Cupp,* 394 U.S. 731 (1969); *Schneckloth v. Bustamonte,* 412 U.S. 218 (1973); *United States v. Matlock,* 415 U.S. 164 (1974); *United States v. Watson,* 423 U.S. 411 (1976). It may be made of the person of a validly arrested individual, *United States v. Robinson,* 414 U.S. 218 (1973); *United States v.*

Edwards, 415 U.S. 800 (1974); *Michigan v. DeFillippo,* 443 U.S. 31, 35-36 (1979), either immediately preceding the arrest, *Rawlings v. Kentucky,* 448 U.S. 98, 110-11 (1980), or at any time thereafter while s/he is still in possession of effects that s/he was carrying or wearing at the time of the arrest, *United States v. Edwards, supra.* If the arrested person is jailed, a warrantless "inventory" search of everything in his or her possession, including closed containers, may be made at the lockup. *Illinois v. LaFayette,* 462 U.S. 640 (1983). And, within a limited range (*Chimel v. California,* 395 U.S. 752 (1969); *United States v. Chadwick, subparagraph (A) supra,* 433 U.S. at 14-16; *Lo-Ji Sales, Inc. v. New York, subparagraph (A) supra,* 442 U.S. at 326; *see James v. Louisiana,* 382 U.S. 36 (1965) (per curiam); *Vale v. Louisiana,* 399 U.S. 30 (1970); *Cardwell v. Lewis,* 417 U.S. 583, 591-92 n.7 (1974) (plurality opinion); *id.* at 599 n.4 (dissenting opinion, agreeing with the plurality on this point)), a warrantless search may be made of the immediate site at the time of a valid arrest, *Hill v. California,* 401 U.S. 797 (1971); *New York v. Belton,* 453 U.S. 454, 457-61 (1981). An arrest, in turn, is constitutionally valid only if it is authorized by local law and is based upon a determination of probable cause to believe that the arrested person has committed a criminal offense. *See, e.g., Hayes v. Florida,* 470 U.S. 811, 813-16 (1985). Local law in every jurisdiction authorizes the issuance of arrest warrants on a magistrate's finding of probable cause (*see Steagald v. United States,* subparagraph (A) *supra,* 451 U.S. at 213); and arrests made under a warrant so issued satisfy the requirements of the Fourth Amendment, *Shadwick v. City of Tampa,* 407 U.S. 345, 350 (1972); *Baker v. McCollan,* 443 U.S. 137, 142-43 (1979), provided that the issuing magistrate was "supplied with sufficient information to support an independent judgement that probable cause exists," *Whiteley v. Warden,* 401 U.S. 560, 564 (1971), but not otherwise, *ibid.* Local law in most jurisdictions also authorizes warrantless arrests for felonies and for misdemeanors constituting a breach of the peace or committed in the presence of the arresting officer, upon an officer's own determination of probable cause. These warrantless arrests are constitutional when made in a public place, *United States v. Watson, supra; Michigan v. DeFillippo, supra,* 443 U.S. at 36-38, if the officer in fact had adequate grounds for finding probable cause, *Draper v. United States,* 358 U.S. 307 (1959); *Rawlings v. Kentucky, supra,* 448 U.S. at 110-11, but not otherwise, *Henry v. United States,* 361 U.S. 98 (1959); *Taylor v. Alabama,* 457 U.S. 687 (1982). In order to enter a person's home for the purpose of arresting him or her, however, either a valid arrest warrant or a valid search warrant is required; the arresting officer's determination of probable cause alone is not sufficient, *Payton v. New York,* 445 U.S. 573 (1980); *Welsh v. Wisconsin,* 466 U.S. 740 (1984), except in cases of hot pursuit or other exigent circumstances, *Warden v. Hayden,* 387 U.S. 294, 298-99 (1967); *United States v. Santana,* 427 U.S. 38 (1976); *Payton v. New York, supra,* 445 U.S. 583 (dictum). And subject only to the latter exceptions, *Steagald v. United States,* subparagraph (A) *supra,* 451 U.S. at 221-22, entry into a home for the purpose of arresting someone other than a resident requires a valid search warrant, *ibid.* An officer having probable cause to make an arrest but who does not make an arrest is also permitted to conduct a warrantless search of the person of an individual who would otherwise likely destroy evidence on his or her person before a warrant could be obtained, *Cupp v. Murphy,* 412 U.S. 291 (1973), "to the very limited [extent] . . . necessary to preserve . . . highly evanescent evidence," *id.* at 296.

(C) An officer may stop a pedestrian or an automobilist briefly on the street for questioning if the officer has a reasonable suspicion that s/he is engaged in criminal activity, *Terry v. Ohio,* 392 U.S. 1, 16-23 (1968); *Delaware v. Prouse,* 440 U.S. 648, 655-63 (1979) (dictum); *see United States v. Brignoni-Ponce,* 422 U.S. 873, 878-85 (1975) (dictum), or is wanted in connection with an earlier felony, *United States v. Hensley,* 469 U.S. 221 (1985), but the officer may not protract this detention longer than is needed to allow the person stopped to be "questioned briefly where [s/he is] . . . found," *Dunaway v. New York,* 442 U.S. 200, 212 (1979); *cf. Florida v. Royer,* 460 U.S. 491, 498-507 (1983) (plurality opinion); *id.* at 509-11 (concurring opinion of Justice Brennan), or to allow "the police diligently [to pursue] . . . a means of investigation . . . likely to confirm or dispel their suspicions quickly," *United States v. Sharpe,* 470 U.S. 675, 686 (1985). Absent such a "particularized and objective basis for suspecting the particular person stopped of criminal activity," *United*

States v. Cortez, 449 U.S. 411, 417-18 (1981), even brief on-the-street detentions are unconstitutional. *United States v. Brignoni-Ponce, supra,* 422 U.S. at 882-84, 885-87; *Delaware v. Prouse, supra; Brown v. Texas,* 443 U.S. 47, 51-53 (1979); *Reid v. Georgia,* 448 U.S. 438, 440-41 (1980) (per curiam); *Florida v. Royer, supra,* 460 U.S. at 497-98 (plurality opinion) (dictum); *id.* at 511-12 (concurring opinion of Justice Brennan). An officer executing a valid search warrant may detain occupants of the premises during the limited time required for the search. *Michigan v. Summers,* 452 U.S. 692 (1981). In street-stop cases, and perhaps in these latter cases as well, the officer who conducts these temporary detentions may "frisk" the detained persons to the extent necessary to discover weapons (but to no greater extent, *Sibron v. New York,* 392 U.S. 40, 65-66 (1968); *Florida v. Royer, supra,* 460 U.S. at 499-500 (plurality opinion); *id.* at 509-11 (concurring opinion of Justice Brennan)), if the officer is "able to point to particular facts from which he reasonably inferred that the individual was armed and dangerous," *Sibron v. New York, supra,* 392 U.S. at 64 (dictum); *Adams v. Williams,* 407 U.S. 143 (1972); *Pennsylvania v. Mimms,* 434 U.S. 106 (1977) (per curiam); *New York v. Class,* 106 S. Ct. 960, 967-68 (1986) (dictum), but may not "place[] a hand on the person of a citizen in search of anything" (*Sibron v. New York, supra,* 392 U.S. at 64) without such facts, *Ybarra v. Illinois,* 444 U.S. 85, 92-94 (1979); *Dunaway v. New York, supra,* 442 U.S. at 209 n.11 (dictum). If the person stopped is in or near an automobile, the same rules govern searches of those areas of the passenger compartment that might contain a weapon. *Michigan v. Long,* 463 U.S. 1032 (1983).

(D) A warrantless search may be made of a motor vehicle that is capable of being moved out of reach during the time necessary to obtain a warrant, *Coolidge v. New Hampshire,* subparagraph (A) *supra,* if—and only if —the searching officer has probable cause, *see Almeida Sanchez v. United States,* 413 U.S. 266 (1973), to believe that the vehicle contains criminal objects, *Carroll v. United States,* 267 U.S. 132 (1925); *Chambers v. Maroney,* 399 U.S. 42 (1970); *Colorado v. Bannister,* 449 U.S. 1 (1980) (per curiam); *Michigan v. Thomas,* 458 U.S. 259 (1982) (per curiam); *United States v. Ross,* 456 U.S. 798 (1982) (extending the authorization to closed containers within the car that are capable of concealing the criminal objects sought); *United States v. Johns,* 469 U.S. 478 (1985) (extending *Ross* to uphold delayed searches of containers removed from a seized vehicle). This *"Carroll* rule" is one of several that relax the warrant requirement in automobile-search cases. See paragraph [246] *infra;* and *see California v. Carney,* 471 U.S. 386 (1985) (extending the rule to a mobile home parked in a public parking lot). It has not been authoritatively extended to searches of other potentially mobile containers, *United States v. Chadwick,* subparagraph (A) *supra,* 433 U.S. at 11-13; *United States v. Ross, supra,* 456 U.S. at 809-12 (dictum); *United States v. Place,* 462 U.S. 696 (1983). However, highly mobile containers (such as luggage in transit) may be seized and briefly detained for the purpose of conducting further investigation when there are reasonable grounds to suspect that these containers are concealing contraband or other seizable objects, *id.* at 703-6; and if probable cause appears, they may be detained for a longer period so as to permit the officers to get a warrant to open them, *id.* at 701-2 (dictum); *United States v. Jacobsen,* 466 U.S. 109, 121-22 (1984); *Segura v. United States,* 468 U.S. 796, 805-13 (1984) (dictum). Searches without warrants — including building searches — have also been sustained on particularized showings of "an emergency situation demanding immediate action": for example, when police officers "reasonably believe that a person . . . is in need of immediate aid," *Mincey v. Arizona,* 437 U.S. 385, 392 (1978) (dictum); *Thompson v. Louisiana,* 469 U.S. 17, 21-22 (1984) (dictum); *see Michigan v. Tyler,* subparagraph (A) *supra,* 436 U.S. at 509, or when they are in hot pursuit of a fleeing felony suspect and have probable cause both for arrest and for the belief that the suspect is within the place searched, *Warden v. Hayden,* subparagraph (B) *supra; United States v. Santana,* subparagraph (B) *supra; Steagald v. United States,* subparagraph (B) *supra,* 451 U.S. at 221-22 (dictum). These cases have sometimes been described as presenting situations of "exigent circumstances" (*e.g., Payton v. New York,* subparagraph (B) *supra,* 445 U.S. at 583); and the "exigent circumstances" exception to the warrant requirement may also extend to some nonautomobile cases in which there is an individualized showing of probable cause to believe that criminal objects will be rapidly removed or destroyed and in which there is no means short of search to preserve them while a warrant is being sought, *Johnson v. United States,* 333 U.S. 10, 14-15 (1948) (dictum), and cases cited together with *Johnson* in paragraph [240](C)(3)(e) *infra.* This latter extension, if it exists, demands a compelling demonstration on the facts of the particular case that a warrant could not practicably have been obtained, *Vale v. Louisiana,* subparagraph (B) *supra,* 399 U.S. at 34-35; *United States v. Chadwick,* subparagraph (A) *supra,* 433 U.S. at 11-16 — a more explicit demonstration than is required in automobile cases under the *Carroll* rule, *see, e.g., Chambers v. Maroney, supra,* 399 U.S. at 47-52.

(E) Routine searches of persons, vehicles, and mail entering the United States across an international boundary are permitted without either warrant or probable cause, *United States v. Ramsey,* 431 U.S. 606 (1977); *California Bankers Ass'n v. Shultz,* 416 U.S. 21, 62-63 (1974) (dictum); *United States v. Montoya de Hernandez,* 473 U.S. 531, 537-38 (1985) (dictum); but this authority does not extend beyond the border and its functional equivalents, *see Almeida-Sanchez v. United States,* subparagraph (D) *supra; United States v. Ortiz,* 422 U.S. 891 (1975); *Torres v. Puerto Rico,* 442 U.S. 465, 472-74 (1979). *Cf. United States v. Martinez-Fuerte,* 428 U.S. 543 (1976). Searches without warrant or probable cause are also permitted of licensed premises in connection with the administrative regulation of such trades as gun and liquor dealerships and junkyards, *United States v. Biswell,* 406 U.S. 311 (1972); *New York v. Burger,* 107 S. Ct. 2636 (1987), and of automobiles and their contents properly taken into police custody in connection with traffic regulation, *South Dakota v. Opperman,* 428 U.S. 364 (1976); *Colorado v. Bertine,* 107 S. Ct. 738 (1987). Except in these latter vehicle cases, the border and "regulated industries" cases, the weapons "frisk" cases, consent cases, and certain situations in which "'special [governmental] needs, beyond the normal need for law enforcement, make the warrant and probable-cause requirement impracticable,'" *Griffin v. Wisconsin,* 107 S. Ct. 3164, 3167 (1987) (searches of probationers' homes by probation officers); *see also New Jersey v. T.L.O.,* 469 U.S. 325 (1985) (searches of public school children by school officials on school premises); *O'Connor v. Ortega,* 107 S. Ct. 1492 (1987) (work-related searches of government employees' offices by their employers or supervisors), all searches of protected premises, persons, or objects, with or without a warrant, thus must rest upon a showing of probable cause that an object to be seized or a person to be arrested has been criminally involved, *see, e.g., Almeida-Sanchez v. United States,* subparagraph (D) *supra,* 413 U.S. at 269-70; *Griffin v. Wisconsin, supra,* 107 S. Ct. at 3169-70; *Arizona v. Hicks,* 107 S. Ct. 1149, 1153-54 (1987); and on proper challenge to a search and seizure, judicial review of the question of probable cause, as well as of the other requisites for valid search under the circumstances, is required. *E.g., Whiteley v. Warden,* 401 U.S. 560 (1971); *Torres v. Puerto Rico, supra,* 442 U.S. at 471.

[231] **Same.** The preceding paragraph summarizes the restrictions that the Fourth Amendment imposes upon *searches and seizures* of *protected persons, places, and objects.* The italicized phrases are words of art, used to distinguish those law enforcement activities that the amendment regulates from those that it does not. The question *what is a search* is discussed in subpart (A) of this paragraph. The question *what is a seizure* is better addressed in specific contexts: "seizures" of persons are treated in paragraph [236](B) *infra;* "seizures" of premises are treated in paragraph [240](E) *infra;* "seizures" of objects are treated in paragraphs [239] (subpoenaed objects), [246](C), (D) and (E) (automobiles), and [247](C) and [248](D) (other objects) *infra.* The question *what persons, places, and objects does the Fourth Amendment protect* against searches and seizures is discussed in subpart (B) of the present paragraph.

(A) (1) Any physical entry into premises by law enforcement officers (*Johnson v. United States,* 333 U.S. 10, 13, 16-17 (1948); *Lo-Ji Sales, Inc. v. New York,* 442 U.S. 319, 325-26 (1979)) or any physical penetration of premises by a surveillance device (*Silverman v. United States,* 365 U.S. 505 (1961)), is a search.

(2) In 1967, the Supreme Court, overruling its earlier decisions, held that electronic surveillance conducted without physical penetration into areas where an expectation of privacy is justified is also a search. *Katz v. United States,* 389 U.S. 347 (1967); *see Smith v. Maryland,* 442 U.S. 735, 739-40 (1979). In *United States v. Karo,* 468 U.S. 705 (1984), it held that governmental monitoring of an electronic "beeper" which had been in-

troduced into a suspected drug manufacturer's home by being secreted in a can of chemicals sold to the suspect by an informer was a Fourth Amendment search because, while "less intrusive than a full-scale search, . . . it does reveal a critical fact about the interior of the premises that the Government is extremely interested in knowing and that it could not have otherwise obtained without a warrant." *Id.* at 715. The critical fact was no longer, as before *Katz,* that "there was a technical trespass on the space occupied by the beeper. The existence of a physical trespass is only marginally relevant to the question of whether the Fourth Amendment has been violated, . . . for an actual trespass is neither necessary nor sufficient to establish a constitutional violation." *Id.* at 712-13. The important fact was that "the Government [had] surreptitiously employ[ed] an electronic device to obtain information [from within a house] that it could not have obtained by observation from outside the curtilage of the house," *id.* at 715.

(3) Whether other forms of surveillance into premises from the outside constitute searches apparently depends on the degree of privacy that the premises afford and that the ordinary conventions of society lead people to expect to enjoy inside those premises. *Compare Regalado v. California,* 374 U.S. 497 (1963) (per curiam) (police observation into an occupied hotel room through a peephole in the door is a search), *with United States v. Dunn,* 107 S. Ct. 1134 (1987) (police observation, with a flashlight, into the partly open front of a barn after crossing a perimeter fence and an interior fence "designed and constructed to corral livestock, not to prevent persons from observing what lay inside the enclosed areas" [*id.* at 1140] is not a search). In general, the Court seems disinclined to treat visual observation as a search when it is made from vantage points accessible to any members of the public, *see Texas v. Brown,* 460 U.S. 730, 737-40 (1983) (plurality opinion); *New York v. Class,* 106 S. Ct. 960, 965-66 (1986); *cf. California v. Greenwood,* 108 S. Ct. 1625, 1628-29 (1988), even though the access and the means of observation may be difficult and uncommon, *see California v. Ciraolo,* 106 S. Ct. 1809 (1986) (Fourth Amendment offers no protection against naked-eye observation of marijuana growing in a homeowner's fenced back yard by police investigators who overflew

the yard in a private plane operating in navigable airspace at an altitude of 1000 feet; Court intimates that the result might be different in the case of surveillance that discloses less readily observable domestic activity, *id.* at 1814 n.3); *Dow Chemical Co. v. United States,* 106 S. Ct. 1819 (1986) (Fourth Amendment offers no protection against observation of uncovered ground areas within a fenced industrial compound by government agent using a precision aerial mapping camera mounted in a plane which overflew the compound in navigable airspace at altitudes up to 12,000 feet; Court intimates that the result might be different if such an observation were made of "an area immediately adjacent to a private home, where privacy expectations are most heightened," *id.* at 1826 n.4, or if the industrial compound had been observed "by using highly sophisticated surveillance equipment not generally available to the public, such as satellite technology," *id.* at 1826); *Florida v. Riley,* 109 S. Ct. 693 (1989) (Fourth Amendment offers no protection against naked-eye observation of marijuana growing in an incompletely roofed greenhouse in a homeowner's fenced back yard by police investigators who overflew the greenhouse in a helicopter at an altitude of 400 feet; "[a]ny member of the public could legally have been flying over Riley's property in a helicopter at the altitude of 400 feet and could have observed Riley's greenhouse," *id.* at 697; plurality opinion intimates that the result might be different if "the helicopter interfered with . . . normal use of the greenhouse or of other parts of the curtilage" or if "intimate details connected with the use of the home or curtilage were observed," *ibid.;* concurring opinion necessary for a majority intimates that the result would have been different if Riley had proved factually that "the public can[not] generally be expected to travel over residential backyards at an altitude of 400 feet," *id.* at 699 (concurring opinion of Justice O'Connor), or if the police helicopter had flown at "altitudes lower than that," *ibid.*). Police use of searchlights and binoculars does not alone constitute a Fourth Amendment search. *See Texas v. Brown, supra,* 460 U.S. at 739-40, *and United States v. Dunn, supra,* 107 S. Ct. at 1141, both citing *United States v. Lee,* 274 U.S. 559 (1927).

(4) The thrust of the *Katz* opinion is to make the fact of governmental intrusion into privacy, rather than the means by

which the intrusion is accomplished, the focus of attention. *See also Terry v. Ohio,* 392 U.S. 1, 16-19 (1968), and particularly its footnote 15; *Skinner v. Railway Labor Executives' Ass'n,* 109 S. Ct. 1402, 1412-13 (1989). Ordinarily, some degree of intrusion into privacy is required before any police activity will be characterized as a search. *See United States v. Dionisio,* 410 U.S. 1, 13-15 (1973); *United States v. Miller,* 425 U.S. 435, 440, 442-43 (1976); *Pennsylvania v. Mimms,* 434 U.S. 106, 111 (1977) (per curiam); *Smith v. Maryland,* subparagraph (2) *supra,* 442 U.S. at 739-41; *Washington v. Chrisman,* 455 U.S. 1, 8-9 (1982); *United States v. Knotts,* 460 U.S. 276, 280-85 (1983); *Illinois v. Andreas,* 463 U.S. 765, 771-73 (1983); *United States v. Jacobsen,* 466 U.S. 109, 113-15, 119, 122-24 (1984); *California v. Greenwood,* subparagraph (3) *supra,* 108 S. Ct. at 1628-29; *cf. Fisher v. United States,* 425 U.S. 391, 400-1 (1976) (dictum); *United States v. Martinez-Fuerte,* 428 U.S. 543, 554-55 (1976) (dictum); *and compare United States v. Santana,* 427 U.S. 38, 42 (1976), *with G.M. Leasing Corp. v. United States,* 429 U.S. 338, 353-58 (1977). The intrusion does not have to be very great. Thus in cases dealing with police examination of closed containers such as luggage in transit, the courts have held that mere surface inspection is not a search for Fourth Amendment purposes but that handling of the container which causes the disclosure of otherwise concealed matter is, even though the handling does not involve opening the container. *See* cases cited in paragraph [248](B) *infra.* And in *Arizona v. Hicks,* 107 S. Ct. 1149 (1987), the Supreme Court held that a police officer who had gained lawful admittance to a private apartment and there saw an assortment of stereo components which he suspected of being stolen committed a search within the Fourth Amendment when he moved some of the components about in order to uncover and read the serial number on a turntable, because this "action . . . exposed to view concealed portions of the apartment or its contents [and thereby] . . . produce[d] a new invasion of [the tenant's] . . . privacy [going beyond that which was entailed by the initial] . . . entry," *id.* at 1152. The benchmark of a search seems to be whether or not the surveillance is capable of "expos[ing] noncontraband items that otherwise would remain hidden from public view." *United States v. Place,* 462 U.S. 696, 707 (1983). If it could disclose nothing which was previously shielded from perception (*see United States v. Jacobsen, supra,* 466 U.S. at 118-120) or nothing except that a shielded object is or is not contraband (*see United States v. Place, supra,* 462 U.S. at 707; *United States v. Jacobsen, supra,* 466 U.S. at 122-24); *cf. Skinner v. Railway Labor Executives' Ass'n, supra,* 109 S. Ct. at 1417-18), then it is not within the regulation of the Fourth Amendment.

(5) The same distinction between observing what is already revealed and prying into matters that are not accessible to observation is reflected in the "plain view" doctrine, which holds that "objects falling in the plain view of an officer who has the right to be in a position to have that view' are not thereby the products of a "search" in the Fourth Amendment sense. *Harris v. United States,* 390 U.S. 234, 236 (1968). *See Michigan v. Tyler,* 436 U.S. 499, 508, 509-10 (1978); *Colorado v. Bannister,* 449 U.S. 1, 3-4 (1980) (per curiam); *Washington v. Chrisman,* subparagraph (4) *supra,* 455 U.S. at 5-6, 8-9; *Michigan v. Clifford,* 464 U.S. 287, 294, 299 (1984) (plurality opinion); *United States v. Hensley,* 469 U.S. 221, 235 (1985); *Mincey v. Arizona,* 437 U.S. 385, 393 (1978) (dictum); *Illinois v. Andreas, supra,* 463 U.S. at 771-72 (dictum); *Thompson v. Louisiana,* 469 U.S. 17, 22 (1984) (per curiam) (dictum). "'[P]lain view' provides grounds for seizure of an item when an officer's access to an object has some prior justification under the Fourth Amendment," *Texas v. Brown,* subparagraph (3) *supra,* 460 U.S. at 738 (plurality opinion), or requires no Fourth Amendment justification because the officer's perception of the object is obtained from a location and in a manner that involves no antecedent "search," *see id.* at 738-40, if—and only if—the perception so acquired gives the officer "'*probable cause to associate the [object] . . . with criminal activity.*'" *Id.* at 738 (plurality opinion) (original emphasis). *See Arizona v. Hicks,* subparagraph (4) *supra,* 107 S. Ct. at 1153-54. "What the 'plain view' cases have in common is that the police officer in each of them had a prior justification for an intrusion in the course of which he came inadvertently across a piece of evidence incriminating the accused. . . . In each case, this initial intrusion [was] . . . justified by a warrant or by an exception such as 'hot pursuit' or search incident to a lawful arrest, or by an extraneous valid reason for the officer's presence. . . . [P]lain view *alone* is never enough to justify the warrantless seizure of evidence." *Coolidge v. New Hampshire,* 403 U.S. 443, 466-68 (1971)

(plurality opinion; original emphasis); *see also Lo-Ji Sales, Inc. v. New York,* 442 U.S. 319, 326 (1979); *Washington v. Chrisman,* subparagraph (4) *supra,* 455 U.S. at 9 n.5.

(B) (1) The notion of protected persons, places, and objects is rooted in the Fourth Amendment's text, which restricts its "special protection . . . to . . . 'persons, houses, papers, and effects.'" *Hester v. United States,* 265 U.S. 57, 59 (1924). But the interpretation of these terms, like the interpretation of the terms "searches" and "seizures," has increasingly been shaped by "the touchstone of . . . the question whether a person has a 'constitutionally protected reasonable expectation of privacy,'" *Oliver v. United States,* 466 U.S. 170, 177 (1984). *See, e.g., Rawlings v. Kentucky,* 448 U.S. 98, 104-6 (1980). An individual is protected in his or her home or hotel room, *Payton v. New York,* 445 U.S. 573, 589-90 (1980); *Stoner v. California,* 376 U.S. 483 (1964); in a friend's apartment that s/he has "permission to use" and where s/he keeps belongings and has slept "'maybe a night,'" *Jones v. United States,* 362 U.S. 257 (1960), as explained in *Rakas v. Illinois,* 439 U.S. 128, 141 (1978); in his or her place of business, *G.M. Leasing Corp. v. United States,* subparagraph (A)(4) *supra,* 429 U.S. at 353-54, and authorities cited; *Michigan v. Tyler,* subparagraph (A)(5) *supra,* 436 U.S. at 504-5; *Donovan v. Dewey,* 452 U.S. 594, 598 & n.6 (1981) (dictum); *New York v. Burger,* 107 S. Ct. 2636, 2642 (1987) (dictum), even though s/he shares it with employees or co-workers, *Marshall v. Barlow's, Inc.,* 436 U.S. 307, 311-15 (1978); *Mancusi v. DeForte,* 392 U.S. 364 (1968); *O'Connor v. Ortega,* 107 S. Ct. 1492, 1498 (1987) (plurality opinion) (dictum); *id.* at 1505 (Justice Scalia, concurring); *id.* at 1508-10 (dissenting opinion); in his or her automobile, *Preston v. United States,* 376 U.S. 364 (1964); *cf. Delaware v. Prouse,* 440 U.S. 648, 662-63 (1979); and even in a taxicab, telephone booth, or locker that s/he temporarily occupies, *Rios v. United States,* 364 U.S. 253 (1960) (cab); *Lanza v. New York,* 370 U.S. 139, 143 (1962) (dictum) (same); *Katz v. United States,* subparagraph (A)(2) *supra,* 389 U.S. at 352 (phone booth); *United States v. Karo,* subparagraph (A)(2) *supra,* 468 U.S. at 720 n.6 (dictum) (locker); and this is so even if s/he opens his or her house to a considerable group of invitees (as for an illegal crap game), *Recznik v. City of Lorain,* 393 U.S. 166 (1968), or opens his or her shop to customers generally, *LoJi Sales, Inc. v. New York,* subparagraph (A)(1) *supra,* 442 U.S. at 329; see paragraph [240](C)(3)(b) *infra.* But if s/he opens the premises to all comers for the transaction of illegal business and if an undercover police agent enters with his or her acquiescence in the same manner that any other customer might, then s/he has no Fourth Amendment grievance. *Lewis v. United States,* 385 U.S. 206 (1966); *United States v. White,* 401 U.S. 745 (1971); *Maryland v. Macon,* 472 U.S. 463 (1985). Nor does the Fourth Amendment protect objects that s/he has abandoned, *Abel v. United States,* 362 U.S. 217, 240-41 (1960), or the contents of garbage bags that s/he has placed out on the curb for pickup by the trash collector, *California v. Greenwood,* subparagraph (A)(3) *supra,* or records that s/he has permanently delivered into the keeping of another person, at least when that person is expected to make their contents known to government authorities, *Couch v. United States,* 409 U.S. 322, 336 n.19 (1973); *cf. United States v. Miller,* subparagraph (A)(4) *supra,* 425 U.S. at 442-43; *United States v. Payner,* 447 U.S. 727, 731-32 & n.4 (1980); *Securities and Exchange Commission v. Jerry T. O'Brien, Inc.,* 467 U.S. 735, 743 (1984). The Amendment does not protect property owners against trespasses by officers on vacant lands and outlying fields, even when these are posted and fenced, *Hester v. United States, supra; Air Pollution Variance Board v. Western Alfalfa Corp.,* 416 U.S. 861 (1974); *Oliver v. United States, supra,* although it does protect the "curtilage" around a dwelling house because "the curtilage is the area to which extends the intimate activity associated with the 'sanctity of a man's home and the privacies of life,'" *id.,* 466 U.S. at 180 (dictum); *see California v. Ciraolo,* subparagraph (A)(3) *supra,* 106 S. Ct. at 1812 (dictum); *Dow Chemical Co. v. United States,* subparagraph (A)(3) *supra,* 106 S. Ct. at 1825 (dictum); *United States v. Dunn,* subparagraph (A)(3) *supra,* 107 S. Ct. at 1139-40 (dictum); *United States v. Mullin,* 329 F.2d 295 (4th Cir. 1964).

(2) Prior to *Katz v. United States,* subparagraph (A)(2) *supra,* many courts viewed issues of the scope of Fourth Amendment protection as a matter of drawing territorial lines defining constitutionally protected areas. *E.g., Marullo v. United States,* 328 F.2d 361, 330 F.2d 609 (5th Cir. 1964); *Jones v. United States,* 339 F.2d 419 (5th Cir. 1964); *Smayda v. United States,* 352 F.2d 251 (9th Cir.

1965). The *Katz* opinion, although not entirely rejecting the notion of "constitutionally protected areas," does emphasize that the notion cannot "serve as a talismanic solution to every Fourth Amendment problem." 389 U.S. at 351 n.9. Because the "Fourth Amendment protects people, not places," *id.* at 351, it applies to governmental intrusions into "what [the individual] . . . seeks to preserve as private," *ibid.;* into the privacy upon which he justifiably relie[s] . . .," *id.* at 353; into areas "in which there [is] . . . a reasonable expectation of freedom from governmental intrusion," *Mancusi v. DeForte, supra,* 392 U.S. at 368. *See also Rakas v. Illinois,* subparagraph (B)(1) *supra,* 439 U.S. at 143; *United States v. Salvucci,* 448 U.S. 83, 91-92 (1980) (dictum). This new focus upon the protection of "people, not places" (*see also United States v. Chadwick,* 433 U.S. 1, 7 (1977); *Ybarra v. Illinois,* 444 U.S. 85, 91-92 (1979)) and of justifiable expectations of privacy may qualify to some extent the earlier conception that the Fourth Amendment does not restrict surveillance in public-use areas or in places, such as jails and prisons, where "surveillance has traditionally been the order of the day," *Lanza v. New York,* subparagraph (B)(1) *supra,* 370 U.S. at 143 (dictum). That proposition doubtless continues to be valid with regard to surveillance on the public streets insofar as it monitors only activities that "would . . . have been visible to the naked eye," *United States v. Knotts,* subparagraph (A)(4) *supra,* 460 U.S. at 285, and that the actor who conducted them in public thereby "voluntarily conveyed to anyone who wanted to look," *id.* at 281, even though the government's actual means of observing them involved sensory enhancement by technological snooping devices. *United States v. Karo,* subparagraph (A)(2) *supra,* 468 U.S. at 713-14, 721; *see Texas v. Brown,* subparagraph (A)(3) *supra,* 460 U.S. at 739-40 (plurality opinion); *United States v. Santana,* subparagraph (A)(4) *supra,* 427 U.S. at 42; *Terry v. Ohio,* subparagraph (A)(4) *supra,* 392 U.S. at 22-23 (by implication); *cf. G.M. Leasing Corp. v. United States,* subparagraph (A)(4) *supra,* 429 U.S. at 351-52. It also continues to be valid for even more intrusive surveillance in jails and prisons. *Bell v. Wolfish,* 441 U.S. 520, 556-60 (1979); *Hudson v. Palmer,* 468 U.S. 517, 524-30 (1984). But it may no longer hold for particularly intrusive forms of surveillance that are not reasonably to be anticipated in the places or circumstances in which they are employed, such as electronic eavesdropping into private conversations. *Cf. New Jersey v. T.L.O.*, 469 U.S. 325, 337-39 (1985) (dictum) (recognizing that the Fourth Amendment protects a schoolchild's interest in the privacy of a purse which she carries onto public school premises, notwithstanding "the pervasive supervision to which children in the schools are necessarily subject," *id.* at 338); *Griffin v. Wisconsin*, 107 S. Ct. 3164 (1987) (dictum) (recognizing that a "probationer's home, like anyone else's, is protected by the Fourth Amendment[ ]," *id.* at 3167, notwithstanding the "importance of [probation] supervision," *id.* at 3168); *Oliver v. United States*, subparagraph (B)(1) *supra*, 466 U.S. at 179 n.10 (dictum) ("An individual who enters a place defined to be 'public' for Fourth Amendment analysis does not lose all claims to privacy or personal security"); *Dow Chemical Co. v. United States*, subparagraph (A)(3) *supra*, 106 S. Ct. at 1826-27 & n.4 (dictum); *and see* Amsterdam, *Perspectives on the Fourth Amendment*, 58 MINN. L. REV. 349, 403 (1974) (suggesting that the question "whether, if the particular form of surveillance practiced by the police is permitted to go unregulated by constitutional restraints, the amount of privacy and freedom remaining to citizens would be diminished to a compass inconsistent with the aims of a free and open society [is] . . . the judgment that the fourth amendment inexorably requires the Court to make"). Rather than turning Fourth Amendment protection on mere geography, the approach of the recent cases is to read *Katz* as holding "that the application of the Fourth Amendment depends on whether the person invoking its protection can claim a 'justifiable,' a 'reasonable,' or a 'legitimate expectation of privacy' that has been invaded by governmental action," *Smith v. Maryland*, subparagraph (A)(2) *supra*, 442 U.S. at 740, and to treat this question as requiring inquiry into two subquestions: *first*, "whether the individual, by his conduct, has 'exhibited an actual (subjective) expectation of privacy,'" and, *second*, "whether the individual's subjective expectation of privacy is 'one that society is prepared to recognize as "reasonable,"'" *ibid. See, e.g., United States v. Knotts*, subparagraph (A)(4) *supra*, 460 U.S. at 280-85; *United States v. Jacobsen*, subparagraph (A)(4) *supra*, 466 U.S. at 113, 122-25; *Oliver v. United States*, subparagraph (B)(1) *supra*, 466 U.S. at 177-81, 182-84; *Hudson v. Palmer*, *supra*, 468 U.S. at 524-25; *United States v. Karo*, subparagraph (A)(2) *supra*, 468 U.S. at 712,

714-16; *New Jersey v. T.L.O., supra,* 469 U.S. at 337-39; *Maryland v. Macon,* 472 U.S. 463, 469 (1985); *New York v. Class,* subparagraph (A)(3) *supra,* 106 S. Ct. at 965-66, 968-69; *California v. Ciraolo,* subparagraph (A)(3) *supra,* 106 S. Ct. at 1811-13; *California v. Greenwood,* subparagraph (A)(3) *supra,* 108 S. Ct. at 1628-29; *Florida v. Riley,* subparagraph (A)(3) *supra,* 109 S. Ct. 696 (plurality opinion); *id.* at 697 (concurring opinion of Justice O'Connor); *Michigan v. Clifford,* subparagraph (A)(5) *supra,* 464 U.S. at 292 (plurality opinion); *O'Connor v. Ortega,* subparagraph (B)(1) *supra,* 107 S. Ct. at 1497-99 (plurality opinion).

(3) The *Katz* concern for privacy apparently expands but does not exhaust the Fourth Amendment's protection, for although "[t]hat Amendment protects individual privacy against certain kinds of governmental intrusion . . . its protections go further, and often have nothing to do with privacy at all." *Katz v. United States,* subparagraph (A)(2) *supra,* 389 U.S. at 350. *See, e.g., Tennessee v. Garner,* 471 U.S. 1 (1985). It protects certain kinds of property interests — reflected in the constitutional phrases *houses, papers,* and *effects* — independently of any relation that these may have to the privacy of their owner's "person," *see Spinelli v. United States,* 393 U.S. 410, 412 n.2 (1969); *Alderman v. United States,* 394 U.S. 165, 176-80 (1969); *United States v. Chadwick,* subparagraph (B)(2) *supra,* 433 U.S. at 14-16 & n.10; *Mincey v. Arizona,* subparagraph (A)(5) *supra,* 437 U.S. at 391-92; *Walter v. United States,* 447 U.S. 649 (1980); *United States v. Place,* subparagraph (A)(4) *supra,* 462 U.S. at 705-6, 707-10; *United States v. Van Leeuwen,* 397 U.S. 249, 251-52 (1970) (dictum); *Rakas v. Illinois,* subparagraph (B)(1) *supra,* 439 U.S. at 144 n.12 (dictum); and it also protects a range of interests that have been variously described in terms of "personal security," "liberty," and "dignity," *see Davis v. Mississippi,* 394 U.S. 721, 726 (1969); *Terry v. Ohio,* subparagraph (A)(4) *supra,* 392 U.S. at 17; *Delaware v. Prouse,* subparagraph (B)(1) *supra,* 440 U.S. at 653-55, 656-57, 662-63; *Florida v. Royer,* 460 U.S. 491, 502 (1983) (plurality opinion); *Winston v. Lee,* 470 U.S. 753, 758-62 (1985); *United States v. Ortiz,* 422 U.S. 891, 895 (1975) (dictum); *United States v. Martinez-Fuerte,* subparagraph (A)(4) *supra,* 428 U.S. at 554 (dictum); *Michigan v. Summers,* 452 U.S. 692, 698-99 (1981) (dictum); *Immigration and Naturalization Service v. Delgado,* 466

U.S. 210, 215 (1984) (dictum); *New Jersey v. T.L.O.*, subparagraph (B)(2) *supra*, 469 U.S. at 337 (dictum). See paragraphs [236]-[238], [240](A), [245](C), [246](F), [248](A) *infra*.

[232] **The Fifth Amendment privilege.** (A) At its earliest English origins, the privilege was concerned principally with protecting against the compulsion of self-incriminating testimony by legal process. The Fifth Amendment still has that function. It permits a person who is subpoenaed before the grand jury, a criminal investigating agency, a civil court, an administrative or legislative investigatory body, or any other subpoena-assisted tribunal to decline to answer potentially incriminating questions. *Counselman v. Hitchcock*, 142 U.S. 547 (1892); *Malloy v. Hogan*, 378 U.S. 1 (1964); *Lefkowitz v. Turley*, 414 U.S. 70, 77 (1973); *Maness v. Meyers*, 419 U.S. 449, 463-65 (1975); *Lefkowitz v. Cunningham*, 431 U.S. 801 (1977); *Pillsbury Co. v. Conboy*, 459 U.S. 248 (1983); *Baxter v. Palmigiano*, 425 U.S. 308, 316 (1976) (dictum); *United States v. Mandujano*, 425 U.S. 564, 572-76, 584 (1976) (plurality opinion) (dictum); *United States v. Washington*, 431 U.S. 181, 189 (1977) (dictum); *Zurcher v. Stanford Daily*, 436 U.S. 547, 561-62 n.8 (1978) (dictum). See paragraph [161] *supra*. If the person is compelled to answer notwithstanding a valid claim of the privilege (*see Lefkowitz v. Turley*, *supra*, 414 U.S. at 78; *Minnesota v. Murphy*, 465 U.S. 420, 426-29 (1984)) or if the person's freedom of choice to assert the privilege is overborne (*see Garner v. United States*, 424 U.S. 648, 654 n.9, 656-65 (1976); *Lefkowitz v. Cunningham*, *supra*), nothing s/he discloses may thereafter be used as evidence against him or her in a criminal proceeding. *Garrity v. New Jersey*, 385 U.S. 493 (1967); *Murphy v. Waterfront Commission*, 378 U.S. 52 (1964); *New Jersey v. Portash*, 440 U.S. 450 (1979); *United States v. Mandujano*, *supra*, 425 U.S. at 576 (plurality opinion) (dictum); *and see Kastigar v. United States*, 406 U.S. 441, 460-62 (1972). Similarly, the Fifth Amendment forbids the government to extract incriminatory information through disclosure requirements enforced by criminal penalties, *Marchetti v. United States*, 390 U.S. 39 (1968); *Grosso v. United States*, 390 U.S. 62 (1968); *Garner v. United States*, *supra*, 424 U.S. at 650, 662-65 (dictum); *cf. Albertson v. Subversive Activities Control Board*, 382 U.S. 70 (1965), except in a narrow range

of situations in which recordkeeping or disclosure may be required "in an essentially noncriminal and regulatory area of inquiry," *id.* at 79, *see Marchetti v. United States, supra,* 390 U.S. at 55-57, explaining *Shapiro v. United States,* 335 U.S. 1, 32-35 (1948); *cf. California v. Byers,* 402 U.S. 424 (1971). The privilege has, however, also grown beyond its origins. By a process of constant accretion it has come today to be at once the mainstay of modern Anglo-American "accusatorial" criminal procedure and the symbolic expression of a cluster of values concerned with personal self-respect, individual dignity, and independence. *See Murphy v. Waterfront Commission, supra,* 378 U.S. at 55; *Maness v. Meyers, supra,* 419 U.S. at 461; *Carter v. Kentucky,* 450 U.S. 288, 299-300 (1981); *DeLuna v. United States,* 308 F.2d 140, 144-50 (5th Cir. 1962), *rehearing denied,* 324 F.2d 375 (5th Cir. 1963); *see also* LEVY, ORIGINS OF THE FIFTH AMENDMENT (1968); *Culombe v. Connecticut,* 367 U.S. 568, 583-84 n.25 (1961) (plurality opinion). It has long been construed in this country as forbidding any sort of compulsive force directed by a government officer against an individual to cause the individual to disclose self-incriminating information, *Bram v. United States,* 168 U.S. 532 (1897); and thus it gives, as the Supreme Court has unequivocally declared, a right of silence in the police station as well as in the courtroom. *Miranda v. Arizona,* 384 U.S. 436 (1966); *Doyle v. Ohio,* 426 U.S. 610, 617 (1976); *Tague v. Louisiana,* 444 U.S. 469, 470 (1980) (per curiam); *Edwards v. Arizona,* 451 U.S. 477, 481-82 (1981); *Berkemer v. McCarty,* 468 U.S. 420, 428-29 (1984); *Arizona v. Roberson,* 108 S. Ct. 2093, 2100 (1988); *Kolender v. Lawson,* 461 U.S. 352, 360 n.9 (1983) (dictum); *Colorado v. Spring,* 107 S. Ct. 851, 856 (1987) (dictum). *See Estelle v. Smith,* 451 U.S. 454, 466-67 (1981); *Michigan v. Tucker,* 417 U.S. 433, 439-43 (1974) (dictum); *Brown v. Illinois,* 422 U.S. 590, 600-2 (1975) (dictum); *Michigan v. Mosley,* 423 U.S. 96, 99-104 (1975) (dictum). "Under the Fifth Amendment, a criminal defendant may not be compelled to testify against himself. In that sense, the exclusion of involuntary confessions derives from the Amendment itself." *United States v. Raddatz,* 447 U.S. 667, 678 n.4 (1980) (dictum). Accordingly, since the incorporation of the Fifth Amendment privilege into the Fourteenth Amendment in 1964 (see paragraph [227](A) *supra*), it has been recognized that the "standard of voluntariness [of confessions] which [had previously] . . . evolved in state cases under the Due Process Clause of the Fourteenth Amendment [(see paragraph [228] *supra*)] is the same general standard which applied in federal prosecutions—a standard grounded in the policies of the privilege against self-incrimination," *Davis v. North Carolina*, 384 U.S. 737, 740 (1966); *cf. Miller v. Fenton*, 106 S. Ct. 445, 449-50 (1985). See paragraph [363](C), (E) *infra*. And since 1964, it has also been held that the privilege protects against *state* extraction of communications which incriminate an individual at *federal* law, and vice versa. *Murphy v. Waterfront Commission, supra.*

(B) To call the privilege into play, therefore, only four elements need be found.

(1) There must be some sort of *compulsion. See Hoffa v. United States*, 385 U.S. 293 (1966); *Andresen v. Maryland*, 427 U.S. 463, 472-77 (1976); *United States v. Washington*, subparagraph (A) *supra*, 431 U.S. at 186-90; *Lakeside v. Oregon*, 435 U.S. 333, 339 (1978); *South Dakota v. Neville*, 459 U.S. 553, 562-64 (1983); *United States v. Doe*, 465 U.S. 605, 610-12 (1984); *Colorado v. Connelly*, 107 S. Ct. 515, 523-24 (1986). The compulsion may be relatively mild and indirect, such as the threatened loss of a government job, *Garrity v. New Jersey*, subparagraph (A) *supra*, or government contracts, *Lefkowitz v. Turley*, subparagraph (A) *supra*, or the threat of adverse inferences being drawn from a criminal defendant's failure to take the stand, *Griffin v. California*, 380 U.S. 609 (1965); *Carter v. Kentucky*, subparagraph (A) *supra*, 450 U.S. at 301, 305; *Lakeside v. Oregon, supra*, 435 U.S. at 339 (dictum), or the oppressive atmosphere of police in-custody interrogation, *Miranda v. Arizona*, subparagraph (A) *supra; Roberts v. United States*, 445 U.S. 552, 560-61 (1980) (dictum); *Minnesota v. Murphy*, subparagraph (A) *supra*, 465 U.S. at 429-31, 433; *Arizona v. Mauro*, 107 S. Ct. 1931, 1936-37 (1987) (dictum); *compare Oregon v. Mathiason*, 429 U.S. 492 (1977) (per curiam); *California v. Beheler*, 463 U.S. 1121 (1983) (per curiam); *United States v. Washington*, subparagraph (A) *supra*, 431 U.S. at 187 n.5 (dictum). The threat that a party's silence or claim of the privilege in civil litigation or administrative proceedings may be considered adversely by the factfinder in its weighing of other evidence is, however, not sufficient compulsion to trigger the

privilege, *Baxter v. Palmigiano,* subparagraph (A) *supra,* 425 U.S. at 316-20 (prison disciplinary proceedings); *Minnesota v. Murphy,* subparagraph (A) *supra,* 465 U.S. at 436 n.7 (dictum) (probation revocation proceedings); *cf. United States v. Washington,* subparagraph (A) *supra,* 431 U.S. at 191 (grand jury proceedings); *see also United States v. Rylander,* 460 U.S. 752, 758-59 (1983); nor is the threat that an individual may be required to undergo criminal prosecution for failing to make statutorily required disclosures, so long as a good-faith assertion of the privilege is recognized as a sufficient defense to such a prosecution, *Garner v. United States,* subparagraph (A) *supra,* 424 U.S. at 661-65 & n.18; *cf. Selective Service System v. Minnesota Public Interest Research Group,* 468 U.S. 841, 857-58 (1984). The question is whether the individual is confronted with a threat of "potent sanctions" or "substantial penalties" or "grave consequences solely because he refused to . . . give self-incriminating testimony." *Lefkowitz v. Cunningham,* subparagraph (A) *supra,* 431 U.S. at 805, 807; *see Minnesota v. Murphy,* subparagraph (A) *supra,* 465 U.S. at 434-39.

(2) The compulsion must ordinarily be directed *against the individual who will be incriminated if the disclosure sought to be compelled is made,* not against another party. *Couch v. United States,* 409 U.S. 322 (1973); *United States v. Nobles,* 422 U.S. 225, 233-34 (1975); *Fisher v. United States,* 425 U.S. 391, 396-401 (1976); *Securities and Exchange Commission v. Jerry T. O'Brien, Inc.,* 467 U.S. 735, 742-43 (1984).

(3) The compulsion must be directed to extracting a kind of material that the Supreme Court has characterized as *"communications"* or *"testimony,"* *Schmerber v. California,* 384 U.S. 757, 764 (1966), as distinguished from corporal or physical objects or demonstrations, *see United States v. Dionisio,* 410 U.S. 1 (1973); *and see Fisher v. United States,* subparagraph (B)(2) *supra,* 425 U.S. at 408-11; *Washington v. Chrisman,* 455 U.S. 1, 6 n.3 (1982); *South Dakota v. Neville,* subparagraph (B)(1) *supra,* 459 U.S. at 560-62; *United States v. Doe,* subparagraph (B)(1) *supra,* 465 U.S. at 610-12 & n.10; *Doe v. United States,* 108 S. Ct. 2341, 2345-50 (1988); *California v. Byers,* subparagraph (A) *supra,* 402 U.S. at 431-34 (plurality opinion); *United States v. Nobles,* subparagraph (B)(2) *supra,* 422 U.S. at 233 n.7 (dic-

tum). This element is discussed further in the following subparagraph [232](C).

(4) The material that is sought to be extracted by compulsion must present a *"realistic threat of incrimination,"* Fisher v. United States, subparagraph (B)(2) *supra,* 425 U.S. at 412 (emphasis added), as distinguished from "a mere imaginary possibility," *Mason v. United States,* 244 U.S. 362, 366 (1917), or "remote possibilities out of the ordinary course of law," *Heike v. United States,* 227 U.S. 131, 144 (1913). *See Grosso v. United States,* subparagraph (A) *supra,* 390 U.S. at 65-67; *Haynes v. United States,* 390 U.S. 85, 95-97 (1968); *compare United States v. Apfelbaum,* 445 U.S. 115, 128-31 (1980). A sufficient threat is established if the material "would furnish a link in the chain of evidence needed to prosecute the claimant [of the privilege] for a . . . crime," *Hoffman v. United States,* 341 U.S. 479, 486 (1951); see paragraph [161](E) *supra,* or if the material would provide "an 'investigatory lead,' [or produce] . . . evidence . . . by focusing investigation on a witness as a result of his [or her] compelled disclosures," *Kastigar v. United States,* subparagraph (A) *supra,* 406 U.S. at 460; *see id.* at 453-54, 461-62. The threat to which the individual is exposed by the compelled disclosure must be a threat of criminal or "quasi-criminal" sanctions, *see United States v. Ward,* 448 U.S. 242, 251-55 (1980); it is apparently sufficient if the information disclosed can be used *either* to establish criminal guilt *or* to enhance criminal punishment (that is, for purposes of increasing sentence), *Estelle v. Smith,* subparagraph (A) *supra,* 451 U.S. at 462-63 (so holding at least when the information was used to establish the factual predicate for a death sentence); but an exposure to civil liability—even to involuntary civil commitment, *Allen v. Illinois,* 106 S. Ct. 2988 (1986), and to some sorts of civil penalties enforced by suits brought on behalf of the state, *United States v. Ward, supra*—does not implicate the Fifth Amendment privilege. *See United States v. Apfelbaum, supra,* 445 U.S. at 125 (dictum).

(C) The notion that the Fifth Amendment is concerned solely with "testimonial self-incrimination," *Fisher v. United States,* subparagraph (B)(2) *supra,* 425 U.S. at 399, derives contemporary currency from *Schmerber v. California,* subparagraph (B)(3) *supra,* which espoused the notion as a ground for holding that the amendment did not forbid the involuntary extraction of a blood sample from a drunk-driving suspect for chemical analysis. The line between "testimonial" and "nontestimonial" self-incrimination is far from clear, as is evidenced by the recurring problems of police lineups in which the suspects are made to turn, walk, gesture, and speak for voice identification. The question that is probably dispositive of these cases is whether the concept of "'communications' or 'testimony,'" *id.*, 384 U.S. at 764, denotes *discourse* — the communication of informative content — or rather focuses on the distinction between *willed* and *unwilled* acts of an accused, prohibiting the compulsion of a person's exercise of will to incriminate himself or herself as amounting to a violation of human personality. The Supreme Court is presently committed to the *discourse* concept. *See, e.g., Doe v. United States,* subparagraph (B)(3) *supra,* 108 S. Ct. at 2347 ("in order to be testimonial, an accused's communication must itself, explicitly or implicitly, relate a factual assertion or disclose information"); *Estelle v. Smith,* subparagraph (A) *supra,* 451 U.S. at 463-65 (pretrial psychiatric examination of a capital defendant violated the Fifth Amendment when opinion testimony of the psychiatrist based on this examination was used by the prosecution to show probable future dangerousness in support of a death sentence; the psychiatrist's "diagnosis . . . was not based simply on his observation of [the defendant, but] . . . rested on statements [which the defendant] . . . made, and remarks he omitted, in reciting the details of the crime," *id.* at 464; the "Fifth Amendment privilege . . . is directly involved here because the State used as evidence against [the defendant] . . . the substance of his disclosures during the . . . examination," *id.* at 464-65). Thus the Court has found no Fifth Amendment obstacle to compelling suspects to produce handwriting and printing exemplars, *Gilbert v. California,* 388 U.S. 263 (1967); *United States v. Mara,* 410 U.S. 19 (1973); *United States v. Euge,* 444 U.S. 707, 718 (1980), or to speak for voice identification, *United States v. Wade,* 388 U.S. 218 (1967); *United States v. Dionisio,* subparagraph (B)(3) *supra,* or to execute a document authorizing the release of his or her bank records to government investigators, *Doe v. United States,* subparagraph (B)(3) *supra.* Doubtless these decisions will stand until the composition of the Court changes substantially. But they are the kind of decisions that, over a long period of time, tend to be reconsidered and overturned. Like the line of search-incident-to-arrest cases overruled by *Chimel v. California,* 395 U.S. 752 (1969), they represent the product of an unthinking process by which a "'hint'" tossed out the *Schmerber* opinion "was, without persuasive justification, 'loosely turned into dictum and finally elevated to a decision.'" *See* 395 U.S. at 760. In drawing the line between testimonial and nontestimonial extractions, the *Schmerber* Court noted Wigmore's collection of cases from "both federal and state courts . . . usually [holding] . . . that [the Fifth Amendment] . . . offers no protection against compulsion to . . . write or speak for identification . . . or to make a particular gesture," 384 U.S. at 764 — matters not at all in issue in *Schmerber.* The Court then concluded that, "[a]lthough we agree that this distinction [between "communications" and "real or physical evidence"] is a helpful framework for analysis, we are not to be understood to agree with past applications in all instances." *Ibid.* *Dicta* in *Wade* and *Gilbert* next proceeded to rely uncritically upon the same line of cases to reject Fifth Amendment attacks against compulsion of a suspect to speak and write for identification, 388 U.S. at 221-23, 266-67, without mentioning the *Schmerber caveat* or noting (a) that the federal and state cases referenced by *Schmerber* themselves generally depend upon Wigmore's analysis of the privilege against self-incrimination; (b) that the Court had expressly said in *Schmerber* that it was not "to be understood as adopting the Wigmore formulation," 384 U.S. at 763 n.7; (c) that Wigmore, who was "consistently unfriendly to the privilege" and whose writings "are an inexhaustible quarry of quotations apt for use against the policy of the privilege" (*DeLuna v. United States,* subparagraph (A) *supra,* 308 F.2d at 145), based his analysis upon an obdurate insistence that the privilege be restricted to its historical origins; (d) that the Supreme Court had previously rejected that approach, saying that "[to] apply the privilege narrowly or begrudgingly — to treat it as an historical relic, at most merely to be tolerated — is to ignore its development and purpose," *Quinn v. United States,* 349 U.S. 155, 162 (1955); *see also Ullman v. United States,* 350 U.S. 422, 426 (1956); *Miranda v. Arizona,* subparagraph (A) *supra,* 384 U.S. at 458-63; and (e) that, even as an historical matter, Wigmore's view of the privilege was unduly narrow, *see* LEVY, ORIGINS OF THE FIFTH AMENDMENT 325-32, 495-97 (1968). Furthermore, there is no suggestion in *Wade* and *Gilbert* that the parties argued or that the Court seriously considered the alternative possible distinction between "testimonial" and "nontestimonial" compulsion, turning upon whether an individual has been forced by an act of *will* to furnish evidence against himself and thus be "made the deluded instrument of his own conviction." II HAWKINS, PLEAS OF THE CROWN 595 (8th ed. 1824). Justice Fortas's opinion did make the point briefly, 388 U.S. at 261; but Justice Fortas had also dissented in *Scherber* and so did not forcefully emphasize the extent to which *Wade* and *Gilbert* were distinguishable from that decision. The *Wade-Gilbert dicta* finally emerged as holdings in *Dionisio* and *Mara,* over Justice Marshall's dissent urging that the true line between "testimonial" and "nontestimonial" compulsion for Fifth Amendment purposes lies between cases in which an individual is compelled to furnish "active cooperation" in the production of self-incriminating material, 410 U.S. at 37, and those in which s/he is not. Although the Marshall position gives no solace to defendants in the lower courts — or even in the Supreme Court of the United States, probably, for some years to come — it should not be overlooked by counsel with an eye to the future. Pushed persistently enough for long enough, it is likely eventually to prevail. Indeed, recent decisions cutting back the scope of Fifth Amendment protection against the compelled production of documents, the contents of which communicate incriminating information (*e.g., Fisher v. United States,* subparagraph (B)(2) *supra,* 425 U.S. at 405-14 & n.11; *United States v. Doe,* subparagraph (B)(1) *supra,* 465 U.S. at 610-612; see paragraph [163](B) *supra*), have apparently unwittingly deprived the *discourse* approach to self-incrimination of any intelligible foundation.

(D) Only natural persons have a Fifth Amendment privilege against self-incrimination. No privilege may be claimed either on behalf of corporations, partnerships, or unincorporated associations or by individuals on their own behalf in respect to papers and records of these organizations held by the individual in a representative capacity. *See California Bankers Ass'n v. Shultz,* 416 U.S. 21, 55 (1974); *Bellis v. United States,* 417 U.S. 85 (1974); *Braswell v. United States,* 108 S. Ct. 2284 (1988), and cases cited. The Fifth Amendment does, however, forbid the compulsion of an individual to produce records of a sole proprietorship when the act of production would itself incriminate him or her. *United States v. Doe,* subparagraph (B)(1) *supra.*

[233] The Sixth and Fifth Amendment rights to counsel. (A) (1) The Supreme Court has construed the Sixth Amendment to give a criminal defendant the right to counsel, including the right to court-appointed counsel if s/he is indigent (*Gideon v. Wainwright,* 372 U.S. 335 (1963); *Argersinger v. Hamlin,* 407 U.S. 25 (1972); *Baldasar v. Illinois,* 446 U.S. 222 (1980)), not merely at trial but at any pretrial proceeding that is a "critical stage" of the prosecution. *See, e.g., United States v. Henry,* 447 U.S. 264, 269 (1980); *Estelle v. Smith,* 451 U.S. 454, 469-70 (1981); *Maine v. Moulton,* 106 S. Ct. 477, 484 (1985); *Holloway v. Arkansas,* 435 U.S. 475, 489 (1978) (dictum), and cases cited; *compare Gerstein v. Pugh,* 420 U.S. 103, 122-23 (1975). The "critical stage" phraseology was coined in a context that involved a defendant's needs for the services of a lawyer performing the traditional advocate's function — presenting and preserving legal contentions in a judicial proceeding. Thus *Hamilton v. Alabama,* 368 U.S. 52 (1961), held arraignment a "critical stage" because the defense of insanity, if not pleaded at arraignment, might be lost. However, the decision in *White v. Maryland,* 373 U.S. 59 (1963) (per curiam), gave the doctrine a significant new turn. Preliminary hearing was there held to be a "critical stage" because the defendant, without counsel, entered a guilty plea at preliminary hearing that was subsequently used in evidence against him at trial. Hence emerged the notion that, under some circumstances, a defendant had a right to counsel *for the purpose of protecting him or her against improper procedures that produced incriminating evidence,* that is, of preserving the defendant's rights and guarding the defendant's interests in the *investigative* process. *See also Arsenault v. Massachusetts,* 393 U.S. 5 (1968) (per curiam); *Brewer v. Williams,* 430 U.S. 387 (1977); *Moore v. Illinois,* 434 U.S. 220 (1977); *United States v. Henry, supra; Estelle v. Smith, supra; Satterwhite v. Texas,* 108 S. Ct. 1792, 1796 (1988); *Patterson v. Illinois,* 108 S. Ct. 2389, 2395-96 n.6 (1988); *United States v. Morrison,* 449 U.S. 361, 364-65 (1981) (dictum). The notion developed apace in *Escobedo v. Illinois,* 378 U.S. 478 (1964), in which the Court required exclusion of a police station confession obtained by interrogation following the denial of an arrested person's request to be permitted to consult his attorney. *Miranda v. Arizona,* 384 U.S. 436 (1966), made clear that the role of the attorney, as conceived in *Escobedo,* was to support the arrestee effectively in the exercise of his or her privilege against self-incrimination. *See Arizona v. Roberson,* 108 S. Ct. 2093, 2100 (1988); *see also Fare v. Michael C.,* 442 U.S. 707, 719-22 (1979); *United States v. Gouveia,* 467 U.S. 180, 188 n.5 (1984); *Moran v. Burbine,* 106 S. Ct. 1135, 1140-41, 1143 (1986); *Connecticut v. Barrett,* 107 S. Ct. 828, 831-32 (1987). *Miranda* accordingly declared inadmissible all incriminating statements made by persons undergoing custodial interrogation without prior warning and waiver of their right to counsel (including appointed counsel) as well as of the Fifth Amendment privilege. *Edwards v. Arizona,* 451 U.S. 477 (1981); *Tague v. Louisiana,* 444 U.S. 469 (1980) (per curiam); *Berkemer v. McCarty,* 468 U.S. 420 (1984); *Smith v. Illinois,* 469 U.S. 91 (1984) (per curiam); *Michigan v. Mosley,* 423 U.S. 96, 99-100 (1975) (dictum).

(2) *Escobedo* and *Miranda* are treated in more detail in paragraph [363](D), (E) *infra.* Here it suffices to note that the right to counsel given by those decisions applies only when a person who is in "custody" (*see Oregon v. Mathiason,* 429 U.S. 492 (1977) (per curiam); *California v. Beheler,* 463 U.S. 1121 (1983) (per curiam); *New York v. Quarles,* 467 U.S. 649, 654 n.4, 655 (1984) (dictum); *cf. Minnesota v. Murphy,* 465 U.S. 420, 429-31 (1984))—in the sense that his or her "freedom of action is curtailed to a 'degree associated with formal arrest,'" *Berkemer v. McCarty,* subparagraph (1) *supra,* 468 U.S. at 440—is subjected to some form of "interrogation," *see Rhode Island v. Innis,* 446 U.S. 291 (1980); *Arizona v. Mauro,* 107 S. Ct. 1931, 1934-36 (1987); and that the right may be waived, *see North Carolina v. Butler,* 441 U.S. 369 (1979); *Wyrick v. Fields,* 459 U.S. 42 (1982) (per curiam); *Oregon v. Elstad,* 470 U.S. 298 (1985); *Colorado v. Connelly,* 107 S. Ct. 515 (1986); *Colorado v. Spring,* 107 S. Ct. 851 (1987); *Connecticut v. Barrett,* subparagraph (1) *supra.* Indeed, in *Moran v. Burbine,* 106 S. Ct. 1135 (1986), the Supreme Court found a valid waiver of the right to counsel when a suspect undergoing interrogation in custody was "informed of his rights pursuant to *Miranda* . . . and execut[ed] a series of written waivers," *id.* at

1138, even though an attorney who phoned the police station on his behalf and offered to represent him during any police questioning had been falsely assured by officers that he would not be interrogated until the following day. The Court held that because the right to counsel and to warnings under *Miranda* "are 'not themselves rights protected by the Constitution but . . . instead measures to insure that the [suspect's] right against compulsory self-incrimination [is] protected,'" *id.* at 1143, this right to counsel cannot be asserted by a lawyer on the suspect's behalf but is one to be exercised or forgone by the suspect personally. It noted that the suspect in *Burbine* was not aware of the attorney's efforts to reach him, and it reasoned that, "[a]lthough highly inappropriate, even deliberate [police] deception of an attorney could not possibly affect a suspect's decision to waive his *Miranda* rights unless he were at least aware of the incident." *Id.* at 1142. The *Escobedo* decision, in which an attorney asking to see an arrested suspect at the police station was turned away by officers who then "incorrectly told the *suspect* that his lawyer '"didn't want to see" him,'" was explicitly distinguished on the latter ground. *Id.* at 1142 (emphasis in original). Significantly, *Burbine* emphasized that "[n]othing we say today disables the States from adopting different requirements for the conduct of [state] . . . employees and officials as a matter of state law," *id.* at 1145; and several state courts have subsequently repudiated *Burbine* under their state constitutions, excluding all or some confessions obtained by in-custody interrogation after police officers had thwarted efforts by a lawyer to gain access to an arrested suspect. *E.g., People v. Houston,* 42 Cal.3d 595, 724 P.2d 1166, 230 Cal. Rptr. 141 (1986); *State v. Stoddard,* 206 Conn. 157, 537 A.2d 446 (1988).

(3) A separate development, *Massiah v. United States,* 377 U.S. 201 (1964), excludes statements made to a police spy by a defendant in the absence of counsel following indictment and appears to condemn the fruits of any conversation pursued by a government agent for investigative purposes (*cf. Weatherford v. Bursey,* 429 U.S. 545 (1977)) with an uncounseled defendant following the initiation of adversary judicial proceedings (see subparagraph (B)(1) *infra*), *Brewer v. Williams,* subparagraph (1) *supra,* 430 U.S. at 398-99; *United States v. Henry,* subparagraph (1)

supra, 447 U.S. at 270 ("[t]he question . . . is whether . . . a Government agent 'deliberately elicited' incriminating statements from [the defendant in the absence of counsel]"); *Maine v. Moulton,* subparagraph (1) *supra,* 106 S. Ct. at 487 ("knowing exploitation by the State of an opportunity to confront the accused without counsel being present is as much a breach of the State's obligation not to circumvent the right to the assistance of counsel as is the intentional creation of such an opportunity"); *Kuhlmann v. Wilson,* 106 S. Ct. 2616, 2630 (1986) ("the defendant must demonstrate that the police and their informant took some action, beyond merely listening, that was designed deliberately to elicit incriminating remarks"); *Rhode Island v. Innis, supra,* 446 U.S. at 300 n.4 (dictum), unless the defendant has knowingly and voluntarily waived the right to counsel, *Brewer v. Williams,* subparagraph (1) *supra,* 430 U.S. at 401-6. The application of *Massiah* in *United States v. Wade,* 388 U.S. 218 (1967), requiring counsel at a postindictment police lineup, makes it clear that the presence of counsel may be required to protect other interests of the accused during police investigation, in addition to the interest against compelled self-incrimination. The Sixth Amendment "requires that we scrutinize *any* pretrial confrontation of the accused to determine whether the presence of his counsel is necessary to preserve the defendant's basic right to a fair trial as affected by his right meaningfully to cross-examine the witnesses against him and to have effective assistance of counsel at the trial itself. It calls upon us to analyze whether potential substantial prejudice to defendant's rights inheres in the particular confrontation and the ability of counsel to help avoid that prejudice." 388 U.S. at 227. *See United States v. Morrison, supra,* 449 U.S. at 364-65 (dictum). Applying this test, the Court held in *Gilbert v. California,* 388 U.S. 263 (1967), that counsel was *not* required to be present when handwriting exemplars were taken from an accused. *See also United States v. Euge,* 444 U.S. 707, 718 n.13 (1980) (dictum). (The *Wade* rule was announced prospectively and applies only to lineups staged after June 12, 1967. *See Stovall v. Denno,* 388 U.S. 293 (1967).)

(4) Thus the Court's decisions recognize two overlapping but not congruent rights to counsel during the investigative phases of a criminal prosecution. *Michigan v. Jackson,* 106 S. Ct. 1404, 1407-8

(1986). The first, whose principal expression is *Miranda,* was developed by extension of the "critical stage" analysis of Sixth Amendment cases but has now come to be seen as an adjunct of the Fifth Amendment privilege against self-incrimination — one of the "procedural safeguards . . . necessary to protect a defendant's Fifth . . . Amendment privilege," *Rhode Island v. Innis, supra,* 446 U.S. at 297. Indeed, the Court has gone so far as to say that this "right to counsel . . . is based not on the Sixth and Fourteenth Amendments, but rather on the Fifth and Fourteenth Amendments as interpreted in the *Miranda* opinion." *Rhode Island v. Innis, supra,* 446 U.S. at 300 n.4; *see also Edwards v. Arizona, supra,* 451 U.S. at 481-82. It therefore applies only in situations in which a defendant is in jeopardy of making self-incriminating disclosures, that is, "testimonial" statements (see paragraph [232](B)(3), (C) *supra*), but it applies to all such situations in which "custodial interrogation" is found, whether they occur before or after the initiation of adversary proceedings, *Edwards v. Arizona, supra; Arizona v. Roberson, supra.* A second right to counsel, stemming from *Massiah* and *Wade,* is based exclusively on the Sixth Amendment (and its incorporation into the Fourteenth, see paragraphs [57-A](B)(1), [227] *supra*); it attaches only upon the initiation of adversary criminal proceedings (as discussed more fully in subparagraph (B)(1) *infra*), but it then attaches whether or not the defendant is in custody, *see Massiah v. United States, supra; Maine v. Moulton,* subparagraph (1) *supra; United States v. Henry, supra,* 447 U.S. at 273-74 n.11 (dictum), or is interrogated, *see Rhode Island v. Innis, supra,* 446 U.S. at 300 n.4 (dictum); *cf. Kuhlmann v. Wilson,* subparagraph (3) *supra,* 106 S. Ct. at 2629, and whether or not the defendant's Fifth Amendment interests are in jeopardy, *see United States v. Wade, supra; Michigan v. Jackson, supra,* 106 S. Ct. at 1409 n.5. The distinct nature of these two rights to counsel during police investigation should be kept in mind: One may protect the defendant in circumstances in which the other does not (*see Estelle v. Smith, supra,* 451 U.S. at 470 n.14; *Edwards v. Arizona, supra,* 451 U.S. at 480-82 n.7; *Arizona v. Roberson, supra,* 108 S. Ct. at 2100)); and even when both are applicable, they may have different incidents — for example, different requisites for valid waiver (*see Patterson v. Illinois, supra,* 108 S. Ct. at 2397 n.9 (dictum) ("there will be cases where a waiver which would be valid under *Miranda* will not suffice for Sixth Amendment purposes"); *Wyrick v.*

Fields, supra, 459 U.S. at 49 (holding the Fifth Amendment right to counsel waived while noting that "Sixth Amendment issues . . . are not before us"); *id.* at 52-55 (dissenting opinion of Justice Marshall); *cf. Fields v. Wyrick,* 706 F.2d 879 (8th Cir. 1983) (on remand)). The *Miranda* right is considered further in paragraph [363](E) *infra;* the *Massiah-Wade* right is the subject of the following subparagraph (B) and also of paragraphs [363](F) and [374] *infra.*

(B) Two developments since *Wade* qualify and complicate the *Massiah-Wade* Sixth Amendment right to counsel:

(1) In *Kirby v. Illinois,* 406 U.S. 682 (1972), the Supreme Court refused to require the exclusion of a witness's testimony that he had identified the defendant in the police station, shortly following the defendant's arrest, in the absence of a lawyer. The defendant neither asked for counsel nor was told, as *Wade* requires, of his right to counsel. Although the witness was brought to the station to view the defendant, there was no formally staged showup or lineup because as soon as the witness entered the room where the defendant was sitting, he saw and identified the defendant. Writing for four members of the Court, Justice Stewart noted that the identification in *Wade* had occurred after indictment, and he distinguished *Wade* on the ground that "a person's Sixth and Fourteenth Amendment right to counsel attaches only at or after the time that adversary judicial proceedings have been initiated against him," 406 U.S. at 688, "whether by way of formal charge, preliminary hearing, indictment, information, or arraignment," *id.* at 689. (*See also United States v. Mandujano,* 425 U.S. 564, 581 (1976) (plurality opinion) (dictum)). Four Justices dissented in *Kirby* on the ground that *Wade* was controlling, and Justice Powell concurred in the result with a one-sentence opinion saying only that he "would not extend the Wade-Gilbert *per se* exclusionary rule." 406 U.S at 691. Since Justice Powell's vote was necessary to make up a majority, the meaning of the *Kirby* decision is entirely confused, but subsequent opinions treat the case as establishing the rule that "until such time as the "'government has committed itself to prosecute, and . . . the adverse positions of government and defendant have solidified'" the Sixth Amendment right to counsel does not attach," *Moran v. Burbine,* subparagraph

(A)(1) *supra,* 106 S. Ct. at 1147; *see United States v. Gouveia,* subparagraph (A)(1) *supra,* 467 U.S. at 187 ("the right to counsel attaches only at or after the initiation of adversary judicial proceedings against the defendant"; *see also id.* at 188-89). Controversy among the Justices on this point apparently continues, with different opinions conveying different intimations about it, depending on the identity of the author. *Compare Burbine and Gouveia with Maine v. Moulton,* subparagraph (A)(1) *supra,* 106 S. Ct. at 487 ("[t]he Sixth Amendment guarantees the accused, at least after the initiation of formal charges, the right to rely on counsel as a 'medium' between him and the State"; *see also id.* at 484). In the present posture of the law, defense counsel can plausibly argue that a right to counsel arises in some situations prior to indictment or information, on either of two theories:

(a) Justice Stewart's plurality opinion in *Kirby* itself recognizes that the "initiation of adversary judicial . . . proceedings" which triggers the Sixth Amendment right to counsel may be marked by "formal charge" *or* by "preliminary hearing" *or* by "arraignment." 406 U.S. at 689. *See also Estelle v. Smith,* subparagraph (A)(1) *supra,* 451 U.S. at 469-70 (dictum). Subsequent cases demonstrate that although the filing of a formal charging paper, such as an indictment, is, of course, a sufficient condition to bring the Sixth Amendment into play (*id.* at 469), it is not an indispensable condition. *See Moore v. Illinois,* subparagraph (A)(1) *supra,* 434 U.S. at 226-29 (*Wade* right to counsel attaches at preindictment preliminary hearing); *Brewer v. Williams,* subparagraph (A)(1) *supra,* 430 U.S. at 398-99 (*Massiah* right to counsel attaches when defendant is ordered to be committed following preliminary arraignment); *Michigan v. Jackson,* subparagraph (A)(2) *supra,* 106 S. Ct. at 1407 & n.3 (preliminary arraignment suffices to establish the "'initiation of adversary judicial proceedings'" within *Kirby*). The requirement of a "formal charge" should be satisfied by the filing of a criminal complaint, although that issue was reserved in *Edwards v. Arizona,* subparagraph (A)(1) *supra,* 451 U.S. at 480-82 n.7. Arguably, it should be satisfied by booking, *see City of Tacoma v. Heater,* 67 Wash.2d 733, 409 P.2d 867, 871

(1966), at least where the magistrate's proceedings are handled for the state by the police rather than by the District Attorney, since in these cases booking represents the point at which "the government has committed itself to prosecute, and . . . the adverse positions of government and defendant have solidified," *Kirby v. Illinois, supra,* 406 U.S. at 689, quoted with approval in *United States v. Gouveia, supra,* 467 U.S. at 189, and in *Moran v. Burbine, supra,* 106 S. Ct. at 1147. And as soon as a prosecuting attorney becomes involved in the case in any fashion, it can be contended that the requisite "adversary judicial proceedings" have commenced, in light of the Sixth Amendment's concern to assure against the "imbalance in the adversary system" which exists when a legally untrained and uncounseled defendant stands against "a professional prosecuting official." *See United States v. Ash,* 413 U.S. 300, 309 (1973), discussed in subparagraph (B)(2) *infra; Wardius v. Oregon,* 412 U.S. 470 (1973), paragraph [270](H) *infra.*

(b) Neither the prevailing opinion in *Kirby* nor any of its progeny have purported to overrule *Miranda* or *Escobedo,* which clearly provide some right to counsel before the "initiation of adversary judicial proceedings." Those cases are commonly distinguished on the ground that, in both, the right to counsel derived not from the Sixth Amendment but from the necessity to provide adequate protection for the Fifth. *Kirby v. Illinois, supra,* 406 U.S. at 688, 689; *United States v. Gouveia, supra,* 467 U.S. at 188 n.5; *see also Brewer v. Williams,* subparagraph (A)(1) *supra,* 430 U.S. at 397; *United States v. Mandujano, supra,* 425 U.S. at 581 n.6 (plurality opinion); *cf. Garner v. United States,* 424 U.S. 648, 657 (1976); *Doyle v. Ohio,* 426 U.S. 610, 617 (1976). But there is nothing unique about the Fifth Amendment privilege against self-incrimination from the standpoint of the need for an ancillary right to counsel to protect it: "'[T]he right to be represented by counsel . . . affects [a person's] . . . ability to assert any other rights he [or she] may have,'" *United States v. Cronic,* 466 U.S. 648, 654 (1984). *Wade,* for example, seemed most concerned with the right to counsel as a means of protecting the defendant's interest in fair adversarial testing of the prosecution's identification evidence at trial, *see* 388 U.S. at 227-37 — an interest that is itself vouchsafed by the Sixth Amendment Confrontation Clause, *see id.* at 235; paragraph [360] *infra*. Arguably, then, the reason no right to counsel was found in *Kirby* was simply because, on the facts of that particular case, the analysis required by *Wade,* "whether potential substantial prejudice to the defendant's rights inheres in the particular confrontation and the ability of counsel to help avoid that prejudice," 388 U.S. at 227, showed no prejudice or jeopardy to any federal constitutional right which a lawyer might have helped Kirby to avert. *See Patterson v. Illinois,* subparagraph (A)(1) *supra,* 108 S. Ct. at 2398: "[W]e have defined the scope of the right to counsel by a pragmatic assessment of the usefulness of counsel to the accused at the particular proceeding, and the dangers to the accused of proceeding without counsel." By contrast, such prejudice would exist and would call for application of the reasoning of *Miranda* and *Wade* by which "we have extended an accused's right to counsel to certain 'critical' pretrial proceedings" (*United States v. Gouveia, supra,* 467 U.S. at 189; *see also Maine v. Moulton,* subparagraph (A)(1) *supra,* 106 S. Ct. at 484) whenever any other federal constitutional right is threatened with overreaching: for example, in the case of the right to confrontation, when

(i) a formal showup or lineup is conducted that is "not intended merely to secure information, but [is] . . . specifically designed to elicit [identification evidence]," *cf. Clewis v. Texas,* 386 U.S. 707, 711 (1967), since in such a case, trial is little more than an appeal from the police station, *see Maine v. Moulton, supra,* 106 S. Ct. at 484, quoting *United States v. Wade, supra,* 388 U.S. at 224;

(ii) the defendant is requested or required to *do* something during an identification confrontation, with regard to which counsel's advice or assistance might supply protective guidance (*cf. Estelle v. Smith,* subparagraph (A)(1) *supra,* 451 U.S. at 469-71; *Satterwhite v. Texas,* subparagraph (A)(1) *supra,* 108 S. Ct. at 1796; and see the following subparagraph (B)(2));

(iii) the witness's identification is less immediate or positive than in the *Kirby* case (*see Neil v. Biggers,* 409 U.S. 188 (1972) (per Justice Powell));

(iv) the witness fails to identify the defendant at trial, thereby making his or her pretrial identification both crucial and suspect and justifying its exclusion as necessary for "the safeguarding of constitutional claims of innocence" (*see* Justice Powell's concurring opinion in *Schneckoth v. Bustamonte,* 412 U.S. 218, 274 (1973)), and "essential 'to protect the fairness of the trial itself'" (*United States v. Ash, supra,* 413 U.S. at 322 (concurring opinion of Justice Stewart)); or

(v) other circumstances in the conduct of a lineup, showup, or identification confrontation introduce a risk of unreliability which, while insufficient to constitute an independent violation of the defendant's Due Process rights under *Manson v. Brathwaite,* 432 U.S. 98 (1977), paragraph [228] *supra,* make the absence of counsel at the identification particularly hurtful from the standpoint of "the prevention of unfairness and the lessening of the hazards of eyewitness identification at the lineup [or other confrontation] itself," *United States v. Wade, supra,* 388 U.S. at 235; *see Kirby v. Illinois, supra,* 406 U.S. at 690 (plurality opinion), acknowledging that "when the police do abuse identification procedures . . . [, s]uch abuses are not beyond the reach of the Constitution."

(2) In *United States v. Ash,* subparagraph (B)(1) *supra,* the Court refused to extend *Wade's* right to counsel so as to require the presence of a defendant's lawyer at postindictment, pretrial exhibitions of photographs by the prosecutor to a prosecution witness for identification. The Court's opinion recognizes two primary purposes of the Sixth Amendment: (a) to provide "counsel as a guide through complex legal technicalities," 413 U.S. at 307, "as a spokesman for, or advisor to, the accused," *id.* at 312, and (b) "to minimize the imbalance in the adversary system that otherwise resulted with the creation of a professional prosecuting official," *id.* at 309. Pretrial stages of a criminal case are therefore "critical," requiring counsel under *Hamilton v. Alabama,* subparagraph (A)(1) *su-*

pra, if, but only if, the defendant is "confronted . . . by the procedural system, or by his expert adversary, or by both." 413 U.S. at 310. A photographic identification is not "critical" in this sense because, "[s]ince the accused himself is not present . . ., no possibility arises that the accused might be misled by his lack of familiarity with the law or overpowered by his professional adversary." *Id.* at 317. Conversely, counsel would be necessary when required "to produce equality in a trial-like adversary confrontation." *Ibid. See also Geders v. United States,* 425 U.S. 80, 88-89 (1976); *Cuyler v. Sullivan,* 446 U.S. 335, 343 (1980) (dictum) ("[u]nless a defendant charged with a serious offense has counsel able to invoke the procedural and substantive safeguards that distinguish our system of justice, a serious risk of injustice infects the trial itself"); *Kimmelman v. Morrison,* 106 S. Ct. 2574, 2583 (1986) ("[t]he essence of an ineffective assistance claim is that counsel's unprofessional errors so upset the adversarial balance between defense and prosecution that the trial was rendered unfair and the verdict rendered suspect"). Under this reasoning, after the "initiation of adversary . . . proceedings" within the meaning of subparagraph (B)(1) *supra,* the defendant should be entitled to have a lawyer present in any situation when:

(a) counsel's advice, based upon legal knowledge, would be useful to the defendant in guiding what the defendant says or does — including all situations in which the defendant is asked by investigators to make any response requiring judgment or choice (*see Estelle v. Smith,* subparagraph (A)(1) *supra; Satterwhite v. Texas,* subparagraph (A)(1) *supra; compare Massiah v. United States,* subparagraph (A)(3) *supra; Beatty v. United States,* 389 U.S. 45 (1967) (per curiam), *rev'g* 377 F.2d 181 (5th Cir. 1967); *Brewer v. Williams,* subparagraph (A)(1) *supra; and United States v. Henry,* subparagraph (A)(1) *supra, with Gilbert v. California,* subparagraph (A)(3) *supra*) and all other situations involving "government efforts to elicit information from the accused" (*Michigan v. Jackson,* subparagraph (A)(4) *supra,* 106 S. Ct. at 1408), or

(b) the defendant is personally confronted by a prosecuting attorney (*see Moore v. Illinois,* subparagraph (A)(1) *supra,* 434 U.S. at 228; *cf. United States v. Gouveia,* 467 U.S. 180,

189 (1984) (dictum) (the purpose of the Sixth Amendment is "protecting the unaided layman at critical confrontations with his adversary"); *Evitts v. Lucey,* 469 U.S. 387, 394-95 n.6 (1985) (dictum) ("[o]ur cases dealing with the right to counsel . . . have often focused on the defendant's need for an attorney to meet the adversary presentation of the prosecutor"), or

(c) the defendant's legal rights may be prejudiced in the absence of a professionally trained advocate to present or preserve them (*see Hamilton v. Alabama,* subparagraph (A)(1) *supra; cf. Wheat v. United States,* 108 S. Ct. 1692, 1696 (1988) (dictum) ("an unaided layman may have little skill in arguing the law or in coping with an intricate procedural system"); *Strickland v. Washington,* 466 U.S. 668, 685 (1984) (dictum) ("[t]he right to counsel plays a crucial role in the adversarial system embodied in the Sixth Amendment, since access to counsel's skill and knowledge is necessary to accord defendants the 'ample opportunity to meet the case of the prosecution' to which they are entitled"); *McCoy v. Court of Appeals,* 108 S. Ct. 1895, 1900 (1988) (dictum) ("[t]he 'guiding hand of counsel' . . . is essential for the evaluation of the prosecution's case, the determination of trial strategy, [and] the possible negotiation of a plea bargain [as well as at trial]").

(C) The Sixth Amendment also restricts governmental investigative activity that invades the privacy of communications between a criminal defendant and defense counsel. *United States v. Morrison,* subparagraph (A)(1) *supra,* 449 U.S. at 364-65 (dictum), and cases cited; *United States v. Seale,* 461 U.S. 345, 364-66 (7th Cir. 1972); *cf. Patterson v. Illinois,* subparagraph (A)(1) *supra,* 108 S. Ct. at 2393 n.3. The boundaries of this principle are discussed in *Weatherford v. Bursey,* subparagraph (A)(3) *supra.* See paragraph [363](G) *infra.*

[234] Has anything happened that may give rise to an issue under the constitutional doctrines relating to illegally obtained evidence?

(A) Was the defendant stopped or accosted, arrested, or taken into custody by the authorities at any time? If so, see paragraph [235] *infra*.

(B) Was the defendant's body or clothing inspected or any physical examination of the defendant made or any tests made on the defendant's body or on any object or fluid, hair, or like substance taken from the defendant's body? If so, see paragraph [238] *infra*.

(C) Has the defendant made any statement to the authorities? If so, see paragraph [363] *infra*.

(D) Has the defendant appeared pursuant to a subpoena to testify or to produce books, records, or things before any government agent or agency? If so, see paragraph [239] *infra*.

(E) Were the defendant's home or office, place of work, or any premises with which s/he has more than transitory connections entered by the authorities? If so, see paragraph [240] *infra*.

(F) Were any premises entered by the authorities while the defendant was in them? If so, see paragraph [242] *infra*.

(G) Was surveillance of any sort maintained by the authorities into or around any premises described in items (E) or (F) *supra*? If so, see paragraph [243] *infra*.

(H) Were yards or grounds around any premises described in items (E) or (F) *supra* entered or put under surveillance by the authorities? If so, see paragraph [244] *infra*.

(I) Was any telephone owned or used by the defendant tapped? If so, see paragraph [245] *infra*.

(J) Was the defendant's automobile stopped, seized, entered, or inspected by the authorities? If so, see paragraph [246] *infra*.

(K) Was any automobile in which the defendant was riding or of which s/he had temporary possession stopped, seized, entered, or inspected by the authorities? If so, see paragraph [246](F) *infra*.

(L) Was any physical object seized from the defendant's possession or inspected in the defendant's possession by the authorities? If so, see paragraph [247] *infra*.

(M) Was any physical object belonging to the defendant inspected or seized by the authorities? If so, see paragraph [248] *infra*.

(N) Were any documents or records relating to the defendant inspected or seized by the authorities? If so, see paragraph [248](G) *infra.*

(O) Were informers, "special agents," or other sorts of police spies used in the investigation of the defendant? If so, see paragraph [249] *infra.*

(P) Did private persons cooperate with the authorities in the investigation of the defendant? If so, see paragraph [250] *infra.*

[235] Defendant stopped, accosted, arrested, or taken into custody. If the defendant was stopped, accosted, arrested, or taken into custody by the authorities, there are two principal areas of legal challenge:

(A) *The stopping, accosting, or arrest* [see paragraph [236] *infra*];

(B) *Postarrest custodial treatment* [see paragraph [237] *infra*].

[236] The stopping, accosting, or arrest. (A) If a defendant has been unconstitutionally detained or arrested, all evidence obtained as a result of the detention or arrest is inadmissible. This includes:

(1) *Any physical object or substance seized without a warrant at or after the time of arrest, the validity of whose seizure depends on the arrest. Beck v. Ohio,* 379 U.S. 89 (1964); *Sibron v. New York,* 392 U.S. 40, 62-66 (1968); *Whiteley v. Warden,* 401 U.S. 560 (1971); *compare Maryland v. Macon,* 472 U.S. 463, 467-68, 471 (1985). As noted in paragraphs [229]-[230] *supra,* a search of a person or of a constitutionally protected area or a search or seizure of a protected object may ordinarily be made only under the authorization of a search warrant. See also paragraphs [240](C), [247](A), [248](C) *infra.* Two major exceptions to this rule are the doctrines allowing warrantless searches incident to arrest (paragraph [240](C)(3)(d) *infra*) and warrantless "frisks" (that is, weapons pat-downs) incident to investigative detentions (subparagraph (D) *infra*). These searches and the seizure of objects found by them are, however, unconstitutional if the arrest or detention is unconstitutional. *E.g., United States v. Di Re,* 332 U.S. 581 (1948); *Henry v. United States,* 361 U.S. 98 (1959). Similarly, if an unconstitutionally arrested or detained person attempts to drop or to

throw away objects or exposes them to police when attempting to discard them, their observation and seizure are tainted by the arrest or detention. *Reid v. Georgia,* 448 U.S. 438 (1980) (per curiam); see paragraph [247](D) *infra.*

(2) *Any observation made at or after the time of arrest, whose validity depends on the arrest. Johnson v. United States,* 333 U.S. 10 (1948). Another exception to the rule requiring that searches be authorized by a search warrant is the doctrine permitting entry into premises, under certain circumstances, for the purpose of arresting a person reasonably believed to be inside. (In some of these circumstances the police are required to have an *arrest* warrant; in others they may enter without a warrant of any sort. See paragraph [240] (C) (3) (c), (e) *infra.*) The validity of such an entry, and of all observations made in the course of it, however, depends on the constitutionality of the arrest or intended arrest. *Johnson v. United States, supra; Massachusetts v. Painten,* 368 F.2d 142 (1st Cir. 1966), *cert. dismissed,* 389 U.S. 560 (1968).

(3) *Confessions or statements made in custody after the arrest or otherwise induced by pressures flowing from the arrest* "unless intervening events break the causal connection between the illegal arrest and the confession so that the confession is ""'sufficiently an act of free will to purge the primary taint.'""" *Taylor v. Alabama,* 457 U.S. 687, 690 (1982). *Wong Sun v. United States,* 371 U.S. 471 (1963); *Brown v. Illinois,* 422 U.S. 590 (1975); *Dunaway v. New York,* 442 U.S. 200 (1979); *Lanier v. South Carolina,* 106 S. Ct. 297 (1985) (per curiam); *Oregon v. Elstad,* 470 U.S. 298, 306 (1985) (dictum). *Compare Rawlings v. Kentucky,* 448 U.S. 98, 106-10 (1980); and *cf. United States v. Ceccolini,* 435 U.S. 268, 273-79 (1978) (dictum).

(4) *Any physical object or substance or observation obtained by a search or seizure whose validity depends upon consent, when the consent is given in custody after the arrest or otherwise induced by pressures flowing from the arrest. Florida v. Royer,* 460 U.S. 491 (1983). Still another exception to the warrant requirement is the principle allowing warrantless searches and seizures with consent of the party affected. See paragraph [240](C)(3)(a) *infra.* The consent relied upon, however, is ineffective if made under conditions of confinement that would render a confession or in-

criminating statement inadmissible, and for the same reasons. *See* the *Watson* and *Klapholz* cases cited in paragraph [237](B) *infra*. Accordingly, the *Wong Sun* rule, subsection (3) *supra*, invalidates consent given by a defendant in custody following an unconstitutional arrest. *Cf. United States v. Watson*, 423 U.S. 411, 414 (1976) (dictum).

(5) *Fingerprint exemplars taken after the arrest. Davis v. Mississippi*, 394 U.S. 721 (1969); *Hayes v. Florida*, 470 U.S. 811 (1985); *Bynum v. United States*, 262 F.2d 465 (D.C. Cir. 1959); *see Taylor v. Alabama*, subparagraph (3) *supra*, 457 U.S. at 692-93 (dictum), and, by the same logic, any other evidence obtained through physical custody of the defendant — lineup identifications, body-test results, and so forth.

(6) *Evidence derived from any of the foregoing sources.* See paragraph [251] *infra*.

(B) (1) "[W]henever a police officer accosts an individual and restrains his freedom to walk away, he has 'seized' that person" for purposes of the Fourth Amendment's regulation of "seizures" and hence for purposes of the exclusionary consequences just described. *Terry v. Ohio*, 392 U.S. 1, 16 (1968). *See, e.g., United States v. Brignoni-Ponce*, 422 U.S. 873, 878 (1975): *Brown v. Texas*, 443 U.S. 47, 50 (1979); *Reid v. Georgia*, subparagraph (A)(1) *supra*, 448 U.S. at 440; *United States v. Ward*, 488 F.2d 162, 168 (9th Cir. 1973) (en banc); *Cupp v. Murphy*, 412 U.S. 291, 294 (1973) (dictum); *Michigan v. Summers*, 452 U.S. 692, 696 & n.5 (1981) (dictum); *United States v. Jacobsen*, 466 U.S. 109, 113 n.5 (1984) (dictum); *cf. United States v. Martinez-Fuerte*, 428 U.S. 543, 554-60 (1976); *Berkemer v. McCarty*, 468 U.S. 420, 436-40 (1984). The restraint may be physical, *Sibron v. New York*, 392 U.S. 40, 67 (1968); *see Brower v. County of Inyo*, 109 S. Ct. 1378 (1989), or it may take the form of a command to "stand still" or to "come along" or any other gesture or expression indicating that the person is not free to go as s/he pleases. *Dunaway v. New York*, subparagraph (A)(3) *supra*, 442 U.S. at 203, 207 n.6; *Florida v. Royer*, subparagraph (A)(4) *supra*, 460 U.S. at 501-4 & n.9 (plurality opinion); *id.* at 511-12 (concurring opinion of Justice Brennan); *Kelley v. United States*, 298 F.2d 310 (D.C. Cir. 1961); *cf. Terry v. Ohio, supra*, 392 U.S. at 19 n.16; *Sibron v. New York, supra*, 392 U.S. at 63. *Compare Oregon v. Mathiason*, 429 U.S. 492 (1977) (per curiam); *California v. Beheler*, 463

U.S. 1121 (1983) (per curiam); *United States v. Euge,* 444 U.S. 707, 718 (1980); *United States v. Mendenhall,* 446 U.S. 544, 554 (1980) (opinion of Justice Stewart, announcing the judgment of the Court). The Fourth Amendment is not called into play by "law enforcement officers . . . merely approaching an individual on the street or in another public place, by asking him if he is willing to answer some questions, by putting questions to him if the person is willing to listen . . . [even if] the officer identifies himself as a police officer. . . . The person approached, however, need not answer any questions put to him; indeed, he may decline to listen to the questions at all and may go on his way. . . . He may not be detained even momentarily without [triggering Fourth Amendment protections that require] reasonable, objective grounds for doing so; and his refusal to listen or answer does not, without more, furnish those grounds." *Florida v. Royer,* subparagraph (A)(4) *supra,* 460 U.S. at 497-98 (plurality opinion); *see also Florida v. Rodriguez,* 469 U.S. 1, 5-6 (1984) (per curiam). "What has evolved from our cases is a determination that an initially consensual encounter between a police officer and a citizen can be transformed into a seizure or detention within the meaning of the Fourth Amendment, 'if, in view of all the circumstances surrounding the incident, a reasonable person would have believed that he was not free to leave.'" *Immigration and Naturalization Service v. Delgado,* 466 U.S. 210, 215 (1984); *see also id.* at 216-17; *Michigan v. Chesternut,* 108 S. Ct. 1975, 1979 (1988); *Florida v. Royer,* subparagraph (A)(4) *supra,* 460 U.S. at 502 (plurality opinion); *id.* at 514 (dissenting opinion of Justice Blackmun); *id.* at 523 n.3 (dissenting opinion of Justice Rehnquist); *United States v. Mendenhall, supra,* 446 U.S. at 554 (opinion of Justice Stewart, announcing the judgement of the Court). The operative test is whether the police behavior "would . . . have communicated to a reasonable person that he [or she] was not at liberty to ignore the police presence and go about his [or her] business." *Michigan v. Chesternut, supra,* 108 S. Ct. at 1977; *see also id.* at 1981. (It may also be relevant that the officers had an undeclared intention to restrain the person so that s/he "would not have been free to leave . . . had . . . [s/he] asked to do so," *Florida v. Royer,* subparagraph (A)(4) *supra,* 460 U.S. at 503 (plurality opinion), but the cases are at odds on this point. *Compare Royer and Dunaway v. New York,* subparagraph (A)(3) *supra,* 442 U.S. at 203, 212, *with United States v. Mendenhall, supra,* 446 U.S. at 554 n.6 (opinion of Justice Stewart, announcing the judgment of the Court); *Berkemer v. McCarty, supra,* 468 U.S. at 442; *United States v. Hensley,* 469 U.S. 221, 234-35 (1985); *Michigan v. Chesternut, supra,* 108 S. Ct. at 1980 n.7.)

(2) Following the "stop-and-frisk" cases, *Terry* and *Sibron,* subparagraph (B)(1) *supra,* it is useful to distinguish two categories of restraints: "arrests" and "detentions." As will appear below, the line between the categories is far from clear. Ordinarily, defense counsel will be interested in establishing that a particular restraint was an arrest rather than a detention (or that an arrest occurred earlier, rather than later, in a sequence of events involving increasing degrees of restraint) because the requirements for lawful arrest (subparagraph (C) *infra*) are more demanding than those for lawful detention (subparagraph (D) *infra*), and once an unlawful arrest occurs, it taints everything that follows (see subparagraph (A) *supra*). But this is not invariably so. If, for example, an officer who has probable cause to arrest X proceeds to stop and search X, X's lawyer may be advised to argue that the stopping was not an arrest, since the permissible scope of search of a person upon probable cause without an arrest is considerably narrower than the permissible scope of search of a person incident to arrest. *See Cupp v. Murphy,* subparagraph (B)(1) *supra;* paragraph [230](B) *supra;* paragraphs [238](A), [247](A) *infra; cf. Michigan v. Long,* 463 U.S. 1032, 1035 n.1, 1049-50 n.14, 1052 n.16 (1983). (Although *Rawlings v. Kentucky,* subparagraph (A)(3) *supra,* 448 U.S. at 111, permits a search incident to arrest to be made immediately preceding the arrest as a part of a single course of action, this is the only exception to the general rule that "a search incident to a lawful arrest may not precede the arrest," *Sibron v. New York,* subparagraph (B)(1) *supra,* 392 U.S. at 67. See paragraph [240](C)(3)(d) *infra.*)

(3) Counsel who is arguing that a client was arrested can probably urge persuasively that an arrest is made out whenever a person is restrained by an officer who

(a) announces or visibly manifests an intention to take the person into custody for the purpose of confining him or her or of charging him or her with an offense, *see Rios v. United States,* 364 U.S. 253, 261-62 (1960); *compare United States v. Hensley,* subparagraph (B)(1) *supra,* 469 U.S. at 234-35; *or*

(b) restrains the person for more than a "momentary" period, *Rios v. United States, supra,* 364 U.S. at 262 — more than "briefly," *Terry v. Ohio,* subparagraph (B)(1) *supra,* 392 U.S. at 10; *Berkemer v. McCarty,* subparagraph (B)(1) *supra,* 468 U.S. at 439 (dictum); *see Dunaway v. New York,* subparagraph (A)(3) *supra,* 442 U.S. at 212 (stops are limited to "brief and narrowly circumscribed intrusions"); *United States v. Place,* 462 U.S. 696 (1983) (first holding that "the limitations applicable to investigative detentions of the person should define the permissible scope of an investigative detention of the person's luggage on less than probable cause," *id.* at 708-9; then noting that "[a]lthough we have recognized the reasonableness of seizures longer than the momentary ones involved in *Terry* . . . and *Brignoni-Ponce, see Michigan v. Summers,* [subparagraph (B)(1) *supra,* 452 U.S. at 700 n.12 (dictum)], the brevity of the invasion of the individual's Fourth Amendment interests is an important factor in determining whether the seizure is so minimally intrusive as to be justifiable on reasonable suspicion," 462 U.S. at 709; and finally invalidating a 90-minute detention of an air traveler's luggage on reasonable suspicion: "[A]lthough we decline to adopt any outside time limitation for a permissible *Terry* stop, we have never approved a seizure of the person for the prolonged 90-minute period involved here and cannot do so on the facts presented by this case," *id.* at 709-10); *cf. United States v. Brignoni-Ponce,* subparagraph (B)(1) *supra,* 422 U.S. at 878, 880-82; *Florida v. Royer,* subparagraph (A)(4) *supra,* 460 U.S. at 498-500 (plurality opinion); *id.* at 509-11 (concurring opinion of Justice Brennan); *United States v. Martinez-Fuerte,* subparagraph (B)(1) *supra,* 428 U.S. at 558, 566-67 (dictum); *but compare United States v. Sharpe,* 470 U.S. 675 (1985) ("We reject the contention that a 20-minute stop is unreasonable when the police have acted diligently and a suspect's actions contribute to the added delay about which he complains," *id.* at 688; "Obviously, if an investigative stop continues indefinitely, at some point it can no longer be justified as an investigative stop. But our cases impose no rigid time limitation on *Terry* stops. While it is clear that 'the brevity of the invasion . . . is an important factor . . . ,' we have emphasized the need to consider the law enforcement purposes to be served by the stop as well as the time reasonably needed to effectuate those purposes," *id.* at 685); *United States v. Montoya de Hernandez,* 473 U.S. 531, 542-43 (1985) (27-hour airport detention of suspected alimentary canal smuggler deplaning from an international flight sustained as a border seizure; "we have . . . consistently rejected hard-and-fast time limits");

(c) removes the person from the immediate site of the initial encounter, *see Davis v. Mississippi,* subparagraph (A)(5) *supra,* 442 U.S. at 212; *Dunaway v. New York,* subparagraph (A)(3) *supra; United States v. Sharpe, supra,* 470 U.S. at 684 n.4 (dictum); *Seals v. United States,* 325 F.2d 1006 (D.C. Cir. 1963); *Kelley v. United States,* subparagraph (B)(1) *supra,* at least when such a move is more than minimal, *see Hayes v. Florida,* subparagraph (A)(5) *supra,* or is not justified by demonstrable "reasons of safety and security," *Florida v. Royer,* subparagraph (A)(4) *supra,* 460 U.S. at 504-5 (plurality opinion); *or*

(d) detains the person in an isolated setting where s/he is "alone with . . . police officers," *Florida v. Royer,* subparagraph (A)(4) *supra,* 460 U.S. at 502 (plurality opinion); *see also Berkemer v. McCarty,* subparagraph (B)(1) *supra,* 468 U.S. at 438-39. In any event, "[t]here is no doubt that at some point in the investigative process, police procedures can qualitatively and quantitatively be so intrusive with respect to a suspect's freedom of movement and privacy interests as to trigger the full protection of the Fourth and Fourteenth Amendments. . . . And our view continues to be that the line is crossed when the police, without probable cause or a warrant, forcibly remove a person from his home or other place in which he is entitled to be and transport him to the police station, where he is detained, although briefly, for investigative purposes." *Hayes v. Florida,* subparagraph (A)(5) *supra,* 470 U.S. at 815-16. *Compare Oregon v. Mathiason,* subparagraph (B)(1) *supra; California v. Beheler,* subparagraph (B)(1) *supra*. To escape "the general rule that an official seizure of the person must be supported by probable cause, even if no formal arrest is made," *Michigan v. Summers,* subparagraph (B)(1) *supra,* 452 U.S. at 696, a detention must be "significantly less intrusive than an arrest," *id.* at 697, and "[t]he scope of the detention must be carefully tailored to its underlying justification," *Florida v. Royer,* subparagraph (A)(4) *supra,* 460 U.S. at 500 (plurality opinion), which is to say that "an investigative detention must be temporary and last no longer than is necessary to effectuate the purpose of the stop," and "the investigative methods employed should be the least intrusive means reasonably available to verify or dispel the officer's suspicion in a short period of time," *ibid; see also United States v. Sokolow,* 109 S. Ct. 1581, 1587 (1989) (dictum). "Typically, this means that the officer may ask the detainee a moderate number of questions to determine his identity and to try to obtain information confirming or dispelling the officer's suspicions. But the detainee is not obliged to respond. And, unless the detainee's answers provide the officer with probable cause to arrest him, he must then be released." *Berkemer v. McCarty,* subparagraph (B)(1) *supra,* 468 U.S. at 439-40. Officers may also conduct a warrant check, *United States v. Hensley,* subparagraph (B)(1) *supra,* and make observations of the suspect and surroundings pertinent to their suspicions, *see United States v. Sharpe, supra,* so long as they "diligently pursue[ ] a means of investigation that [is] . . . likely to confirm or dispel their suspicions quickly, during which time it [is] . . . necessary to detain the [suspect]," *id.* at 686. "It is the State's burden to demonstrate that the seizure it seeks to justify on the basis of a reasonable suspicion was sufficiently limited in scope and duration to satisfy the conditions of an investigative seizure," *Florida v. Royer,* subparagraph (A)(4) *supra,* 460 U.S. at 500 (plurality opinion); *see also id.* at 509-11 (concurring opinion of Justice Brennan). Detentions for interrogation are particularly likely to be characterized as arrests requiring probable cause under the Fourth Amendment, *see Dunaway v. New York,* subparagraph (A)(3) *supra,* 442 U.S. at 212; *Michigan v. Summers,* subparagraph (B)(1) *supra,* 452 U.S. at 701-2 & n.15 (dictum); *United States v. Sharpe, supra,* 470 U.S. at 683-84 & n.4 (dictum); *Florida v. Royer,* subparagraph (A)(4) *supra,* 460 U.S. at 499 (plurality opinion) (dictum). But counsel arguing that a client was *not* arrested may plausibly contend, in the current obscure state of the law, that neither charging purpose nor prolonged detention nor change of situs nor interrogation alone suffices to constitute an arrest.

(4) Any restraint of liberty that is not an arrest subject to the requirements of the following subparagraph is a detention subject to those of subparagraph (D) *infra.*

(C) An arrest is constitutional if, but only if:

(1) *It is made under authorization of law* (that is, by an officer legally empowered to make arrests under the circumstances for the sort of offense in question), *United States v. Di Re,* 332 U.S. 581 (1948); *cf. Michigan v. DeFillippo,* 443 U.S. 31, 36 (1979); *and*

(2) (a) *It is made under authority of an arrest warrant,*

(i) issued upon a showing of probable cause to believe that the defendant has committed an offense, *Giordenello v. United States,* 357 U.S. 480 (1958), as explained in *Aguilar v. Texas,* 378 U.S. 108, 112 n.3 (1964); *Steagald v. United States,* 451 U.S. 204, 213 (1981) (dictum); *and*

(ii) identifying the defendant with requisite particularity; *or,* alternatively to (a):

(b) *It is made without an arrest warrant, on the basis of facts which give the arresting officer* (or the officers who ordered or requested the arrest, *see United States v. Hensley,* subparagraph (B)(1) *supra,* 469 U.S. at 229-33 (dictum)) *probable cause to believe that the defendant has committed a felony* (or, in many States, a misdemeanor constituting a breach of the peace), *United States v. Watson,* 423 U.S. 411 (1976); *United States v. Santana,* 427 U.S. 38 (1976); *Michigan v. DeFillippo,* subparagraph (C)(1) *supra,* 443 U.S. at 36; *see Gerstein v. Pugh,* 420 U.S. 103, 111-14 (1975); *Ingraham v. Wright,* 430 U.S. 651, 679-80 (1977) (dictum); *Steagald v. United States, supra,* 451 U.S. at 221 (dictum); and *compare Henry v. United States,* 361 U.S. 98 (1959); *Wong Sun v. United States,* 371 U.S. 471 (1963); *Taylor v. Alabama,* subparagraph (A)(3) *supra; and Hayes v. Florida,* subparagraph (A)(5) *supra,* with *Draper v. United States,* 358 U.S. 307 (1959), *and Sibron v.*

New York, subparagraph (B)(1) *supra,* 392 U.S. 40, 66-67 (1968); *or,* alternatively to (a):

(c) *It is made without an arrest warrant, for a misdemeanor or a petty offense constituting a breach of the peace, "on view"* (that is, in the presence of the arresting officer); and

(3) *The arrest is bona fide, not a "sham" or "pretext" for a warrantless search, see United States v. Harris,* 321 F.2d 739 (6th Cir. 1963), and cases cited; *Application of Tomich,* 221 F. Supp. 500, 502 (D. Mont. 1963), *aff'd sub nom. Montana v. Tomich,* 332 F.2d 987 (9th Cir. 1964); *State v. Blair,* 691 S.W.2d 259 (Mo. 1985); *Kehoe v. State,* 521 So.2d 1094, 1096-97 (Fla. 1988) (dictum). But *cf. Scott v. United States,* 436 U.S. 128, 135-38 (1978).

It is unclear whether the rule forbidding warrantless misdemeanor arrests upon probable cause (unless the misdemeanor either constitutes a breach of the peace or was committed in the presence of the arresting officer) is itself a Fourth Amendment limitation. *Cf. Welsh v. Wisconsin,* 466 U.S. 740, 750-53 (1984); *id.* at 756 (dissenting opinion of Justice White); *United States v. Hensley,* subparagraph (B)(1) *supra,* 469 U.S. at 229. It is, however, the common rule at state law; and where it is, it thus becomes a constitutional restriction for the purposes of the exclusionary consequences of. subparagraph (A) *supra,* under the "lawful authorization" principle of subparagraph (C)(1) *supra.* ("Whether an officer is authorized to make an arrest ordinarily depends, in the first instance, on state law." *Michigan v. DeFillippo,* subparagraph (C)(1) *supra,* 443 U.S. at 36.) When an arrest is made with or without a warrant upon probable cause to believe that a particular individual has committed an offense, but the police mistakenly arrest the wrong individual, their arrest is nonetheless legal if (i) they honestly believe that the person arrested is the individual sought and (ii) they have probable cause for this belief. *Hill v. California,* 401 U.S. 797 (1971); *Maryland v. Garrison,* 107 S. Ct. 1013, 1018-19 (1987) (dictum). The "probable cause" concept is discussed in paragraph [241] *infra.*

(D) The requisites of a constitutional "detention" are fuzzy. In the *Terry* and *Sibron* cases, subparagraph (B)(1) *supra,* the Supreme Court held that a state could constitutionally authorize its law enforcement officers to conduct a "stop and frisk" — a brief on-the-street detention for the purpose of inquiry and observation and a "pat-down" for weapons or a similar "self-protective" search — under circumstances giving rise to a rational suspicion of criminal activity but not amounting to the probable cause necessary for arrest and thus for the more intensive search which is permitted incident to arrest. *Terry* and *Sibron* "created an exception to the requirement of probable cause, an exception whose 'narrow scope'. . . [the Supreme] Court 'has been careful to maintain.'" *Ybarra v. Illinois,* 444 U.S. 85, 93 (1979); *see also Dunaway v. New York,* subparagraph (A)(3) *supra,* 442 U.S. at 207-10; *Florida v. Royer,* subparagraph (A)(4) *supra,* 460 U.S. at 498-500 (plurality opinion); *id.* at 509-11 (concurring opinion of Justice Brennan).

(1) The Court's opinions are somewhat clearer concerning the requirements for a "frisk" than concerning those for a "stop." A frisk is constitutional only if

(a) it is made incidentally to a valid accosting or stop;

(b) it is made for the purpose of discovering weapons that might be used against the officer, *see Sibron v. New York,* subparagraph (B)(1) *supra,* 392 U.S. at 64-65; *Ybarra v. Illinois, supra,* 444 U.S. at 93-94; *Michigan v. Long,* subparagraph (B)(2) *supra,* 463 U.S. at 1048-52 & n.16;

(c) the officer can "point to specific and articulable facts which, taken together with rational inferences from those facts, reasonably warrant" the conclusion that s/he "is dealing with an armed and dangerous individual," *Terry v. Ohio,* subparagraph (B)(1) *supra,* 392 U.S. at 21, 27; *see Sibron v. New York,* subparagraph (B)(1) *supra,* 392 U.S. at 63-64; *Ybarra v. Illinois, supra,* 444 U.S. at 92-93; *Michigan v. Long,* subparagraph (B)(2) *supra,* 463 U.S. at 1046-52 & nn.14, 16; *Dunaway v. New York,* subparagraph (A)(3) *supra,* 442 U.S. at 209 n.11 (dictum); and

(d) the frisk is "limited to that which is necessary for the discovery of weapons," *Terry v. Ohio,* subparagraph (B)(1) *supra,* 392 U.S. at 26; *see Sibron v. New York,* subparagraph (B)(1) *supra,* 392 U.S. at 65-66; *United States v. Del Toro,* 464 F.2d 520 (2d Cir. 1972); *People v. Collins,* 1 Cal. 3d 658, 463 P.2d 403, 83 Cal. Rptr. 179 (1970); *State v. Hobart,* 94 Wash. 2d 437, 617 P.2d 429 (1980). *See generally United States v.*

Brignoni-Ponce, subparagraph (B)(1) *supra,* 422 U.S. 880-82; *Pennsylvania v. Mimms,* 434 U.S. 106, 111-12 (1977) (per curiam); *Florida v. Royer,* subparagraph (A)(4) *supra,* 460 U.S. at 499-500 (plurality opinion); *id.* at 510-11 (concurring opinion of Justice Brennan); *Michigan v. Long,* subparagraph (B)(2) *supra,* 463 U.S. at 1049 (dictum).

(In *Michigan v. Long,* subparagraph (B)(2) *supra,* the Court extended *Terry* to hold that police who have stopped a person riding in an automobile may search the passenger compartment of the vehicle and any containers found in it, under the same four conditions; here again, the search is "limited to those areas in which a weapon may be placed or hidden," 463 U.S. at 1049; *see also id.* at 1052 n.16.)

(e) Presumably, a stop may no more be made as the pretext for a frisk than an arrest may be made as the pretext for a search. See subparagraph (C)(3) *supra.*

(2) As for the stop itself, it appears that a stop is valid only under the following circumstances:

(a) It is made on the street or in a public place. (This is the context in which *Terry* and *Sibron* originally recognized the "stop" power. With a single exception, all subsequent decisions of the Supreme Court upholding stops have involved "on-the-street" situations, *Dunaway v. New York,* subparagraph (A)(3) *supra,* 442 U.S. at 210-11, or encounters in similarly public places, such as airport concourses, *Florida v. Rodriguez,* subparagraph (B)(1) *supra; United States v. Mendenhall,* subparagraph (B)(1) *supra,* 446 U.S. at 560-66 (plurality opinion on this point); *Florida v. Royer,* subparagraph (A)(4) *supra,* 460 U.S. at 502-5 (plurality opinion) (dictum). The exception is *Michigan v. Summers,* subparagraph (B)(1) *supra,* holding that officers executing a valid search warrant for contraband in a home have "the limited authority to detain the occupants of the premises while a proper search is conducted," 452 U.S. at 705. In *Summers,* the detained homeowner was, in fact, first encountered by the officers "descending the front steps" as the officers entered, *id.* at 693 [*but see id.* at 702 n.16]; in any event, the possession of the search warrant gave the officers a right of entry independent of the "stop" power. Compare the discussion of the "plain view" doctrine in paragraph

[231](A)(5) *supra;* and *cf. Rawlings v. Kentucky,* subparagraph (A)(3) *supra,* 448 U.S. at 110 & n.5 (dictum).)

(b) The officer has grounds for believing that the person whom s/he stops is presently engaged in criminal activity, *see Reid v. Georgia,* subparagraph (A)(1) *supra,* 448 U.S. at 441; *United States v. Cortez,* 449 U.S. 411, 417 (1981) (dictum), or "was involved in or is wanted in connection with a completed felony" and the police "have been unable to locate . . . [the] person" previously, *United States v. Hensley,* subparagraph (B)(1) *supra,* 469 U.S. at 229.

(c) The grounds for the belief are specific, identifiable facts that, "judged against an objective standard," *Terry v. Ohio,* subparagraph (B)(1) *supra,* 392 U.S. at 21; *see Delaware v. Prouse,* 440 U.S. 648, 654 (1979), give rise to "a reasonable and articulable suspicion that the person seized is engaged in criminal activity," *Reid v. Georgia,* subparagraph (A)(1) *supra,* 448 U.S. at 440; *see Brown v. Texas,* subparagraph (B)(1) *supra,* 443 U.S. at 51-53; *Florida v. Rodriguez,* subparagraph (B)(1) *supra,* 469 U.S. at 5-6; *United States v. Sharpe,* subparagraph (B)(3) *supra,* 470 U.S. at 682 & n.3. Considering "the totality of the circumstances," the "detaining officers must have a particularized and objective basis for suspecting the particular person stopped of criminal activity." *United States v. Cortez, supra,* 449 U.S. at 417-18; *see also United States v. Sokolow,* subparagraph (B)(3) *supra,* 109 S. Ct. at 1581; *Kolender v. Lawson,* 461 U.S. 352, 356 n.5 (1983) (dictum). Conduct or circumstances that "describe a very large category of presumably innocent [persons]" is not sufficient, *Reid v. Georgia,* subparagraph (A)(1) *supra,* 448 U.S. at 441; *Brown v. Texas,* subparagraph (B)(1) *supra,* 443 U.S. at 52; *cf. Ybarra v. Illinois, supra,* 444 U.S. at 91; *compare United States v. Sokolow,* subparagraph (B)(3) *supra;* the "particularized suspicion" must be focused upon "the particular individual being stopped," *United States v. Cortez, supra,* 449 U.S. at 418; *see also United States v. Montoya de Hernandez,* subparagraph (B)(3) *supra,* 473 U.S. at 541-42; *cf. New Jersey v. T.L.O.,* 469 U.S. 325, 342 n.8 (1985) (dictum). Information "completely lacking in indicia of reliability, would either warrant no police response or require further investigation before a forcible stop of a suspect would be authorized."

Adams v. Williams, 407 U.S. 143, 147 (1972) (dictum). *See, e.g., United States v. Mallides,* 473 F.2d 859 (9th Cir. 1973); *Irwin v. Superior Court,* 1 Cal. 3d 423, 462 P.2d 12, 82 Cal. Rptr. 484 (1969), *modified in In re Tony C.,* 21 Cal. 3d 888, 894, 582 P.2d 957, 960, 148 Cal. Rptr. 366, 369 (1978); *cf. United States v. Ramsey,* 431 U.S. 606, 612-15 (1977); *Jernigan v. Louisiana,* 446 U.S. 958, 959-60 (1980) (opinion of Justice White, dissenting from denial of *certiorari*). (The rubric "reasonable suspicion," commonly used by lower courts and commentators in the wake of *Terry* and *Sibron* to characterize this standard of justification required for an investigative stop, was first endorsed by the Supreme Court in *United States v. Brignoni-Ponce,* subparagraph (B)(1) *supra,* 442 U.S. at 881-84. *See Michigan v. Summers,* subparagraph (B)(1) *supra,* 452 U.S. at 698 n.7 (1981); *Florida v. Royer,* subparagraph (A)(4) *supra,* 460 U.S. at 498 (plurality opinion); *United States v. Place,* subparagraph (B)(3) *supra,* 462 U.S. at 702; *United States v. Hensley,* subparagraph (B)(1) *supra,* 469 U.S. at 226-33; *United States v. Sharpe,* subparagraph (B)(3) *supra,* 470 U.S. at 682 & n.3; *United States v. Montoya de Hernandez,* subparagraph (B)(3) *supra,* 473 U.S. at 541-42. Applying the standard in the context of automobile stops by Border Patrol agents (see paragraph [246](C) *infra*), *Brignoni-Ponce* declined to find that the "apparent Mexican ancestry" of three occupants of a car in the Mexican border region constituted "reasonable suspicion" of illegal immigration. *See also Brown v. Texas,* subparagraph (B)(1) *supra; Reid v. Georgia,* subparagraph (A)(1) *supra.*)

It should be noted that *Terry* and *Sibron* assume state law authorization (by state common law in *Terry,* statute in *Sibron*) for stops or detentions not amounting to arrests. Many states had not recognized such detentions prior to *Terry* and *Sibron,* and it is arguable that in these states legislative authorization should be required in order to invest various categories of law enforcement officers with the stop-and-frisk power, consistently with the "lawful authorization" principle that is basic to the Fourth Amendment, see subparagraph (C)(1) *supra; Colonnade Catering Corp. v. United States,* 397 U.S. 72 (1970); *Donovan v. Dewey,* 452 U.S. 594, 599 (1981); *Aiuppa v. United States,* 338 F.2d 146 (10th Cir. 1964).

[237] Postarrest custodial treatment. (A) Although a defendant's initial arrest was constitutional, his or her confinement or treatment after arrest may become unlawful if any of the following occurs:

(1) *S/he is detained for an undue length of time before being taken to a magistrate for preliminary arraignment and a judicial determination of probable cause.* See paragraph [127] *supra,* for a discussion of this complicated principle.

(2) *Following preliminary arraignment, s/he is remanded by the magistrate, without lawful authority, into the custody of the police. See Mitchell v. United States,* 316 F.2d 354 (D.C. Cir. 1963); *cf. Culombe v. Connecticut,* 367 U.S. 568, 611-12, 631-33 (1961). This principle is still relatively undeveloped and is only suggested by the cases cited.

(3) *S/he is denied access to a lawyer, Escobedo v. Illinois,* 378 U.S. 478 (1964); *Michigan v. Jackson,* 106 S. Ct. 1404 (1986), *or other reasonable opportunities for communication, cf. Haynes v. Washington,* 373 U.S. 503 (1963). *See also* the cases dealing with denial of requests for potentially exculpatory physical examinations. *In re Martin,* 58 Cal. 2d 509, 374 P.2d 801, 24 Cal. Rptr. 833 (1962); *Winston v. Commonwealth,* 188 Va. 386, 49 S.E.2d 611 (1948); *City of Tacoma v. Heater,* 67 Wash. 2d 733, 409 P.2d 867 (1966); *cf. California v. Trombetta,* 467 U.S. 479, 485-89 (1984); *Arizona v. Youngblood,* 109 S. Ct. 333 (1988). Some kinds of police investigative activity directed at persons in custody are constitutionally forbidden to be conducted in the absence of defense counsel unless the defendant has been warned of the right to counsel and has effectively waived the right. These include interrogation (as defined in *Rhode Island v. Innis,* 446 U.S. 291, 298-302 (1980), and *Arizona v. Mauro,* 107 S. Ct. 1931, 1934-37 (1987)) carried out by officers in any custodial setting, *Miranda v. Arizona,* 384 U.S. 436 (1966), paragraph [363](E) *infra;* mental examinations that are designed to be used, or to the extent that their results are later sought to be used, in evidence against the detained person on the issues of guilt or penalty, *Estelle v. Smith,* 451 U.S. 454 (1981), paragraphs [180](A), [232](C) *supra; Satterwhite v. Texas,* 108 S. Ct. 1792 (1988); the deliberate eliciting of information from the detained person by police spies or planted snitches after the

juncture that marks the initiation of adversary judicial proceedings (as defined in paragraph [233](B)(1) *supra*), *United States v. Henry,* 447 U.S. 264 (1980), paragraph [363](F) *infra;* and lineups or other identification confrontations occurring after that juncture, *United States v. Wade,* 388 U.S. 218 (1967), paragraph [233](A)(3) *supra; Moore v. Illinois,* 434 U.S. 220 (1977). See generally paragraph [233] *supra.*

(4) *S/he is treated brutally or with indignity or with unnecessary disregard for privacy.* See paragraph [228] *supra;* paragraph [238](B) *infra; cf. Lucero v. Donovan,* 354 F.2d 16, 21-22 (9th Cir. 1965). "The Fourth Amendment's requirement that searches and seizures be reasonable . . . may limit police use of unnecessarily frightening or offensive methods of surveillance and investigation." *United States v. Ortiz,* 422 U.S. 891, 895 (1975) (dictum). *And see Winston v. Lee,* 470 U.S. 753, 760 (1985); *Tennessee v. Garner,* 471 U.S. 1, 7-9 (1985); *United States v. Edwards,* 415 U.S. 800, 808 n.9 (1974) (dictum); *United States v. Ramsey,* 431 U.S. 606, 618 n.13 (1977) (dictum); *Bell v. Wolfish,* 441 U.S. 520, 560 (1979) (dictum); *cf. Skinner v. Railway Labor Executives' Ass'n,* 109 S. Ct. 1402, 1418 (1989); *but see United States v. Montoya de Hernandez,* 473 U.S. 531 (1985).

(5) *S/he is denied admission to bail or other conditional release to which s/he is constitutionally entitled.* See paragraphs [54]-[61] *supra.* Denial of the bail right has not yet been recognized as a ground for excluding evidence obtained during detention, but the point should be urged.

(B) Confessions taken from a detained person in violation of the right to counsel and the related guarantees announced in *Miranda v. Arizona,* subparagraph (A)(3) *supra,* are, on that account alone, excluded from evidence. *Tague v. Louisiana,* 444 U.S. 469 (1980) (per curiam); *Berkemer v. McCarty,* 468 U.S. 420, 429 (1984); *Smith v. Illinois,* 469 U.S. 91 (1984) (per curiam); *Michigan v. Mosley,* 423 U.S. 96, 99-100 (1975) (dictum); see paragraph [363](E) *infra.* Within the limitations discussed in paragraph [127] *supra,* violations of the right against undue delay of preliminary arraignment (subparagraph (A)(1) *supra*) may give rise to a similar *per se* exclusionary rule. The other unlawful conditions of confinement described in subparagraph (A) *supra* are, in present theory, merely factors to be considered as affecting the question whether a confession is involuntary and hence excludable (see paragraphs [127](C), [228] *supra;* paragraph [363](C) *infra*). *Compare Haynes v. Washington,* 373 U.S. 503 (1963), with *Moran v. Burbine,* 106 S. Ct. 1135, 1141-42 (1986). But the later Supreme Court decisions routinely exclude confessions made in the wake of physical brutality, *Sims v. Georgia,* 389 U.S. 404 (1967); *Brooks v. Florida,* 389 U.S. 413 (1967) (per curiam); and the argument is strong that any confession obtained while a person is undergoing illegal conditions of confinement is "'come at by exploitation of that illegality,'" *Wong Sun v. United States,* 371 U.S. 471, 488 (1963), paragraph [251] *infra,* and consequently is required to be excluded. *See* the cases cited with *Wong Sun* in paragraph [236](A)(3) *supra.* Nonconfessional evidence obtained under illegal conditions of detention is also excluded if the manner of obtaining it bears a sufficiently direct relationship to the illegality. *See United States v. Wade,* 388 U.S. 218 (1967); *Gilbert v. California,* 388 U.S. 263 (1967); *Watson v. United States,* 249 F.2d 106 (D.C.Cir 1957); *United States v. Klapholz,* 230 F.2d 494 (2d Cir 1956). For example, the *Wade* and *Gilbert* cases hold that when an accused has been identified in a lineup at which s/he neither had nor validly waived counsel required by the Sixth Amendment (see paragraph [233](A)(3) *supra*), federal and state courts must exclude (a) all evidence concerning the lineup identification itself, *see Moore v. Illinois,* subparagraph (A)(3), *supra,* 434 U.S. at 231-32; and (b) testimony by the lineup witness identifying the accused *at trial* unless the prosecution establishes "by clear and convincing evidence that the in-court identifications were based upon observations of the suspect other than the lineup identification," *United States v. Wade, supra,* 388 U.S. at 240; *compare United States v. Crews,* 445 U.S. 463, 472-73 & n.18 (1980). (Congress purported to overrule one or both of these holdings, in federal criminal trials, by providing in Section 701 of the Omnibus Crime Control and Safe Streets Act of 1968, Pub. L. No. 90-351, 82 Stat. 211, codified as 18 U.S.C. §3502, that the "testimony of a witness that he saw the accused commit or participate in the commission of [a] . . . crime . . . shall be admissible in evidence" at such trials. But since *Wade* and *Gilbert* were constitutional decisions, the statute is patently unconstitutional to the extent that it conflicts with them.)

[238] Body searches, physical examinations, extractions of body fluids, hair, and so forth. (A) (1) Warrantless searches of an arrested person's clothing and body surfaces are routinely permitted incident to a valid arrest. *United States v. Robinson,* 414 U.S. 218 (1973); *Gustafson v. Florida,* 414 U.S. 260 (1973); *Michigan v. DeFillippo,* 443 U.S. 31, 35-36 (1979); *New York v. Belton,* 453 U.S. 454, 457-59 (1981); *cf. Michigan v. Long,* 463 U.S 1032, 1049-50 n.14 (1983) (dictum); *United States v. Ramsey,* 431 U.S. 606, 621 (1977) (dictum); *United States v. Chadwick,* 433 U.S. 1, 14-15 (1977) (dictum); and see generally paragraphs [240](C)(3)(d), [247] *infra.* These searches may be thorough and may be made either at the site of the arrest, *United States v. Robinson, supra,* or at the stationhouse to which the arrested person is taken, *United States v. Edwards,* 415 U.S. 800 (1974).

(2) If the arrested person is to be incarcerated, the police may remove, examine, and inventory everything in his or her possession at the lockup. *Illinois v. LaFayette,* 462 U.S. 640, 645-48 (1983). This "inventory search" power permits the opening, without a warrant, of any container carried by the person, whether or not the police have any reason to suspect its contents and whether or not they could practicably secure the container during the period of the person's incarceration without opening it up. *Ibid.* The Supreme Court opinion establishing the power suggests that it is broader than the ordinary power to search incident to arrest (subparagraph (A)(1) *supra*): "Police conduct that would be impractical or unreasonable — or embarrassingly intrusive — on the street can more readily — and privately — be performed at the station. For example, the interests supporting a search incident to arrest would hardly justify disrobing an arrestee on the street, but the practical necessities of routine jail administration may even justify taking a prisoner's clothes before confining him, although that step would be rare." *Illinois v. LaFayette, supra,* 462 U.S. at 645. The final clause of this sentence, with an adjoining footnote, "We . . . do not discuss here, the circumstances in which a strip search of an arrestee may or may not be appropriate," *id.* at 646 n.2, presumably imply that the power is limited by the principles of the

following subparagraph (B). The only other limitation of the power that might be gleaned from *LaFayette* is that "inventory searches" must be conducted "in accordance with established inventory procedures," *id.* at 648, or not at all. *See also Colorado v. Bertine,* 107 S. Ct. 738, 742-43 & nn.6, 7 (1987) (dictum). A doctrinal basis for this latter limitation can be extrapolated from *LaFayette's* recognition that the "so-called inventory search is not an independent legal concept but rather an incidental administrative step following arrest and preceding incarceration," whose validity is to be determined by the principles of *"Delaware v. Prouse,* 440 U.S. 648, 654 (1979)." *Illinois v. LaFayette, supra,* 462 U.S. at 644. The *Prouse* case is one of a line of decisions stating that administrative searches, when permitted without a warrant, must be conducted pursuant to regular procedures which control "'the discretion of the official in the field,'" *Delaware v. Prouse, supra,* 440 U.S. at 655. See paragraph [246](A)(3), (D)(2) *infra; cf. New Jersey v. T.L.O.,* 469 U.S. 325, 342 n.8 (1985) (dictum); *New York v. Burger,* 107 S. Ct. 2636, 2644, 2648 (1987) (dictum); *Skinner v. Railway Labor Executives' Ass'n,* 109 S. Ct. 1402, 1415 (1989) (dictum). Counsel challenging an inventory search that was not made under "standardized inventory procedures" in effect at the particular lockup, *Illinois v. LaFayette, supra,* 462 U.S. at 648, should invoke this line of authority: "Our decisions have always adhered to the requirement that inventories be conducted according to standardized criteria." *Colorado v. Bertine, supra,* 107 S. Ct. at 742 n.6; *see id.* at 744 (concurring opinion of Justice Blackmun); *id.* at 744-46 (dissenting opinion of Justice Marshall).

(3) A warrantless search may also be made of the person of an individual whom the police have probable cause to arrest, but do not arrest, provided that it is restricted to the "very limited search necessary to preserve" some evidence of "ready destructibility" that the person would otherwise likely destroy. *Cupp v. Murphy,* 412 U.S. 291, 296 (1973). In this situation, "we do not hold that a full *Chimel* search [that is, the extensive search that is permitted incident to an arrest upon probable cause] would [be] . . . justified . . . without a formal arrest and without a warrant." *Ibid.*

(B) Searches that intrude into the body or breach the body wall — and perhaps other intimate personal examinations — are governed by a canon of restrictions that may be inferred from the opinions in *Schmerber v. California,* 384 U.S. 757 (1966) (upholding the extraction of a blood sample from a drunk-driving suspect for chemical analysis), and *Winston v. Lee,* 470 U.S. 753 (1985) (forbidding court ordered surgical removal of a bullet from an armed robbery suspect's chest for ballistics examination). Cardinal among these restrictions are:

(1) The requirement of a search warrant, issued upon a finding of probable cause that incriminating evidence is present in the suspect's body, *Winston v. Lee, supra,* 470 U.S. at 760-61, except that a warrant may be foregone and a body search of a lawfully arrested person may be made upon the arresting officer's own determination of probable cause if the officer reasonably believes that the imminent dissipation of the evidence makes it impracticable to obtain a warrant, *Schmerber v. California, supra,* 384 U.S. at 768-71. (The phrase "clear indication," which the *Schmerber* opinion conjoins with "probable cause," *id.* at 770, has since been construed as not intended to set a "third verbal standard in addition to 'reasonable suspicion' [see paragraph [236](D) *supra*] and 'probable cause' [see paragraph [241] *infra*]," *United States v. Montoya de Hernandez,* 473 U.S. 531, 540-41 (1985). Probable cause remains the ordinary standard, *Winston v. Lee, supra,* 470 U.S. at 760, subject to the possible proviso that reasonable suspicion may suffice in border-search cases involving suspected alimentary-canal and body-cavity smugglers, *see United States v. Montoya de Hernandez, supra,* 473 U.S. at 541-42 & n.4; and see paragraph [246](C) *infra.*)

(2) The requirement that the search or examination be conducted by medical personnel using medically approved methods in a medical environment so as to avoid unnecessary pain or risk of physical injury, *Schmerber v. California, supra,* 384 U.S. at 771-72; *Winston v. Lee, supra,* 470 U.S. at 761; *cf. Rochin v. California,* paragraph [228] *supra;* see paragraph [237](A)(4) *supra.* "*Schmerber* did caution that due process concerns could be involved if the police initiated physical violence while administering the test, refused to respect a reasonable

request to undergo a different form of testing, or responded to resistance with inappropriate force." *South Dakota v. Neville,* 459 U.S. 553, 559 n.9 (1983) (dictum); *see also id.* at 563.

(3) The requirement that the search or examination be conducted in such a manner that its results are reliably probative, *Schmerber v. California,* 384 U.S. at 771.

(4) The requirement that "the State's need for the evidence," *Winston v. Lee, supra,* 470 U.S. at 763, considered in the light of alternative "available . . . evidence," *id.* at 765, be found to outweigh "the individual's dignitary interests in personal privacy and bodily integrity," *id.* at 761, and the "threats to . . . health or safety" involved in the procedure, *id.* at 763, taking any "uncertainty about the medical risks into account," *id.* at 764, as "militat[ing] . . . against finding the operation to be 'reasonable,'" *id.* at 766. *See also Tennessee v. Garner,* 471 U.S. 1, 7-9 (1985).

(C) In addition to the *Schmerber/Lee* requirements:

(1) body searches incident to an illegal arrest are impermissible (see paragraph [236](A) *supra*);

(2) body searches during a period of illegal detention may be impermissible (see paragraph [237](B) *supra*);

(3) tests and examinations that involve the eliciting of "communications" from the accused (such as polygraph tests or the use of "truth serums") — and perhaps others that require his or her willed cooperation (see paragraph [232](C) *supra*) — are impermissible in the absence of a valid waiver of the privilege against self-incrimination and the right to counsel (*Estelle v. Smith,* 451 U.S. 454 (1981), paragraph [180](E)(2) *supra* [psychiatric examination]; *Satterwhite v. Texas,* 108 S. Ct. 1792 (1988) [same]; *see Schmerber v. California, supra,* 384 U.S. at 764 (dictum) ["lie detector tests"]; *South Dakota v. Neville, supra,* 459 U.S. at 561-62 n.12 (dictum) [same]); and

(4) to some unclear extent, tests and examinations whose reliability depends upon careful administration are impermissible if conducted in the absence of counsel and without a valid waiver of the right to counsel, following the initiation of adversary judicial proceedings (*compare United States v. Wade,* 388 U.S. 218 (1967), and *Moore v. Illinois,* 434 U.S. 220 (1977), *with Gilbert v. California,* 388 U.S. 263, 267 (1967); *and*

see the discussion of *Kirby v. Illinois,* 406 U.S. 682 (1972), and *United States v. Ash,* 413 U.S. 300 (1973), in paragraph [233](B) *supra*).

[239] Defendant subpoenaed. Any subpoena-compelled testimony by the defendant or the defendant's subpoena-compelled production of books, records, or papers raises issues under the Self-Incrimination Clause of the Fifth Amendment. *Zurcher v. Stanford Daily,* 436 U.S. 547, 561-62 n.8 (1978) (dictum). See the discussion and authorities cited in paragraphs [161], [163], [232] *supra;* paragraphs [274](B), [363](M) *infra.* Unduly broad or sweeping subpoenas *duces tecum* may also be assailable under the Fourth Amendment. See paragraph [163](C) *supra.*

[240] Entry into premises with which the defendant has more than transitory connections. (A) A defendant's home and office, place of work, and any premises with which s/he has more than transitory connections are ordinarily held protected in the defendant's favor by the Fourth Amendment. *See United States v. Johnson,* 457 U.S. 537 (1982) (dwelling house; "the Fourth Amendment accords special protection to the home," *id.* at 552 n.13); *Chapman v. United States,* 365 U.S. 610 (1961) (dwelling house found, after search, to be used exclusively as site for illegal still); *Griffin v. Wisconsin,* 107 S. Ct. 3164 (1987) (dwelling house; "[a] probationer's home, like anyone else's, is protected by the Fourth Amendment[ ]," *id.* at 3167); *McDonald v. United States,* 335 U.S. 451 (1948) (room in rooming house found, after search, to be used exclusively for operation of numbers game); *Murray v. United States,* 380 U.S. 527 (1965) (per curiam), *vacating* 333 F.2d 409 (10th Cir. 1964) (unleased room occupied from time to time by defendant in rental property owned by defendant's parents); *Jones v. United States,* 362 U.S. 257 (1960), as explained in *Rakas v. Illinois,* 439 U.S. 128, 141-42 (1978) (apartment owned by defendant's friend, who had given defendant a key and permission to use the apartment; defendant kept a change of clothes in the apartment and had slept there "maybe a night"; he was alone in the apartment at the time of the search); *Stoner v. California,* 376 U.S. 483 (1964) (hotel room); *United States v. Jeffers,* 342 U.S. 48 (1951) (hotel room rented by defendant's aunts, who had given defendant a key and permission to use the room at will; he "often entered the room for various purposes," *id.* at 50); *See v. City of Seattle,* 387 U.S. 541 (1967) (locked commercial warehouse); *Marshall v. Barlow's Inc.,* 436 U.S. 307 (1978) (employees' work areas in factory building; "[t]the Warrant Clause of the Fourth Amendment protects commercial buildings as well as private homes," *id.* at 311; "[t]he owner of a business has not, by the necessary utilization of employees in his operation, thrown open the areas where employees alone are permitted to the warrantless scrutiny of Government agents," *id.* at 315); *G.M. Leasing Corp. v. United States,* 429 U.S. 338 (1977) (corporate business premises); *United States v. Lefkowitz,* 285 U.S. 452 (1932) (business office); *Mancusi v. DeForte,* 392 U.S. 364 (1968) (union office shared by defendant and other union officials); *Lo-Ji Sales, Inc. v. New York,* 442 U.S. 319 (1979) (retail book store); *Michigan v. Tyler,* 436 U.S. 499 (1978) (fire-gutted furniture store); *Villano v. United States,* 310 F.2d 680 (10th Cir. 1962) (employee's desk in retail store); *O'Connor v. Ortega,* 107 S. Ct. 1492 (1987) (public hospital administrator's individual office, desk and files); *United States v. Blok,* 188 F.2d 1019 (D.C. Cir. 1951) (employee's desk in government office); *Rosencranz v. United States,* 356 F.2d 310 (1st Cir. 1966) (defendant's unoccupied farm property). See also paragraph [231](B) *supra.* The test of Fourth Amendment protection is whether the defendant "had an interest in connection with the searched premises that gave rise to 'a reasonable expectation [on his part] of freedom from governmental intrusion' upon those premises." *Combs v. United States,* 408 U.S. 224, 227 (1972). See also paragraph [225](C) *supra.* An individual may have "a legitimate expectation of privacy in the premises he was using and therefore . . . claim the protection of the Fourth Amendment with respect to a governmental invasion of those premises, even though his 'interest' in those premises might not have been a recognized property interest at common law." *Rakas v. Illinois, supra,* 439 U.S. at 143 (dictum). See also paragraph [242](B), (C) *infra.* On the other hand, "[o]ne of the main rights attaching to property is the right to exclude others, . . . and one who owns or lawfully possesses or controls property will in all likelihood have a legitimate expectation of privacy by virtue of this right to exclude." *Rakas v. Illinois, supra,* 439 U.S. at 144 n.12.

(B) An entry into a building is a "search" within the Amendment. *Lo-Ji Sales, Inc. v. New York,* subparagraph (A) *supra,* 442 U.S. at 325; *United States v. Karo,* 468 U.S. 705, 714-18 (1984) (dictum). Therefore, if any of the foregoing premises are entered by officers and the entry is illegal within the principles of the following subparagraph (C), all observations made or things seized by the entering officers are excludable. *Johnson v. United States,* 333 U.S. 10 (1948); *Chapman v. United States,* 365 U.S. 610 (1961); *Michigan v. Clifford,* 464 U.S. 287, 298-99 (1984); *Murray v. United States,* 108 S. Ct. 2529, 2532 (1988) (dictum); *Work v. United States,* 243 F.2d 660 (D.C. Cir. 1957); *United States v. Merritt,* 293 F.2d 742 (3d Cir. 1961). Evidence derived from these observations or things is also excludable. See paragraph [251] *infra.*

(C) The Fourth Amendment restrictions on building entries are as follows:

(1) Subject to the exceptions in subpart (3) *infra,* a building entry without a search warrant is unconstitutional. *See* the line of cases from *Agnello v. United States,* 269 U.S. 20 (1925), to *Thompson v. Louisiana,* 469 U.S. 17 (1984) (per curiam), cited in paragraph [229](C) *supra.* Officers executing a valid search warrant may enter the building and search "the entire area in which the object of the search may be found," performing whatever additional "acts of entry or opening may be required to complete the search. Thus a warrant that authorizes an officer to search a home for illegal weapons also provides authority to open closets, chests, drawers, and containers in which the weapon might be found." *United States v. Ross,* 456 U.S. 798, 820-21 (1982) (dictum); *cf. Dalia v. United States,* 441 U.S. 238, 257-58 (1979) (dictum). The limits of allowable search are fixed by the general Fourth Amendment principle that "'[t]he scope of [a] search must be "strictly tied to and justified by" the circumstances which rendered its initiation permissible.'" *New York v. Belton,* 453 U.S. 454, 457 (1981) (dictum), and authorities cited; *see also Mincey v. Arizona,* 437 U.S. 385, 393 (1978); *Arizona v. Hicks,* 107 S. Ct. 1149, 1152-53 (1987); *Florida v. Royer,* 460 U.S. 491, 499-500 (1983) (plurality opinion); *Michigan v. Clifford,* subparagraph (B) *supra,* 464 U.S. at 294-95, 297-98 (plurality opinion); *New Jersey v. T.L.O.,* 469 U.S. 325, 341-42 (1985) (dictum); *United States v.*

Sharpe, 470 U.S. 675, 682 (1985) (dictum); *Maryland v. Garrison,* 107 S. Ct. 1013, 1017 (1987) (dictum); *cf. Tennessee v. Garner,* 471 U.S. 1, 7-9 (1985). Thus the search may not extend into areas that could not contain the objects specified in the warrant, *see United States v. Ross, supra,* 456 U.S. at 824 (dictum): "[A] warrant to search for a stolen refrigerator would not authorize the opening of desk drawers," *Walter v. United States,* 447 U.S. 649, 657 (1980) (plurality opinion) (dictum). Nor may the officers seize anything not specified in the warrant, *Marron v. United States,* 275 U.S. 192, 196-98 (1927); *Bivens v. Six Unknown Named Agents of Federal Bureau of Narcotics,* 403 U.S. 388, 394 n.7 (1971) (dictum); *Marshall v. Barlow's Inc.,* 436 U.S. 307, 323 (1978) (dictum); *cf. Lo-Ji Sales, Inc. v. New York,* subparagraph (A) *supra,* 442 U.S. at 325, except objects coming within the "plain view" doctrine discussed in paragraph [231](A)(5) *supra:* that is, objects which the officer inadvertently encounters while conducting a search of the limited scope just described and which give the officer probable cause to believe that they are contraband or otherwise subject to seizure, *Texas v. Brown,* 460 U.S. 730 (1983); *see, e.g., Rugendorf v. United States,* 376 U.S. 528 (1964), and cases cited together with *Rugendorf* in paragraph [230](A) *supra.* Suspicion falling short of probable cause cannot support these "plain view" seizures or the search of any object (see paragraph [248](A)-(C) *infra*) neither named in the warrant nor capable of concealing one that is. *Arizona v. Hicks, supra,* 107 S. Ct. at 1153-54. (And even probable cause is not sufficient to justify a "plain view" seizure in obscenity cases and other situations in which First Amendment concerns reinforce the warrant requirement of the Fourth. *See Lo-Ji Sales, Inc. v. New York,* subparagraph (A) *supra,* 442 U.S. at 326 n.5 (dictum); *Zurcher v. Stanford Daily,* 436 U.S. 547, 564-65 (1978) (dictum).) Regarding searches of *persons* found on the premises, "a warrant to search a place cannot normally be construed to authorize a search of each individual in that place." *Ybarra v. Illinois,* 444 U.S. 85, 92 n.4 (1979). However, as noted in paragraphs [230](C) and [236](D)(2) *supra,* "a warrant to search for contraband . . . implicitly carries with it the limited authority to detain the occupants of the premises while a proper search [of the premises themselves] is conducted," *Michigan v. Summers,* 452 U.S. 692, 705 (1981). If that search produces probable cause to arrest the occupants (see paragraph [236](C) *supra;* paragraph [241] *infra*), they may then be arrested and searched incident to arrest (see subparagraph (C)(3)(d) *infra*).

(2) A search warrant is valid if, but only if:

(a) *It is issued by a "neutral and detached" judicial officer,* Mancusi v. DeForte, 392 U.S. 364, 371 (1968); *Coolidge v. New Hampshire,* 403 U.S. 443, 449-53 (1971); *Connally v. Georgia,* 429 U.S. 245 (1977) (per curiam); *Lo-Ji Sales, Inc. v. New York,* subparagraph (A) *supra,* 442 U.S. at 326-28; *Dalia v. United States, supra,* 441 U.S. at 255 (dictum): *United States v. Leon,* 468 U.S. 897, 913-14 (1984) (dictum); *cf. Gerstein v. Pugh,* 420 U.S. 103, 116-19 (1975), *who is empowered by law to issue it under the circumstances, Sgro v. United States,* 287 U.S. 206 (1932). In sustaining the power of municipal court clerks to issue arrest warrants for municipal ordinance violations in *Shadwick v. City of Tampa,* 407 U.S. 345 (1972), the Supreme Court was careful to determine that the clerks had "no connection with any law enforcement activity or authority which would distort the independent judgment the Fourth Amendment requires," *id.* at 350-51, and that, although nonlawyers, they met the test of being "capable of determining whether probable cause exists for the requested arrest or search," *id.* at 350, at least with regard to the minor cases to which their authority was limited. *Cf. North v. Russell,* 427 U.S. 328, 337-38 (1976) (dictum).

(b) *It is based upon an affidavit or sworn testimony giving probable cause to believe that seizable items are in the place whose search is authorized. Aguilar v. Texas,* 378 U.S. 108 (1964); *Zurcher v. Stanford Daily, supra,* 436 U.S. at 554, 556-59 & n.6; *Franks v. Delaware,* 438 U.S. 154, 165 (1978); *Dalia v. United States, supra,* 441 U.S. at 255-56; *Steagald v. United States,* 451 U.S. 204, 212-13 (1981); *Griffin v. Wisconsin,* subparagraph (A) *supra,* 107 S. Ct. at 3169-70 (dictum). *Compare United States v. Ventresca,* 380 U.S. 102 (1965), *with Spinelli v. United States,* 393 U.S. 410 (1969). The concept of "probable cause" is discussed in paragraph [241] *infra.* Since the critical question is whether the items are in the place at the time when the search is authorized, the information put forward to supply probable cause must disclose the date when it was received and must not be stale. *Rosencranz v. United States,* 356 F.2d 310 (1st Cir. 1963); *Durham v. United States,* 403 F.2d 190 (9th Cir. 1968); *compare Andresen v. Maryland,* 427 U.S. 463, 478-79 n.9 (1976). (Less stringent requirements surround the issuance of warrants for "administrative" or "civil" searches: for example, building code inspections, health code inspections, fire marshal's examinations. *See Camara v. Municipal Court,* 387 U.S. 523, 534-39 (1967) (dictum); *See v. City of Seattle,* 387 U.S. 541, 543-46 (1967) (dictum); *Marshall v. Barlow's, Inc., supra,* 436 U.S. at 320-23 (dictum); *Michigan v. Tyler,* subparagraph (A) *supra,* 436 U.S. at 506-8 & n.5 (dictum); *Zurcher v. Stanford Daily, supra,* 436 U.S. at 555-56 (dictum); *cf. Griffin v. Wisconsin,* subparagraph (A) *supra,* 107 S. Ct. at 3170 & nn.4, 5. Conversely, stricter procedures must be followed in the issuance of warrants for the seizure of materials supposed to be obscene and of other "materials presumptively protected by the First Amendment," *Fort Wayne Books, Inc. v. Indiana,* 109 S. Ct. 916, 927 (1989), because in those cases the First Amendment requires that the magistrate "'focus searchingly on the question of obscenity,'" *Heller v. New York,* 413 U.S. 483, 489 (1973), and cases cited; *Zurcher v. Stanford Daily, supra,* 436 U.S. at 564-65 (dictum); *but see New York v. P.J. Video, Inc.,* 106 S. Ct. 1610 (1986).)

(c) *It identifies the premises to be searched and the things to be seized with reasonable particularity. Stanford v. Texas,* 379 U.S. 476 (1965); *Lo-Ji Sales, Inc. v. New York,* subparagraph (A) *supra,* 442 U.S. at 325-26; *Dalia v. United States, supra,* 441 U.S. at 255-56 (dictum); *Massachusetts v. Sheppard,* 468 U.S. 981, 988 n.5 (1984) (dictum); *McGinnis v. United States,* 227 F.2d 598 (1st Cir. 1955); *United States v. Hinton,* 219 F.2d 324 (7th Cir. 1955). *Cf. Berger v. New York,* 388 U.S. 41, 55-60 (1967); *Nixon v. Administrator of General Services,* 433 U.S. 425, 461-62 (1977) (dictum). *Compare Andresen v. Maryland, supra,* 427 U.S. at 479-82; *Maryland v. Garrison, supra,* 107 S.

Ct. at 1017-18; *United States v. Kahn,* 415 U.S. 143, 155 n.15 (1974) (dictum).
(Some grounds of invalidity of a search warrant do not have exclusionary consequences. See paragraph [240-A] *infra.*)

(3) A building entry may be made without a warrant:

(a) *On consent of the party affected. See, e.g., Washington v. Chrisman,* 455 U.S. 1, 9-10 (1982). The consent must be voluntary, *Amos v. United States,* 255 U.S. 313 (1921); it must "not be coerced, by explicit or implicit means, by implied threat or covert force . . . no matter how subtly . . . applied," *Schneckloth v. Bustamonte,* 412 U.S. 218, 228 (1973) (dictum); and "'[w]hen a prosecutor seeks to rely upon consent to justify the lawfulness of a search, he has the burden of proving [by a preponderance of the evidence, *see United States v. Matlock,* 415 U.S. 164, 177, 177-78 n.14 (1974)] that the consent was, in fact, freely and voluntarily given,'" *Schneckloth v. Bustamonte, supra,* 412 U.S. at 222, and cases cited; *see also Florida v. Royer,* 460 U.S. 491, 497 (1983) (plurality opinion); *United States v. Mendenhall,* 446 U.S. 544, 557 (1980) (dictum). As with confessions, see paragraph [363](C) *infra,* the test of voluntariness is said to turn upon "the totality of all the surrounding circumstances," *Schneckloth v. Bustamonte, supra,* 412 U.S. at 226: "[A]ccount must be taken of subtly coercive police questions, as well as the possibly vulnerable subjective state of the person who consents," *id.* at 229; *cf. United States v. Watson,* 423 U.S. 411, 424-25 (1976). Courts are loth to find voluntary consent when police entry is sought under a show of apparent authority to enter and is merely acquiesced in by the occupant. *Johnson v. United States,* 333 U.S. 10 (1948); *Bumper v. North Carolina,* 391 U.S. 543 (1968); *Lo-Ji Sales, Inc. v. New York,* 442 U.S. 319, 329 (1979). Valid consent may be obtained from an individual who is in police custody, *United States v. Watson, supra,* 423 U.S. at 424, but "courts have been particularly sensitive to the heightened possibilities for coercion when the 'consent' to a search was given by a person in custody," *Schneckloth v. Bustamonte, supra,* 412 U.S. at 241 n.29. *See, e.g., Judd v. United States,* 190 F.2d 649 (D.C. Cir. 1951); *Higgins v. United States,* 209 F.2d 819 (D.C. Cir.

1954): *United States v. Hall,* 565 F.2d 917 (5th Cir. 1978); *Channel v. United States,* 285 F.2d 217 (9th Cir. 1960); *Guzman v. State,* 283 Ark. 112, 120, 672 S.W.2d 656, 659-60 (1984); *Commonwealth v. Smith,* 470 Pa. 220, 228, 368 A.2d 272, 277 (1977). Consent during a period of *illegal* custody should be *eo ipso* ineffective. *Florida v. Royer, supra,* 460 U.S. at 507-8 (plurality opinion); *id.* at 509 (concurring opinions of Justices Powell and Brennan); see paragraphs [236](A)(4), [237](B) *supra.* At least with regard to persons who have not been taken to the stationhouse or other place of closed confinement, the police may obtain valid consent for a warrantless search without first warning the consenting party of his or her Fourth Amendment rights, *see Coolidge v. New Hampshire,* 403 U.S. 443, 484-90 (1971); *Schneckloth v. Bustamonte, supra; United States v. Matlock, supra,* 415 U.S. at 167 n.2; *United States v. Watson, supra,* 423 U.S. at 424-25; *Florida v. Rodriguez,* 469 U.S. 1, 6-7 (1984) (per curiam); *Edwards v. Arizona,* 451 U.S. 477, 483-84 (1981) (dictum), since "knowledge of a right to refuse is not a prerequisite of a voluntary consent," *Schneckloth v. Bustamonte, supra,* 412 U.S. at 234. Even with respect to these persons, however, "knowledge of the right to refuse consent is one factor to be taken into account" in determining voluntariness, *id.* at 227; *see also United States v. Mendenhall, supra,* 446 U.S. at 558-59; and the Court has not rejected the argument that explicit warnings should be required in the case of persons who *are* in police custody "in the confines of the police station," *United States v. Watson, supra,* 423 U.S. at 424, or in similar settings where "the techniques of police questioning and the nature of custodial surroundings produce an inherently coercive situation," *Schneckloth v. Bustamonte, supra,* 412 U.S. at 247, in which the reasoning of *Miranda v. Arizona,* 384 U.S. 436 (1966), paragraph [363](E) *infra,* appears to be fully applicable, *see Berkemer v. McCarty,* 468 U.S. 420, 437-40 (1984); *Arizona v. Roberson,* 108 S. Ct. 2093, 2100 (1988); *United States v. Washington,* 431 U.S. 181, 187 n.5 (1977) (dictum); *Roberts v. United States,* 445 U.S. 552, 560-61 (1980) (dictum); *Minnesota v. Murphy,* 465 U.S. 420, 429-30 (1984) (dictum); *Moran v.*

Burbine, 106 S. Ct. 1135, 1140 (1986) (dictum); *Arizona v. Mauro,* 107 S. Ct. 1931, 1934, 1936-37 (1987) (dictum). *See Schneckloth v. Bustamonte, supra,* 412 U.S. at 240-41 n.29, 247 n.36. Consent by a party other than the defendant raises difficult problems. A tenant's landlord or hotel manager cannot, without express authority from the tenant, authorize a warrantless police entry. *Chapman v. United States,* 365 U.S. 610 (1961); *Stoner v. California,* 376 U.S. 483 (1964). Consent by a cotenant, such as the defendant's spouse, *Coolidge v. New Hampshire, supra; Roberts v. United States,* 332 F.2d 892 (8th Cir. 1964), or parent, *Maxwell v. Stephens,* 348 F.2d 325 (8th Cir. 1965), is usually sustained. *Cf. Frazier v. Cupp,* 394 U.S. 731 (1969). *But see Payton v. New York,* 445 U.S. 573, 583 (1980) (several police officers, seeking to arrest the defendant, knocked on the door of his home; defendant's three-year-old son opened the door, through which the officers could see the defendant; they entered and arrested him "before [he] . . . had an opportunity either to object or to consent"; *held:* The child's opening of the door did not constitute valid consent to the entry). The question is said to be whether the "third party . . . possessed common authority over or other sufficient relationship to the premises or effects sought to be inspected." *United States v. Matlock, supra,* 415 U.S. at 171. "Common authority is, of course, not to be implied from the mere property interest a third party has in the property. The authority which justifies the third-party consent does not rest upon the law of property, . . . but rests rather on mutual use of the property by persons generally having joint access or control for most purposes, so that it is reasonable to recognize that any of the co-inhabitants has the right to permit the inspection in his own right and the others have assumed the risk that one of their number might permit the common area to be searched." *Id.* at 171 n.7. Consent of the cotenant to enter an area reserved for the defendant's private occupancy or use is ineffective. *Reeves v. Warden,* 346 F.2d 915 (4th Cir. 1965).

(b) *If the premises are held open to the public,* as in the case of a shop, *Maryland v. Macon,* 472 U.S. 463 (1985), commercial office, *United States v. Williams,* 328 F.2d 887 (2d Cir. 1964), motel lobby, *Donovan v. Lone Steer, Inc.,* 464 U.S. 408 (1984), or the common corridors of a multi-unit dwelling, *Jennings v. United States,* 247 F.2d 784 (D.C. Cir. 1957). An officer may enter these places without a warrant or probable cause, as any member of the public might do. But "[w]ithout a warrant he stands in no better position than a member of the public," *Marshall v. Barlow's, Inc.,* 436 U.S. 307, 315 (1978), and may intrude no further than a member of the public would be expected to do. *Lo-Ji Sales, Inc. v. New York,* subparagraph (a) *supra,* 442 U.S. at 329. The officer may not, for example, go beyond the common use portions of the premises. *Baysden v. United States,* 271 F.2d 325 (4th Cir. 1959); *Hughes v. Johnson,* 305 F.2d 67 (9th Cir. 1962). *Cf. Recznik v. City of Lorain,* 393 U.S. 166 (1968).

(c) *For the purpose of making a valid arrest,* provided that either:

(i) the entry is made "in 'hot pursuit' of a fugitive," *Steagald v. United States,* 451 U.S. 204, 221 (1981), citing *United States v. Santana,* 427 U.S. 38 (1976), and *Warden v. Hayden,* 387 U.S. 294 (1967); *compare Welsh v. Wisconsin,* 466 U.S. 740, 753 (1984), or under other "exigent circumstances" (see subparagraph (e) *infra*) that make it impracticable to obtain a warrant, *Steagald v. United States, supra,* 451 U.S. at 213-16, 218, 221-22 (*see particularly id.* at 221 n.14, noting that the mere "'inherent mobility' of persons" sought to be arrested does not suffice to establish this exception to the warrant requirement because the police can cope with that problem "simply by waiting for a suspect to leave the third person's home before attempting to arrest that suspect"); *cf. Payton v. New York,* subparagraph (A) *supra,* 445 U.S. at 583 (dictum), or

(ii) the person sought to be arrested is an occupant of the premises and is the subject of a valid arrest warrant, *id.* at 602-3 (dictum).

(The substantial body of earlier case law permitting warrantless "arrest entries" in circumstances other than these two has been overturned by *Payton* and *Steagald. See United*

States v. Johnson, 457 U.S. 537 (1982); *Pembaur v. City of Cincinnati,* 106 S. Ct. 1292, 1295 & n.5 (1986).) The "hot-pursuit"/"exigent-circumstances" exception to the warrant requirement probably does not apply to arrests for minor offenses, *Welsh v. Wisconsin, supra,* 466 U.S. at 750-753; and neither exception justifies an "arrest entry" unless three additional conditions are met:

(A) The intended arrest itself must be valid within the rules set forth in paragraph [236](C) *supra. E.g., Massachusetts v. Painten,* 368 F.2d 142 (1st Cir. 1966), *cert. dismissed,* 389 U.S. 560 (1968).

(B) There must be probable cause to believe that the person sought to be arrested is within the premises. *E.g., Lankford v. Gelston,* 364 F.2d 197 (4th Cir. 1966); *see Steagald v. United States, supra,* 451 U.S. at 214 n.7 (by implication); *Payton v. New York,* subparagraph (a) *supra,* 445 U.S. at 583, 603 (by implication).

(C) The entry and search may not exceed the bounds appropriate in hunting for a person, and they may not intrude into closed areas too small to contain a human being, *see United States v. Ross,* 456 U.S. 798, 824 (1982) (dictum), unless the officers have probable cause to believe that the person sought to be arrested is armed and that they therefore "need to check the entire premises [for weapons] for safety reasons," *Payton v. New York,* subparagraph (A) *supra,* 445 U.S. at 589 (dictum); *see Warden v. Hayden, supra,* 387 U.S. at 298-300.

Another exception to the warrant requirement, related to, but analytically distinct from, the "arrest entry" exception, was recognized in *Washington v. Chrisman,* 455 U.S. 1 (1982). When a person who has been validly arrested in a location other than his or her home requests and receives permission from the arresting officer to return home prior to being taken to the lockup, the officer may accompany that person into the home, as an exercise of "the arresting officer's authority to maintain custody over the arrested person." *Id.* at 6. *Contra, State v. Chrisman,* 100 Wash. 2d 814, 676 P.2d 419 (1984) (on remand, the Washington Supreme Court rejected the *Washington v. Chrisman* holding on state constitutional grounds).

(d) *Incident to a valid arrest.* "[A] lawful custodial arrest creates a situation which justifies the contemporaneous search without a warrant of the person arrested and of the immediately surrounding area. Such searches have long been considered valid because of the need 'to remove any weapons that [the arrestee] might seek to use in order to resist arrest or effect his escape' and the need to prevent the concealment or destruction of evidence." *New York v. Belton,* 453 U.S. 454, 457 (1981). "The constitutionality of a search incident to an arrest does not depend on whether there is any indication that the person arrested [actually] possesses weapons or evidence. The fact of a lawful arrest, standing alone, authorizes a search." *Michigan v. DeFillippo,* 443 U.S. 31, 35 (1979). *See also Illinois v. LaFayette,* 462 U.S. 640, 644-45 (1983) (dictum); *Michigan v. Long,* 463 U.S. 1032, 1048-50 & n.14 (1983) (dictum). In *Harris v. United States,* 331 U.S. 145 (1947), and *United States v. Rabinowitz,* 339 U.S. 56 (1950), the Supreme Court sustained warrantless searches of the portions of premises surrounding the site of a valid arrest made on those premises. During the next 20 years, the lower courts frequently applied, and generally expanded, the doctrine of "search incident to arrest" — routinely sustaining, for example, thorough searches of large apartments and medium-sized houses without a warrant, "incident" to the arrest of an occupant within one room of the apartment or the house. Searches of this scope were retroactively invalidated in *Von Cleef v. New Jersey,* 395 U.S. 814 (1969), in which the Court took a relatively strict view of its earlier *dicta* that a "search 'can be incident to an arrest only if it is substantially contemporaneous with the arrest and is confined to the immediate vicinity of the arrest,'" *James v. Louisiana,* 382 U.S. 36, 37 (1965), and cases cited. At the same time the Court made clear — also retroactively — that a search of a building cannot be justified incidentally to an arrest outside, even when a homeowner is arrested at the very doorstep. *Shipley v. California,* 395 U.S. 818 (1969); *Vale v. Louisiana,* 399 U.S. 30 (1970). *Compare*

United States v. Santana, 427 U.S. 38 (1976). And in a non-retroactive decision (*see Williams v. United States,* 401 U.S. 646 (1971)), the Court categorically overruled *Harris and Rabinowitz. Chimel v. California,* 395 U.S. 752 (1969). Following the date of the *Chimel* decision, June 23, 1969, no warrantless search incident to arrest may be made that goes beyond the arrestee's wingspan or, as *Chimel* puts it, beyond "the arrestee's person and the area 'within his immediate control'—construing that phrase to mean the area from within which he might gain possession of a weapon [to attack the arresting officer] or destructible evidence." 395 U.S. at 763. *See also United States v. Chadwick,* 433 U.S. 1, 14 (1977); *Lo-Ji Sales, Inc. v. New York,* 442 U.S. 319, 326 (1979). Within this area, a warrantless search incident to arrest is valid, provided that:

(i) the arrest itself is valid, see paragraph [236](A)(1), (C) *supra,* and

(ii) the arrest is not "maneuvered" as a device to justify a warrantless search, *McKnight v. United States,* 183 F.2d 977 (D.C. Cir. 1950) (alternative ground); *United States v. Harris,* 321 F.2d 739 (6th Cir. 1963); *Gilbert v. United States,* 291 F.2d 586 (9th Cir. 1961) (alternative ground), *holding on other issues vacated,* 370 U.S. 650 (1962); *cf.* subparagraph [236](C)(3) *supra.*

For the still more restrictive rule applicable in certain First Amendment cases, *see Roaden v. Kentucky,* 413 U.S. 496 (1973); *cf. Zurcher v. Stanford Daily,* 436 U.S. 547, 564 (1978) (dictum).

(e) Perhaps *if "exceptional circumstances" (a/k/a "exigent circumstances") require immediate entry before the time within which a warrant can be obtained.* Although *dicta* in Supreme Court cases recognize this exception to the warrant requirement, *see, e.g., Johnson v. United States,* 333 U.S. 10, 14-15 (1948); *United States v. Jeffers,* 342 U.S. 48, 51 (1951); *Chapman v. United States,* 365 U.S. 610, 615 (1961); *Michigan v. Tyler,* 436 U.S. 499, 509-10 (1978); *Mincey v. Arizona,* 437 U.S. 385, 392-94 (1978); *Michigan v. Summers,* 452 U.S. 692, 702 n.17 (1981); *Michigan v. Clifford,* 464 U.S. 287, 293 (1984) (plurality opinion); *cf. Torres v. Puerto Rico,* 442 U.S. 465,

471 (1979); *New York v. Belton,* 453 U.S. 454, 457 (1981), the Court has never actually sustained a warrantless building entry on the "exceptional circumstances" theory when the purpose of the entry was to make a search, unassociated with an arrest, for criminal law enforcement purposes. *Welsh v. Wisconsin,* 466 U.S. 740, 749-50 (1984). In *Warden v. Hayden,* 387 U.S. 294 (1967), the Court did approve a building entry by officers without a warrant when the purpose of the entry was to arrest a fugitive and the entry was made in "hot pursuit" of the fugitive (that is, less than five minutes after the fugitive, fleeing directly from the crime scene, was observed entering the building). *Cf. United States v. Santana,* 427 U.S. 38, 42-43 & n.3 (1976); *Steagald v. United States,* 451 U.S. 204, 218, 221-22 (1981) (dictum). Because the fugitive was known to be armed, the Court in *Warden* also approved, under the "exceptional circumstances" principle, a search *within* the building, at least to the extent necessary to find weapons. *Compare Gilbert v. California,* 388 U.S. 263, 269 (1967). And in *Michigan v. Tyler, supra,* the Supreme Court held that firefighting officials require neither "a warrant [n]or consent before entering a burning structure to put out the blaze," 436 U.S. at 509; and, since "[f]ire officials are charged not only with extinguishing fires, but with finding their causes," *id.* at 510, they "need no warrant [or consent] to remain in a building for a reasonable time to investigate the cause of a blaze after it has been extinguished," *ibid. Accord, Michigan v. Clifford, supra,* 464 U.S. at 293-97 (plurality opinion) (dictum). Lower courts have similarly sustained warrantless building entries in a variety of situations in which officers with general peacekeeping responsibilities have gone into premises in the reasonable belief that some person inside is in need of immediate assistance or preventive action to avert serious bodily injury. *United States v. Barone,* 330 F.2d 543 (2d Cir. 1964); *cf. Wayne v. United States,* 318 F.2d 205 (D.C. Cir. 1963); *see Mincey v. Arizona, supra,* 437 U.S. at 392-93 (dictum), and authorities cited; *Thompson v. Louisiana,* 469 U.S. 17, 21 (1984) (per curiam) (dictum). Probably the "exceptional circumstances" exception extends

no further than these situations, although the tenor of some of the Supreme Court *dicta* does. In any event, the exigency that is claimed to justify exemption from the warrant requirement must be affirmatively demonstrated by the prosecution (see paragraph [253](B) *infra*) and must be real and pressing. *See, e.g., Vale v. Louisiana,* 399 U.S. 30, 34-35 (1970); *G.M. Leasing Corp. v. United States,* 429 U.S. 338, 358-59 (1977); *Mincey v. Arizona, supra,* 437 U.S. at 393, 394; *Welsh v. Wisconsin, supra,* 466 U.S. at 749-50; *Thompson v. Louisiana, supra; Eng Fung Jem v. United States,* 281 F.2d 803 (9th Cir. 1960); *State v. Naturile,* 83 N.J. Super. 563, 568-69, 200 A.2d 617, 619 (1964). *Cf. United States v. Caceres,* 440 U.S. 741, 749 (1979) (dictum).

(f) *To enforce administrative codes upon the premises of licensed dealers in regulated industries,* such as gun and liquor distributors, *United States v. Biswell,* 406 U.S. 311 (1972), automobile junkyards, *New York v. Burger,* 107 S. Ct. 2636 (1987), and coin dealers, *Exotic Coins, Inc. v. Beacom,* 474 U.S. 892 (1985) (per curiam), *dismissing appeal from* 699 P.2d 930 (Colo. 1985), to the extent permitted by explicit statutory authorizations of warrantless inspection, *Colonnade Catering Corp. v. United States,* 397 U.S. 72 (1970). *See Donovan v. Dewey,* 452 U.S. 594 (1981); *cf. Wyman v. James,* 400 U.S. 309 (1971). This exception to the warrant requirement is an exceedingly narrow one, limited to "businessmen engaged in . . . licensed and regulated enterprises" subject to a "pervasive system of regulation"; and, even with regard to them, the search is authorized only of the licensed premises. *Almeida-Sanchez v. United States,* 413 U.S. 266, 271 (1973). *See also G.M. Leasing Corp. v. United States,* 429 U.S. 338, 353-58 (1977); *Marshall v. Barlow's Inc.,* 436 U.S. 307, 313-14 (1978); *Delaware v. Prouse,* 440 U.S. 648, 662-63 (1979). In addition, "the regulatory statute . . . must advise the owner of the commercial premises that the search is being made pursuant to the law and has a properly defined scope [that is, it "must be 'sufficiently comprehensive and defined that the owner of commercial property cannot help but be aware that his property will be subject to periodic inspections undertaken for specific purposes'"], and it must limit the discretion of the inspecting officers." *New York v. Burger, supra,* 107 S. Ct. at 2644 (dictum); see also paragraph [238](A)(2) *supra;* paragraph [246](D)(2) *infra.* Except in these "'closely regulated industries,'" *id.* at 4893, warrantless civil or administrative searches, once thought to be sustained by *Frank v. Maryland,* 359 U.S. 360 (1959), are now generally condemned. *Camara v. Municipal Court,* 387 U.S. 523 (1967); *See v. City of Seattle,* 387 U.S. 541 (1967); *Marshall v. Barlow's, Inc., supra,* 436 U.S. at 312-15; *Michigan v. Tyler,* 436 U.S. 499, 504-9 (1978); *Torres v. Puerto Rico,* 442 U.S. 465, 473 (1979); *Michigan v. Clifford, supra,* 464 U.S. at 291-292 (plurality opinion); *Zurcher v. Stanford Daily,* 436 U.S. 547, 555-56 (1978) (dictum); *cf. New Jersey v. T.L.O.,* 469 U.S. 325, 333-35 (1985) (dictum); see subparagraph (C)(2)(b); *supra.* They are said to be sustainable "'[o]nly in those exceptional circumstances in which special needs, beyond the normal need for law enforcement, make the warrant . . . requirement impracticable,'" *O'Connor v. Ortega,* 107 S. Ct. 1492, 1500 (1987) (plurality opinion); *see also id.* at 1506 (concurring opinion of Justice Scalia) (upholding warrantless searches of the individual offices of public employees by their governmental employers "when there are reasonable grounds for suspecting that the search will turn up evidence that the employee is guilty of work-related misconduct, or that the search is necessary for a noninvestigatory work-related purpose such as to retrieve a needed file," *id.* at 1503 (plurality opinion)); *Griffin v. Wisconsin,* 107 S. Ct. 3164 (1987) (upholding warrantless searches of probationers' homes when conducted pursuant to regulations authorizing such searches with the approval of the probationer's supervisor upon reasonable grounds to believe that the search will turn up items that the probationer is forbidden by his or her conditions of probation to possess); *New Jersey v. T.L.O., supra* (implying that warrantless searches of children's public school lockers and desks, if subject to Fourth Amendment restriction at all, *see id.* at 337 n.5, will be sustained "when there are reasonable grounds for suspecting that the search will turn up evidence that the student has violated or is violating either the law or the rules of the school," *id.* at 342). An additional problem in connection with statutorily authorized warrant-less searches is that the invalidity of the underlying statute does not necessarily entail the exclusion of evidence obtained in a search made under its authority. In *Illinois v. Krull,* 107 S. Ct. 1160 (1987), the Supreme Court refused to apply the Fourth Amendment "exclusionary rule to suppress evidence obtained by an officer acting in objectively reasonable reli-ance on a statute" not yet judicially declared unconstitu-tional, *id.* at 1167, even though the statute was later found unconstitutional according to the principles of this subpara-graph. See paragraph [223](C) *supra.* Under *Krull,* suppres-sion is required only if the provisions of the statute "are such that a reasonable officer should have known that the statute was unconstitutional," 107 S. Ct. at 1170 — an "objective" standard of reasonableness, *id.* at 1172, which "requires offi-cers to have a reasonable knowledge of what the law pro-hibits," *United States v. Leon,* 468 U.S. 897, 920 n.20 (1984).

(D) The preceding subparagraph (C) deals with restrictions upon the *circumstances* under which building entries can be made. There are also legal restrictions upon the *manner* of entry. A federal statute, 18 U.S.C. §3109, as construed, provides that a federal officer executing a search warrant may "break open" an outer or inner door or window of a house only after making an announcement of his or her authority and of the purpose for the entry and being refused admittance. *See Miller v. United States,* 357 U.S. 301 (1958). The *Miller* case applied the requirements of the statute to an officer making an entry for the purpose of arrest without a warrant in the District of Columbia, on the explicit ground that the local law of the District held officers to such requirements whether they were entering to search or ar-rest, with or without a warrant. In *Sabbath v. United States,* 391 U.S. 585 (1968), the Court, without explanation, applied the same requirements to a federal officer entering a building to make a warrantless arrest outside the District of Columbia. (*See also Munoz v. United States,* 325 F.2d 23 (9th Cir. 1963).) Al-though this decision is explicable on the narrow ground that the state where the entry occurred (California) had an applicable statute similar to Section 3109 (*cf. United States v. Di Re,* 332 U.S. 581, 589-90 (1948)), the Court's failure to discuss the issue suggests that Section 3109 has now been broadened as a matter of federal common law to cover all entries by federal officers. *Sabbath* further holds that "breaking open" includes any opening of a door, locked or unlocked, forcibly or nonforcibly, by an officer; so, in effect, an announcement of authority and purpose is now required prior to any federal entry except, perhaps, when there is reasonable ground to believe that the announcement would jeopardize the safety of the entering officer or cause the destruction of evidence or would be futile under the circumstances. *See Miller v. United States, supra,* 357 U.S. at 308-10; *Sabbath v. United States, supra,* 391 U.S. at 591; *Ker v. California,* 374 U.S. 23, 38-41, 54-59 (1963); *cf. Dalia v. United States,* 441 U.S. 238, 247-48 (1979); *Washington v. Chrisman,* 455 U.S. 1, 10 n.7 (1982). Congress codified these exceptions in legislation applicable to the District of Columbia, D.C. CODE, §23-591 (1971), as enacted by the District of Columbia Court Reform and Criminal Procedure Act of 1970, Pub. L. No. 91-358, §210(a), 84 Stat. 630, and also provided in it for the issuance of warrants expressly authorizing breaking and entering without announcement. Most states have legislation akin to Section 3109, requiring announcement prior to building entries; some, like the District of Columbia statute, now authorize "no-knock" warrants under specified circumstances. Whether the requirement of announcement has constitutional status remains unresolved in the wake of *Ker v. California, supra.* Arguably it does, under the general Fourth Amendment principle "that the manner in which a warrant is executed is subject to . . . judicial review as to its reasonableness," *Dalia v. United States, supra,* 441 U.S. at 258 (dictum); *cf. Tennessee v. Garner,* 471 U.S. 1, 7-8 (1985) ("[in] many cases . . . this Court, by balancing the extent of the intrusion against the need for it, has examined the reasonableness of the manner in which a search or seizure is conducted"), particularly inasmuch as "physical entry of the home is the chief evil against which the wording of the Fourth Amendment is directed," *United States v. United States District Court for the Eastern District of Michigan,* 407 U.S. 297, 313 (1972); *see also, e.g., Michigan v. Tyler,* 436 U.S. 499, 504 (1978); *Payton v. New York,* 445 U.S. 573, 589-90 (1980); *United States v. Johnson,* 457 U.S. 375, 552 n.13 (1982) [quoted in subparagraph (A) *supra*], and authorities cited; *Welsh v. Wisonsin,* 466 U.S. 740, 748 (1984); *Michigan v. Clifford,* 464 U.S. 287, 296-97 (1984) (plurality opinion); *Oliver v. United States,* 466 U.S. 170, 178-79 (1984) (dictum). Some state courts have explicitly held that the Fourth Amendment embodies the announcement requirement. *E.g., State v. Sundel,* 121 R.I. 638, 643, 402 A.2d 585, 588 (1979); *State v. Coyle,* 95 Wash. 2d 1, 6, 621 P.2d 1256, 1259 (1980). Assuming that it does, the validity of the "no-knock" laws and other state law exceptions to the requirement is left in doubt by the 4-1-4 division of the Supreme Court in *Ker.* (Four Justices there, taking a broad view of Fourth Amendment protection against unannounced police entries, would have recognized only narrow exceptions to the announcement rule. Four Justices thought that if the Fourth Amendment required announcements at all, it tolerated the usual range of state law exceptions to the requirement. Justice Harlan's decisive vote to uphold the entry in *Ker* was based upon the now obsolete theory that the Fourth Amendment is not fully incorporated into the Fourteenth.)

(E) "The [Supreme] Court has not had occasion to consider whether, when officers have probable cause to believe that evidence of criminal activity is on the premises [but lack the additional grounds required to justify a warrantless entry under the principles of subparagraph (C) *supra*], the temporary securing of a dwelling [by posting guards outside] to prevent the removal or destruction of evidence [until a warrant to enter and search can be obtained] violates the Fourth Amendment." *Segura v. United States,* 468 U.S. 796, 809 (1984) (opinion of Chief Justice Burger). Aspects of that issue are debated inconclusively in *id.* at 805-13 (opinion speaking for only two Justices) and *id.* at 822-27 (dissenting opinion for four Justices).

[240-A] Grounds for exclusion of evidence seized pursuant to an invalid warrant. (A) In *United States v. Leon,* 468 U.S. 897 (1984), the Supreme Court held that "the Fourth Amendment exclusionary rule should be modified so as not to bar the [prosecution's] use . . . of evidence obtained by officers acting in reasonable reliance on a search warrant issued by a detached and neutral magistrate but ultimately found to be unsupported by probable cause." *Id.* at 900. The Court reasoned that "the exclusionary rule is designed to deter police misconduct rather than to punish the errors of judges and magistrates." *Id.* at 916. Thus "suppression of evidence obtained pursuant to a warrant should be ordered only on a case-by-case basis and only in those unusual cases in which exclusion will further the purposes of the exclusionary rule." *Id.* at 918. In *Massachusetts v. Sheppard,* 468 U.S. 981 (1984), the Court similarly refused to exclude evidence taken under a search warrant that was invalid because of clerical defects in the magistrate's writeup of the objects to be seized. See paragraph [223](C) *supra.*

(B) Following *Leon* and *Sheppard,* the exclusion of evidence seized under a warrant is required in these situations:

(1) *When the executing officers extend a search or seizure beyond the scope that they can reasonably believe to be authorized by the warrant, or otherwise execute the warrant improperly.* The rule of *Leon* "assumes . . . that the officers properly executed the warrant and searched only those places and for those objects that it was reasonable to believe were covered by the warrant." 468 U.S. at 918 n.19. Thus if the officers enter any area that they know "or should have known" is outside the boundaries of the place that the warrant authorizes to be searched, or if they "discover[ ] that there [are] . . . separate units [within the place described by the warrant and are] therefore . . . put on notice of the risk that they might be in a unit erroneously included within the terms of the warrant," *Maryland v. Garrison,* 107 S. Ct. 1013, 1018 (1987), their conduct is unconstitutional and unprotected by *Leon.* The same is true if:

(a) they seize any objects that they cannot reasonably believe to be covered by the warrant, see paragraph [240](C)(1) *supra; compare Massachusetts v. Sheppard, supra,* 468 U.S. at 989 & n.6;

(b) they extend their search into areas that could not contain objects covered by the warrant, see paragraph [240](C)(1) *supra;* or

(c) they execute the warrant in any manner that violates the Fourth Amendment, see paragraph [240](D) *supra.*

(2) *When officers seeking a warrant know "or even if they should have known" that the premises for which they seek a warrant includes separate units with different occupants and if they fail to limit their*

warrant application to the unit that they are presenting probable cause to search. *See Maryland v. Garrison, supra,* 107 S. Ct. at 1017 (dictum).

(3) *When "the magistrate abandoned his detached and neutral role,"* United States v. Leon, supra, 468 U.S. at 926; *see also id.* at 923. This situation refers to the doctrine described in paragraph [240](C)(2)(a) *supra.*

(4) *When "a warrant is so facially deficient* — i.e., *in failing to particularize the place to be searched or the things to be seized* — *that the executing officers cannot reasonably presume it to be valid."* United States v. Leon, supra, 468 U.S. at 923. The question here appears to be whether a violation of the doctrine described in paragraph [240](C)(2)(c) is glaring.

(5) *When the warrant is issued on the basis of "an affidavit 'so lacking in indicia of probable cause as to render official belief in its existence entirely unreasonable,'"* ibid. — that is, if "a reasonably well-trained officer . . . would have known that his affidavit failed to establish probable cause and that he should not have applied for the warrant," *Malley v. Briggs,* 106 S. Ct. 1092, 1098 (1986). Arguably, this is the case whenever an affidavit is merely conclusory, within the principle of paragraph [241](B)(3) *infra,* since the law has been settled for a half-century that "a merely conclusory statement . . . gives the magistrate virtually no basis at all for making a judgment regarding probable cause," *Illinois v. Gates,* 462 U.S. 213, 239 (1983), citing *Nathanson v. United States,* 290 U.S. 41 (1933).

(6) *When "the magistrate . . . in issuing a warrant was misled by information in an affidavit that the affiant knew was false or would have known known was false except for his reckless disregard of the truth."* United States v. Leon, supra, 468 U.S. at 923. This situation involves a warrant invalidated by the rule of *Franks v. Delaware,* 438 U.S. 154 (1978), discussed in paragraph [241](B)(2)(b) *infra.*

(7) *When the warrant is issued on the basis of evidence produced by earlier unconstitutional police activity and the affidavit does not contain enough independent information to make out probable cause without reference to the tainted evidence. United States v. Karo,* 468 U.S. 705, 719-21 (1984) (dictum). See paragraph [241](B)(8) *infra.*

[241] The concept of "probable cause." (A) Much of the law of the Fourth Amendment is concerned with "probable cause." As indicated in paragraphs [230], [236](C), and [240](C) *supra*, arrest and search warrants are issued only upon a magistrate's finding of probable cause; felony arrests without a warrant are authorized only upon an officer's determination of probable cause; and warrantless searches in most of the situations in which they may be made at all may be made only upon probable cause. See also paragraphs [246](A), [248](C), (D) *infra*. When arrests or searches are challenged, courts must review the findings of probable cause on which their validity depends: the magistrate's finding of probable cause, based on the affidavits before the magistrate, if a warrant was issued; and the police officer's finding of probable cause, based on the information possessed by the officer, if s/he acted without a warrant. (But see paragraph [240-A] *supra*, discussing the limited applicability of the exclusionary rule to evidence seized under warrants issued without probable cause.)

(B) For these purposes the constitutional phrase *probable cause* means "'a reasonable ground for belief,'" *Brinegar v. United States*, 338 U.S. 160, 175 (1949): "Probable cause exists where 'the facts and circumstances within . . . [the officers'] knowledge and of which they had reasonably trustworthy information [are] sufficient in themselves to warrant a man of reasonable caution in the [requisite] belief . . . ,'" *id.* at 175-76. Specifically, probable cause for *arrest* is established when there are reasonable grounds to believe that the particular person sought to be arrested has committed a crime; probable cause for *search* is established when there are reasonable grounds to believe that objects connected to criminal activity or otherwise subject to seizure are presently located in the particular place to be searched. *Zurcher v. Stanford Daily*, 436 U.S. 547, 556-57 n.6 (1978); *Steagald v. United States*, 451 U.S. 204, 213 (1981). There are elaborate definitions of the concept of probable cause, *e.g.*, *Gerstein v. Pugh*, 420 U.S. 103, 111-12 (1975); *Dunaway v. New York*, 442 U.S. 200, 208 n.9 (1979); *Michigan v. DeFillipo*, 443 U.S. 31, 37 (1979); *United States v. Ross*, 456 U.S. 798, 808-9 & n.10 (1982); *Illinois v. Gates*, 462 U.S. 213, 230-40 (1983); *Texas v. Brown*, 460 U.S. 730, 742 (1983) (plurality opinion), and innumerable constructions of it in individual factual situations, *see, e.g., Florida v. Royer,* 460 U.S. 491, 507 (1983) (plurality opinion); *Illinois v. Gates, supra.* Generalization is unhelpful, but a few recurring points, dealing principally with procedural matters, may be noted:

(1) *Different standards of review of the magistrate and of the police officer.* To issue a constitutionally valid search or arrest warrant, a magistrate must make a finding of probable cause. *Griffin v. Wisconsin,* 107 S. Ct. 3164, 3169-70 (1987). Before *United States v. Leon,* 468 U.S. 897 (1984), paragraph [240-A] *supra,* when the validity of a warrant was questioned, "the duty of a reviewing court [was] . . . simply to ensure that the magistrate had a 'substantial basis for . . . conclud[ing]' that probable cause existed." *Illinois v. Gates,* 462 U.S. 213, 238-39 (1983); *see also Massachusetts v. Upton,* 466 U.S. 727, 732-33 (1984) (per curiam). This remains the Fourth Amendment standard for judicial review of the sufficiency of warrant affidavits for other purposes than the federal exclusionary rule, *United States v. Leon, supra,* 468 U.S. at 915 & n.13—for example, for the purpose of quashing an invalid warrant and ordering the return of noncontraband, nonevidentiary material seized pursuant to it—as well as under state constitutional exclusionary rules, see paragraph [227](B) *supra.* Under this standard it is frequently said that courts are to give greater deference to a magistrate's judgment in reviewing the findings of probable cause upon which a warrant has issued than to a police officer's judgment in reviewing the determinations of probable cause on which the officer has acted without a warrant. *United States v. Watson,* 423 U.S. 411, 423 (1976); *Aguilar v. Texas,* 378 U.S. 108, 110-11 (1964); *United States v. Ventresca,* 380 U.S. 102, 105-9 (1965); *Wong Sun v. United States,* 371 U.S. 471, 479-82 (1963); *Illinois v. Gates, supra,* 462 U.S. at 236-37 & n.10; *United States v. Leon, supra,* 468 U.S. at 913-14 (dictum); *Travis v. United States,* 362 F.2d 477, 480 (9th Cir. 1966). The double standard is based upon a recognition that the magistrate's impartial judgment (see paragraph [240](C)(2)(a) *supra*) is more likely to be reliable than the judgment of an "officer engaged in the often competitive enterprise of ferreting out crime," *Johnson v. United States,* 333 U.S. 10, 14 (1948); *see also Payton v. New York,* 445 U.S. 573, 586 n.24 (1980); *Michigan v. Summers,* 452 U.S. 692, 703-4 n.18 (1981), and upon the theory

that stricter judicial review in cases of warrantless police action will encourage the police to seek warrants and will thus support the preference for a warrant that is basic to the Fourth Amendment (see paragraph [229] *supra; cf.* paragraph [246](D)(2) *infra*), *Illinois v. Gates, supra,* 462 U.S. at 236-37 & n.10; *Massachusetts v. Upton, supra,* 466 U.S. at 732-33, 734. For purposes of the federal exclusionary rule after *Leon,* the principle of judicial deference to magistrates' findings of probable cause has been superseded by the still less exacting standard described in paragraph [240-A](B)(5) *supra;* but the language of the pre-*Leon* cases and of *Leon* itself that "in a doubtful or marginal case a search under a warrant may be sustainable where without one it would fall," *United States v. Ventresca, supra,* 380 U.S. at 106, quoted with approval in *United States v. Leon, supra,* 468 U.S. at 914, continues to provide atmospheric support to defense counsel when attacking warrantless police action taken on an officer's judgment of probable cause.

(2) *The factual basis for judicial review in warrant cases.*

(a) It is a disputed question whether the affidavit presented to a magistrate to support the issuance of a warrant stands as the exclusive basis for the magistrate's determination of probable cause or whether it may be supplemented by material presented to the magistrate orally. After *Leon,* the point is of importance for federal exclusionary purposes primarily in cases in which the affidavit is wholly conclusory and therefore arguably invalidates a search under the reasoning of paragraph [240-A](B)(5) *supra.* Under statutes or rules providing for the issuance of warrants "upon affidavit," it is generally held that both the magistrate and any reviewing court are restricted to the "four corners of the affidavit." *See United States v. Sterling,* 369 F.2d 799, 802 n.2 (3d Cir. 1966); *United States v. Hatcher,* 473 F.2d 321, 324 (6th Cir. 1973); *United States v. Anderson,* 453 F.2d 174 (9th Cir. 1971). Similarly, if the governing statute or rule permits the taking of oral testimony before the issuing magistrate but requires that this testimony be recorded and made part of the affidavit (as Federal Rule of Criminal Procedure 41(c)(1) now does), *un*recorded testimony may not be considered by the magistrate or a reviewing court in support of the warrant. *E.g., United States v. Hittle,* 575 F.2d 799 (10th Cir. 1978); *State v.*

Adkins, 346 S.E.2d 762, 766-768 (W. Va. 1986), and authorities cited. In the absence of statutes or rules of these sorts, the cases have ordinarily permitted sworn oral testimony to be used to supplement an affidavit, *see, e.g., United States ex rel. Gaugler v. Brierley,* 477 F.2d 516 (3d Cir. 1973); *United States v. Hill,* 500 F.2d 315 (5th Cir. 1974); *United States v. Berkus,* 428 F.2d 1148 (8th Cir. 1970), despite a few hints that the Fourth Amendment *ex proprio vigore* may require contemporaneous memorialization of the evidentiary basis for a warrant, *see United States v. Anderson, supra,* 453 F.2d at 175; *Christofferson v. Washington,* 393 U.S. 1090 (1969) (opinion of Justice Brennan, dissenting from denial of *certiorari*). (A substantial number of state statutes and, since a 1976 amendment, Federal Rule of Criminal Procedure 41(c)(2) authorize the issuance of warrants upon sworn oral testimony communicated to the magistrate by telephone or other transmitting device, "[i]f the circumstances make it reasonable to dispense with a written affidavit." FED. R. CRIM. P. 41(c)(2)(A). The testimony must be recorded, transcribed, certified by the magistrate, and filed with the court. This process thus supplies the essential safeguards of an affidavit procedure: the fixing and memorializing of the basis for every warrant that is issued. *See State v. Adkins, supra.*) In any event, the Fourth Amendment's requirement of "Oath or affirmation" should preclude a magistrate's resort to *unsworn* oral supplementation of an affidavit, as almost all courts recognize. *See, e.g., Tabasko v. Barton,* 472 F.2d 871 (6th Cir. 1972); *Frazier v. Roberts,* 441 F.2d 1224 (8th Cir. 1971); *State v. Moriarty,* 39 N.J. 502, 189 A.2d 210 (1963). And, certainly, facts known to an affiant but not communicated to the magistrate in any form cannot be invoked to support the warrant upon subsequent judicial review; there seems to be no debate on this basic point. *See Aguilar v. Texas,* subparagraph (B)(1) *supra,* 378 U.S. at 109 n.1; *Whitely v. Warden,* 401 U.S. 560, 565 n.8 (1971); *Stone v. Powell,* 428 U.S. 465, 473 n.3 (1976) (dictum); *Baysden v. United States,* 271 F.2d 325 (4th Cir. 1959); *Lopez v. United States,* 370 F.2d 8, 10 (5th Cir. 1966) (dictum); *cf. Welsh v. Wisconsin,* 466 U.S. 740, 746 n.6 (1984) (facts about suspect's criminal record unknown to arresting officers cannot be considered in judicial review of the legality of the officers' warrantless arrest entry).

(b) A different question is presented when a party challenging a search and seizure made pursuant to a warrant seeks to introduce evidence not laid before the magistrate that *impeaches* the representations of the affidavit. In *Franks v. Delaware*, 438 U.S. 154 (1978), the Supreme Court dealt comprehensively with the subject and held "that, where the defendant makes a substantial preliminary showing that a false statement knowingly and intentionally, or with reckless disregard for the truth, was included by the affiant in the warrant affidavit, and if the allegedly false statement is necessary to the finding of probable cause, the Fourth Amendment requires that a hearing be held at the defendant's request. In the event that at that hearing the allegation of perjury or reckless disregard is established by the defendant by a preponderance of the evidence, and, with the affidavit's false material set to one side, the affidavit's remaining content is insufficient to establish probable cause, the search warrant must be voided and the fruits of the search excluded to the same extent as if probable cause was lacking on the face of the affidavit." *Id.* at 155-56. The rule of *Franks* "has a limited scope, both in regard to when exclusion of the seized evidence is mandated, and when a hearing on allegations of misstatements must be accorded." *Id.* at 167. "To mandate an evidentiary hearing, the challenger's attack must be more than conclusory and must be supported by more than a mere desire to cross-examine. There must be allegations of deliberate falsehood or of reckless disregard for the truth, and those allegations must be accompanied by an offer of proof. They should point out specifically the portion of the warrant affidavit that is claimed to be false; and they should be accompanied by a statement of supporting reasons. Affidavits or sworn or otherwise reliable statements of witnesses should be furnished, or their absence satisfactorily explained. Allegations of negligence or innocent mistake are insufficient. The deliberate falsity or reckless disregard whose impeachment is permitted . . . is only that of the affiant, not of any nongovernmental informant. Finally, if these requirements are met, and if, when material that is the subject of the alleged falsity or reckless disregard is set to one side, there remains sufficient content in the warrant affidavit to support a finding of probable cause, no hearing is required. On the other hand, if the remaining content is insufficient, the defendant is entitled, under the Fourth and Fourteenth Amendments, to his hearing." *Id.* at 171-72.

(3) *Conclusory affidavits.* At least when nothing told to the magistrate *dehors* the affidavit is offered to bolster it, the law is plain that an affidavit is constitutionally insufficient to support a warrant if it merely states the affiant's conclusion on the ultimate fact in issue (for example, that *X* has a sawed-off shotgun in a certain house). *Aguilar v. Texas,* subparagraph (B)(1) *supra; Riggan v. Virginia,* 384 U.S. 152 (1966) (per curiam); *Illinois v. Gates,* subparagraph (B) *supra,* 462 U.S. at 227, 239 (dictum). It must disclose specific factual observations from which that conclusion can be inferred (for example, that on a stated date *Y* observed in *X*'s house a double-barreled shotgun less than 18 inches long), and if the observations are not those of the affiant, it must disclose how the affiant learned of them (for example, that *Y* told the affiant of *Y*'s observations). The theory is that the averments must sufficiently disclose raw facts to permit the magistrate to make an independent determination of their persuasiveness as tending to the conclusion that seizable items are in the place to be searched. *See Nathanson v. United States,* 290 U.S. 41, 47 (1933); *Spinelli v. United States,* 393 U.S. 410, 412-19 (1969); *Franks v. Delaware,* subparagraph (B)(2)(b) *supra,* 438 U.S. at 165; *Illinois v. Gates,* subparagraph (B) *supra,* 462 U.S. at 239.

(4) *Hearsay.*

(a) A magistrate may find probable cause on the basis of information that is hearsay (that is, upon the affiant's relating to the magistrate of circumstances observed and told to the affiant by a third party) if, "given all the circumstances set forth in the affidavit . . ., including the 'veracity' and 'basis of knowledge' of persons supplying hearsay information, there is a fair probability that contraband or evidence of a crime will be found in a particular place." *Illinois v. Gates,* subparagraph (B) *supra,* 462 U.S. at 238. The *Gates* decision repudiated a line of analysis thought by some lower courts to be required by *Spinelli v. United States,* subparagraph (B)(3) *supra,* under which affidavits were held insufficient unless they *both* demonstrated the hearsay declarant's credibility ("veracity" or "reliability") *and* disclosed in detail the manner in which the declarant had obtained the information s/he reported. *See Massachusetts v. Upton,* subparagraph (B)(1) *supra,* 466 U.S. at 732. "We agree . . . that an informant's 'veracity,' 'reliability,' and 'basis of knowledge' are all highly relevant in determining the value of his report. We do not agree, however, that these elements should be understood as entirely separate and independent requirements to be rigidly exacted in every case. . . . Rather, . . . they should be understood simply as closely intertwined issues that may usefully illuminate the common-sense, practical question whether there is 'probable cause' to believe that contraband or evidence is located in a particular place." *Illinois v. Gates,* subparagraph (B) *supra,* 462 U.S. at 230. "[A] deficiency in one [element] may be compensated for, in determining the overall reliability of a tip, by a strong showing as to the other, or by some other indicia of reliability." *Id.* at 233. Thus although an uncorroborated tip from an anonymous informant is insufficient to support a warrant, *id.* at 227, 239, *Gates* upheld a warrant issued on the basis of anonymous information so detailed as to imply that the informant must be highly knowledgeable and accurate, after "independent investigative work" by the police had corroborated a substantial portion of those details relating to conduct which "at least suggested" criminal activity, *id.* at 243-44. Conversely, if "a particular informant is known for the unusual reliability of his predictions of certain types of criminal activities in a locality, his failure, in a particular case, to thoroughly set forth the basis of his knowledge surely should not serve as an absolute bar to a finding of probable cause based on his tip." *Id.* at 233.

(b) Similar rules govern police use of hearsay information to establish probable cause when they act without a warrant. Here again, information from an informant of unknown or doubtful reliability will not alone suffice. *E.g., Wong Sun v. United States,* 371 U.S. 471, 480-81 (1963); *Taylor v. Alabama,* 457 U.S. 687, 688-89 (1982); *cf. Recznik v. City of Lorain,* 393 U.S. 166, 169 (1968) (per curiam). A police officer may rest a determination of probable cause on the observations or knowledge of another person, narrated to the officer, only when additional information gives the officer a solid ground for crediting the narrative. *E.g., Contee v. United States,* 215 F.2d 324 (D.C. Cir. 1954); *Lankford v. Gelston,* 364 F.2d 197 (4th Cir. 1966); *Costello v. United States,* 298 F.2d 99 (9th Cir. 1962).

(c) Both in warrant cases and in cases of police action without a warrant, the requisite support for a hearsay declarant's story may come either from facts that corroborate the story itself (for example, coincident observations of other informants, *e.g., Chambers v. Maroney,* 399 U.S. 42, 44-47 (1970), or observations by the police that suspects are acting as the declarant has predicted they will act, *e.g., Illinois v. Gates,* subparagraph (B) *supra,* 462 U.S. at 242-43, 244-45) or from facts that establish that the declarant is generally trustworthy and dependable (for example, the fact that on previous occasions information received from the declarant proved correct, *e.g., United States v. Ross,* 456 U.S. 798, 817 n.22 (1982); *Costello v. United States,* 324 F.2d 260 (9th Cir. 1963)), or from both (*e.g., Draper v. United States,* 358 U.S. 307, 312-13 (1959); *Andresen v. Maryland,* 427 U.S. 463, 478 n.9 (1976)).

(d) In warrant cases the affiant needs not name the informant. *Jones v. United States,* 362 U.S. 257, 267-72 (1960). But to establish the informant's reliability consistently with the principle of subparagraph (B)(3) *supra,* the affiant must give the magistrate something more than the conclusory averment that the informant is "reliable," *Aguilar v. Texas,* subparagraph (B)(1) *supra,* 378 U.S. at 114-15; the affiant must provide an adequate factual basis for the magistrate's own judgment of reliability, *see United States v. Harris,* 403 U.S. 573, 579-80 (1971) (plurality opinion) (dictum). The common form of averment, in this regard, is that "Three times within the last two months, Mr. *Y* has given information concerning narcotics transactions that was verified by arrest." Defense counsel pressing constitutional objections to a search warrant based on this sort of affidavit should establish at the suppression hearing how many *bad* tips the informant had previously given. Most "confidential informants" have a very bad batting average, and the question has never been squarely put to the courts how high a batting average is necessary to establish the requisite "substantial basis for crediting the hearsay" of such an informant, *Jones v. United States, supra,* 362 U.S. at 269. Although it is certainly not "required that informants used by the police be infallible," *Illinois v. Gates,* subparagraph (B) *supra,* 462 U.S. at 245 n.14, the magistrate's function does call for "a balanced assessment of the relative weights of all the various indicia of reliability (and unreliability) attending an informant's tip," *id.* at 234; *see also Massachusetts v. Upton,* subparagraph (B)(1) *supra,* 466 U.S. at 732; and "magistrates remain perfectly free to exact such assurances [of an informant's credibility] as they deem necessary . . . in making probable-cause determinations," *Illinois v. Gates,* subparagraph (B) *supra,* 462 U.S. at 240; *see also Jones v. United States, supra,* 362 U.S. at 271 (although the magistrate was permitted to credit the informant on the basis of representations of the informant's prior reliability, the magistrate also "might have found the affidavit insufficient and withheld his warrant"). Obviously, a police affiant who follows the usual practice of reciting that an informer has three times previously proved right, although failing to disclose that the informer has four or five times previously proved wrong, is, by this device, disempowering the magistrate to make an independent assessment of credibility and is thus engaged in the sort of misrepresentation that should void the affidavit and warrant under the principles of subsection (B)(2)(b) *supra.* If counsel is challenging an arrest or search defended by the prosecution on the basis of probable cause without a warrant, s/he should pursue the same line of cross-examination, with a view to raising the batting average question frontally.

(5) *Disclosure of the informant's name at the suppression hearing.* Concerning the so-called *informer privilege* and its effect upon the defendant's rights to ask for the names of confidential informants at a suppression hearing, see paragraph [273] *infra.*

(6) *The police dispatch bootstrap.* Frequently Officer *A* concludes that a person is guilty of an offense and conveys that

conclusion to Officer *B* — directly or through some form of police bulletin or dispatch — in connection with a request or directive that the person be arrested. Some courts were inclined to sustain *B*'s arrest of the person in this situation, even though *A* lacked probable cause for *A*'s conclusion, on the theory that *B* had probable cause generated by a communication from an apparently reliable informant — namely, *B*'s fellow officer *A*. This bootstrap was, however, rejected by the Supreme Court in *Whiteley v. Warden,* subparagraph (B)(2)(a) *supra,* on the obvious ground that "an otherwise illegal arrest cannot be insulated from challenge by the decision of the instigating officer to rely on fellow officers to make the arrest," 401 U.S. at 568. After *Whiteley,* police dispatches gain no credibility from the mere fact of their internal transmission. *Cf. Franks v. Delaware,* subparagraph (B)(2)(b) *supra,* 438 U.S. at 163-64 n.6. Unless the transmitting officer has probable cause or the receiving officer adds to the transmission enough independent, reliable information to make out probable cause, an arrest based on the dispatch is illegal. *See United States v. Hensley,* 469 U.S. 221, 230-33 (1985) (dictum) (applying the same principle to determine the legality of stops based on reasonable suspicion).

(7) *The "known criminal" averment.* Affidavits for warrants, and police testimony in support of warrantless arrests and searches, very frequently contain the boilerplate assertion that the person to be arrested or searched is "known to the affiant" or "known to law enforcement officers" to be a gambler, a narcotics dealer, and the like. The *Spinelli* case, subparagraph (B)(3) *supra,* holds that this sort of averment is not merely insufficient to support a finding of probable cause but that it "is entitled to no weight" in the probable-cause determination; that is, it may not "be used to give additional weight to allegations that would otherwise be insufficient." 393 U.S. at 414, 418-19. Because a passage of Chief Justice Burger's *Harris* opinion, subparagraph (B)(4)(d) *supra,* 403 U.S. at 582-83, criticizing this aspect of *Spinelli* was joined by only two other Justices, *Spinelli* remains the law on the point. And clearly an allegation that the person named in the warrant *consorts* with "known" criminals, gamblers, traffickers, and the like, is doubly worthless. *See United States v. Hatcher,* 473 F.2d 321, 323 (6th Cir. 1973).

(8) *Tainted evidence and probable cause.* As indicated in paragraph [251](C) *infra,* items of information that were obtained by anterior illegal police conduct may not be used to support a subsequent probable-cause determination. *Ybarra v. Illinois,* 444 U.S. 85, 92-93 & n.5 (1979). If, for example, officers make an unconstitutional warrantless search of certain premises, they may not thereafter relate their observations on those premises to a magistrate in support of an application for a search warrant for the same or any other premises or for an arrest warrant. A warrant issued — or any police action without a warrant taken — on this basis is invalid unless supported by other evidence that is sufficient, independent of the tainted observations, to establish probable cause. *United States v. Karo,* 468 U.S. 705, 719-21 (1984).

[242] Entry into premises where the defendant is but with which s/he has only temporary connections. (A) The traditional conception that the Fourth Amendment restricts police search-and-seizure activity only insofar as it intrudes into some "constitutionally protected area," *Lanza v. New York,* 370 U.S. 139, 142 (1962), is noted in paragraph [231](B) *supra.* Police activity in "public" common-use areas has generally been held uninhibited by the Amendment, *e.g., Lee v. United States,* 221 F.2d 29 (D.C. Cir. 1954); *cf.* paragraph [240](C)(3)(b) *supra,* except, of course, to the extent that it constitutes the search or seizure of the "persons" or "effects" of individuals located in those areas, *see New Jersey v. T.L.O.,* 469 U.S. 325, 337-43 (1985) (dictum); *O'Connor v. Ortega,* 107 S. Ct. 1492, 1497 (1987) (plurality opinion) (dictum); paragraphs [247], [248] *infra;* see also paragraph [240](C)(1) *supra.*

(B) Nevertheless, individuals have been given protection in some sorts of "public" places in which it is customary to allow temporary exclusive occupancy with a measure of privacy — an occupied taxicab, *Rios v. United States,* 364 U.S. 253, 262 n.6 (1960); *but see Rakas v. Illinois,* 439 U.S. 128, 149 n.16 (1978) (dictum); an occupied pay telephone booth, *Katz v. United States,* 389 U.S. 347 (1967); an occupied public lavatory cabinet, *Bielicki v. Superior Court,* 57 Cal. 2d 602, 371 P.2d 288, 21 Cal.

Rptr. 552 (1962); a rented locker in a commercial storage facility, *United States v. Karo,* 468 U.S. 705, 720 n.6 (1984) (dictum). *Compare Hudson v. Palmer,* 468 U.S. 517 (1984) (no Fourth Amendment protection of prison cell); *see also Block v. Rutherford,* 468 U.S. 576, 589-91 (1984); *Bell v. Wolfish,* 441 U.S. 520, 556-57 (1979). A temporary occupant of one of these places can complain of police entries—or surveillance, to the extent that surveillance is deemed to be a "search," see paragraph [243] *infra*—made while s/he is in possession.

(C) The effect of *Katz v. United States,* 389 U.S. 347 (1967), paragraphs [231](A) *supra* and [243](A), (C) *infra,* which announces a view of the Fourth Amendment that is focused upon the protection of personal privacy, may expand (or render superfluous) the concept of "protected areas," so as to bring within Fourth Amendment control any police surveillance that offends an individual's "reasonable expectation of freedom from governmental intrusion," *Mancusi v. DeForte,* 392 U.S. 364, 368 (1968); *see also United States v. Karo,* subparagraph (B) *supra,* 468 U.S. at 714 (dictum), even in public use areas. This seems the plain implication of *Katz's* oft-quoted formula that "the Fourth Amendment protects people, not places," 389 U.S. at 351. *See United States v. Chadwick,* 433 U.S. 1,7 (1977); *Ybarra v. Illinois,* 444 U.S. 85, 91 (1979); *United States v. Salvucci,* 448 U.S. 83, 93 (1980) (dictum); *United States v. Knotts,* 460 U.S. 276, 280-82 (1983) (dictum); *Illinois v. Andreas,* 463 U.S. 765, 771 (1983) (dictum); paragraph [231](B) *supra.* "An individual who enters a place defined to be 'public' for Fourth Amendment analysis does not lose all claims to privacy or personal security." *Oliver v. United States,* 466 U.S. 170, 179 n.10 (1984) (dictum); *see also New Jersey v. T.L.O.,* subparagraph (A) *supra,* 469 U.S. at 337-43 (dictum). It is noteworthy, as far as electronic surveillance is concerned (see paragraph [243] *infra*), that the congressional legislation which now regulates this area in response to *Katz* forbids warrantless device-assisted interception of any "oral communication," 18 U.S.C. §2511(1)(a), which is defined as "any oral communication uttered by a person exhibiting an expectation that such communication is not subject to interception under circumstances justifying such expectation," 18 U.S.C. §2510(2), without regard to the *locus* of the communication. And in nonelectronic surveillance cases the Supreme Court's increasing tendency to deny Fourth Amendment protection to areas of private property which "do not provide the setting for those intimate activities that the Amendment is intended to shelter from government interference or surveillance," *Oliver v. United States, supra,* 466 U.S. at 179; *see also Dow Chemical Co. v. United States,* 106 S. Ct. 1819 (1986); *California v. Ciraolo,* 106 S. Ct. 1809 (1986); *United States v. Dunn,* 107 S. Ct. 1134 (1987), implies the corollary that "intimate activities" should be given Fourth Amendment protection from surveillance wherever they are carried on, provided that their nature and the circumstances under which they are conducted exhibit "'an expectation of privacy that society is prepared to consider reasonable,'" *United States v. Karo,* subsection (B) *supra,* 468 U.S. at 712, quoting *United States v. Jacobsen,* 466 U.S. 109, 113 (1984); see paragraph [243] *infra*—such as, for example, private conversations held in open places but out of the ordinary hearing range of third parties, or other "'intimate associations, objects or activities . . . imperceptible to police or fellow citizens'" except through highly intrusive surveillance technologies, *California v. Ciraolo, supra,* 106 S. Ct. at 1814 n.3; *see also Florida v. Riley,* 109 S. Ct. 693, 697 (1989) (finding no Fourth Amendment protection against helicopter surveillance of a backyard greenhouse but noting that the result might be different if "intimate details connected with the use of the home or curtilage were observed").

(D) The question whether the restrictions imposed upon governmental surveillance in semipublic areas are identical to those that the Amendment imposes on governmental intrusions into private premises, such as a home, apartment, or office (see paragraph [240] *supra*), is also unsettled. The *Katz* opinion itself suggests that the restrictions are identical, *see* 389 U.S. at 354-59; but the notion which has emerged in other Fourth Amendment contexts, that differing degrees of intrusiveness require differing degrees of justification (*see Schmerber v. California,* 384 U.S. 757, 769-70 (1966); *Terry v. Ohio,* 392 U.S. 1, 18 n.15 (1968); *United States v. Place,* 462 U.S. 696, 702-10 (1983); *Winston v. Lee,* 470 U.S. 753, 759-67 (1985); *Tennessee v. Garner,* 471 U.S. 1, 7-11 (1985); *New York v. Burger,* 107 S. Ct. 2636, 2643 (1987)), might support the contrary conclusion.

(E) When a police entry is made into premises that are clearly private—for example, a home or an apartment—but that belong to someone other than the defendant, the question whether the defendant can complain of the entry was traditionally conceived as an issue of "standing." *See, e.g., Brown v. United States,* 411 U.S. 223 (1973); *United States v. Janis,* 428 U.S. 443, 447 n.16 (1976); *Stone v. Powell,* 428 U.S. 465, 488-89 (1976), and cases cited. As noted in paragraph [225](C) *supra,* the opinion in *Rakas v. Illinois,* 439 U.S. 128 (1978), changed the terminology but not the substance of the inquiry. *See United States v. Karo,* subparagraph (B) *supra,* 468 U.S. at 716-17 n.4. A defendant may not obtain the suppression of evidence produced by a search or seizure that did not invade the defendant's own privacy or property interests. *Brown v. United States, supra; Rakas v. Illinois, supra; United States v. Payner,* 447 U.S. 727 (1980); *United States v. Salvucci,* 448 U.S. 83 (1980); *Rawlings v. Kentucky,* 448 U.S. 98 (1980); *United States v. Ceccolini,* 435 U.S. 268, 275-76 (1978) (dictum). However, when the defendant's relationship to searched premises is such that s/he "could legitimately expect privacy in the areas which were the subject of the search and seizure [that s/he seeks] . . . to contest," s/he is entitled to challenge the legality of that search and seizure. *Rakas v. Illinois, supra,* 439 U.S. at 149 (dictum). Examples of sufficient relationships pertinent in the present context are found in the *Murray, Jones, Jeffers, Mancusi, Villano, O'Connor,* and *Blok* cases cited in paragraph [240](A) *supra.*

[243] **Police surveillance.** (A) Traditionally, surveillance into premises without a physical trespass upon the premises was thought not to be a Fourth Amendment "search." Tom-peeping and eavesdropping were insulated from Fourth Amendment restriction by the doctrine that "the eye cannot commit a search" nor can the ear. *See, e.g., Polk v. United States,* 291 F.2d 230 (9th Cir. 1961), 314 F.2d 837 (9th Cir. 1963); *Anspach v. United States,* 305 F.2d 48, 960 (10th Cir. 1962). The Supreme Court applied these concepts in the famous case of *Olmstead v. United States,* 277 U.S. 438 (1928), to hold that telephone wiretapping was not a "search" and in *Goldman v. United States,* 316 U.S. 129 (1942), to hold that no "search" had been conducted by officers who moni-

tored conversations in a suspect's room by means of an electronic sound-amplifying device placed against the party wall in an adjoining room. During almost 40 years, the Court—although indicating increasing disaffection with *Olmstead*—subjected electronic surveillance to Fourth Amendment restriction only when the surveillance involved some form of physical trespass. *See Silverman v. United States,* 365 U.S. 505 (1961) (involving an electronic device inserted within the perimeter of a suspect's premises); *Clinton v. Virginia,* 377 U.S. 158 (1964) (per curiam), *rev'g* 204 Va. 275, 130 S.E.2d 437 (1963) (same); *Hoffa v. United States,* 387 U.S. 231 (1967) (involving an electronic device planted on a suspect's premises by trespassing officers); *Berger v. New York,* 388 U.S. 41 (1967) (same). Finally, on December 18, 1967, *Olmstead* and *Goldman* were expressly overruled in *Katz v. United States,* 389 U.S. 347 (1967). *Katz* held specifically that the monitoring of conversations through an electronic listening and recording device attached to the outside of a public telephone booth was a Fourth Amendment search; and it said more generally that "electronically listening to and recording . . . words [spoken in an area of] . . . privacy upon which [a person] . . . justifiably relied" would constitute a search without regard to "the presence or absence of a physical intrusion into any given enclosure." 389 U.S. at 353; see paragraph [231](A) *supra. Accord, United States v. Karo,* 468 U.S. 705 (1984) (dictum) (the monitoring of an electronic beeper placed inside a container of chemicals sold by a government agent to drug manufacturing suspects and taken by them into "a private residence, a location not open to visual surveillance, violates the Fourth Amendment rights of those who have a justifiable interest in the privacy of the residence," *id.* at 714; "[t]he monitoring of an electronic device such as a beeper is, of course, less intrusive than a full-scale search, but it does reveal a critical fact about the interior of the premises [namely, that the container of chemicals was there] that the Government is extremely interested in knowing and that it could not have otherwise obtained without a warrant," *id.* at 715). (The *Katz* decision has been held nonretroactive and applies only to surveillance conducted after its date. *Desist v. United States,* 394 U.S. 244 (1969); *Kaiser v. New York,* 394 U.S. 280 (1969).)

(B) Congress responded to *Katz* by legislation comprehensively regulating the subject of electronic surveillance (together with telephone wiretapping, paragraph [245] *infra*). The Omnibus Crime Control and Safe Streets Act of 1968, Pub. L. No. 90-351, §802, 82 Stat. 212, codified as 18 U.S.C. §§2510-20, broadly prohibits electronic eavesdropping and wiretapping, creates criminal and civil liability for violators, declares the fruits of forbidden electronic eavesdropping or wiretapping inadmissible in any state or federal judicial, administrative, or legislative proceedings *but also* excepts from these bans eavesdropping and tapping conducted for law enforcement purposes under the authorization of 18 U.S.C. §§2516-19. The latter sections authorize (a) the issuance of electronic surveillance or wiretap orders by federal judges, upon application of the Attorney General or a specially designated Assistant Attorney General (*see United States v. Giordano*, 416 U.S. 505 (1974)), for the purpose of investigating specified federal offenses and (b) the issuance of similar orders by state judges, in states that so provide by statute, upon application of the "principal prosecuting attorney" of the state or of one of its political subdivisions, for the purpose of investigating specified state law offenses punishable by imprisonment for more than one year and "designated in [the] applicable State statute." 18 U.S.C. §2516. In either instance, judges may issue orders only upon written and sworn applications containing detailed averments of the matters described in 18 U.S.C. §2518(1) and upon finding (1) that there is probable cause to believe that a person is committing, has committed, or is about to commit one of the specified offenses; (2) that there is probable cause to believe that particular communications concerning the offense will be obtained through the authorized surveillance or tap; (3) that there is probable cause to believe that the facilities or places to be tapped or put under surveillance are used in connection with the commission of the offense, or are leased to, listed in the name of, or commonly used by, the person committing the offense; and (4) that "normal investigative procedures have been tried and have failed or reasonably appear to be unlikely to succeed if tried or to be too dangerous." 18 U.S.C. §2518(3). The application and order must set forth the name of every person who is reasonably believed to be committing the offense and whose communications are expected to be intercepted, *United States v. Donovan,* 429 U.S. 413, 423-28 (1977), but need not name persons likely to be overheard unless there is probable cause (that is, grounds for reasonable belief) that they are implicated in the offense, *United States v. Kahn,* 415 U.S. 143 (1974). (The *Kahn* opinion contains *dictum* to the effect that "when there is probable cause to believe that a particular telephone is being used to commit an offense but no particular person is identifiable, a wire interception order may, nevertheless, properly issue under the statute." *Id.* at 157.) A surveillance order impliedly authorizes covert entry into private premises for the purpose of installing listening devices; no "explicit authorization of the entry is . . . required," *Dalia v. United States,* 441 U.S. 238, 259 n.22 (1979), although "the 'preferable approach' would be for Government agents . . . to make explicit to the authorizing court their expectation that some form of surreptitious entry will be required to carry out the surveillance," *ibid.,* and their failure to do so may perhaps be deemed relevant when "the manner in which a warrant is executed is subject[ed] to later judicial review as to its reasonableness," *id.* at 258. The authorizing order must contain specified recitations restricting its scope, 18 U.S.C. §2518(4), and it may not authorize surveillance or taps "for any period longer than is necessary to achieve the objective of the authorization, nor in any event longer than thirty days," 18 U.S.C. §2518(5), although extensions may be granted upon new showings sufficient to authorize initial issuance of an order. *Ibid.* "The plain effect of the detailed restrictions of §2518 is to guarantee that wiretapping or bugging occurs only when there is a genuine need for it and only to the extent that it is needed." *Dalia v. United States, supra,* 441 U.S. at 250 (dictum). Warrantless eavesdropping and tapping are authorized only in "an emergency situation" involving conspiracies that threaten the national security or characterize "organized crime," and, in these cases, subsequent judicial approval must be obtained within 48 hours. 18 U.S.C. §2518(7). (Warrantless electronic surveillance upon consent of one party to a communication is discussed in paragraph [245](A) *infra.*) Detailed provisions are made concerning the execution of surveillance orders (*see, e.g., Scott v. United States,* 436 U.S. 128 (1978), construing the provision of Section 2518(5) requiring that surveillance be conducted "in such a way as to minimize the interception of [noncriminal] communications"), the *post facto* service of inventories upon persons affected (*see United States v. Donovan, supra; United States v. Chun,* 503 F.2d 533 (9th Cir. 1974)), pretrial service of the application and order upon parties to any proceeding when the fruits of the surveillance or tap are to be offered in evidence, and motions to suppress the evidentiary use of these fruits. 18 U.S.C. §2518(8)-(10). Violations of some, but not all, of the procedural provisions of the 1968 statute require the suppression of evidence obtained through electronic surveillance, *United States v. Chavez,* 416 U.S. 562 (1974); *United States v. Giordano, supra; United States v. Donovan, supra,* 429 U.S. at 432-40, whereas violations of the Fourth Amendment uniformly entail suppression, *Berger v. New York, supra; Katz v. United States, supra,* subject only to the qualifications of paragraphs [223](C) and [240-A] *supra.* Counsel handling an electronic surveillance case should consult the statutory provisions against the background of the constitutional restrictions upon electronic surveillance announced in *Berger,* 388 U.S. at 53-64; *Katz,* 389 U.S. at 354-59; and *Osborn v. United States,* 385 U.S. 323, 327-30 (1966) — restrictions that are similar, but may not be identical, to those of the statute. *Dicta* throughout the opinion in *United States v. United States District Court for the Eastern District of Michigan,* 407 U.S. 297 (1972), appear to give the Supreme Court's constitutional blessing to the statute in general (*see also Nixon v. Administrator of General Services,* 433 U.S. 425, 463-65 (1977) (dictum)), but they would not preclude attack upon particular aspects or instances of statutorily authorized surveillance under the constitutional standards of *Berger, Katz,* and *Osborn. See United States v. Chun, supra,* 503 F.2d at 537-38. (The *Eastern District* decision rejected the Government's contention that warrantless electronic surveillance approved by the President was constitutional in certain "national security" cases involving suspected domestic subversion. It did not determine what constitutional restrictions might apply to electronic surveillance in "foreign intelligence" cases. The latter subject is now regulated in detail by Title I of the Foreign Intelligence Surveillance Act of 1978, Pub. L. No. 95-511, 92 Stat. 1783, codified as 50 U.S.C. §§1801-11.)

(C) It is unclear to what extent *Katz* upsets the previous law holding *nonelectronic,* nontrespassory surveillance immune against Fourth Amendment regulation. *Katz's* legitimate-expectation-of-privacy formulation of Fourth Amendment coverage has been regularly quoted by the Supreme Court in non-electronic cases arising after *Katz, e.g., Mancusi v. DeForte,* 392 U.S. 364, 368 (1968); *Combs v. United States,* 408 U.S. 224, 227 (1972); *Couch v. United States,* 409 U.S. 322, 336 n.19 (1973); *United States v. Miller,* 425 U.S. 435, 442 (1976); *United States v. Santana,* 427 U.S. 38, 42 (1976); *United States v. Chadwick,* 433 U.S. 1, 7, 11-13 (1977); *Michigan v. Tyler,* 436 U.S. 499, 505-6, 510 n.6 (1978); *Rakas v. Illinois,* 439 U.S. 128, 143-44 & n.12 (1978); *Brown v. Texas,* 433 U.S. 47, 51 (1979); *Ybarra v. Illinois,* 444 U.S. 85, 91 (1979); *Rawlings v. Kentucky,* 448 U.S. 98, 104-5 (1980); *Donovan v. Dewey,* 452 U.S. 594, 598-99 (1981); *United States v. Place,* 462 U.S. 696, 706-7 (1983); *Illinois v. Andreas,* 463 U.S. 765, 771 (1983); *Oliver v. United States,* 466 U.S. 170, 177 (1984); *New York v. Class,* 106 S. Ct. 960, 965-66 (1986); *California v. Greenwood,* 108 S. Ct. 1625, 1628-29 (1988); *Skinner v. Railway Labor Executives' Ass'n,* 109 S. Ct. 1402, 1412-13 (1989); *Texas v. Brown,* 460 U.S. 730, 740 (1983) (plurality opinion); *Michigan v. Clifford,* 464 U.S. 287, 292-93 (1984) (plurality opinion); *cf. Nixon v. Administrator of General Services,* subparagraph (B) *supra,* 433 U.S. at 458. It is, therefore, arguable that the "Amendment now affords protection against the uninvited ear," *Alderman v. United States,* 394 U.S. 165, 171 (1969), whether or not electronically assisted, so long as the ear intrudes into areas in which governmental intrusion is justifiably not expected, see paragraph [242](B), (C) *supra.* In *Regalado v. California,* 374 U.S. 497 (1963) (per curiam), the Supreme Court seems to have held that police surveillance through peepholes routinely drilled in hotel room doors (apparently by collaboration of the police and hotel management in "high crime" areas) was a Fourth Amendment search. That conclusion seems plainly correct under *Katz* and should extend to other forms of Tom-peeping that violate reasonable expectations of privacy. *See Texas v. Gonzales,* 388 F.2d 145 (5th Cir. 1968); *cf. Arizona v. Hicks,* 107 S. Ct. 1149, 1152 (1987) ("taking action . . . which exposed to view concealed portions of the apartment or its contents . . . produce[d an] . . .

invasion of . . . privacy" and constituted a search). Although there have been several post-*Katz* cases in the Supreme Court holding that particular instances of police surveillance did not constitute a "search" for Fourth Amendment purposes, the Court has been careful to point out in each that the activities witnessed by the officers were exposed to observation by the public at large. *Texas v. Brown, supra,* 460 U.S. at 740 (plurality opinion) (officer used flashlight to examine the interior of an automobile stopped on a public street; "[t]he general public could peer into the interior of Brown's automobile from any number of angles; . . . [t]here is no legitimate expectation of privacy . . . shielding that portion of the interior of an automobile which may be viewed from outside the vehicle by either inquisitive passersby or diligent police officers"); *New York v. Class, supra,* 106 S. Ct. at 966 (same); *United States v. Knotts,* 460 U.S. 276, 281-85 (1983) (officers traced movements of an automobile on the highways and onto an exposed area of private grounds by means of a beeper planted in a container of chemicals purchased by the driver; "[v]isual surveillance from public places along [the automobile's] . . . route or adjoining [the] . . . premises [which it entered from the public thoroughfare] would have sufficed to reveal all of [the] . . . facts [which] . . . the police [obtained by use of the beeper]," *id.* at 282; *see also United States v. Karo,* subparagraph (A) *supra,* 468 U.S. at 713-14); *Dow Chemical Co. v. United States,* 106 S. Ct. 1819 (1986), paragraph [231](A)(3) *supra* (government used an aerial mapping camera to photograph unroofed areas within a fenced, 2000-acre chemical manufacturing facility; "[a]ny person with an airplane and an aerial camera could readily duplicate [the photographs obtained by the government]," *id.* at 1823; the government "was not employing some unique sensory device that, for example, could penetrate the walls of buildings . . . but rather a conventional, albeit precise, commercial camera commonly used in map-making," *id.* at 1826); *California v. Ciraolo,* 106 S. Ct. 1809 (1986), paragraph [231](A)(3) *supra* (police obtained an airplane, flew over the back yard of a homeowner suspected of cultivating marijuana, and thus observed plants invisible from the ground because of a 10-foot fence; their observations "took place within public navigable airspace," *id.* at 1813, and "[a]ny member of the public flying in this airspace who glanced down could have seen everything that these officers observed," *ibid.*); *Florida v. Riley,* 109 S. Ct. 693, 697 (1989) (police flew a helicopter at an altitude of 400 feet above a backyard greenhouse and thus observed marijuana invisible from the ground because of enclosing walls, fences, and foliage; "[a]ny member of the public could legally have been flying over Riley's property in a helicopter at the altitude of 400 feet and could have observed Riley's greenhouse"); *United States v. Dunn,* 107 S. Ct. 1134 (1987), paragraph [231](A)(3) *supra* (government agents climbed the perimeter fence surrounding a 198-acre ranch, crossed cattle fields and several interior fences, approached a barn enclosed by locked wooden gates, and, by "shining a flashlight through the netting on top of the gates, peered into the barn," *id.* at 1137-38; "the fences were designed and constructed to corral livestock, not to prevent persons from observing what lay inside the enclosed areas," *id.* at 1140; and the officers "merely stood, outside the curtilage of the house and in the open fields upon which the barn was constructed, [looking] . . . into the barn's open front," *id.* at 1141); *California v. Greenwood, supra,* 108 S. Ct. at 1628-29 ("[i]t is common knowledge that plastic garbage bags left on or at the side of a public street are readily accessible to animals, children, scavengers, snoops, and other members of the public"); *cf. Oliver v. United States, supra,* 466 U.S. at 179. These cases apply the "plain view" doctrine (see paragraph [231](A)(5) *supra*) to hold that it is not a "search" for officers to observe objects or activities whose owners or practitioners have exposed them to the risk of indiscriminate public scrutiny, and this is so even though the officers used means of observation differing from those which an ordinary citizen would have used. *Cf. United States v. Santana, supra.* Their negative implication, reinforced by their reliance on the principle that "the Fourth Amendment 'has never been extended to require law enforcement officers to shield their eyes when passing by a home on public thoroughfares,'" *United States v. Dunn, supra,* 107 S. Ct. at 1141, quoting *California v. Ciraolo, supra,* 106 S. Ct. at 1812, is that police surveillance does constitute a "search" insofar as it penetrates into privacies that have *not* been exposed to the risk of indiscriminate public scrutiny. This is consistent with the central teaching of

Katz: "What a person knowingly exposes to the public, even in his own home or office, is not a subject of Fourth Amendment protection. . . . But what he seeks to preserve as private, even in an area accessible to the public, may be constitutionally protected." 389 U.S. at 351-52.

(D) Concerning police surveillance or monitoring of communications between an individual and his or her attorney, see paragraph [363](G) *infra*.

[244] **Yards, grounds, and outbuildings.** (A) Fourth Amendment protection is not given to what *Hester v. United States*, 265 U.S. 57, 59 (1924), called "the open fields": privately owned grounds and outbuildings that are not situated close to the owner's dwelling. *E.g., Air Pollution Variance Board v. Western Alfalfa Corp.*, 416 U.S. 861 (1974); *Oliver v. United States*, 466 U.S. 170 (1984); *see also Dow Chemical Co. v. United States*, 106 S. Ct. 1819, 1825-27 (1986). Protection is given to outbuildings within the "curtilage," *e.g., United States v. Mullin*, 329 F.2d 295 (4th Cir. 1964), and probably to open ground areas within the curtilage as well, *e.g., Hobson v. United Stetes*, 226 F.2d 890 (8th Cir. 1955); *Polk v. United States*, 291 F.2d 230 (9th Cir. 1961), *aff'd after remand*, 314 F.2d 837 (9th Cir. 1963); *cf. Dow Chemical Co. v. United States, supra*, 106 S. Ct. at 1826 (dictum). *Curtilage* refers to "the land immediately surrounding and associated with the home"—"the area to which extends the intimate activity associated with the 'sanctity of a man's home and the privacies of life.'" *Oliver v. United States, supra*, 466 U.S. at 180. *See also California v. Ciraolo*, 106 S. Ct. 1809, 1812 (1986) ("[t]he protection afforded the curtilage is essentially a protection of families and personal privacy in an area intimately linked to the home, both physically and psychologically, where privacy expectations are most heightened"). The curtilage is, in other words, the area devoted to domestic use immediately around a dwelling and usually, but not invariably, fenced in with the dwelling. *E.g., Walker v. United States*, 225 F.2d 447 (5th Cir. 1955); *Baxter v. United States*, 188 F.2d 119 (6th Cir. 1951). For any particular dwelling it is to be "defined . . . by reference to the factors that determine whether an individual reasonably may expect that an area immediately adjacent to the home will remain private." *Oli-*

ver v. United States, supra, 466 U.S. at 180. Four factors are said to be particularly significant: "the proximity of the area claimed to be curtilage to the home, whether the area is included within an enclosure surrounding the home, the nature of the uses to which the area is put, and the steps taken by the resident to protect the area from observation by people passing by." *United States v. Dunn,* 107 S. Ct. 1134, 1139 (1987). However, "these factors are useful analytical tools only to the degree that, in any given case, they bear upon the centrally relevant consideration — whether the area in question is so intimately tied to the home itself that it should be placed under the home's 'umbrella' of Fourth Amendment protection." *Ibid.* Thus the *Dunn* "factors" can be emphasized when they support counsel's position and deemphasized when they do not. And in the common situation of police entry into a fenced urban or suburban yard, counsel can plausibly argue for the clear-cut rule that the fence line marks the curtilage, *see, e.g., California v. Ciraolo, supra,* 106 S. Ct. at 1812 (dictum); *Florida v. Riley,* 109 S. Ct. 693, 696 (1989) (plurality opinion) (dictum); *Weaver v. United States,* 295 F.2d 360 (5th Cir. 1961); *Hobson v. United States, supra,* in light of the Supreme Court's observation that "for most homes, the boundaries of the curtilage will be clearly marked," *Oliver v. United States, supra,* 466 U.S. at 182 n.12, and the Court's simultaneous recognition of the desirability of avoiding "the difficulties created for courts, police, and citizens by an ad hoc, case-by-case definition of Fourth Amendment standards to be applied in differing factual circumstances," *id.* at 181; *see also Dow Chemical Co. v. United States, supra,* 106 S. Ct. at 1826 n.3; *United States v. Dunn, supra,* 107 S. Ct. at 1140.

(B) Substantial separate closed structures on residential property — garages, for example — are generally held protected by the Fourth Amendment without reference to the ordinary indicia of "curtilage," such as fencing in. *Taylor v. United States,* 286 U.S. 1 (1932); *State v. Daugherty,* 94 Wash. 2d 263, 616 P.2d 649 (1980).

(C) Areas protected within subparagraphs (A) and (B) *supra* are ordinarily thought to be given the same *degree* of protection as private dwellings themselves, and the restrictions described in paragraph [240] *supra* are therefore applied. *E.g., Taylor v. United*

States, subparagraph (B) *supra; Rosencranz v. United States,* 356 F.2d 310 (1st Cir. 1966). *But see Marullo v. United States,* 328 F.2d 361 (5th Cir. 1964), *rehearing denied,* 330 F.2d 609 (5th Cir. 1964).

[245] Telephone wiretapping. (A) Telephone wiretapping was banned by §605 of the Federal Communications Act of 1934, 48 Stat. 1103, 47 U.S.C. §605 (1964). The Supreme Court construed the statute as rendering wiretap evidence inadmissible in federal prosecutions, even when the tap was made by state officers acting without federal participation and in compliance with a state law allowing tapping. *Benanti v. United States,* 355 U.S. 96 (1957). In *Schwartz v. Texas,* 344 U.S. 199 (1952), the Court held that Section 605 did not require the exclusion of wiretap evidence in state criminal prosecutions; but *Schwartz* was overruled—nonretroactively—on June 17, 1968. *Lee v. Florida,* 392 U.S. 378 (1968); *see Fuller v. Alaska,* 393 U.S. 80 (1968) (per curiam). On June 19, 1968, Section 605 was amended to conform to the detailed congressional regulation of wiretapping and electronic eavesdropping contemporaneously enacted as 18 U.S.C. §§2510-20. That regulation is described in paragraph [243](B) *supra.* The only substantive point requiring additional mention here is that under the new statute, warrantless wiretapping or other interception of a telephone communication (or, indeed, any electronic monitoring of any communication) may be made lawfully by a law enforcement officer (or by any person, under most relevant circumstances) if the officer or person "is a party to the communication or [if] one of the parties to the communication has given prior consent to such interception." 18 U.S.C. §2511(2)(c), (d). This provision appears to broaden somewhat the exception carved out of former Section 605 by *Rathbun v. United States,* 355 U.S. 107 (1957). *See Lee v. Florida, supra,* 392 U.S. at 381-82. Its validity—now that telephone wiretapping has been brought within the purview of the Fourth Amendment by *Katz v. United States,* 389 U.S. 347 (1967), paragraphs [231](A), [243](A), (C) *supra*—raises questions akin to those raised by "bugged" informers, paragraph [249] *infra.* Although the law on the latter subject is a conceptual shambles, see *ibid.,* the present practical bottom line is plain enough: "Neither the Constitution nor any Act of Congress [im-

poses any restraints upon electronic monitoring or recording of conversations] . . . by Government agents with the consent of one of the conversants." *United States v. Caceres*, 440 U.S. 741, 744 (1979); *see id.* at 749-52.

(B) The use of a pen register (a device that records the numbers dialed from a telephone instrument but does not monitor the conversation on the line or even indicate whether the call has been completed) is not subject to the restrictions of 18 U.S.C. §§2510-20, *United States v. New York Telephone Co.*, 434 U.S. 159 (1977), nor does it constitute a "search" subject to Fourth Amendment constraints, *Smith v. Maryland*, 442 U.S. 735 (1979).

(C) A party has standing to complain of an unlawful wiretap if *either* (1) s/he is a party to the tapped conversation *or* (2) his or her telephone is tapped, whether or not s/he is a party to the conversation. *Alderman v. United States*, 394 U.S. 165, 176-80 (1969); *Rakas v. Illinois*, 439 U.S. 128, 144 n.12 (1978) (dictum); *United States v. Karo*, 468 U.S. 705, 716-17 n.4 (1984) (dictum).

(D) Concerning the tapping of telephone conversations between an individual and his or her attorney, see paragraph [363](G) *infra*.

[246] Automobile stoppings, searches, and inspections. (A) Automobiles are the subject of a specialized Fourth Amendment jurisprudence stemming from *Carroll v. United States*, 267 U.S. 132 (1925).

(1) As presently interpreted, *Carroll* permits warrantless stopping and search of moving vehicles if, and only if, the searching officers have probable cause to believe that seizable objects are concealed in the vehicle. *Almeida-Sanchez v. United States*, 413 U.S. 266 (1973); *Marshall v. Barlow's Inc.*, 436 U.S. 307, 315 n.10 (1978) (dictum); *compare Chambers v. Maroney*, 399 U.S. 42 (1970), *and Colorado v. Bannister*, 449 U.S. 1 (1980) (per curiam), *with Preston v. United States*, 376 U.S. 364 (1964), *and Dyke v. Taylor Implement Mfg. Co.*, 391 U.S. 216 (1968). *See also California v. Carney*, 471 U.S. 386 (1985) (extending the *Carroll* rule to a motor home parked in a downtown parking lot). (If there is probable cause to believe that such objects may be concealed in any part of the vehicle, then every part of the vehicle and every container within it which is capable of holding the

seizable object may be searched. *United States v. Ross,* 456 U.S. 798 (1982); *United States v. Johns,* 469 U.S. 478, 482-83 (1985). The only limitation on the scope of the search is that it may not extend into areas incapable of holding the object. *United States v. Ross, supra,* 456 U.S. at 820-21, 823-24 (dictum). If there is probable cause merely to believe that seizable objects may be contained within some particular receptacle carried in the vehicle, then the receptacle may be seized but neither it nor any other portion of the vehicle may be searched without a warrant. *Id.* at 812-13, 824 (dictum), explaining *United States v. Chadwick,* 433 U.S. 1 (1977), and *Arkansas v. Sanders,* 442 U.S. 753 (1979); *see also United States v. Place,* 462 U.S. 696, 701 & n.3 (1983) (dictum); *United States v. Johns, supra,* 469 U.S. at 482-83 (dictum)). The theory of *Carroll* plainly was that the basic Fourth Amendment warrant requirement (see paragraph [229] *supra*) must be relaxed for automobile searches because the mobility of an automobile makes the securing of a warrant impracticable. But it remained unclear during many years whether impracticability needed to be shown in particular situations, *see Staples v. United States,* 320 F.2d 817, 820 (5th Cir. 1963), or whether impracticability was established as a matter of law in some or all vehicles cases, *see United States v. Francolino,* 367 F.2d 1013 (2d Cir. 1966). Many lower courts appear to have taken the view that vehicle searches could invariably be made upon probable cause without a warrant, whether or not the particular vehicle was likely to be (or even capable of being) removed during the time required to obtain a warrant. That conception is no longer tenable after *Coolidge v. New Hampshire,* 403 U.S. 443 (1971). Although *Coolidge* holds on its facts little more than that an almost totally immobilized automobile cannot be searched without a warrant under *Carroll,* it unquestionably marks a watershed by establishing that except in circumstances "where 'it is not practicable to secure a warrant,' . . . the 'automobile exception,' despite its label, is simply irrelevant." 403 U.S. at 462 (plurality opinion). After *Coolidge,* arguably, dispensation from the warrant requirement is justified only when there are reasonable grounds to apprehend that a vehicle will be moved before a warrant can be gotten. The *Carroll* rule applies, in short, "[w]hen a vehicle is being used on the highways, or if it is readily capable of such use and is found stationary in a place not regularly used for residential purposes — temporary or otherwise." *California v. Carney, supra,* 471 U.S. at 392.

(2) *Chambers v. Maroney,* 399 U.S. 42 (1970), holds that if a warrantless search of a vehicle might have been made at the site of its initial stopping because its mobility at that time brought it within the *Carroll* rule, the car may alternatively be seized and later searched at a place to which it is removed by police — at least when no additional invasion of privacy interests results from this delay and when the delay is not inordinate (*see United States v. Johns,* subparagraph (1) *supra,* 469 U.S. at 487, citing Justice White's dissenting opinion in *Coolidge,* subparagraph (1) *supra,* 403 U.S. at 523). *Chambers* retrospectively explains *Cooper v. California,* 386 U.S. 58 (1967), on the same ground. *Accord, Texas v. White,* 423 U.S. 67 (1975); *Michigan v. Thomas,* 458 U.S. 259 (1982) (per curiam) ("the justification to conduct . . . a warrantless search does not vanish once the car has been immobilized; nor does it depend upon a reviewing court's assessment of the likelihood in each particular case that the car would have been driven away, or that its contents would have been tampered with, during the period required for the police to obtain a warrant"); *Florida v. Meyers,* 466 U.S. 380 (1984) (per curiam). The same rule permitting delayed searches applies to closed containers found in the vehicle. *United States v. Johns,* subparagraph (1) *supra.* (There is no inconsistency between the *Coolidge* rule that the applicability of the *Carroll* doctrine in the first instance depends upon a particularized inquiry into a vehicle's mobility at the time it is initially encountered by police officers and the holdings in *Chambers, White, Thomas,* and *Meyers* that no particularized inquiry should be made regarding the vehicle's mobility at the time of a delayed search. *Carroll's* rationale for permitting a warrantless search when the vehicle is first encountered is the impracticability of obtaining a warrant at that time, whereas *Chambers'* rationale for permitting the search to be delayed has nothing to do with the impracticability of obtaining a warrant at the time when the search is eventually made. *Chambers'* rationale is simply that, once an officer is authorized to make a warrantless search under *Carroll,* there is no good reason

to insist that s/he make it on the street instead of at the station house. *See United States v. Ross, supra,* 456 U.S. at 807 n.9.)

(3) *Cady v. Dombrowski,* 413 U.S. 433 (1973), held that officers who had properly taken an automobile into their custody in connection with routine traffic-control duties (specifically, a disabled vehicle that had crashed into a bridge abutment and was "a nuisance along the highway," *id.* at 443) could search it without a warrant when (a) they had reasonable grounds to believe that there was something in it (specifically, a gun) that might be harmful to the public if it fell "into untrained or perhaps malicious hands," *ibid.,* and (b) they apparently lacked the resources to prevent this danger by taking the car to a police lot or "posting . . . a police guard," *id.* at 447, and (c) the officer conducting the search had no purpose to look for criminal evidence, *ibid.* Language in the opinion and in *South Dakota v. Opperman,* 428 U.S. 364 (1976), suggested more broadly that warrantless "inventory" searches — "a routine practice of securing and inventorying the automobiles' contents," *id.* at 369 — might be sustained as "administrative caretaking functions," *id.* at 370 n.5, whenever a car is taken into police custody upon any legitimate ground (such as the arrest of its operator); and this broader rule has apparently now been accepted by the Supreme Court, *Colorado v. Bertine,* 107 S. Ct. 738 (1987), subject only to the qualifications (a) that inventory searches must "be conducted according to standardized criteria," *id.* at 742 n.6 — for example, criteria "related to the feasibility and appropriateness of parking and locking a vehicle rather than impounding it," *id.* at 743 — and (b) that the particular search not be made "in bad faith or for the sole purpose of investigation," *id.* at 742. *See also Harris v. United States,* 390 U.S. 234 (1968); *United States v. Chadwick,* 433 U.S. 1, 10 n.5, 13-14 nn.7-8 (1977) (dictum); *compare Illinois v. LaFayette,* 462 U.S. 640, 643-48 (1983), paragraph [238](A)(2) *supra.* (The requirements that any discretion which is allowed to the police under the applicable regulations be "exercised according to standard criteria and on the basis of something other than suspicion of evidence of criminal activity," *Colorado v. Bertine, supra,* 107 S. Ct. at 743; *see also South Dakota v. Opperman, supra,* 428 U.S. at 376, are a reflection of the general principle that administrative searches "must be based on a 'plan containing

specific neutral criteria,'" *Torres v. Puerto Rico,* 442 U.S. 465, 473 (1979) — that is, "a plan embodying explicit, neutral limitations on the conduct of individual officers," *Brown v. Texas,* 443 U.S. 47, 51 (1979) — in order to avert the "'grave danger' of abuse of discretion [by the police]," *Delaware v. Prouse,* 440 U.S. 648, 662 (1979), which is a central concern of the Fourth Amendment, see subparagraph (D)(2) *infra.* See also paragraphs [238](A)(2), [240](C)(3)(f) *supra.*) Unlike *Carroll* searches, "inventory searches" may be made without probable cause. *See United States v. Ross, supra,* 456 U.S. at 809 n.11 (dictum). (Notably, state constitutional rules governing inventory searches are frequently more restrictive than is the federal Fourth Amendment caselaw; this is an area in which defense attorneys are particularly advised to follow the suggestion of paragraph [227](B) *supra* and invoke state law principles as alternative grounds for challenging searches and seizures. *See, e.g., State v. Daniel,* 589 P.2d 408, 417 (Alaska 1979); *State v. Opperman,* 247 N.W.2d 673, 675 (S.D. 1976).)

(4) The short of it is that the Supreme Court's automobile-search decisions are in considerable confusion because the oft-repeated *Carroll* principle that "for the purposes of the Fourth Amendment there is a constitutional difference between houses and cars" (*Chambers v. Maroney,* subparagraph (2) *supra,* 399 U.S. at 52; *United States v. Ortiz,* 422 U.S. 891, 896 n.2 (1975); *and see G.M. Leasing Corp. v. United States,* 429 U.S. 338, 351-53 (1977)) is said to rest upon both the consideration that "the inherent mobility of automobiles creates circumstances of such exigency that . . . rigorous enforcement of the warrant requirement is impossible," *South Dakota v. Opperman,* subparagraph (3) *supra,* 428 U.S. at 367; *see also, e.g., California v. Carney,* subparagraph (1) *supra,* 471 U.S. at 390-91 ("[t]he capacity to be 'quickly moved' was clearly the basis of the holding in *Carroll,* and our cases have consistently recognized ready mobility as one of the principal bases of the automobile exception [to the warrant requirement]," *id.* at 390), and the consideration that the "expectation of privacy with respect to one's automobile is significantly less than that relating to one's home or office," *South Dakota v. Opperman, supra,* 428 U.S. at 367; *see also United States v. Martinez-Fuerte,* 428 U.S. 543, 561, 564-65 (1976); *Rakas v. Illinois,* 439

U.S. 128, 148 & n.15 (1978); *United States v. Knotts,* 460 U.S. 276, 281-82 (1983); *United States v. Johns,* subparagraph (1) *supra,* 469 U.S. at 484; *California v. Carney,* subparagraph (1) *supra,* 471 U.S. at 391-92; *New York v. Class,* 106 S. Ct. 960, 965-66 (1986); *United States v. Chadwick, supra,* 433 U.S. at 12-13 (dictum); *cf. Texas v. Brown,* 460 U.S. 730, 740 (1983) (plurality opinion). The extent to which either of these considerations supports warrantless automobile searches in the absence of the other (as, for example, in cases in which automobiles are relatively immobile or when searches intrude into invisible, closed, or locked inner portions of an automobile) is unclear; the considerations themselves involve matters of degree and not of kind (see subparagraph (1) *supra* regarding mobility; and *see United States v. Ortiz, supra,* 422 U.S. at 896 n.2 ("[t]he degree of the invasion of privacy in an automobile search may vary with the circumstances")). Still a third consideration sometimes voiced in the automobile cases — "the extensive [noncriminal] regulation of motor vehicles and traffic," *Cady v. Dombrowski, supra,* 413 U.S. at 441; *see South Dakota v. Opperman, supra,* 428 U.S. at 368-69; *California v. Carney,* subparagraph (1) *supra,* 471 U.S. at 392; *New York v. Class, supra,* 106 S. Ct. at 965; *United States v. Chadwick,* subparagraph (1) *supra,* 433 U.S. at 13 (dictum); *Marshall v. Barlow's, Inc.,* subparagraph (1) *supra,* 436 U.S. at 315 n.10 (dictum) — bears an ambiguous relationship to the first two and seems to have little independent weight, *see Delaware v. Prouse, supra,* 440 U.S. at 662-63. It is therefore not surprising that the Court frequently flounders in deciding auto-search cases, *see, e.g., Cardwell v. Lewis,* 417 U.S. 583 (1974), paragraph [248](B) *infra,* and that its decisions in this area provide few coherent principles for application by the lower courts.

(B) (1) Automobiles may be subjected to a warrantless search of limited scope incidental to the valid arrest of their drivers or occupants, under the doctrine of "search incident to arrest" described in paragraph [240](C)(3)(d) *supra.* But these searches may be made without a warrant only at the immediate time and place of the arrest. *See Preston v. United States,* subparagraph (A)(1) *supra; Dyke v. Taylor Implement Mfg. Co.,* subparagraph (A)(1) *supra; Chambers v. Maroney,* subparagraph (A)(1) *supra,* 399 U.S. at 47; *Cardwell v. Lewis,* subparagraph (A)(4) *supra,* 417

U.S. at 591-92 n.7 (plurality opinion); *id.* at 599 n.4 (dissenting opinion of four Justices); *United States v. Chadwick,* subparagraph (A)(1) *supra,* 433 U.S. at 14-15. The search may extend throughout the passenger compartment of the vehicle, *United States v. Hensley,* 469 U.S. 221, 235-36 (1985), and may include the opening of any closed container and the examination of its contents, *New York v. Belton,* 453 U.S. 454, 460-63 (1981). This encompasses "closed or open glove compartments, consoles, or other receptacles located anywhere within the passenger compartment, as well as luggage, boxes, bags, clothing, and the like." *Id.* at 460-61 n.4. It "encompasses only the interior of the passenger compartment . . . and does not encompass the trunk." *Ibid.; see also id.* at 462.

(2) When the driver or occupant of an automobile is the object of a valid investigative "stop" (see subparagraph (D) *infra*) or when an automobile is validly stopped to ticket the driver for a traffic violation, a warrantless "search of the passenger compartment of [the] . . . automobile, limited to those areas in which a weapon may be placed or hidden, is permissible if the police officer possesses a reasonable belief . . . that the suspect [driver or occupant] is dangerous and the suspect may gain immediate control of weapons [from the vehicle]." *Michigan v. Long,* 463 U.S. 1032, 1049 (1983), paragraph [236](D)(1) *supra; New York v. Class,* subparagraph (A)(4) *supra,* 106 S. Ct. at 967-68. Unlike a search incident to arrest, which is authorized by the mere fact of a valid arrest, this latter sort of weapons search requires *both* a valid stop *and* reasonable grounds to believe that the driver or occupant is dangerous and may grab a weapon from the car to use against the officers. *Michigan v. Long, supra,* 463 U.S. at 1046-53 & nn.14, 16.

(C) A dictum in the *Carroll* opinion said that every person entering the United States across an international boundary could be stopped routinely and required "to identify himself as entitled to come in, and his belongings as effects which may be lawfully brought in." *Carroll v. United States,* subparagraph (A) *supra,* 267 U.S. at 154. *See also United States v. Ramsey,* 431 U.S. 606, 616-19 (1977); *United States v. Montoya De Hernandez,* 473 U.S. 531, 537-40 (1985); *United States v. Ross,* subparagraph (A)(1) *supra,* 456 U.S. at 823 (dictum). Under this constitutional "border search" doctrine and congressional legislation authorizing warrantless vehicle searches for aliens "within a reasonable distance from any external boundary," 8 U.S.C. §1357(a)(3) (1970) (interpreted by regulations of the Attorney General as 100 miles), the lower federal courts prior to 1973 sustained both stops and searches of automobiles, without a warrant or probable cause, by immigration officers operating either at fixed "checkpoints" or in "roving patrols" within this expansively defined border region. However, on June 21, 1973, the Supreme Court of the United States, in *Almeida-Sanchez v. United States,* 413 U.S. 266, limited the border search doctrine to the "border itself [or] . . . its functional equivalents," 413 U.S. at 272. The *Almeida Sanchez* case (which has been held nonretroactive, *United States v. Peltier,* 422 U.S. 531 (1975); *Bowen v. United States,* 422 U.S. 916 (1975)) dealt with a roving patrol search; but it has since been applied to checkpoint searches as well. *United States v. Ortiz,* 422 U.S. 891 (1975). Under *Almeida-Sanchez* and *Ortiz,* automobiles may not be *searched* at places other than the border and its functional equivalents without either a warrant or probable cause. Brief warrantless *stops* of vehicles in border regions may be made by roving patrols of immigration agents upon "reasonable suspicion" not amounting to probable cause (a concept borrowed from the stop-and-frisk cases, paragraph [236](B), (D) *supra*) that a particular vehicle contains illegal aliens. *United States v. Brignoni-Ponce,* 422 U.S. 873, 880-84 (1975); *United States v. Villamonte-Marquez,* 462 U.S. 579, 587-89 (1983) (dictum) (discussing the border-search doctrines applicable to automobiles while developing a somewhat different rule for ships "located in waters offering ready access to the open sea"). "The officer may question the driver and passengers about their citizenship and immigration status, and he may ask them to explain suspicious circumstances, but any further detention or search must be based on consent or probable cause." *United States v. Brignoni-Ponce, supra,* 422 U.S. at 881-82. Similar stops of all or selected vehicles may be made routinely at fixed checkpoints within the border area, without warrant, probable cause, or "reasonable suspicion," *United States v. Martinez-Fuerte,* 428 U.S. 543 (1976), although (1) the "claim that a particular exercise of [administrative] discretion in locating or operating a checkpoint is unreasonable is subject to post-stop judicial review," 428 U.S. at 559, and (2) routine checkpoint stops, like roving-patrol stops made upon "reasonable suspicion," must be limited to "brief questioning" and may not include either prolonged detention or search in the absence of "consent or probable cause," *id.* at 566-67. The detention of an individual known to have just entered the country may be extended for a reasonable time for further investigation upon a "reasonable suspicion" that s/he is smuggling contraband in a manner that will be disclosed by the investigation. *United States v. Montoya De Hernandez, supra,* 473 U.S. at 540-44. (The opinions in *Ortiz* and *Brignoni-Ponce* purport to reserve the question whether searches and more extensive detentions in connection with immigration stops (either by roving patrols or at fixed checkpoints) may be made without reasonable suspicion or probable cause concerning the individual vehicle stopped, under the authorization of a search warrant "issued to stop cars in a designated area on the basis of conditions in the area as a whole," 422 U.S. at 882 n.7; *see also* 422 U.S. at 897 n.3. This question was generated by Justice Powell's concurring opinion in *Almeida-Sanchez,* which adopts the concept of an "areal" search warrant from the Supreme Court's building-code cases (*see Camara v. Municipal Court,* 387 U.S. 523 (1967), noted in paragraph [240](C)(2)(b) *supra*) and suggests that such a warrant might validate immigration searches in border areas. Since Justice Powell's concurrence was necessary to make up a 5-4 majority in *Almeida-Sanchez* and the Court has not become more sympathetic to Fourth Amendment rights since his departure, the likelihood is strong that "areal" search warrants will be sustained in border-region immigration cases. See also *United States v. Martinez-Fuerte, supra,* 428 U.S. at 555, 564 n.18.) The "border search" doctrine is limited to *international* borders; it does not apply to interstate boundary lines. *Torres v. Puerto Rico,* 442 U.S. 465, 472-73 (1979); *One 1958 Plymouth Sedan v. Pennsylvania,* 380 U.S. 693, 702 (1965) (by implication).

(D) In two other common situations, automobiles may be stopped for investigation upon "reasonable suspicion."

(1) Officers having a reasonable suspicion that a car's occupants are presently engaged in criminal activity or are wanted for arrest for a felony are permitted to pull the car over in

order to question the occupants. *E.g., United States v. Hensley,* 469 U.S. 221 (1985); *United States v. Sharpe,* 470 U.S. 675 (1985); *United States v. Bugarin-Casas,* 484 F.2d 853 (9th Cir. 1973). This rule developed out of the stop-and-frisk doctrine described in paragraph [236](B), (D) *supra*: decisions allowing pedestrians to be stopped for questioning on reasonable suspicion, *e.g., Terry v. Ohio,* 392 U.S. 1 (1968), were extended to allow the accosting of a driver seated in a parked vehicle, *Adams v. Williams,* 407 U.S. 143 (1972), and then to allow the frisking of a driver previously halted for a traffic violation, *Pennsylvania v. Mimms,* 434 U.S. 106 (1977) (per curiam). At about the same time, the "reasonable suspicion" standard of the stop-and-frisk cases was imported into the border-search area, see subparagraph (C) *supra,* and there applied to vehicular border stops, *see, e.g., United States v. Brignoni Ponce,* subparagraph (C) *supra; United States v. Cortez,* 449 U.S. 411 (1981). Against this background it was not surprising that the Supreme Court came eventually to suggest in dictum that vehicle stops in nonborder regions could be made without a warrant on "reasonable suspicion . . . that either the vehicle or an occupant is . . . subject to seizure for violation of law," *Delaware v. Prouse,* 440 U.S. 648, 663 (1979); *see also Illinois v. Batchelder,* 463 U.S. 1112, 1117 n.3 (1983) (per curiam), and finally to so hold in the *Hensley* case, *supra.* The origin of the principle continues to dictate its particulars: (a) Reasonable suspicion is a necessary as well as a sufficient condition for a stop; *e.g., United States v. Ward,* 488 F.2d 162 (9th Cir. 1973) (en banc); *United States v. Hensley, supra,* 469 U.S. at 226, 229 (dictum); *cf. United States v. Brignoni-Ponce,* 422 U.S. 873 (1975). (b) The stop must not "be so lengthy or intrusive as to exceed the permissible limits of a *Terry* stop," *United States v. Hensley, supra,* 469 U.S. at 235; and the question whether it is "too long in duration to be justified as an investigative stop [requires a consideration] . . . whether the police diligently pursued a means of investigation that was likely to confirm or dispel their suspicions quickly, during which time it was necessary to detain the [automobile's occupants]," *United States v. Sharpe, supra,* 470 U.S. at 686. See paragraph [236](B)(3) *supra.* (c) The person and the automobile stopped may be frisked for weapons under the circumstances and within the limitations described in paragraph [236](D) *supra;* see also subparagraph (B) *supra.*

(2) Before *Delaware v. Prouse,* 440 U.S. 648 (1979), lower federal courts and state courts frequently sustained automobile stops without a warrant, probable cause, or reasonable suspicion by officers empowered to enforce traffic codes who asserted that the stops were made for the purpose of checking operator's licenses or vehicle registrations. *See, e.g., Berry v. United States,* 369 F.2d 386 (3d Cir. 1966). The courts essentially permitted these "license-check" stops to be made indiscriminately unless they were palpable pretexts for criminal investigations, *see Montana v. Tomich,* 332 F.2d 987 (9th Cir. 1964); and *cf. Colorado v. Bannister,* subparagraph (A)(1) *supra,* 449 U.S. at 4 n.4 (dictum). Neither searches nor frisks were permitted without additional justification, but the "plain view" doctrine (paragraph [231](A)(5) *supra*) was applied to uphold any visual observations that the officer made through the windows of the stopped car while questioning the driver and examining his or her license. In *Prouse,* the Supreme Court substantially curtailed this kind of vehicle stop. It held that roving patrol officers cannot constitutionally flag down an automobile "in order to check [the] . . . driver's license and the registration of the automobile" unless "there is at least articulable and reasonable suspicion that a motorist is unlicensed or that an automobile is not registered." 440 U.S. at 663. It suggested, however, that it might sustain other "methods for spot checks that involve less intrusion or that do not involve the unconstrained exercise of discretion" by police officers, *ibid.,* and it included "[q]uestioning of all oncoming traffic at roadblock-type stops [as] . . . one possible [constitutional] alternative," *ibid.* (The Court and all parties appear to have assumed the constitutionality of such a "routine driver's license checkpoint" in the subsequent case of *Texas v. Brown,* 460 U.S. 730, 733 (1983) (plurality opinion).) The Court also noted in *Prouse* that its holding there did not "cast doubt on the permissibility of roadside truck weigh-stations and inspection checkpoints, at which some vehicles may be subject to further detention for safety and regulatory inspection than are

others." 440 U.S. at 663 n.26. In the wake of *Prouse,* the validity of various spot-check practices that involve the stopping of vehicles at roadblocks or other fixed checkpoints without at least a reasonable suspicion that the particular vehicle stopped is being operated in violation of an applicable regulatory law (for example, stops for safety-equipment tests, for pollution-emission tests, for agricultural produce inspections and game wardens' inspections, and for observation of signs of drunk driving as well as inspection of operators' licenses and registration papers) appears to turn upon three considerations. *First* is the extent to which some sort of spot check is necessary and will likely be effective to enforce the regulatory scheme in question. *See Delaware v. Prouse, supra,* 440 U.S. at 658-61. (Counsel challenging a checkpoint stop should contend that the standard of necessity is high. In the border-search area, where routine checkpoint stops have been upheld, see subparagraph (C) *supra,* the Supreme Court has repeatedly emphasized "the enormous difficulties of patrolling a 2,000-mile open border," *United States v. Cortez, supra,* 449 U.S. at 418, and the vital national importance of patrolling it effectively. *See, e.g., Almeida-Sanchez v. United States,* subparagraph (C) *supra,* 413 U.S. at 273; *United States v. Brignoni-Ponce,* subparagraph (D)(1) *supra,* 422 U.S. at 878-79, 881; *United States v. Martinez-Fuerte,* subparagraph (C) *supra,* 428 U.S. at 551-57.) *Second* is the extent to which the visibility and regularity of the spot-check practice are likely to reduce motorists' apprehensions of danger and the feeling that they are being singled out for official scrutiny. *See Delaware v. Prouse, supra,* 440 U.S. at 657. *Third* is the extent to which the spot-check procedures limit and control the exercise of discretion by individual officers in determining which vehicles to stop and which ones to detain for longer or shorter periods. *Id.* at 653-55, 661-63. This last factor is probably the most significant. For the Supreme Court's Fourth Amendment decisions have increasingly recognized that restricting police discretion in the execution of the search-and-seizure power is the Amendment's central purpose. *See, e.g., Johnson v. United States,* 333 U.S. 10, 13-17 (1948); *McDonald v. United States,* 335 U.S. 451, 455-56 (1948); *Beck v. Ohio,* 379 U.S. 89, 97 (1964); *See v. City of*

Seattle, 387 U.S. 541, 545 (1967); *United States v. United States District Court for the Eastern District of Michigan,* 407 U.S. 297, 316-17 (1972); *United States v. Martinez-Fuerte,* subparagraph (C) *supra,* 428 U.S. at 558-59, 566; *G.M. Leasing Corp. v. United States,* subparagraph (A)(4) *supra,* 429 U.S. at 357; *Marshall v. Barlow's, Inc.,* subparagraph (A)(4) *supra,* 436 U.S. at 323-24; *Mincey v. Arizona,* 437 U.S. 385, 394-95 (1978); *Brown v. Texas,* subparagraph (A)(3) *supra,* 443 U.S. at 51; *Steagald v. United States,* 451 U.S. 204, 220 (1981); *Donovan v. Dewey,* 452 U.S. 594, 599, 601, 605 (1981); *New York v. Burger,* 107 S. Ct. 2636, 2644 (1987) (dictum); *cf. Torres v. Puerto Rico,* subparagraph (C) *supra,* 442 U.S. at 473; *Colorado v. Bertine,* subparagraph (A)(3) *supra,* 107 S. Ct. at 742-43 & nn.6, 7; *Skinner v. Railway Labor Executives' Ass'n,* 109 S. Ct. 1402, 1415 (1989). As in other fields of constitutional law in which excessive discretion embodied in a statutorily or administratively prescribed procedure may void it, factual evidence of divergent and particularly of discriminatory police practices in the administration of the procedure should be admissible and persuasive on this last issue. *See, e.g., Yick Wo v. Hopkins,* 118 U.S. 356 (1886); *Niemotko v. Maryland,* 340 U.S. 268 (1951); *Shuttlesworth v. City of Birmingham,* 394 U.S. 147 (1969).

(E) Automobiles may, of course, be stopped for traffic violations. See paragraph [236](C)(2)(c) *supra; United States v. Robinson,* 414 U.S. 218 (1973); *New York v. Class,* subparagraph (A)(4) *supra.* An officer making this sort of stop may order the driver out of the car, whether the officer proposes to arrest the driver or merely to give the driver a summons. *Pennsylvania v. Mimms,* subparagraph (D)(1) *supra; New York v. Class,* subparagraph (A)(4) *supra,* 106 S. Ct. at 967. In the former case, the officer may conduct a complete search of the driver's person, as with any other arrest (see paragraph [238](A) *supra*); in the latter, the officer may frisk the driver and search the passenger compartment of the car for weapons if, but only if, the conditions of paragraph [236](D) *supra* are met. *United States v. Robinson, supra; Pennsylvania v. Mimms,* subparagraph (D)(1) *supra; Michigan v. Long,* subparagraph (B) *supra.* The officer may also demand to see the driver's license and registration papers and may examine the car's Vehicle Identification Number; if the VIN is not observable from outside the car, s/he may enter the passenger compartment and move anything obscuring the VIN, to the extent necessary to read it. *New York v. Class,* subparagraph (A)(4) *supra.* But see paragraph [236](C)(3) *supra,* relating to "sham" or "pretext" arrests.

(F) The defendant has standing to complain of an unconstitutional automobile search if (1) the automobile belongs to the defendant, even though it is out of his or her possession at the time of the search, *see e.g., Cash v. Williams,* 455 F.2d 1227 (6th Cir. 1972), as long as the defendant has not given up possession of the vehicle in a manner that deprives him or her of any remaining legitimate expectation of privacy in it, *see generally Rakas v. Illinois,* subparagraph (A)(4) *supra;* paragraphs [242](C), [243](C) *supra,* or (2) the automobile is in the defendant's lawful possession, under circumstances that comport the possessor's ordinary right to exclude undesired intrusions by others, *see Rakas v. Illinois,* subparagraph (A)(4) *supra,* 439 U.S. at 144 n.12 (dictum), or (3) the defendant is a lawful occupant of the vehicle at the time of the search, and the search invades an area of the vehicle in which, as a lawful occupant, the defendant has "any legitimate expectation of privacy," *id.* at 150 n.17 (dictum).

[247] Taking of papers or objects from the defendant — the "dropsie" problem. (A) Manual examination of the defendant's body or clothing by officers or the opening by officers of any closed container that the defendant is carrying is a Fourth Amendment "search" and is unlawful unless made under the authority of a warrant or within some exception to the warrant requirement, *Sibron v. New York,* 392 U.S. 40 (1968); *Torres v. Puerto Rico,* 442 U.S. 465 (1979); *Ybarra v. Illinois,* 444 U.S. 85 (1979); *New Jersey v. T.L.O.,* 469 U.S. 325, 337-38 (1985) (dictum); *White v. United States,* 271 F.2d 829 (D.C. Cir. 1959), such as the exception for search incident to a valid arrest, *see United States v. Robinson,* 414 U.S. 218 (1973), or the related *Cupp v. Murphy* and "stop and frisk" exceptions, see generally paragraphs [230](B), [236], [238](A), [240](C)(3)(d) *supra.* Most body searches are made incident to arrest, so their validity usually depends upon that of the underlying arrest. *E.g., Beck v. Ohio,* 379 U.S. 89 (1964); see paragraph [236](C) *supra.* As noted in paragraph [238](A) *supra,* the clothing and body surfaces of a validly arrested individual may be searched "without a warrant, and . . . whether or not there is probable cause to believe that the person arrested may have a weapon or is about to destroy evidence." *United States v. Chadwick,* 433 U.S. 1, 14 (1977) (dictum); compare paragraph [236](D) *supra,* dealing with "frisks" incident to nonarrest "stops." The *Chadwick* case implies that large locked receptacles, such as luggage, may also be taken from the arrested person as a matter of routine incident to arrest, but it states explicitly (although in *dictum*) that they may not thereafter be *opened* without a warrant based upon probable cause. 433 U.S. at 14-16 & n.10. *See also United States v. Place,* 462 U.S. 696, 701 n.3 (1983) (dictum). This latter proposition is contrary to *dictum* in *New York v. Belton,* 453 U.S. 454 (1981), which upholds an arresting officer's opening of a zippered pocket in a leather jacket found on the seat of a car following arrest of the car's occupants and says that the scope of search incident to arrests of motorists extends to "the contents of any containers found within the passenger compartment," *id.* at 460, including "luggage, boxes, [and] bags," *id.* at 460-61 n.4, "whether [the container] . . . is open or closed," *id.* at 461. See paragraph [246](B) *supra; cf. Michigan v. Long,* 463 U.S. 1032, 1048-51 (1983). The opinion in *United States v. Ross,* 456 U.S. 798 (1982), doubly compounds the confusion, first, by saying gratuitously that "[a] container carried at the time of arrest *often* may be searched without a warrant and even without any specific suspicion concerning its contents," *id.* at 823 (emphasis added), and, second, by asserting (in the different context of a *Carroll* vehicle search, see paragraph [246](A) *supra*) that "a traveler who carries a toothbrush and a few articles of clothing in a paper bag or knotted scarf [may] claim an equal right to conceal his possessions from official inspection as the sophisticated executive with the locked attaché case," *id.* at 822. This latter observation appears to rule out any distinction between "paper bags, locked trunks, lunch buckets, and orange crates," *ibid.,* so far as the Fourth Amendment privacy interests of the respective possessors of these containers are concerned. Within the framework of the search-incident-to-arrest doctrine, the containers might still be distinguished, allowing search of the paper bag and not the trunk, on the ground that the arrestee's ability to seize weapons or destructible evidence from the former is greater. *That* distinction is, however, difficult to reconcile with the holding of *United States v. Robinson, supra,* 414 U.S. at 235, paragraphs [230](B), [238](A), [240](C)(3)(d) *supra,* that "[t]he authority to search the person incident to a lawful custodial arrest, while based upon the need to disarm and to discover evidence, does not depend on what a court may later decide was the probability in a particular arrest situation that weapons or evidence would in fact be found upon the person of the suspect." *Belton* not merely quotes this *Robinson* language but draws from it the conclusion that the power of search incident to arrest encompasses "containers [which are] . . . such that they could hold neither a weapon nor evidence of the criminal conduct for which the suspect was arrested." 453 U.S. at 461. Differences in the accessibility of various containers to the arrestee can hardly be thought decisive of the application of a doctrine that permits search of containers that could not hold a weapon or evidence in the first place. So *Belton* rests the search incident-to-arrest power not upon the risk that the arrestee may grab the contents of the container but upon the concept that a "lawful custodial arrest justifies the infringement of any privacy interest the arrestee may have" in containers within his or her reach. *Ibid.* But if this is so, the question arises why the search-incident-to-arrest power is restricted to the area within the arrestee's reach, as *Belton* concedes that it is. *Id.* at 457-58, 460. *Chadwick* squarely holds that the privacy interests inhering in "property in the possession of a person arrested in public" (433 U.S. at 14) but outside of his or her reach are *not* dissipated by the fact of a lawful custodial arrest. 433 U.S. at 13-16. And it adds that "[u]nlike searches of the person, *United States v. Robinson,* 414 U.S. 218 (1973) . . ., searches of possessions within an arrestee's immediate control cannot be justified by any reduced expectations of privacy caused by the arrest." *Id.* at 16 n.10. Obviously, the Supreme Court's pronouncements regarding the permissibility of a warrantless incidental search of closed containers carried by an arrested person at the time of arrest are in utter confusion. In this disheveled state of the law, counsel should seek to develop any facts or arguments relating to his or her particular client's (1) special efforts "to preserve as private" the contents of any container seized from the client and searched following arrest, *see Katz v. United States,* 389 U.S. 347, 351 (1967), as, for example, by sealing or locking it, and (2) inability to get at those contents physically at and after the time when s/he was accosted by the arresting officer. Counsel should then urge that these circumstances bring the case within *Chadwick,* not *Belton.* (Note, however, that if the client is jailed, a warrantless search of the container at the jail will be sustained under *Illinois v. LaFayette,* 462 U.S. 640 (1983), paragraph [238](A)(2) *supra,* unless counsel can avoid *LaFayette* on the grounds suggested in the concluding sentences of that subparagraph.)

(B) In *New Jersey v. T.L.O.,* 469 U.S. 325 (1985), the Supreme Court announced a unique set of Fourth Amendment rules governing searches of the persons and personal possessions of schoolchildren on school premises. These rules apply "only [to] searches carried out by school authorities acting alone and on their own authority" as distinguished from searches by law enforcement officers and "searches conducted by school officials in conjunction with or at the behest of law enforcement agencies." *Id.* at 341 n.7. The validity of such a search "depend[s] simply on [its] . . . reasonableness, under all the circumstances. . . . Determining the reasonableness of any search involves a twofold inquiry: . . . 'whether the . . . action was justified at its inception,' . . . [and] whether the search as actually conducted 'was reasonably related in scope to the circumstances which justified [its inception]. . . .' Under ordinary circumstances, a search of a student by a teacher or other school official will be 'justified at its inception' when there are reasonable grounds for suspecting that the search will turn up evidence that the student has violated or is violating either the law or the rules of the school. Such a search will be permissible in its scope when the measures adopted are reasonably related to the objectives of the search and not excessively intrusive in light of the age and sex of the student and the nature of the infraction." *Id.* at 341-42.

(C) A police demand that a defendant disclose or hand over an object in his or her possession is treated as a search, *see Kelley v. United States,* 298 F.2d 310 (D.C. Cir. 1961); *United States v. Hallman,* 365 F.2d 289 (3d Cir. 1966); *cf. Brower v. County of Inyo,*

109 S. Ct. 1378, 1382 (1989) (dictum), and is governed by the rules of the preceding subparagraphs. See paragraph [248](C) *infra*. When such demands are made and obeyed, the critical issue is likely to be whether the defendant's obedience amounted to a valid, voluntary "consent," constituting an effective waiver of Fourth Amendment rights under the principles of paragraph [240](C)(3)(a) *supra. See, e.g., Florida v. Royer,* 460 U.S. 491 (1983); *Florida v. Rodriguez,* 469 U.S. 1 (1984) (per curiam). An officer's physical taking, or announcement that the officer is taking, an observable object from the defendant's person is a seizure, *United States v. Place,* subparagraph (A) *supra,* 462 U.S. at 707, and is governed by similar rules, *id.* at 700-2; see paragraph [248](D) *infra,* in the absence of valid consent.

(D) Police will frequently testify that, when approached or accosted, the defendant threw away an incriminating object, which was then picked up by the officers, or that the defendant disclosed the object to their sight in an attempt to hide it somewhere away from his or her person. This testimony is calculated to invoke the doctrines that the observation of objects "placed . . . in plain view" is not a search, *Rawlings v. Kentucky,* 448 U.S. 98, 106 (1980) (dictum); *see, e.g., Rios v. United States,* 364 U.S. 253, 262 (1960); paragraph [231](A)(5) *supra,* and that it is neither a search nor a seizure to pick up "abandoned" objects thrown on a public road, *California v. Greenwood,* 108 S. Ct. 1625 (1988); *see, e.g., Lee v. United States,* 221 F.2d 29 (D.C. Cir. 1954). In these "dropsie" or "throw-away" cases, the defense can prevail by showing (a) that the defendant was illegally arrested or detained prior to the time of the alleged "drop," *Rios v. United States, supra; Reid v. Georgia,* 448 U.S. 438 (1980) (per curiam); *Williams v. United States,* 237 F.2d 789 (D.C. Cir. 1956); *United States v. Beck,* 602 F.2d 726 (5th Cir. 1979); *Commonwealth v. Harris,* 491 Pa. 402, 421 A.2d 199 (1980); *State v. Bennett,* 430 A.2d 424 (R.I. 1981); see paragraph [236](B), (C), (D) *supra,* or was induced to make the "drop" by other unconstitutional police actions, *see United States v. Newman,* 490 F.2d 993 (10th Cir. 1974); *People v. Shabaz,* 424 Mich. 42, 378 N.W.2d 451 (1985); *State v. Dineen,* 296 N.W.2d 421 (Minn. 1980); *Commonwealth v. Barnett,* 484 Pa. 211, 398 A.2d 1019 (1979); (b) that the object "dropped" fell into a constitutionally protected area, *Rios v.*

United States, supra; Work v. United States, 243 F.2d 660 (D.C. Cir.
1957); see paragraphs [231](B), [240](A), [242], [244] *supra;* or
(c) that the police "dropsie" story is a fabrication, as it often is.
Officers should be cross-examined by defense counsel on what
they did prior to the "drop" that caused the defendant to disclose
to them incriminating matters that were otherwise well concealed. If plainclothes police are involved, this fact, together
with the fact that the defendant had not previously encountered
the officers, should be brought out. Even the habitual credulity
of judges with regard to police testimony is sometimes shaken by
accounts of a defendant's tossing away incriminating and valuable objects at the mere approach of unannounced, unknown,
and unidentifiable police.

[248] **Search and seizure of objects belonging to the defendant, not in the defendant's possession.** (A) A defendant
has standing to complain whenever objects belonging to him or
her are searched or seized, even though not in the defendant's
possession or on the defendant's premises. *Walter v. United States,*
447 U.S. 649 (1980); *Holzhey v. United States,* 223 F.2d 823 (5th
Cir. 1955); *and see Rakas v. Illinois,* 439 U.S. 128, 142 n.11
(1978) (dictum). However, because the mere observation of visible external characteristics of an object is not a search (see paragraph [231](A)(5) *supra,* discussing the "plain view" doctrine;
subparagraph (B) *infra*), the owner of an object has no Fourth
Amendment grievance if police officers view the object either by
seeing it where the owner has exposed it to viewing by the general public, *Rawlings v. Kentucky,* 448 U.S. 98, 106 (1980) (dictum); see paragraphs [243](C), [247](D) *supra,* or while making
a search that does not otherwise intrude upon any privacy interest of the object's owner, *United States v. Salvucci,* 448 U.S. 83
(1980); see paragraph [242](E) *supra.* And once the police see an
object whose external appearance gives them probable cause to
believe that it is contraband or an instrument, fruit, or evidence
of crime, they may seize it without a warrant. *See Texas v. Brown,*
460 U.S. 730 (1983); *United States v. Jacobsen,* 466 U.S. 109, 120-
22 (1984); *United States v. Johns,* 469 U.S. 478, 486 (1985) (dictum). The upshot is that if a search of some other individual's
property or person uncovers visibly criminal objects belonging

to the defendant, the defendant can complain of neither that search nor the ensuing seizure of the objects. *Rakas v. Illinois, supra; Rawlings v. Kentucky, supra.* It is in this sense, and this sense only, that *United States v. Salvucci, supra,* "decline[s] to use possession of a seized good as a substitute for a factual finding that the owner of the good had a legitimate expectation of privacy in the area searched." 448 U.S. at 92. If an object is *not* visibly contraband or crime-related in the sense that its observable attributes provide probable cause for inferring its criminal character (*see Arizona v. Hicks,* 107 S. Ct. 1149, 1153-54 (1987)), then the owner can complain of its seizure wherever it may be; and the owner can always complain of any *search* of the object within the principles of the following subparagraph. *See Walter v. United States, supra.* In short, "the Fourth Amendment provides protection to the owner of every container that conceals its contents from plain view." *United States v. Ross,* 456 U.S. 798, 822-23 (1982) (dictum), quoted with approval in *New Jersey v. T.L.O.,* 469 U.S. 325, 337 (1985); *see also O'Connor v. Ortega,* 107 S. Ct. 1492, 1497 (1987) (plurality opinion) (dictum).

(B) Surface inspection of objects made by officers without anterior search of persons or premises has not generally been regarded as a "search" of the object, even though it may involve some handling. *Romero v. United States,* 318 F.2d 530 (5th Cir. 1963); *cf. Arizona v. Hicks,* subparagraph (A) *supra,* 107 S. Ct. at 1154 (dictum) ("a truly cursory inspection—one that involves merely looking at what is already exposed to view, without disturbing it—is not a 'search' for Fourth Amendment purposes"). Handling that results in the disclosure of concealed contents is, however, a "search," *Corngold v. United States,* 367 F.2d 1 (9th Cir. 1966); *see Arizona v. Hicks,* subparagraph (A) *supra,* 107 S. Ct. at 1152-53, even if it does not amount to opening the object up, *Hernandez v. United States,* 353 F.2d 624 (9th Cir. 1965). Prosecutors often rely upon *Cardwell v. Lewis,* 417 U.S. 583 (1974), to argue that surface inspections of objects do not constitute "searches" even when they disclose information that would not be revealed by ordinary sight or touch. *Cardwell,* however, does not so hold. The Court there divided 4-4 on the legality of taking tire casts and paint scrapings from an automobile without a warrant; and even the four Justices who sustained this police action concluded only that "where probable cause exists, a warrantless examination of the exterior of a car is not unreasonable under the Fourth [Amendment]. . . ." 417 U.S. at 592. Probable cause is, of course, unnecessary and irrelevant unless there is a search; so eight Justices in *Cardwell* may be said to have concluded (despite some ambiguous language in the plurality opinion, *id.* at 590-92) that exterior inspections *do* constitute searches insofar as they disclose anything which common observation would not. The Court's sole deviations from this principle since the modernization of the concept of "searches" in *Katz v. United States,* 389 U.S. 347 (1967), paragraphs [231](A), [242](C), [243](A), (C) *supra,* involve investigative techniques that detect the presence of contraband substances but reveal no other information to the investigator. In *United States v. Place,* 462 U.S. 696, 707 (1983), the Court held that "[a] 'canine sniff' [of closed luggage] by a well-trained narcotics detection dog [does] . . . not constitute a 'search' within the meaning of the Fourth Amendment" because the canine sniff "does not expose noncontraband items that otherwise would remain hidden from public view, as does, for example, an officer's rummaging through the contents of the luggage. . . . [T]he sniff discloses only the presence or absence of narcotics, a contraband item. . . . In these respects, the canine sniff is *sui generis.* We are aware of no other investigative procedure that is so limited both in the manner in which the information is obtained and in the content of the information revealed by the procedure." *Ibid.* Subsequently, in *United States v. Jacobsen,* subparagraph (A) *supra,* 466 U.S. at 123, the Court applied a similar analysis in concluding that a "chemical test that merely discloses whether or not a particular substance is cocaine does not compromise any legitimate interest in privacy" and therefore does not constitute a search, so long as the substance tested came into the hands of the police in a constitutionally unobjectionable manner. *See also Skinner v. Railway Labor Executives' Ass'n,* 109 S. Ct. 1402, 1417-18 (1989).

(C) Searches of objects off protected premises are generally governed by the same rules as those governing searches of premises, described in paragraph [240] *supra. United States v. Chadwick,* 433 U.S. 1 (1977); *Torres v. Puerto Rico,* 442 U.S. 465, 471 & n.4 (1979); *United States v. Ross,* 456 U.S. 798, 809-12

(1982) (dictum); *see also id.* at 812-13, explaining *Arkansas v. Sanders*, 442 U.S. 753 (1979). Thus a search warrant is ordinarily required (see paragraphs [229](C) and [240](C)(1) *supra*): "The Court in *Chadwick* refused to hold that probable cause generally supports the warrantless search of luggage" or other containers. *United States v. Johns*, subparagraph (A) *supra*, 469 U.S. at 482 (dictum). There is language in a few Supreme Court opinions suggesting that under the "exigent circumstances" doctrine (see paragraph [240](C)(3)(e) *supra*), highly mobile objects—for example, a commercial airline passenger's baggage while it is in transit—may be searched on probable cause without a warrant. *See Florida v. Royer*, 460 U.S. 491, 497 (1983) (plurality opinion) ("it is unquestioned that without a warrant to search Royer's luggage [which was checked at an airport for boarding on a departing flight] and in the absence of probable cause and exigent circumstances, the validity of the search depended on Royer's purported consent"); *cf. United States v. Chadwick, supra*, 433 U.S. at 11-16. But if this exception to the warrant requirement exists, it depends upon a showing that the circumstances of the particular case made the obtaining of a warrant impracticable. *Walter v. United States*, subparagraph (A) *supra*, 447 U.S. at 654, 658 n.10 (opinion of Justice Stevens announcing the judgment of the Court); *compare Corngold v. United States*, subparagraph (B) *supra, with* the *Romero* and *Hernandez* cases in the same subparagraph. Even in regard to baggage in transit, there is no generic presumption of impracticability as there is in motor vehicle cases (see paragraph [246](A) *supra*). Rather, the prosecution has the burden of proving impracticability on the facts. See paragraph [253](B) *infra*. And it should not be able to make the necessary showing to justify a warrantless *search* when, instead of searching any particular object, the police could have detained it briefly during the time required to seek a warrant. See the following subparagraph. "Even when government agents may lawfully seize . . . a package to prevent loss or destruction of suspected contraband, the Fourth Amendment requires that they obtain a warrant before examining [its] . . . contents. . . ." *United States v. Jacobsen*, subparagraph (A) *supra*, 466 U.S. at 114. *Cf. Segura v. United States*, 468 U.S. 796, 806-10 (1984) (opinion of Chief Justice Burger).

(D) Of course, even the brief detention of an object is itself a "seizure" subject to the Fourth Amendment's prohibition of unreasonable seizures. "A 'seizure' of property occurs when there is some meaningful interference with an individual's possessory interests in that property." *United States v. Jacobsen,* subparagraph (A) *supra,* 466 U.S. at 113. *See also id.* at 120, 124-25; *United States v. Karo,* 468 U.S. 705, 712-13 (1984); *Maryland v. Macon,* 472 U.S. 463, 469 (1985); *Arizona v. Hicks,* 107 S. Ct. 1149, 1152 (1987). "In the ordinary case, the Court has viewed a seizure of personal property as *per se* unreasonable within the meaning of the Fourth Amendment unless it is accomplished pursuant to a judicial warrant issued upon probable cause and particularly describing the items to be seized . . . Where law enforcement authorities have probable cause to believe that a container holds contraband or evidence of a crime, but have not secured a warrant, the Court has interpreted the Amendment to permit seizure of the property, pending issuance of a warrant to examine its contents, if the exigencies of the circumstances demand it or some other recognized exception to the warrant requirement is present." *United States v. Place,* subparagraph (B) *supra,* 462 U.S. at 701. In *Place,* the Court analogized to *Terry v. Ohio,* 392 U.S. 1 (1968), paragraph [236](B), (D) *supra,* to hold that, in addition, an officer who has reasonable suspicion, not amounting to probable cause, that an air traveler is carrying narcotics in his or her luggage may "detain the luggage briefly to investigate the circumstances that aroused his [or her] suspicion, provided that the investigative detention is properly limited in scope." *United States v. Place,* subparagraph (B) *supra,* 462 U.S. at 706. *See also Arizona v. Hicks,* 107 S. Ct. 1149, 1154 (1987) (dictum). On the facts of *Place,* a 90-minute detention was found to be too long and hence unconstitutional, particularly inasmuch as the police were forewarned of the traveler's arrival and could have arranged to conduct their investigation more expeditiously. 462 U.S. at 709-10; *and see United States v. Sharpe,* 470 U.S. 675, 684-85 (1985) (dictum) (treating the latter fact as decisive of *Place*).

(E) "Letters and other sealed packages are in the general class of effects in which the public at large has a legitimate expectation of privacy; warrantless searches of such effects are presumptively unreasonable." *United States v. Jacobsen,* subparagraph

(A) *supra,* 466 U.S. at 114 (1984) (dictum). First-class domestic mail may be opened only under a warrant. 39 U.S.C. §4057; *Oliver v. United States,* 239 F.2d 818 (8th Cir. 1957); *see United States v. Van Leeuwen,* 397 U.S. 249, 251-52 (1970) (dictum). Other classes of domestic mail may be opened without a warrant or probable cause for postal inspection pursuant to postal regulations. *Santana v. United States,* 329 F.2d 854 (1st Cir. 1964). Incoming international mail may be opened without a warrant or probable cause, upon "reasonable cause to suspect there is merchandise [therein] which was imported contrary to law," 19 U.S.C. §482 — a standard that has been analogized to the "reasonable suspicion" required for stop-and-frisk (see paragraph [236](D) *supra*) and sustained as constitutional under the border-search doctrine (see paragraph [246](C) *supra*). *United States v. Ramsey,* 431 U.S. 606, 611-15 (1977). *Cf. Illinois v. Andreas,* 463 U.S. 765, 769 & n.1 (1983). Authorities who have opened mail or other containers shipped by carrier and have found contraband or who have been alerted to contraband in such containers as a result of the carrier's opening them will often reseal the container and make a "controlled delivery" of it to its consignee in order to catch the latter in possession. The *Andreas* case holds that if the initial opening was lawful, the "owner's privacy interest in that [container] . . . is lost," and therefore "the subsequent reopening of the container is not a 'search' within the . . . Fourth Amendment" unless, because of "a gap in surveillance" during the controlled delivery, "there is a substantial likelihood that the contents of the container have been changed" between the initial opening and the reopening. *Id.* at 771-73. *Andreas* speaks only to the second opening of the container itself. If the police enter private premises or open other containers in order to locate the one previously opened, *those* are searches requiring Fourth Amendment justification. In the absence of exigent circumstances (see paragraph [240](C)(3)(e) *supra*), they will ordinarily require a warrant despite the officers' knowledge that the offending container is somewhere on the premises or in the other containers searched, for "'[i]t is settled doctrine that probable cause for belief that certain articles subject to seizure are in a dwelling cannot of itself justify a search without a warrant.'"

Payton v. New York, 445 U.S. 573, 588 n.26 (1980); see paragraphs [229], [240](C)(1) *supra*.

(F) Searches of objects out of possession of their owners frequently occasion litigation of the issue of "abandonment." *See Abel v. United States*, 362 U.S. 217 (1960); *cf.* paragraph [247](D) *supra*. The "abandonment" doctrine predates *Katz v. United States*, 389 U.S. 374 (1967), paragraphs [231](A), [242](C), [243](A), (C) *supra*, and now appears to be undergoing assimilation into *Katz's* "reasonable-expectation-of-privacy" framework for Fourth Amendment analysis. *See Couch v. United States*, 409 U.S. 322 (1973), paragraph [231](B)(1) *supra*. In post-*Katz* terms, the "abandonment" question can be framed as whether the way in which the owner has disposed of the object "manifested a subjective expectation of privacy . . . that society accepts as objectively reasonable," *California v. Greenwood*, 108 S. Ct. 1625, 1628 (1988).

(G) Fourth Amendment objections to governmental acquisition or inspection of records relating to an individual are similarly subject to analysis within the *Katz* framework. They are said to require an examination of "the nature of the particular documents . . . in order to determine whether there is a legitimate 'expectation of privacy' concerning their contents," *United States v. Miller*, 425 U.S. 435, 442 (1976); *see also United States v. Payner*, 447 U.S. 727, 731-32 (1980). Ordinarily, "when a person communicates information to a third party even on the understanding that the communication is confidential, [s/he] . . . cannot object if the third party conveys that information or records thereof to law enforcement authorities" either voluntarily or in response to compulsory process. *Securities and Exchange Commission v. Jerry T. O'Brien, Inc.*, 467 U.S. 735, 743 (1984); see also paragraph [231](B)(1) *supra*. But the Fourth Amendment does offer some protection against record subpoenas that are excessively broad. See paragraph [163](C) *supra*.

[249] Informers and police spies. (A) The Supreme Court has generally refused to apply the Fourth Amendment as a restriction upon the duplicitous activities of undercover officers, "special agents," and other disguised police spies. Even when these types secure admittance to private premises by concealing or misrepresenting their identities, their entries have been exempted from any Fourth Amendment control — at least when they are not armed with electronic recording or transmitting devices. *Lewis v. United States,* 385 U.S. 206 (1966); *Hoffa v. United States,* 385 U.S. 293 (1966). Electronically rigged police spies were similarly treated for a time, *see On Lee v. United States,* 343 U.S. 747 (1952); *Lopez v. United States,* 373 U.S. 427 (1963). Then the opinion in *Osborn v. United States,* 385 U.S. 323 (1966), suggested that electronic surveillance of a suspect by means of a "bugged" informer might be subjected to the same restrictions as other forms of clandestine electronic surveillance: that is, to an exacting warrant requirement. See paragraph [243](A), (B), *supra.* Finally, a plurality of the Court, as an alternative ground of decision in *United States v. White,* 401 U.S. 745 (1971), reverted to *On Lee. White* is deprived of intelligible meaning by the incomprehensible basis upon which Justice Black's concurring vote — necessary to make up a majority — was put. Although *White* has since been cited with approval in majority opinions, *United States v. Caceres,* 440 U.S. 741, 744 n.2, 749-52 (1979); *Smith v. Maryland,* 442 U.S. 735, 743-44 (1979); *and see United States v. Karo,* 468 U.S. 705, 716 n.4 (1984), none of these later cases involves a police spy who acquired entry to private premises by concealing his or her identity as a government agent; and the Court has recognized (in still another context) that entries achieved by subterfuge are no more or less intrusive than entries by stealth. *Dalia v. United States,* 441 U.S. 238, 253 n.14 (1979); *see also Gouled v. United States,* 255 U.S. 298 (1921). It is doubtless a forlorn hope that the present Supreme Court of the United States could be persuaded to acknowledge that *White* is nonauthoritative and that *On Lee* is wrong, but counsel might want to argue to any reasonably progressive state court that these decisions should not be followed in the construction of the applicable *state* constitutional guarantee against unreasonable searches and seizures. The federal Fourth Amendment jurisprudence relating to police spies hardly deserves emulation at the state constitutional level. It is surely unpersuasive to say, for example, that although "[t]he owner of a business has not, by the necessary utilization of employees in his operation, thrown open the areas where employees alone are permitted to the warrantless scrutiny of Government agents [seeking to make a forthright, nonforcible entry]," *Marshall v. Barlow's, Inc.*, 436 U.S. 307, 315 (1978), nevertheless the same government agents can secure entry to the same area with constitutional impunity by posing falsely as employees. For more detailed criticism of *On Lee* and its progeny, *see* Amsterdam, *Perspectives on the Fourth Amendment*, 58 MINN. L. REV. 349, 406-9 (1974); and for a well-reasoned state decision requiring a warrant before a transmitter-equipped informer may enter a private home, *see People v. Beavers*, 393 Mich. 554, 227 N.W. 2d 511 (1975).

(B) After the initiation of adversary proceedings against a defendant (see paragraph [233](B)(1) *supra*), the Sixth Amendment as applied in *Massiah v. United States*, 377 U.S. 201 (1964), paragraph [233](A)(3) *supra* and paragraph [363](F) *infra*, forbids planted snitches and other government spies from eliciting incriminating admissions by striking up conversations with him or her. *United States v. Henry*, 447 U.S. 264 (1980); *Maine v. Moulton*, 474 U.S. 159 (1985); *Beatty v. United States*, 389 U.S. 45 (1967) (per curiam), *rev'g* 377 F.2d 181 (5th Cir. 1967); *Patterson v. Illinois*, 108 S. Ct. 2389, 2399 n.9 (1988) (dictum). *Cf. Weatherford v. Bursey*, 429 U.S. 545, 554 (1977). To establish a violation of this rule, the defendant must show that the spy "took some action, beyond merely listening, that was designed deliberately to elicit incriminating remarks." *Kuhlmann v. Wilson*, 106 S. Ct. 2616, 2630 (1986).

[250] **Investigative activity by private individuals.** (A) The Fourth Amendment does not prohibit the prosecution's evidentiary use of objects obtained by private individuals through activities that would constitute unconstitutional searches and seizures if conducted by government agents. *Burdeau v. McDowell*, 256 U.S. 465 (1921); *United States v. Jacobsen*, 466 U.S. 109, 113 (1984); *United States v. Janis*, 428 U.S. 433, 456 n.31 (1976) (dictum); *Walter v. United States*, 447 U.S. 649, 656, 660, 662 (1980) (dictum); *Colorado v. Connelly*, 107 S. Ct. 515, 521 (1986) (dictum).

(B) Private conduct is, however, brought within the inhibitions of the Amendment, paragraphs [240]-[248] *supra,* if government agents encourage or participate in the private activity (*see Skinner v. Railway Labor Executives' Ass'n,* 109 S. Ct. 1402, 1411-12 (1989)), for example, by (a) asking the private party to make a search, *Corngold v. United States,* 367 F.2d 1 (9th Cir. 1966) (alternative ground); *People v. Barber,* 94 Ill. App. 3d 813, 419 N.E.2d 71, 50 Ill. Dec. 204 (1981); *cf. Commonwealth v. Dembo,* 451 Pa. 1, 301 A.2d 689 (1973); or (b) accompanying the private party who makes a search, *Nicaud v. State ex rel. Hendrix,* 401 So. 2d 43 (Ala. 1981), even though they do not initiate the intent to search, *Green v. Yeager,* 223 F. Supp. 544 (D.N.J. 1963), *aff'd per curiam,* 332 F.2d 794 (3d Cir. 1964), and even though the officers themselves wait outside protected premises while the private party enters, *Moody v. United States,* 163 A.2d 337 (M.C.A.D.C. 1960). *See also, e.g., State v. Scrotsky,* 39 N.J. 410, 189 A.2d 23 (1963); *Commonwealth v. Borecky,* 277 Pa. Super. 244, 419 A.2d 753 (1980).

(C) The Fourth Amendment does govern searches and seizures made by government employees in the conduct of any public function; it is not limited to law enforcement activity. *E.g., New Jersey v. T.L.O.,* 469 U.S. 325 (1985) (on-campus searches of children's possessions by public school officials); *O'Connor v. Ortega,* 107 S. Ct. 1492 (1987) (searches of government employees' workplaces by their supervisors or administrative officials); *National Treasury Employees Union v. Von Raab,* 109 S. Ct. 1384, 1390 (1989) (drug testing of government employees); see also paragraph [240](C)(3)(f) *supra.*

(D) Coercive conduct by private parties that compels an individual to make self-incriminating disclosures arguably requires the exclusion of any evidence disclosed as a result, even though government officers had no hand in the coercion. *See People v. Berv,* 51 Cal. 2d 286, 332 P.2d 97 (1958). The argument proceeds from the premises that "[i]t is the 'extortion of information from the accused,' . . . the attempt to force him 'to disclose the contents of his own mind,' . . . that implicates the Self-Incrimination Clause, *Doe v. United States,* 108 S. Ct. 2341, 2348 (1988), and that "the exclusion of involuntary confessions derives from the Amendment itself," *United States v. Raddatz,* 447 U.S. 667, 678 n.4 (1980) (dictum), rather than from a policy of deterrence of governmental misconduct, *see Mincey v. Arizona,* 437 U.S. 385, 397-98 (1978); *New Jersey v. Portash,* 440 U.S. 450, 458-60 (1979); but see paragraphs [228] *supra* and paragraph [251](A)(2) *infra*. There is language in *Colorado v. Connelly,* subparagraph (A), *supra,* 107 S. Ct. at 522, to the effect that "coercive police activity is a necessary predicate to the finding that a confession is not 'voluntary' within the meaning of the Due Process Clause of the Fourteenth Amendment." But this is dictum insofar as it speaks to the present issue; in *Connelly,* no external coercion was applied to the defendant by anybody, police *or* private citizens; Connelly's claim of involuntariness was based solely on the ground that his own mental illness impaired his ability to make a free and rational choice to confess.

[251] **Derivative evidence.** (A) When government agents have violated the restrictions of the Fourth Amendment or of the federal wiretap and electronic surveillance laws, not only evidence directly obtained by the violation but also "derivative evidence," that is, evidence to which the police are led "'by exploitation of that illegality,'" *Wong Sun v. United States,* 371 U.S. 471, 488 (1963); *see also Brown v. Illinois,* 422 U.S. 590, 597-603 (1975), is excluded. *Silverthorne Lumber Co. v. United States,* 251 U.S. 385 (1920); *Nardone v. United States,* 308 U.S. 338 (1939); *United States v. Giordano,* 416 U.S. 505, 529-34 (1974); *Oregon v. Elstad,* 470 U.S. 298, 305-6 (1985) (dictum); 18 U.S.C. §2518(10)(a).

(1) "*Wong Sun, supra,* articulated the guiding principle for determining whether evidence derivatively obtained from a violation of the Fourth Amendment is admissible against the accused at trial: 'The exclusionary prohibition extends as well to the indirect as the direct products of such invasions.' 371 U.S., at 484. . . . As subsequent cases have confirmed, the exclusionary sanction applies to any 'fruits' of a constitutional violation — whether such evidence be tangible, physical material actually seized in an illegal search, items observed or words overheard in the course of the unlawful activity, or confessions or statements of the accused obtained during an illegal arrest and detention." *United States v. Crews,* 445 U.S. 463, 470 (1980) (dictum). It also applies to the testimony of witnesses that has a sufficiently close "causal connection" to the constitutional violation, *United States v. Ceccolini,* 435 U.S.

268, 274 (1978); *see id.* at 274-75 (dictum), although in order to exclude "live-witness testimony . . . , a closer, more direct link between the illegality and that kind of testimony is required," *id.* at 278; *see also id.* at 280, except perhaps "where the search was conducted by the police for the specific purpose of discovering potential witnesses," *id.* at 276 n.4; *see also id.* at 279-80. The possible chains of causal connection may be elaborate, *e.g.*, *Smith v. United States,* 344 F.2d 545 (D.C. Cir. 1965); *United States v. Tane,* 329 F.2d 848 (2d Cir. 1964), and counsel should be alert to follow them out. "[T]he question" of the excludability of any particular piece of evidence is said to be "whether the chain of causation proceeding from the unlawful conduct has become so attenuated or has been interrupted by some intervening circumstance so as to remove the 'taint' imposed upon that evidence by the original illegality." *United States v. Crews, supra,* 445 U.S. at 471. *Compare Dunaway v. New York,* 442 U.S. 200, 216-19 (1979), *and Taylor v. Alabama,* 457 U.S. 687, 689-93 (1982), *with Rawlings v. Kentucky,* 448 U.S. 98, 106-10 (1980); *and see United States v. Ceccolini, supra,* 435 U.S. at 276 ("we have declined to adopt a *'per se* or "but for" rule' that would make inadmissible any evidence, whether tangible or live-witness testimony, which somehow came to light through a chain of causation that began with an illegal arrest"); *id.* at 273-74. Evidence obtained by the prosecution following an unconstitutional search or seizure is not excluded if the prosecutor shows that (a) the prosecution's knowledge of the evidence and access to it derived from an "independent source" unconnected with the search or seizure, *Segura v. United States,* 468 U.S. 796 (1984); *Murray v. United States,* 108 S. Ct. 2529 (1988), or (2) the evidence "ultimately or inevitably would have been discovered by lawful means" in the course of events even if the search or seizure had not produced it, *Nix v. Williams,* 467 U.S. 431, 444 (1984) (Sixth Amendment decision placed on grounds equally applicable to the Fourth Amendment exclusionary rule).

(2) When illegal activity by government agents has been shown and may have led to evidence proffered by the prosecution, the prosecutor has the burden of demonstrating that the evidence is untainted. *See Harrison v. United States,* 392

U.S. 219, 224-26 (1968); *Brown v. Illinois, supra,* 422 U.S. at 604; *Dunaway v. New York, supra,* 442 U.S. at 218; *Rawlings v. Kentucky, supra,* 448 U.S. at 107, 110; *Taylor v. Alabama, supra,* 457 U.S. at 690; *United States v. Paroutian,* 299 F.2d 486 (2d Cir. 1962), *aff'd after remand,* 319 F.2d 661 (2d Cir. 1963); *cf. Alderman v. United States,* 394 U.S. 165, 183 (1969) (dictum); *and compare Mt. Healthy City School District Board of Education v. Doyle,* 429 U.S. 274, 286-87 (1977). In *Nix v. Williams,* 467 U.S. 431, 444 n.5 (1984), the Supreme Court implies that "the usual burden of proof" on this issue is "a preponderance of the evidence." It may, however, be greater in situations in which the illegality is peculiarly likely to have tainted the sort of evidence that the prosecution is offering or when there is peculiar "difficulty in determining" questions of cause and effect because these involve "speculative elements." *Ibid.* Both considerations were mentioned in *Nix* as distinguishing *United States v. Wade,* 388 U.S. 218, 240 (1967), paragraphs [233](A)(3), [237](B) *supra,* which held that the prosecutor's burden of proof in showing that in-court identification testimony is not tainted by the witness's exposure to the defendant in an earlier, unconstitutional identification confrontation is "clear and convincing evidence." *See also Moore v. Illinois,* 434 U.S. 220, 225-26 (1977) (dictum). *And see Kastigar v. United States,* 406 U.S. 441, 461-62 (1972), subparagraph (B) *infra,* holding that when a defendant has given compelled testimony under an immunity grant, the prosecution bears "the heavy burden of proving that all of the evidence it proposes to use was derived from legitimate independent sources." *See also Braswell v. United States,* 108 S. Ct. 2284, 2295 (1988). Both *Nix* and *Wade* were Sixth Amendment right-to-counsel cases; *Kastigar* and *Braswell* were Fifth Amendment self-incrimination cases; the Supreme Court has not squarely addressed the prosecution's burden of proving its evidence untainted following a Fourth Amendment search-and seizure violation. But there appears to be no reason to distinguish among kinds of constitutional violations when it comes to the standards for determining whether derivative evidence is "'purged of the primary taint.'" *Johnson v. Louisiana,* 406 U.S. 356, 365 (1972). The *Nix* opinion derived its statement of the "usual burden of proof at suppression hearings" from Fourth and Fifth Amendment caselaw (*see also Colorado v. Connelly,* 107 S. Ct. 515, 523 (1986)); *Wade's* companion case, *Gilbert v. California,* 388 U.S. 263, 272-73 (1967), expressly adopted principles of taint that were first announced in the Fourth Amendment context (*see also Moore v. Illinois, supra,* 434 U.S. at 226, 231; *cf. Weatherford v. Bursey,* 429 U.S. 545, 552 (1977) (dictum)); the Court in *Harris v. New York,* 401 U.S. 222, 224-25 (1971), relied upon a Fourth Amendment case, *Walder v. United States,* 347 U.S. 62 (1954), when deciding the exclusionary consequences of a *Miranda* violation; and it later treated *Harris* as authoritative in another Fourth Amendment case, *United States v. Havens,* 446 U.S. 620, 624-27 (1980). The exclusionary rules that enforce the Fourth, Fifth, and Sixth Amendments are said to have the same essential purpose: "to deter — to compel respect for the constitutional guaranty in the only effectively available way — by removing the incentive to disregard it," *Elkins v. United States,* 364 U.S. 206, 217 (1960). *See Colorado v. Connelly, supra,* 107 S. Ct. at 521; *Linkletter v. Walker,* 381 U.S. 618, 633, 636-37 (1965) (Fourth Amendment); *Stone v. Powell,* 428 U.S. 465, 484-88 (1976) (same); *Immigration and Naturalization Service v. Lopez-Mendoza,* 468 U.S. 1032, 1041 (1984) (same); *Illinois v. Krull,* 107 S. Ct. 1160, 1165-66 (1987) (same); *Johnson v. New Jersey,* 384 U.S. 719, 729-31 (1966) (Fifth Amendment); *Stovall v. Denno,* 388 U.S. 293, 297 (1967) (Sixth Amendment); *see generally United States v. Peltier,* 422 U.S. 531, 535-42 (1975); *United States v. Caceres,* 440 U.S. 741, 754 (1979); *Michigan v. DeFillippo,* 443 U.S. 31, 38 n.3 (1979); *United States v. Payner,* 447 U.S. 727, 735-36 n.8 (1980); *United States v. Johnson,* 457 U.S. 537, 561 (1982); *compare Manson v. Brathwaite,* 432 U.S. 98, 112-13 & n.13 (1977); *United States v. Crews, supra,* 445 U.S. at 473 n.19. Rules for litigating issues of taint under all three Amendments are therefore presumptively similar. *But see Oregon v. Elstad, supra,* 470 U.S. at 306-9 (*Miranda* violations treated differently).

(3) A brief passage in *Brown v. Illinois, supra,* 422 U.S. at 604, indicates that "the purpose and flagrancy of . . . official misconduct are . . . relevant" in determining the scope of

taint that flows from Fourth Amendment violations. *See also Dunaway v. New York, supra,* 442 U.S. at 218; *Rawlings v. Kentucky, supra,* 448 U.S. at 109-10; *Taylor v. Alabama, supra,* 457 U.S. at 690, 693. The *Brown* case itself involved the question of the admissibility of a confession following an illegal arrest (as did *Dunaway, Rawlings,* and *Taylor*); the *Brown* majority opinion leaves unclear whether the "flagrancy" principle is limited to that issue or is applicable to determinations of taint in other contexts. Arguably, "flagrancy" is uniquely relevant in connection with the inquiry whether confessions, "(verbal acts, as contrasted with physical evidence)," 422 U.S. at 600, are tainted by unconstitutional police treatment of a suspect because the *degree* of official disregard of a suspect's rights is uniquely likely to affect the suspect's choice to confess. *See Oregon v. Elstad, supra,* 470 U.S. at 312-13. The *Brown* majority notes specifically that "[t]he manner in which Brown's arrest was effected gives the appearance of having been calculated to cause surprise, fright, and confusion." 422 U.S. at 605. On the other hand, the majority supports its "flagrancy" statement with a footnote citing lower court decisions that involved both confessional and nonconfessional evidence, *id.* at 604 n.9, and it purports, at the outset of its opinion, to be explicating the principles announced in *Wong Sun v. United States, supra,* "to be applied where the issue is whether statements *and other evidence* obtained after an illegal arrest or search should be excluded," 422 U.S. at 597 (emphasis added). A concurring opinion by Justice Powell explains the relevance of "flagrancy" by reference to a notion that has also appeared in a number of other Supreme Court opinions (see paragraph [253](E) *infra*): that the exclusionary rule "is most likely to be effective" in cases of willful or gross police violations of the Constitution. 422 U.S. at 611. If this is indeed its rationale, the flagrancy principle should extend to all exclusionary-rule issues: "In view of the deterrent purposes of the exclusionary rule[,] consideration of official motives may play some part in determining whether application of the exclusionary rule is appropriate . . . ," *Scott v. United States,* 436 U.S. 128, 135-36 (1976) (dictum); *see also id.* at 139 n.13; *United States v. Leon,* 468 U.S. 897, 911 (1984).

(4) The *Alderman case, supra,* holds that once unconstitutional or unlawful surveillance has been judicially established, a defendant is entitled to full disclosure of all surveillance logs or transcripts concerning which s/he has standing to complain, for the purpose of the inquiry into the issue of taint. Apparently, these logs need not be disclosed in their entirety until after illegality has been found, although the court "'must develop the relevant facts and decide if the . . . electronic surveillance was unlawful.'" *Giordano v. United States,* 394 U.S 310, 312 (1969). The question of standing may also be determined without full disclosure of the logs, at least if that question is not factually complex. *Taglianetti v. United States,* 394 U.S. 316 (1969). Claims of unlawful surveillance conducted before June 19, 1968, are subject to special rules found in 18 U.S.C. §3504.

(B) Traditionally, "derivative evidence" emanating from a coerced confession was not inadmissible. The reason is obvious. The common-law prohibition of coerced confessional evidence was based on fear of its unreliability; physical objects or witnesses to which the confession led were no less reliable than if they had been discovered without benefit of the coercion. By contrast, the federal constitutional rules excluding coerced confessions (or confessions obtained in violation of the *Escobedo, Miranda,* and *Massiah* decisions, see paragraph [363](D), (E), (F) *infra*), do not depend upon concern for possible unreliability, *see Rogers v. Richmond,* 365 U.S. 534 (1961); *Johnson v. New Jersey,* 384 U.S. 719, 729 n.9 (1966), but rather involve an exclusionary sanction, like the exclusionary rule of the Fourth Amendment, designed to deter impermissible police behavior by forbidding use of its fruits. See paragraph [228] *supra* and subparagraph (A)(2) *supra.* For this reason evidence derived from confessions or admissions obtained in disregard of the federal restrictions on police conduct in eliciting statements from suspects must, like evidence derived from Fourth Amendment violations, be excluded. *See Brewer v. Williams,* 430 U.S 387, 406-7 n.12 (1977) (testimony that defendant, after confessing, led police to murder victim's body); *People v. Ditson,* 57 Cal. 2d 415, 369 P.2d 714, 20 Cal. Rptr. 165 (1962) (considered dictum). The Supreme Court acknowledged as much in *Kastigar v. United States,* 406 U.S. 441, 461-62 (1972), an opinion concerned with derivative evidence issues arising in the wake of subpoena-compelled testimony under an immunity grant, see paragraph [161](C) *supra.* "In holding that the immunity provided by [a federal immunity-grant] . . . statute is coextensive with the Fifth Amendment privilege, the Court implicitly concluded that the privilege prohibits 'the use of compelled testimony, as well as evidence derived directly and indirectly therefrom.'" *Doe v. United States,* 108 S. Ct. 2341, 2346 n.6 (1988). Comparing the respective positions of "a defendant against whom incriminating evidence has been obtained through a grant of immunity" with "a defendant who asserts a Fifth Amendment coerced-confession claim," *Kastigar v. United States, supra,* 406 U.S. at 461, the Court concluded that the only difference was that the latter defendant "must first prevail in a voluntariness hearing before his confession and evidence derived from it become inadmissible." *Id.* at 462. The plain implication is that, once involuntariness of a confession *is* shown, the derivative-evidence rules of *Kastigar* apply, imposing "on the prosecution the affirmative duty to prove that the evidence it proposes to use is derived from a legitimate source wholly independent of the [confession]." *Id.* at 460; *see also Pillsbury Co. v. Conboy,* 459 U.S. 248, 255 (1983). *Cf. Michigan v. Tucker,* 417 U.S. 433 (1974), reserving questions of the application of the derivative-evidence principle to violations of the *Miranda* rules occurring after the *Miranda* decision, 417 U.S. at 447, but apparently accepting the proposition that the "fruits" of a coerced confession must be excluded, *id.* at 445-46. Note that *Oregon v. Elstad,* subparagraph (A) *supra,* also leaves unsettled the general applicability of derivative-evidence principles to *Miranda* violations. *Elstad* applies more restrictive rules of taint to second confessions made after a first confession obtained in violation of *Miranda* than may apply to second confessions made after a first involuntary confession, see paragraph [363](N) *infra,* but is unclear in its implications for other derivative-evidence issues arising under *Miranda.*

(C) Illegally obtained evidence or information that may not be used in court (see subparagraphs (A) and (B) *supra*) also may not be used to justify any subsequent police action. The fruits of an illegal search, for example, may not be used to supply the probable cause required for a later arrest, *Johnson v. United*

States, 333 U.S. 10 (1948), or search, *see United States v. Paroutian,* subparagraph (A)(2) *supra; cf. New Jersey v. T.L.O.,* 469 U.S. 325, 344 (1985) (dictum), or for the issuance of a warrant, *United States v. Giordano,* subparagraph (A) *supra,* 416 U.S. at 529-34; *Steagald v. United States,* 451 U.S. 204 (1981) (by implication); *Hair v. United States,* 289 F.2d 894 (D.C. Cir. 1961). When they are so used, the products of the second police action are tainted by the illegality of the first, *see Alderman v. United States,* subparagraph (A)(2) *supra,* 394 U.S. at 177 (dictum); *United States v. Karo,* 468 U.S. 705, 719 (1984) (dictum), unless the prosecution shows "sufficient untainted evidence" (that is, information not derived in any way from the first action) to justify the later one, *ibid.* This evidence must be "genuinely independent of [the] . . . earlier, tainted [police action]," a condition that cannot be met if either (1) the police "decision to seek [a] . . . warrant [or conduct the second search] was prompted by what they had seen during the initial entry," or (2) "information obtained during that entry was presented to the Magistrate and affected his decision to issue the warrant [or is necessary to justify the second search without a warrant, if it was so made]." *Murray v. United States,* subparagraph (A)(1) *supra,* 108 S. Ct. at 2535-36.

(D) Problems relating to the use of illegally obtained evidence at preliminary hearing and before the grand jury are discussed in paragraph [172](D) *supra.*

(E) When illegally obtained evidence is improperly admitted at trial and the defendant thereupon adduces evidence to explain it away, the latter evidence is tainted and inadmissible at a subsequent trial. *Harrison v. United States,* 392 U.S. 219 (1968); *McDaniel v. North Carolina,* 392 U.S. 665 (1968) (per curiam); *Oregon v. Elstad,* subparagraph (A) *supra,* 470 U.S. at 316-17 (dictum). The same principle should apply to any explanatory or responsive evidence that a defendant may have given at earlier stages of the criminal proceeding — at preliminary hearing or before the grand jury — whether or not the magistrate's bindover or the indictment can be quashed on account of the receipt of the illegal evidence to which the defendant responded, *see* paragraph [172](D) *supra.*

[252] **The motion for suppression.** Even more than other pretrial motions (see paragraph [222](B), (C) *supra*), motions to suppress evidence should be carefully drafted so as not to disclose the factual theories of the defense that underlie the motion. Police are deeply interested in sustaining their arrests, searches, and confessions and will frequently conform their testimony to fit whatever theories validate their conduct. They should be educated as little as possible in advance.

[253] **Conduct of the hearing on the motion to suppress.** (A) For the same reason counsel should ordinarily invoke the rule on witnesses at any suppression hearing (see paragraph [348] *infra*) so as to exclude all officers from the courtroom except the one on the stand.

(B) Although the defendant has the burden proving an illegal search and seizure on a motion to suppress (*Rawlings v. Kentucky,* 448 U.S. 98, 104-5 (1980); compare paragraph [251](A)(2) *supra,* dealing with the issue of taint, and paragraph [366] *infra,* dealing with the issues of voluntariness and waiver of *Miranda* rights in connection with confessions), the defendant's burden is carried in the first instance by showing merely that s/he was subjected to a search or seizure without a warrant. The prosecution then bears the burden of persuasion with regard to any facts that it contends bring the case within some exception to the warrant requirement (see paragraphs [229]-[230] *supra*). *McDonald v. United States,* 335 U.S. 451, 456 (1948); *United States v. Jeffers,* 342 U.S. 48, 51 (1951); *Wrightson v. United States,* 222 F.2d 556 (D.C. Cir. 1955); *cf. Vale v. Louisiana,* 399 U.S. 30, 34 (1970); *Florida v. Royer,* 460 U.S. 491, 500 (1983) (plurality opinion); *Schneckloth v. Bustamonte,* 412 U.S. 218, 219, 222 (1973) (dictum). Counsel should therefore seek a stipulation from the prosecutor that the search and seizure were warrantless and, when the stipulation is made, should insist that the prosecutor proceed with his or her witnesses, allowing subsequent opportunity for rebuttal testimony by the defense. To request such a stipulation in open court at the beginning of the hearing will force the prosecutor to make it or look obstructive to the court. If the prosecutor will not stipulate, counsel should ask leave to proceed only to the extent of showing that there was a search or seizure conducted without a warrant, reserving further testimony for rebuttal. This procedure should obviously not be followed if counsel has good reason to want to take the officers' testimony on direct examination—when, for example, (1) the officers are known to be unintelligent or unprepared and the prosecutor is an experienced and able examiner who can effectively shape their testimony on direct, or (2) the rules of evidence in a particular jurisdiction permit parties to lead and impeach their own witnesses, or (3) the judge will permit the officers to be called as hostile witnesses (see paragraph [410] *infra*). But in most jurisdictions the greater latitude allowed to lead and to impeach witnesses on cross than on direct examination makes it wise for defense counsel to force the prosecutor to call the officers on direct whenever possible.

(C) Counsel will often find it helpful to ask each officer to draw his or her own diagram of the scene of the arrest, search, or seizure in issue and to describe the events in detail in relation to the diagram. Diagrams drawn by each officer should be removed from view before the entry of the next police witness, and counsel should ask the court not only for leave to remove the diagram after the testimony of the first witness but also for a ruling precluding the use of that diagram by the prosecutor in examining subsequent prosecution witnesses. The policy underlying the rule on witnesses supports such a request, and by keeping from each police witness the diagrams drawn by the others, visibly inconsistent versions of the affair can sometimes be elicited that will persuade the court or an appellate court to discredit the officers. To make the best record for an appellate court, counsel should have the officers draw their diagrams with a marker on graph paper rather than use a blackboard.

(D) As at trial, the operation of the rule on witnesses does not exclude the defendant. S/he has a right to be present while all testimony in the case is taken (see paragraphs [341], [348] *infra*), and it is usually best for the defense that s/he testify last, so as to meet the police testimony effectively.

(E) Counsel presenting a suppression motion frequently find that they can establish a marginal case of unconstitutional police conduct on the basis of police testimony alone, whereas the defendant's version of the relevant events portrays the officers' behavior as considerably more egregious and blatantly unlawful. It is a difficult question whether to put the defendant on the stand in this situation. Many judges believe that defendants are prone to exaggerate police misconduct; they are slow to credit any defendant's testimony, particularly when it consists of horror stories. Therefore, calling the defendant to testify entails the risk of irritating the judge to such an extent that s/he will strain the facts and the law to uphold the police. In addition, putting the defendant on the stand has collateral dangers. The defendant's testimony at the hearing on the motion to suppress may not subsequently be used against him or her in the prosecutor's case in chief at trial on the issue of guilt, *Simmons v. United States,* 390 U.S. 377 (1968); *Brown v. United States,* 411 U.S. 223, 228 (1973) (dictum); *United States v. Salvucci,* 448 U.S. 83, 89-90 (1980) (dictum); but the law is unclear whether it may be used by the prosecution for impeachment if the defendant elects to take the stand at trial and testifies inconsistently in any regard with his or her testimony on the motion, *see id.* at 93-94 & n.9; and see paragraph [394] *infra.* In any event, it is unwise to give a prosecutor an unnecessary opportunity to cross-examine the defendant before trial — an opportunity that may be used for discovery to improve the prosecution's presentation of its own evidence at trial and that will certainly be used, at the least, for "batting practice." (In federal cases Federal Rule of Evidence 104(d) may be invoked to limit the scope of cross-examination of the defendant.) On the other hand, there are significant defense advantages in presenting evidence, if it is at all credible, that depicts police behavior as atrocious. The Supreme Court has already held (in a decision of uncertain breadth) that the scope of taint attending an unconstitutional search and seizure may depend in part on the flagrancy of the unconstitutionality. *See Brown v. Illinois,* 422 U.S. 590, 603-5 (1975), discussed in paragraph [251](A)(3) *supra.* The Court may, indeed, be moving toward a general limitation of the exclusionary rule to cases in which "the law enforcement officer had knowledge, or may properly be charged with knowledge, that the search was unconstitutional," *United States v. Peltier,* 422 U.S. 531, 542 (1975), as distinguished from cases in which "law enforcement officials reasonably believed in good faith that their *conduct* was in accordance with the law . . .," *id.* at 538 (emphasis in original). *See United States v. Janis,* 428 U.S. 433, 454 n.28, 458-59 n.35 (1976); *Stone v. Powell,* 428 U.S. 465, 490-91 n.29 (1976); *id.* at 537-42 (dissenting opinion of Justice White); *Illinois v. Gates,* 462 U.S. 213, 217 (1983); *id.* at 246, 254-67 (concurring opinion of Justice White); *United States v. Leon,* 468 U.S. 897 (1984); *Illinois v. Krull,* 107 S. Ct. 1160 (1987); *California v. Greenwood,* 108 S. Ct. 1625, 1631 (1988); *but see Taylor v. Alabama,* 457 U.S. 687, 693 (1982); *cf. United States v. Johnson,* 457 U.S. 537, 559-61 (1982); *Arizona v. Hicks,* 107 S. Ct. 1149, 1155 (1987). Even apart from these doctrinal developments, trial (and appellate) judges who can be persuaded that the police have behaved abominably are naturally more likely to rule in the defendant's favor on any close questions in the case. Additional considerations for and against putting the defendant on the stand at a suppression hearing are akin to those involved in the decision whether to put the defendant on the stand at trial (see paragraph [390] *infra;* and *cf.* paragraph [388] *infra*), particularly if the judge conducting the hearing will later be the trial judge or sentencing judge or both. If the defendant *is* called to testify at the hearing, the advice in paragraph [59] *supra* and in paragraphs [395] and [466] *infra,* is applicable: When possible, counsel should corroborate the defendant's testimony by independent witnesses or evidence, since the defendant is the witness most likely to be disbelieved in his or her own behalf. The rule of the *Simmons* case, *supra,* that a defendant's testimony may not be used against the defendant at trial (at least in the prosecution's case in chief) is arguably applicable to any other evidence that the defendant introduces at a suppression hearing because the logic of the rule — that the defendant may not constitutionally be required to choose between the vindication of Fourth Amendment rights and the privilege against self-incrimination, *see United States v. Kahan,* 415 U.S. 239, 242 (1974) (per curiam) — can plausibly be extended to any sort of evidence that the defense is compelled to present in court (*cf. Harrison v. United States,* 392 U.S. 219 (1968), paragraph [251](E) *supra*) in order to assert the defendant's rights against the governmental illegality that necessitated the motion to suppress. *Cf. Fisher v. United States,* 425 U.S. 391, 399-400 n.5 (1976) (dictum); *Andresen v. Maryland,* 427 U.S. 463, 472 & n.6

(1976) (dictum). This extension, however, is far from clear, *cf.*
United States v. Nobles, 422 U.S. 225, 233-34 (1975), and counsel
cannot afford to rely on it in the present state of the law.

(F) The rules of evidence applicable at criminal trials are (except for privileges) somewhat relaxed at suppression hearings:
Hearsay is, for example, admissible if it is found to be sufficiently reliable. *United States v. Matlock,* 415 U.S. 164, 172-77
(1974); *United States v. Raddatz,* 447 U.S. 667, 679 (1980) (dictum). (In federal cases *see also* Fed. R. Evid. 104(a), 1101(d)(1).)
A footnote in *United States v. Crews,* 445 U.S. 463, 473 n.18
(1980), speaks ambiguously to the question whether illegally obtained evidence itself may be used to establish any fact supporting the prosecution's position on the motion to suppress.

**[253-A] Presenting defensive evidence at trial to rebut
prosecution evidence which has been admitted over the objection that it was illegally obtained.** Evidence that the defense presents in response to the court's improper admission of
illegally obtained evidence by the prosecution is thereby tainted
and cannot be used by the prosecution at a subsequent trial. See
paragraph [251](E) *supra.* But the case that lays down this rule,
Harrison v. United States, 392 U.S. 219 (1968), appears to leave
some room for the prosecution to establish subsequently that
any particular piece of defense evidence was presented not in
rebuttal of the improperly admitted prosecution evidence but for
other reasons. To guard against this possibility, counsel whose
pretrial suppression motion has been denied should ordinarily
(a) renew at trial all pretrial objections to the evidence s/he
moved to suppress, *see United States v. Raddatz,* 447 U.S. 667, 678
n.6 (1980) (dictum); paragraph [224](D) *supra,* and (b) approach the bench, before presenting any defensive evidence,
and state for the record that s/he is presenting the evidence that
will follow "solely under the compulsion of the court's rulings on
the prosecution's evidence, to which I have objected, and to reply to that evidence without waiving my pretrial or trial objections." (Of course, this statement may not be advised in particular cases: for example, in a bench trial when the principal tactic
of the defense is to deny guilt and impress the court with the
candor of the defendant, that is, to "come clean.")

XVI. MOTIONS FOR A CHANGE OF VENUE AND FOR DISQUALIFICATION OF A JUDGE

[254] Initial venue and change of venue. The general principles governing initial venue in criminal cases are sketched in paragraph [174] *supra.* As that paragraph indicates, a charging paper filed in the wrong venue is generally subject to a motion to quash or to dismiss; but in some jurisdictions the defendant's remedy may be merely a motion for transfer to the court of proper venue. When the applicable venue rule would allow prosecution of a particular offense in more than one court, ordinarily the prosecutor has the initial option. After the commencement of the prosecution, statutes or rules may permit either party to move for a change of venue to another court in which the prosecution could properly have been begun. In the absence of an explicit statutory authorization, the prosecutor may not ordinarily seek a change of venue, *Jackson v. Superior Court,* 13 Cal. App. 3d 440, 91 Cal. Rptr. 565 (1970); and in no event may the prosecutor obtain a change of venue, over the defendant's objection, to a place where the prosecution could not initially have been brought, consistent with the state and federal constitutional guarantees mentioned in paragraph [174]. The defendant, however, is allowed a venue change to other places under certain circumstances.

[255] Grounds for a defensive motion for change of venue. A defendant may ordinarily obtain a change of venue for one or more of the following reasons. Local practice must be considered for particulars.

(A) *Because of inability to obtain a fair trial in the court in which the charge is pending.*

(1) Public hostility against the defendant, public belief that the defendant is guilty, public outrage over the offense, and prejudicial news reporting or editorializing that vilifies the defendant or discloses inadmissible evidence against the defendant may all be shown in support of this ground. In addition to the state law right to a venue change, the federal constitutional guarantee of a fair trial by an impartial jury is

implicated here. *See Sheppard v. Maxwell,* 384 U.S. 333 (1966), and cases cited together with *Sheppard* in paragraph [315](C) *infra.* "This Court has long recognized that adverse publicity can endanger the ability of a defendant to receive a fair trial. . . . To safeguard the due process rights of the accused, a trial judge has an affirmative constitutional duty to minimize the effects of prejudicial pretrial publicity." *Gannett Co. v. DePasquale,* 433 U.S. 368, 378 (1979). "Trial courts must be especially vigilant to guard against any impairment of the defendant's right to a verdict based solely upon the evidence and the relevant law." *Chandler v. Florida,* 449 U.S. 560, 574 (1981) (dictum). The federal right does not necessarily require change of venue as a remedy. Other procedural devices may sometimes be effective to insulate a jury from the effects of inflammatory publicity and similar prejudicing influences — a continuance, sequestration of the jurors, or scrupulous interrogation on the *voir dire,* for example. *See Dobbert v. Florida,* 432 U.S. 282, 302-3 (1977); *Nebraska Press Ass'n v. Stuart,* 427 U.S. 539, 563-64 (1976) (dictum); *Richmond Newspapers, Inc. v. Virginia,* 448 U.S. 555, 581 (1980) (plurality opinion) (dictum). But if these devices are not employed or are insufficient, vindication of the federal fair trial rights demands a venue change. *Groppi v. Wisconsin,* 400 U.S. 505 (1971); *Coleman v. Kemp,* 778 F.2d 1487 (11th Cir. 1985), *rehearing en banc denied,* 782 F.2d 896 (11th Cir. 1986). And, of course, the defendant may not be required to waive other significant rights, such as the right to a jury trial (see paragraph [315](A) *infra*) or a speedy trial (see paragraphs [309]-[311] *infra*), as the price of a fair trial. *Cf. Jackson v. Denno,* 378 U.S. 368 (1964); *Simmons v. United States,* 390 U.S. 377, 389-94 (1968), and cases cited following *Simmons* in paragraph [180](E) *supra.*

(2) When a defendant charged in county *A* moves for a change of venue to county *B* on the grounds that s/he cannot get a fair trial in *A,* the court is ordinarily allowed discretion to transfer the case instead to county *C.* The defendant's right is only to get out of *A,* not to get into *B.* For this reason considerable caution is advised before counsel decides to file a change-of-venue motion. Counsel should ascertain from knowledgeable local attorneys or court personnel *where,* in

granting such motions, the court (or this particular judge) has been sending cases; and, after investigating those localities, counsel should thoroughly review the risks and costs of being transferred there. In particular, the pattern has developed in a number of metropolitan counties to transfer venue almost invariably to one or more nearby rural counties—possibly because it is thought that the jurors there will have been less exposed to inflammatory publicity but more likely simply because court calendars in the rural counties are not so badly backlogged. These counties may be unmitigated disaster areas for the transferred defendant. Adverse publicity there may be less voluminous and less provable without being less pervasive in fact. Even if it is less pervasive, the local jurors may also be (a) less sophisticated and skeptical in their reactions to the adverse publicity to which they *have* been exposed; (b) more homogeneous (see paragraphs [332], [340] *infra*); (c) more punitive; (d) less likely to include members of a minority defendant's race and social class; and (e) unprovably but unmistakably hostile to "foreigners"—including both defendants and their lawyers.

(3) Statutes sometimes delimit the geographic bounds within which a venue change may be allowed. If circumstances render fair trial anywhere within the area of allowed change impossible, the statutes may be attacked as unconstitutional. *See Groppi v. Wisconsin, supra; Nebraska Press Ass'n v. Stuart, supra,* 427 U.S. at 563 n.7 (dictum).

(B) *In the interest of justice, for the convenience of the parties and witnesses.*

(C) *Under federal practice, for the purpose of the defendant's pleading guilty and disposing of the prosecution in the district of arrest.* This procedure allows a defendant to avoid the necessity of returning to the district where the crime was alleged to have been committed if s/he is not going to contest guilt and wishes to expedite disposition. Federal Criminal Rule 20 should be consulted.

[256] The motion for change of venue on the ground that a fair trial cannot be had. In some jurisdictions a motion for venue change from a court in which the defendant asserts that s/he cannot be fairly tried must await the conclusion of *voir dire* examination of prospective jurors (see paragraphs [326]-[340] *infra*): only after an attempt to empanel a fair jury has been made and, in the opinion of the presiding judge, has failed, may venue be shifted. In other jurisdictions a motion for change of venue may be made before trial. Local practice governing the timeliness of motions should be checked. The motion is customarily supported by affidavits, and the defendant is allowed an evidentiary hearing if the motion and affidavits are facially sufficient. The following sorts of evidence should be considered by counsel who is attempting to prove that a fair trial cannot be had in the locality.

(1) *Newspaper clippings, videotapes, audiotapes, and TV or radio scripts.* These may be attached as riders to affidavits and presented as exhibits at a hearing. The prosecutor will ordinarily stipulate their authenticity; if s/he does not, the news reporters or editorial personnel who published them will have to be called to authenticate them. If the news media are uncooperative, subpoenas *duces tecum* are in order. *See Coleman v. Zant,* 708 F.2d 541, 546-48 (11th Cir. 1983). Counsel should be sure particularly to put into the record tapes and texts of publicity containing inadmissible inculpatory or inflammatory material. *Cf. Gannett Co. v. DePasquale,* 443 U.S. 368, 378 (1979).

(2) *Testimony of persons knowledgeable about public opinion.* Individuals whose occupations bring them in touch with prevalent public opinions may be called as witnesses or their affidavits attached to a motion. News reporters, political ward leaders, and members of the service trades (cab drivers, bartenders, barbers, delivery people, shopkeepers, and so forth) are frequently used. After a foundation is laid by showing that the witness (a) has occasion to talk to a great many persons daily and (b) has, in fact, discussed this case with a great many persons, s/he may be asked such questions as (i) what proportion of the persons to whom s/he talked discussed the case; (ii) whether they expressed the view that the defendant was guilty; (iii) whether they expressed the view that the crime was atrocious or that the perpetrator should be shot; and (iv) (if local practice demands this question) whether they expressed the view that the defendant could not get a fair trial in the locality. In a number of jurisdictions a change of venue

apparently depends upon the answer to this last question—obviously, a wholly unrealistic test. Counsel should urge its abandonment—and, if necessary, its unconstitutionality—on the ground that the same circumstances which are likely to make trial unfair are likely to make the local populace bad judges of whether a fair trial is possible. *Cf. Irvin v. Dowd*, 366 U.S. 717, 728 (1961); *Holbrook v. Flynn*, 106 S. Ct. 1340, 1346-47 (1986) (dictum). Usually the witness may also be asked (v) whether s/he has an opinion as to whether the defendant can receive a fair trial locally and (vi) what that opinion is. S/he will be permitted to answer only if s/he has demonstrated sufficient contact with public attitudes to qualify as an expert.

(3) *Opinion polls.* Counsel should consider commissioning an opinion poll to establish through accepted polling techniques the nature and pervasiveness of public attitudes about the defendant and the case. Useful questions include: (a) Have you ever heard of . . . [name of defendant], who is accused of . . . [crime]? (b) Do you think s/he is guilty? (c) Do you know that s/he has made a confession? (d) Have you heard that s/he has a criminal record? [Other publicized inadmissible matters should be made the subject of separate questions.] (e) Have you read . . . [or seen, or heard] [specified news stories]? (f) Do you think that most people in . . . County believe s/he is guilty? [This question is preferable to "Do you think s/he can get a fair trial in . . . County," but local law may require that the latter question be asked. See subparagraph (2) *supra.*] Commercial attitude-polling organizations or advertising firms with expertise in consumer studies may be retained to do the job. Professors of psychology, sociology, communications, or advertising at neighboring universities may be competent to design a poll and may be willing to conduct it with student assistance at a cost cheaper than that which a commercial pollster would charge.

(4) *Summoning passersby.* At the hearing on a motion for change of venue, the court may be asked to have the marshal bring in the first 20 or 25 persons who pass by on the street outside the courthouse. This procedure was developed in the era predating modern opinion-polling methods and is some-

times recognized by statute or local practice. It is obviously dangerous and should not be used if an opinion poll is possible.

(5) *Evidence of petitions, resolutions, speeches, and so forth.* If petitions relating to the case have been circulated or resolutions passed or speeches made at public meetings, these may be proved by observers. Since only the making of these sorts of declarations is to be proved and not the truth of what is declared, there is, of course, no hearsay problem.

(6) *Evidence of news conferences, press releases, and so forth by the police and the prosecutor.* It is desirable to prove, if it is so, that adverse publicity emanated from state officials. This has been an important consideration in cases holding that defendants were denied a fair trial by reason of inflammatory publicity or the publication of inadmissible evidence. *E.g., United States ex rel. Bloeth v. Denno,* 313 F.2d 364 (2d Cir. 1963). *See Nebraska Press Ass'n v. Stuart,* 427 U.S. 539, 554-55 (1976).

[257] **Same.** If a pretrial motion for change of venue is denied, counsel can usually not afford to rest on the record made at the hearing of the motion but must also conduct intensive *voir dire* examination of the panel at the trial to establish the prospective jurors' hostility to the defendant or their exposure to the prejudicial publicity of which counsel complains (see paragraphs [335]-[336] *infra*). *Dobbert v. Florida,* 432 U.S. 282, 301-3 (1977). A challenge to the venire or the panel may also be advised. See paragraphs [324], [327] *infra.* Requests to the court for other protective measures — continuance, sequestration — will improve counsel's record. If prejudicial publicity has continued between the time of the pretrial hearing and the trial, counsel should submit affidavits documenting its content, extensiveness, and date of publication and should renew the motion for a change of venue on the record previously made and this augmentation of it. The same procedure should be repeated during trial and at the time of postrial motions whenever significant additional inflammatory matter is published unless the jury is sequestered. The temporal proximity of inflammatory publications to the jury's deliberations is an important factor in appellate and post-conviction consideration of claims that the defendant was improperly denied a change of venue or a fair trial because of such

publications, *see, e.g., Patton v. Yount,* 467 U.S. 1025 (1984), and counsel should accordingly be careful to update the record periodically until after verdict.

[258] Motion for disqualification of a judge. (A) Statutes provide varying procedures by which counsel may object to a particular judge's presiding at the trial or hearing pretrial matters in the case. The statutes may or may not specify particular grounds for challenge: personal interest in the outcome of the case, relationship to a party, bias, and so forth. Local practice must be consulted with regard to the appropriate form of the challenge (affidavit of bias, motion for recusation, and so forth) and the time when it must be made. Under some procedures the filing of a facially sufficient affidavit or motion requires that the judge recuse himself or herself, without inquiry into the truth of the matters of fact averred; under other procedures the underlying factual questions are heard before the judge challenged or another judge. In addition to the statutory grounds and procedures for recusation, a defendant has a constitutional right not to be tried before a judge who is (a) biased in fact or (b) subject to influences that are likely to render an ordinary person in the judge's position biased, *see Tumey v. Ohio,* 273 U.S. 510 (1927); *Ward v. Village of Monroeville,* 409 U.S. 57 (1972); *cf. Mayberry v. Pennsylvania,* 400 U.S. 455 (1971); *Johnson v. Mississippi,* 403 U.S. 212 (1971); *Taylor v. Hayes,* 418 U.S. 488 (1974); *Connally v. Georgia,* 429 U.S. 245, 247-50 (1977) (per curiam); *Aetna Life Ins. Co. v. Lavoie,* 106 S. Ct. 1580 (1986); *Withrow v. Larkin,* 421 U.S. 35, 47 (1975) (dictum); *Marshall v. Jerrico, Inc.,* 446 U.S. 238, 242-43 (1980) (dictum); and the defendant is entitled to put allegations of bias into the record in any manner necessary to present them to the court and save them for review, *see Holt v. Virginia,* 381 U.S. 131 (1965); *In re Little,* 404 U.S. 553 (1972). Ordinarily, a written motion with supporting affidavits is desirable to protect the record. Before filing such a motion or invoking statutory recusation procedures, counsel may want to consider making an informal request to the judge to reassign the case "in the interest of the appearance of the most complete impartiality, and just to avoid any question of possible factors in the background of this case that might be thought to affect your Honor's attitude toward the case in any way." This kind of informal request is insufficient to make a record for appeal, and it should be followed by a formal motion if counsel means to stand on the point. But the initial soft-sell approach permits a graceful way out that will be accepted by some judges who would feel obliged to resist a formal motion making specific allegations of bias against them. Counsel can be both tactful and effective by emphasizing that actual bias is not required to support recusal: "'The guiding consideration is that the administration of justice should reasonably appear to be disinterested as well as be so in fact." *Public Utilities Commission v. Pollak,* 343 U.S. 451, 466-67 (1952) (Frankfurter, Circuit Justice), quoted with approval in *Liljeberg v. Health Services Acquisition Corp.,* 108 S. Ct. 2194, 2207 (1988).

(B) In some jurisdictions there is a procedure—sometimes called a motion for change of venue, sometimes called an affidavit of bias—which is actually used (by law or custom) as a form of peremptory challenge to the judge. It may not require any assertion of bias, or it may require simply an allegation of bias in conclusory form that the judges do not take seriously or resent. If the practice of "affidaviting" a judge is accepted by the local bench and bar as a routine forum-shopping device, then it may ordinarily be safely used, without incurring judicial wrath, even though in form it calls for allegations of bias. But counsel should always carefully investigate and determine both the general local attitudes toward these procedures and the known past reactions of the individual judge in question, since what is mere stock pleading in one locality—or to one judge—may be taken as a deadly insult in another locality or by another judge. Ordinarily, motions or affidavits for removal of a judge under these peremptory challenge procedures are timely only if filed before the judge has taken any action in the case; sometimes they are required to be filed within a specific time after its assignment to the judge.

XVII. MOTIONS FOR SEVERANCE OR FOR CONSOLIDATION

[259] Joinder; dismissal or severance for misjoinder. Rules authorizing the joinder in a single charging paper of more than one offense against one defendant or of more than one defendant charged with an offense or offenses vary considerably among the jurisdictions. Typical authorizations of joinder, which conversely serve to restrict the circumstances under which joinder is permissible, are described summarily in paragraph [178] *supra,* together with a few of the constructional problems that the authorizations raise. Ordinarily offenses and defendants joined in one indictment or information are jointly tried. If the indictment or information misjoins them, the remedy in some jurisdictions is dismissal; in others, merely severance. Motions attacking misjoinder may be required to be made before or at arraignment, or it may be sufficient to make them before trial. Local practice concerning the procedures and the time limitations, as well as the precise terms of the joinder rules, must be consulted. Objections to joinder not seasonably made are waived, and trial judges frequently exercise a discretion to permit the joinder by stipulation or waiver of otherwise nonjoinable charges or defendants. Courts differ on the question whether the propriety of joinder is controlled by the allegations of the charging paper or by the proofs at trial. The problem arises when a factual circumstance that is prerequisite to joinder under the applicable statute or rule (for example, "common scheme") is alleged but not proved. Some courts hold that the prosecution goes to trial on joined charges at its peril and that if the allegations warranting joinder are not proved, the defendant or defendants are entitled to a mistrial and severance on motion. Other courts require that to support a mistrial motion, not merely misjoinder but prejudice by reason of the misjoinder needs to be shown. Still others treat the initial joinder as proper and will declare a mistrial only if the joinder proves prejudicial in the specialized sense of the following paragraph. The difference between the second and third positions is one of degree. Courts that treat the failure of proof as a matter of misjoinder are somewhat more inclined to find prejudice (since error *has* occurred, and the sole remaining question is whether it was harmless) than are those that treat the joinder as technically proper and ask only whether it is so prejudicial that it should nonetheless be disallowed.

[260] Severance by reason of prejudicial joinder. Although charges or defendants are properly joined in the charging paper, a defendant may move that they be severed for trial if s/he would be prejudiced by trying them together. Prejudice in this sense is a practical, rather than a doctrinal, conception, and the various potential harms mentioned in paragraphs [263]-[264] *infra* may be urged upon the court in support of a severance motion. In many localities counsel will find that the judges are obdurate in favor of joint trials to the fullest extent allowed by law and that they are reluctant to grant a severance whenever joinder is technically permissible because of the supposed saving of court time. In these localities, particularly, the inquiry into "prejudice" is likely to turn into a balancing of the economies and other considerations favoring or disfavoring joint trial, and counsel is wise to point out (when this is true) that there is going to be so little evidentiary overlap with regard to the joined charges or defendants that not much time will be saved by a single trial instead of several. Similarly, if the joint trial is going to give rise to practical problems not involved in separate trials or if it will require rulings by the trial judge that may be assailable on appeal (for example, a ruling on the admissibility of one codefendant's confession that arguably incriminates another, see paragraphs [264](A), [362] *infra*), a court can often be convinced that the risk of error and reversal makes the supposed efficiency of the single trial illusory. A cardinal problem here, as with the required showing of prejudice generally, is that at the time of the hearing on a pretrial motion for severance, most of what will occur at trial remains largely speculative. After trial has begun and if prejudice develops, a motion for mistrial and severance may be made; but by this time the judge has an interest in not having wasted the court hours already invested, and s/he will be particularly loth to grant the motion. Counsel can sometimes turn these several related problems to advantage, however. If, on a pretrial motion, counsel can convince the court that the case is one in which trial problems may arise depending on the nature of the prosecutor's proof, the court will frequently ask the prosecutor what the proof is going to be — for example, whether a codefendant's confession will be used and whether it will incriminate the defendant. Motions for severance, therefore, have considerable discovery potential and may result in the disclosure of advance information about the prosecutive evidence that counsel could not obtain by regular discovery procedures.

[261] Consolidation. When offenses or defendants are charged in separate indictments of informations, the cases may ordinarily be consolidated for trial if, but only if, they could have been properly joined initially in a single indictment or information. Consolidation may be ordered on stipulation or on joint motion of the parties or on motion of one of them, or it may be effected informally by the prosecutor's listing the cases for trial together, with the acquiescence of the defense. If the prosecution and defense are agreed that joint trial is desirable, the court will probably accept a stipulation consolidating even those charges which could not technically be joined. When a defendant is going to plead guilty, it is generally wise to bring all of his or her pending charges on at the same time for disposition by plea or dismissal. Separate sentencing judges will probably know, in any event, about the other charges (see paragraph [465] *infra*), and the likelihood of concurrent sentencing ordinarily is strongly increased if a defendant lets one judge impose sentence for everything at one time. Similarly, if the defendant is going to plead guilty to some charges but go to trial on others, counsel should ask the prosecutor (and, if necessary, the court) to defer arraignment on the guilty plea charges until after the return of a verdict on the trial charges. Thus sentencing proceedings on the various convictions can be consolidated. Counsel should not have the defendant plead guilty on the plea charges before trial on the others because news of this may leak to the jury and the pleas could possibly, in some jurisdictions, be used to impeach the defendant if s/he testifies at trial. See paragraphs [390](F), [394] *infra*.

[262] Joinder or consolidation of jury-tried and bench-tried cases. It is not necessarily fatal to joint trial that some charges are going to be tried to a jury and others to the court. In a number of localities it is standard procedure to conduct simultaneous jury and bench trials, with the judge sitting as the trier of fact on the bench-tried charges and sending the others out to the jury. Other courts do not seem to do this, and in those courts the defendant can obtain a *de facto* severance by waiving jury trial on some charges but not on others. In many jurisdictions, however, the waiver is only effective if it is agreed to by the prosecutor and accepted by the court (see paragraph [316] *infra*), and one or the other may well decline to agree to a jury waiver in some, but not all, cases that would otherwise be jointly tried.

[263] Considerations favoring and disfavoring joint trial of multiple charges against one defendant. If all the charges against a defendant arise from the same episode or transaction, such as the ordinary housebreaking-robbery-rape, it is probably in the defendant's interest that they be tried together. The same proof, and all the proof, would likely be admitted at separate trials; and the more trials there are, the more chance there is that the defendant will lose something. S/he has, in any event, not much choice, since most courts will compel a joint trial in this situation, whether the defendant wants one or not. When separate charges arise from different episodes or from such far-flung aspects of one episode that trial on one charge would take shape substantially differently from trial on another, the choice between joint and separate trial is more difficult. Among the factors that my affect judgment are the answers to the following questions:

(A) *What will be the effect of the trier's knowing that the defendant is charged with several offenses, quite apart from any proof of his or her guilt of those offenses?* Generally, the more a defendant is charged with, the worse s/he looks. Jurors tend to operate on the principle that where there's smoke, there's fire. At the outset of the trial, when they are forming critical first impressions of the case that may affect their perceptions of much of the proof that follows, they know little about the defendant except what s/he is charged with. If the charges are several, s/he starts with several sins. In some cases, however, there may be countervailing considerations. If the defendant is obviously overcharged—if for example, s/he breaks a few coin boxes in public telephone booths and is charged, for each booth, with burglary, theft, and malicious destruction—the cumulative weight of the overcharging may make out a case of persecution that will sway a jury in the defendant's favor.

(B) *What will be the effect on the trier of the cumulation of evidence?* Again, generally, the more there is against a defendant, the worse. But this may depend on whether the evidence comes from several sources or from one. If two package store proprietors give the same jury "pretty sure" identifications of the defendant as the person who robbed them, conviction is more likely than if separate juries heard the identifying witnesses. On the other hand, if a defendant's young daughter in an incest-sodomy case relates that the defendant had intercourse with her on several occasions, proof that the defendant was not at home on one of the occasions may convince the jury that the whole story is a fabrication.

(C) *Will one defense depreciate another?* If a defendant has a weak or unconvincing defense to one charge and a more substantial defense to another, the incredibility of the former is likely to attaint the latter. Or both defenses may be believable separately but unbelievable together, as when a defendant charged with two rapes pleads alibi to the first and consent to the second.

(D) *Is it desirable to put the defendant on the stand in one case but not in the other?* If so, separate trials are essential. Apart from problems of cross-examination, a defendant cannot practicably take the stand and leave part of the charges against him or her unanswered.

(E) *Is there a "clinching" piece of evidence in one case that would not be admissible in the other if it were tried separately?* If so, the item may "clinch" both cases, as when a defendant charged with two holdups left a fingerprint at the scene of one.

(F) *What are the legal consequences for sentencing of successive and simultaneous convictions, respectively?* The rules governing sentencing on multiple charges and the terms of recidivist sentencing statutes must be carefully studied. See paragraph

[464](B), (G) *infra.* Increased penalties may be available for successive but not simultaneous convictions.

(G) *To what extent will a unitary wrap-up of all charges against the defendant expedite the presentation and disposition of the case and tend to ameliorate the sentencing in the event of conviction?* There may be substantial advantages to the defendant in a joint trial. Character witnesses and experts may be willing to be available once but not twice. All other things being equal, the defendant probably has a better chance of receiving concurrent sentences on two convictions after a single trial before a single judge than after two trials before different judges, or even the same judge. The prosecutor's habits and intentions must also be considered. If the defendant is tried on only one of several pending charges, the prosecutor may "dead-list" the others (that is, not bring them on for trial) and may lodge them as detainers against the defendant who is committed to serve a sentence of imprisonment on the first charge. The detainers will not only hang over the defendant's head; they may make the defendant ineligible for parole. See paragraph [205](D) *supra.* The prosecutor may or may not be required to bring the dead-listed charges on for trial upon the defendant's demand. See paragraphs [309]-[311] *infra.*

[264] Considerations favoring and disfavoring joint trial of several defendants. These considerations are exceedingly complex, and only a few of the more important ones can be sketched here.

(A) *Will evidence be admitted at a joint trial that could not be admitted at the defendant's trial if s/he were tried separately?* A principal item of concern is the codefendant's confession, which is inadmissible against the defendant both as hearsay and by force of the Sixth Amendment Confrontation Clause (see paragraph [360] *infra*), *e.g., Lee v. Illinois,* 106 S. Ct. 2056 (1986), but may be admitted "limited" by jury instructions to use against the codefendant at a joint trial. These instructions, of course, are not heeded by juries. Although *Bruton v. United States,* 391 U.S. 123 (1968), gives a joined defendant the constitutional right to exclude a codefendant's confession from their joint trial if it mentions and explicitly incriminates the defendant, *Bruton* does not bar the admission of a codefendant's confession that contains no reference to the defendant or is redacted to eliminate any reference to the defendant, *Richardson v. Marsh,* 107 S. Ct. 1702 (1987). Yet this kind of confession can also be extremely damaging to the defendant, particularly when it factually contradicts the theory of his or her defense or when the facts are such that both defendants are probably guilty if either one is. *Bruton* is also subject to qualifications of presently unclear scope that may permit the admission of a codefendant's confession directly implicating the defendant, under some circumstances. *See Cruz v. New York,* 107 S. Ct. 1714, 1719 (1987) (dictum), paragraph [362] *infra.* Certain nonconfessional evidence that would be inadmissible against the defendant at a severed trial may be admissible and hurtful at a joint trial: for example, evidence of the codefendant's prior convictions admitted to impeach the codefendant if s/he testifies, see paragraphs [381], [390](F), [394] *infra.*

(B) *Conversely, will evidence be excluded at a joint trial that would be admitted against the defendant at a separate trial?* Products of an illegal search and seizure of the codefendant may be admissible against the defendant because the defendant lacks standing to complain of the illegality. See paragraphs [225](C), [242](E), [248](A) *supra.* At a joint trial they might have to be excluded, although this point is not clear. *See McDonald v. United States,* 335 U.S. 451 (1948).

(C) *What are the relative strengths of the defensive cases of the defendant and codefendant(s)?* Defendants with weak defenses tend to look particularly bad in comparison to those who have stronger defenses. Defendants who take the stand cast those who do not in the worst possible light. In this last situation it has been held error to permit the testifying defendant's lawyer to comment on the failure of the codefendant to take the stand. *De Luna v. United States,* 308 F.2d 140 (5th Cir. 1962), *rehearing denied,* 324 F.2d 375 (5th Cir. 1963). The same opinion indicates, however, that it would also be error, as against the testifying defendant, to preclude his or her counsel from making this sort of comment at a joint trial. The practical consequence appears to be that when one defendant will testify and the other will not, severance may be had at the option of either. *But cf. Richardson v. Marsh,* subparagraph (A) *supra,* 107 S. Ct. at 1708-9.

(D) *What is the apparent relative blameworthiness of the defendant and the codefendant(s)?* Joint trial invites the jury to assess degrees of culpability. Particularly when the jury fixes sentence or when convictions of lesser included offenses are possible, the jury may mete out a sort of rough justice among codefendants according to their culpability. This suggests that the least culpable defendant has the most to gain from joint trial. But counsel cannot count on his or her defendant appearing least culpable unless the stories of prosecution witnesses or irrefutable physical circumstances—for example, relative size and age—make the favorable comparison strongly evident. Otherwise, the codefendants and their attorneys will also be vying to look the best of the bunch. In this and other situations of antagonistic defenses, separate trial should be sought.

(E) *Is there something particularly attractive or unattractive about the codefendant(s)?* The jury's positive or negative reactions to a codefendant may rub off on the defendant at a joint trial.

(F) *Can counsel cooperate and work well with counsel for the codefendant(s)?* Do their defensive theories or trial strategies conflict?

(G) *Will the number of defendants tend to protract the trial and wear the jury out?* Will it leave the jury confused and unable to identify the individual defendants? In "mass trials," when there is considerable evidence of wrong-doing, the jury usually convicts everybody in sight.

(H) *What are the local rules, and what is the local practice, regarding limitation of the procedural rights of joined defendants?* For example, will counsel's cross-examination of prosecution witnesses be cut off as "cumulative" of that of counsel for a codefendant? Will each joined defendant be permitted the full number of peremptory challenges to which s/he would be entitled at a separate trial, or will the defendants be required to apportion peremptories?

(I) *If trial is severed, who is likely to be tried first?* Prior trial of the codefendants may allow defense counsel full discovery of the prosecution's case in advance of his or her own trial. On the other hand, if they are convicted, they may turn state's evidence in an attempt to win sentencing consideration.

XVIII. DISCOVERY PROCEEDINGS;
PRETRIAL CONFERENCE

[265] Traditional limitations of criminal discovery. It is frequently said that no discovery was allowed by the common law in criminal cases. This is not strictly accurate; and, at least since Chief Justice Marshall presided at the trial of Aaron Burr, American trial courts have exercised a discretionary power to compel the production of materials requested by a defendant and found by the court to be necessary for adequate preparation of the defense. *United States v. Burr,* 25 Fed. Cas. 30 (No. 14,692d) (C.C.D. Va. 1807). It is true that the power was seldom used before the second half of the twentieth century and that in some states even recent decisions categorically deny the authority of a criminal court to order the prosecution to make any pretrial disclosure of evidence to the defense. A considerable trend away from the latter view has developed since the 1940's. With increasing frequency trial judges have been willing to order some discovery by the prosecution, and their orders have been sustained by appellate courts. Statutes and court rules have been promulgated, authorizing and in some cases requiring court-ordered disclosure of information and material in the possession of the prosecution. Nevertheless, this development has been far less extensive than the parallel development of civil discovery. In no state today does criminal procedure reflect the completely "open-book" policy that is characteristic of contemporary codes of civil procedure. In a number of states there has been only small progress away from the "closed-book" policy of the common law. The retarded state of criminal discovery is particularly evident in three regards. First, there are very few provisions for self-operating discovery mechanisms, like the interrogatories and depositions allowed in civil practice, by which one party may call upon the other for disclosure or may use court process for investigation, without a prior court order. Criminal discovery, instead, must be specifically requested of, and authorized in each particular by, the court. Second, criminal discovery is largely discretionary with the court and may not be demanded as a matter of right. Third, the kinds of information that will be ordered disclosed and the procedures by which it will be ordered disclosed are far more restricted than in civil matters.

[266] Checklist of self-help discovery devices. (A) In this state of the art, considerable self-help efforts by resourceful defense counsel are demanded. In the early stages of a criminal case, there are a number of proceedings that, although not designed for the purpose of allowing discovery, may often be used to get it. These have been discussed elsewhere in the *Guidelines,* and tactics for enhancing the discovery potential of the proceedings have been noted. An index follows:

(1) *Discussions with the prosecutor and the police.* [Paragraphs [91]-[105], [108], [116], [179] *supra.*] The possibility of obtaining a judicial order compelling the police to talk to counsel is considered in paragraph [116] *supra.* The discovery potential of plea negotiation with the prosecutor cannot be overemphasized. See paragraphs [206]-[219] *supra.*

(2) *Habeas corpus immediately following arrest, challenging the legality of the arrest.* [Paragraph [38] *supra.*]

(3) *Applications for bail or for the reduction of bail.* [Paragraphs [54]-[72] *supra;* see particularly paragraphs [58](A), [59].]

(4) *Preliminary hearing.* [Paragraphs [124]-[147] *supra;* see particularly paragraphs [139]-[144].]

(5) *Habeas corpus to challenge the bindover.* [Paragraph [146] *supra.*]

(6) *Arrangement of transcription of grand jury proceedings; motion to quash the indictment on grounds of procedural or evidentiary defects before the grand jury.* [Paragraphs [160], [172] *supra.*] Observing the grand jury room to identify witnesses who are called to it is also possible, although unnecessary in most cases when local practice requires the endorsement of names of witnesses on the indictment. See paragraphs [165], [183] *supra.*

(7) *Plea of double jeopardy when the defendant has been previously tried for related matters.* [Paragraph [177] *supra.*]

(8) *Motions to suppress illegally obtained evidence.* [Paragraphs [159], [184], [223]-[253] *supra;* see particularly paragraph [253](B), (C); and see paragraph [222](B) *supra.*]

(9) *Motions for severance or for consolidation.* [Paragraphs [259]-[264] *supra;* see particularly paragraph [260].]

(10) *Depositions to preserve the testimony of witnesses who may become unavailable.* [Paragraph [284] *infra.*]

(11) *Trial subpoenas.* [Paragraphs [285]-[291] *infra.*]

(12) *A pretrial conference.* [Paragraphs [275]-[276] *infra.*]

(B) In particular cases there may be other adventitious discovery opportunities, such as the coroner's inquest in homicide cases (paragraph [123-A] *supra*) or a prior trial resulting in a mistrial. Whenever there are recorded prior proceedings relating to a case, counsel should obtain and inspect the transcript. If notes of testimony have not been transcribed and counsel's client is an indigent, counsel should move the court for their transcription at public expense, as required by the Equal Protection Clause. *See Roberts v. LaVallee,* 389 U.S. 40 (1967) (transcript of preliminary hearing); *Britt v. North Carolina,* 404 U.S. 226 (1971) (dictum) (transcript of prior trial resulting in mistrial); *United States ex rel. Wilson v. McMann,* 408 F.2d 896 (2d Cir. 1969) (same); *Peterson v. United States,* 351 F.2d 606 (9th Cir. 1965) (same); *State ex rel. Marshall v. Eighth Judicial District Court,* 80 Nev. 478, 396 P.2d 680 (1964) (same); *Beasley v. State,* 81 Nev. 431, 404 P.2d 911 (1965) (transcript of prior trial of severed codefendants). *Compare Bounds v. Smith,* 430 U.S. 817, 822 n.8 (1977), *with United States v. MacCollum,* 426 U.S. 317 (1976); and see generally paragraphs [298]-[301] *infra.* In federal practice *see* FED. R. CRIM. P. 5.1 (c), dealing with defense access to recordings and transcripts of preliminary examinations.

(C) A number of jurisdictions have enacted freedom of information laws (commonly called FOIL's), some of them patterned on the federal Freedom of Information Act, 5 U.S.C. §552. Although not intended to provide discovery to criminal defendants, these laws may be written sufficiently broadly to reach certain government records that defense counsel would like to examine. *See, e.g., United States Department of Justice v. Julian,* 108 S. Ct. 1606 (1988). Unless the local statute explicitly forbids its use by parties to litigation against the government, counsel may find it profitable to follow the statutory procedures for requesting access to any records that arguably fall within its compass. FOIL requests are ordinarily submitted in writing directly to the governmental agency whose records are sought; if the agency does not produce them, a civil action is brought against the agency to compel production. The FOIL specifies the court or courts in which the civil action may be brought and the procedure for bringing it.

[267] **Formal discovery devices — the bill of particulars and the list of witnesses.** These are discussed in paragraph [183] *supra.*

[268] **Other formal discovery devices — in general.** (A) Local practice varies widely with regard to whether and which discovery procedures, other than the bill of particulars and witness list, are available. A checklist of particular devices that may be recognized, or that the courts might be persuaded to recognize, in any jurisdiction follows in paragraph [271](A) *infra.* Authorities from various jurisdictions and arguments supporting the recognition of these several devices are found in the following texts and articles, most of which are outspoken in favor of broadened criminal discovery. AMERICAN BAR ASSOCIATION PROJECT ON MINIMUM STANDARDS FOR CRIMINAL JUSTICE, STANDARDS RELATING TO DISCOVERY AND PROCEDURE BEFORE TRIAL (1970); Brennan, *The Criminal Prosecution: Sporting Event or Quest for Truth?,* 1963 WASH. U. L. Q. 279; Calkins, *Criminal Justice for the Indigent,* 42 U. DET. L. J. 305, 334-35, 337-39 (1965); Calkins, *Grand Jury Secrecy,* 63 MICH. L. REV. 455 (1965); Capra, *Access to Exculpatory Evidence: Avoiding the* Agurs *Problems of Prosecutorial Discretion and Retrospective Review,* 53 FORDHAM L. REV. 391 (1984); Carlson, *False or Suppressed Evidence: Why a Need for the Prosecutorial Tie,* 1969 DUKE L.J. 1171; Fletcher, *Pre-Trial Discovery in State Criminal Cases,* 12 STAN. L. REV. 293 (1960); Goldstein, *The State and the Accused: Balance of Advantage in Criminal Procedure,* 69 YALE L. J. 1149, 1172-98 (1960); Krantz, *Pretrial Discovery in Criminal Cases: A Necessity for Fair and Impartial Justice,* 42 NEB. L. REV. 127 (1962); Louisell, *Criminal Discovery: Dilemma Real or Apparent?* 49 CALIF. L. REV. 56 (1961); Nakell, *Criminal Discovery for the Defense and the Prosecution — The Developing Constitutional Considerations,* 50 N.C. L. REV. 437 (1972); Nakell, *The Effect of Due Process on Criminal Defense Discovery,* 62 KY. L. J.

58 (1973-74); Rezneck, *The New Federal Rules of Criminal Procedure*, 54 GEO. L. J. 1276 (1966); Traynor, *Ground Lost and Found in Criminal Discovery*, 39 N.Y.U. L. REV. 228, 749 (1964); Westen, *The Compulsory Process Clause*, 73 MICH. L. REV. 71, 121-31 (1974); Bureau Draft, *A State Statute to Liberalize Criminal Discovery*, 4 HARV. J. ON LEGIS. 105 (1966); Note, *Discovery Depositions: A Proposed Right for the Criminal Defendant*, 51 S. CALIF. L. REV. 467 (1978); Note, *Disclosure of Grand Jury Minutes to Challenge Indictments and Impeach Witnesses in Federal Criminal Cases*, 111 U. PA. L. REV. 1154 (1963). A suggested general approach to defense counsel's argument for broadened discovery rights is contained in paragraph [269] *infra;* constitutional considerations that may be advanced to support those rights are enumerated in paragraph [270] *infra.*

(B) In any particular case counsel may adopt one of two polar positions concerning discovery or take a stance somewhere between them. At one pole counsel may limit his or her discovery requests to what s/he is highly likely to get, and by this attitude of undemanding reasonableness attempt to persuade the court to exercise its discretion in favor of discovery in areas in which the local practice favors discovery but allows the court discretionary power to deny it. At the other pole counsel can go for broke and demand everything that a liberal and enlightened criminal procedure would allow to the defense. See paragraph [271](B) *infra.* If s/he takes the latter approach or some less extreme version of it that involves asking for a measure of discovery that local practice has not yet recognized, four points of technique are advised:

(1) *Counsel should always ask the prosecutor for whatever is wanted before moving the court for an order.* Judges understandably dislike being asked for compulsive orders when it is not clear that compulsion is necessary. Conversely, the prosecutor's denial of a request leaves the prosecution to blame for the necessity of bothering the court with whatever motions the defense is thereby required to file.

(2) *To the extent possible, counsel should make discovery requests highly specific, identifying the material that is wanted with particularity* (see the discussion of *United States v. Agurs*, 427 U.S. 97 (1976), and *United States v. Bagley*, 473 U.S. 667 (1985), in

paragraph [270](G) *infra; and see Pennsylvania v. Ritchie,* 107 S. Ct. 989, 1002 n.15 (1987)) *and describing its relevance and importance for the preparation of the defense unless self-evident* (*cf. United States v. Valenzuela-Bernal,* 458 U.S. 858, 867-71, 873 (1982). Counsel should support the requests by affidavit averring that the prosecutor has (or has control over) the material, that the defendant needs it to prepare adequately to present his or her defense, and that defense counsel has attempted to obtain the material by other means but has been unable to get it. *Cf. California v. Trombetta,* 467 U.S. 479, 489-90 (1984).

(a) Of course, counsel will not always know what the prosecutor has that the defense needs. It is one of the purposes of discovery to find out. But counsel should have some idea, for example, that the prosecution has interviewed particular witnesses. In this case a request for a production order should seek the statements of those witnesses by name *as well as* the "statements of all other witnesses made in connection with this case," and the request should be accompanied by an affidavit showing that the named witnesses have refused to talk to counsel or to a defense investigator.

(b) The problem confronting counsel here is that courts will often deny an overly broad or unspecific discovery request as a "fishing expedition," even though some of the materials included within it would be ordered produced if they were designated with greater particularity. On the other hand, a discovery request limited to materials that defense counsel has sufficient information to identify with particularity may fail to cover some items that are crucial to the defense and that the court might, in its discretion, order produced if described generically rather than specifically. One device for dealing with this problem is to frame discovery requests in the form of a series of concentric circles of increasing breadth and generality, for example (in an armed robbery prosecution):

(I) The following real or physical objects or substances:

(A) The "thing of value" that it is alleged in Count One of the indictment the defendant took from the complainant, John Smith, on or about May 1, 1988;

(B) Any other thing that it is claimed was taken from John Smith during the course of the robbery alleged in Count One;

(C) The "pistol" described by Detective James Hall at page 6, line 4 of the transcript of the preliminary hearing herein;

(D) Any other weapon that it is claimed was used by the defendant during the course of the robbery alleged in Count One of the indictment;

(E) Any other thing that it is claimed was used by the defendant as an instrumentality or means of committing the robbery alleged in Count One;

(F) Any real or physical object or substance that:

(1) the District Attorney intends to offer into evidence at any trial or hearing in this case;

(2) the District Attorney is retaining in his or her custody or control for potential use as evidence at any trial or hearing in this case;

(3) is being retained for potential use as evidence at any trial or hearing in this case by, or within the custody or control of:

(a) any personnel of the Oak City Police Department;

(b) any personnel of the State Bureau of Investigation;

(c) any personnel of the Oakland County Criminalistics Laboratory;

(d) [following paragraphs designate other relevant agencies];

(4) has been submitted to any professional personnel [as defined in a "Definitions" paragraph of the discovery request, encompassing all forensic science experts and investigators] for examination, testing, or analysis in connection with this case by:

(a) the District Attorney;

(b) any person previously described by paragraph (I)(F)(3)(a),(b),(c), or (d);

(5) has been gathered or received in connection with the investigation of this case by:

(a) the District Attorney;

(b) any personnel previously described by paragraph (I)(F)(3)(a),(b),(c), or (d);

(6) is relevant to:

(a) the robbery alleged in Count One of the indictment;

(b) the identity of the perpetrator of that robbery;

(c) the investigation of that robbery;

(d) the physical or mental state, condition, or disposition of the defendant at the time of:

(i) that robbery;

(ii) the confession allegedly made by the defendant, described by Detective James Hall at page 10, lines 12-23 of the transcript of the preliminary hearing herein;

(iii) any other confession, admission, or incriminating statement allegedly made by the defendant;

(iv) the present;

(G) Every real or physical object or substance within the categories previously described by paragraphs (I)(A) through (I)(F), which hereafter comes into the possession, custody, or control of, or is, or hereafter becomes, known to:

(1) the District Attorney;

(2) any person previously described by paragraph (I)(F)(3)(a),(b),(c), or (d).

(II) [Following paragraphs describe other categories of materials — defendant's statements, witnesses' statements, police and investigative reports and records, lab test results, exculpatory materials, and so forth — in a similar manner.]

Discovery requests in this form have the virtue of covering everything that might be discoverable, whether known or unknown to defense counsel, while insulating counsel's requests for narrower or more specific categories of items from denial on the ground that the broader or more general categories are impermissible "fishing expeditions" or include undiscoverable material.

(3) *When no procedure is authorized in criminal cases to obtain the sort of information counsel wants, counsel should ask the court to adopt procedures locally recognized in civil cases or procedures authorized in criminal cases for other purposes.* Particularly when the *substance* of what counsel wants the court to do is novel, it is important to make the court feel that the *method* of proceeding is ordinary and not unnatural. If counsel wants a physical examination of the complaining witness, for example, it is helpful to point to the provisions in the civil procedure code or rules authorizing such an examination and to follow their technical details as far as is practicable. If counsel wants the compulsory process of the court to obtain the story of a police witness, s/he may follow the deposition procedures authorized in criminal cases for perpetuating the testimony of a witness who is likely to be unavailable for trial, or s/he may ask the court by order to permit the defense to proceed with a deposition as under civil practice.

(4) *Counsel should include in every proposed discovery order that seeks a class of items or a generic sort of information some such phrase as: "and all like matter that hereafter comes into the possession of, or becomes known to, the attorney for the prosecution."*

[269] Same—the general position of the defense on discovery. (A) Arguing in support of specific discovery requests, counsel will find it helpful to take the position that the same general policy which supports "wide-open" discovery in civil cases is equally applicable in criminal cases. "We have elected to employ an adversary system of criminal justice in which the parties contest all issues before a court of law. The need to develop all relevant facts in the adversary system is both fundamental and comprehensive." *United States v. Nixon,* 418 U.S. 683, 709 (1974). The quest for truth at trial is better served, under an adversary system, if the evidence of one party does not come as a surprise to the other but, having been disclosed in advance while there is still time to check it out through adequate investigation, appears in court subject to meaningful cross-examination and rebuttal. This assures "the reliability of the adversarial testing process." *Kimmelman v. Morrison,* 106 S. Ct. 2574, 2589 (1986).

(B) The arguments against this eminently civilized approach to criminal cases are essentially two:

First, it is said that criminal defendants, more than civil litigants, once forewarned are likely to flee the jurisdiction, bribe or intimidate witnesses, or engage in other misbehavior. Counsel may concede that these dangers, if they are real, justify curbing criminal discovery. But quite apart from the fact that there has never been any adequate showing made to support the proposition that the dangers *are* greater in criminal cases generically than in civil cases (*compare NLRB v. Robbins Tire & Rubber Co.,* 437 U.S. 214, 239-41 (1978), finding a special danger of witness intimidation in NLRB proceedings because of the "'peculiar character of labor litigation,'" *id.* at 240), it is evident that the supposed dangers are differentially present in different sorts of criminal cases and in different sorts of discovery requests. No amount of argument about generalities can make concerns for flight, bribery, or intimidation anything other than preposterous when the defendant is an indigent, is jailed in default of bail, and wants production of the police report. Counsel should, therefore, urge that the liberality of civil discovery practice is appropriate unless the prosecutor can make some particularized showing that in *this* case and with respect to *this* discovery request the speculative dangers have some factual substance to them.

Second, the objection is mounted against criminal discovery that it is a "one-way street": that the privilege against self-incrimination precludes the prosecutor from obtaining discovery against the defendant and that it is inefficient or unfair to give the defendant unilateral discovery against the prosecutor. Defense counsel can disarm this argument if s/he is willing to offer reciprocal disclosure to the prosecution. If s/he is not, s/he may at least be able to point to recent judicial developments suggesting that the Fifth Amendment is *not* an absolute bar to criminal discovery in favor of the prosecution but would permit the prosecutor to obtain disclosure of the products of defense investigation in an appropriate case, see paragraph [274] *infra*—a point that can often be made consistently with arguing vigorously that the present case is not an appropriate one. Yet even if the Fifth Amendment were an absolute bar—or to the extent that it is a bar—the "one-way street" objection is nonetheless logically unsound. That is so because the "one-way street" in question is no anomolous creation of criminal discovery but is the very hallmark of the American accusatorial system of criminal procedure, preferred and, in large measure, commanded by the Fifth Amendment itself. *See Murphy v. Waterfront Commission,* 378 U.S. 52, 55 (1964). The Fifth Amendment privilege against self-incrimination embodies "'a judgment . . . that the prosecution should [not] be free to build up a criminal case, in whole or in part, with the assistance of enforced disclosures by the accused.'" *Ullmann v. United States,* 350 U.S. 422, 427 (1956). No one would suppose that because it protects the defendant from being compelled to incriminate himself or herself, the prosecution should be permitted to incriminate the defendant with perjurious or unreliable evidence. See paragraph [270](E) *infra.* The efficiency and fairness of prescreening the prosecution's evidence for veracity and reliability are not diminished simply because the overriding policy of the Fifth Amendment makes impossible what would be equally, but independently, desirable if constitutionally permissible: the prescreening of defense evidence as well. Any aversion to one-way streets, in this context, is nothing more or less than a rejection of basic Fifth Amendment values. Such a rejection is particularly indefensible because the best founded attacks on the policy of the privilege against self-incrimination have always rested upon its tendency to protect the guilty, whereas it is the innocent who are particularly hurt by denial of discovery on "one-way street" logic. Furthermore, the realities of criminal investigation are a one-way street the other way. Police and prosecutors have resources to gather and preserve evidence incomparably greater than those of the accused. *See Wardius v. Oregon,* 412 U.S. 470, 475-76 n.9 (1973). If equal advantage *were* the measure of fairness in criminal procedure—which the

Fifth Amendment denies—discovery in favor of the defense would nevertheless be required in virtually all situations.

[270] Same—the constitutional concerns. There are a number of constitutional guarantees that, in varying degrees, support various defensive requests for discovery. Counsel should be alert to these.

(A) *The Sixth Amendment right to counsel.* This right, incorporated into the Fourteenth Amendment by *Gideon v. Wainwright,* 372 U.S. 335 (1963), guarantees more than that the defendant should have a lawyer. It assures "effective aid in the preparation and trial of the case." *Powell v. Alabama,* 287 U.S. 45, 71 (1932); *see Strickland v. Washington,* 466 U.S. 668, 684-88 (1984). "[T]he essential aim of the [Sixth] Amendment is to guarantee an effective advocate for each criminal defendant . . . ," *Wheat v. United States,* 108 S. Ct. 1692, 1697 (1988), and the Amendment is violated when defense counsel is required to operate under circumstances that render his or her services ineffective, *Ferguson v. Georgia,* 365 U.S. 570 (1961); *Brooks v. Tennessee,* 406 U.S. 605 (1972); *Geders v. United States,* 425 U.S. 80 (1976); *Cuyler v. Sullivan,* 446 U.S. 335, 344 (1980) (dictum); *Perry v. Leeke,* 109 S. Ct. 594, 599 (1989) (dictum). "[T]he right to the assistance of counsel has been understood to mean that there can be no restrictions upon the function of counsel in defending a criminal prosecution in accord with the traditions of the adversary factfinding process that has been constitutionalized in the Sixth and Fourteenth Amendments." *Herring v. New York,* 422 U.S. 853, 857 (1975). For example, the Sixth Amendment has repeatedly been held to condemn eve-of-trial appointments of counsel that leave the lawyer inadequate time to prepare for trial. *E.g., Jones v. Cunningham,* 313 F.2d 347 (4th Cir. 1963); *Martin v. Virginia,* 365 F.2d 549 (4th Cir. 1966); *Roberts v. United States,* 325 F.2d 290 (5th Cir. 1963); *Townsend v. Bomar,* 331 F.2d 19 (6th Cir. 1964); see also the cases cited in paragraph [53] *supra; compare United States v. Cronic,* 466 U.S. 648 (1984). Timely appointment of counsel was required by *Powell v. Albabama, supra,* the fountainhead of all right-to-counsel cases, because during the pretial period "consultation, thoroughgoing investigation and preparation were vitally important." 287 U.S. at 57. If adequate *time* to prepare is a constitutional mandate, adequate *information* to prepare is arguably no less necessary. For, as the Supreme Court has recognized in *Coleman v. Alabama,* 399 U.S. 1, 9 (1970), and *Adams v. Illinois,* 405 U.S. 278, 281-82 (1972), paragraph [131] *supra,* the pretrial gathering of this information is a vital part of the effective assistance of counsel that the Constitution commands. "An accused is entitled to be assisted by an attorney . . . who plays the role necessary to ensure that the trial is fair." *Strickland v. Washington, supra,* 466 U.S. at 685. A key component of a fair trial is that the "evidence [be] subject to adversarial testing." *Ibid.*; *see also United States v. Cronic, supra,* 466 U.S. at 656 ("[t]he right to the effective assistance of counsel is . . . the right of the accused to require the prosecution's case to survive the crucible of meaningful adversarial testing"). And a failure to obtain pretrial discovery of the prosecution's case "puts at risk . . . the reliability of the adversarial testing process." *Kimmelman v. Morrison,* 106 S. Ct. 2574, 2589 (1986).

(B) *The right to fair notice of charges.* In *Cole v. Arkansas,* 333 U.S. 196, 201 (1948), the Supreme Court recognized the "principle of procedural due process . . . that notice of the specific charge, and a chance to be heard in a trial of the issues raised by that charge, if desired, are among the constitutional rights of every accused in a criminal proceeding in all courts, state or federal." *See also Dunn v. United States,* 442 U.S. 100, 106-7 (1979). "These standards no more than reflect a broader premise that has never been doubted in our constitutional system: that a person cannot incur the loss of liberty for an offense without notice and a meaningful opportunity to defend." *Jackson v. Virginia,* 443 U.S. 307, 314 (1979). "Notice, to comply with due process requirements, must be given sufficiently in advance of scheduled court proceedings so that reasonable opportunity to prepare will be afforded, and it must 'set forth the alleged misconduct with particularity.'" *In re Gault,* 387 U.S. 1, 33 (1967) (a juvenile proceeding). This principle may—though it probably need not—be derived from the express right given an accused by the Sixth Amendment "to be informed of the nature and cause of the accusation." *See Faretta v. California,* 422 U.S. 806, 818 (1975) (dictum); *Herring v. New York,* subparagraph (A) *supra,* 422 U.S. at 856-57. Even in noncriminal matters, the Supreme Court has found a due process right to adequate notice of the issues posed for adjudication in a proceeding affecting individual interests. *E.g., Morgan v. United States,* 304 U.S. 1 (1938); *Gonzales v. United States,* 348 U.S. 407 (1955); *Goldberg v. Kelly,* 397 U.S. 254, 267-68 (1970) (dictum); *cf. Wolff v. McDonnell,* 418 U.S. 539, 563-64 (1974); *Goss v. Lopez,* 419 U.S. 565, 578-82 (1975); *Vitek v. Jones,* 445 U.S. 480, 494-96 (1980); *but see Greenholtz v. Inmates of the Nebraska Penal and Correctional Complex,* 442 U.S. 1, 14 n.6 (1979). A *dictum* in *United States v. Agurs,* 427 U.S. 97, 112 n.20 (1976), says that "the notice component of due process refers to the charge rather than the evidentiary support for the charge"; but the line between these two will often be shadowy.

(C) *The Sixth Amendment right to confrontation.* As noted in paragraph [360] *infra,* the Supreme Court held in 1965 that the Due Process Clause imposes upon the states the requirement of the Sixth Amendment that a criminal accused have the right "to be confronted with the witnesses against him." The *Pointer* and *Douglas* decisions cited in that paragraph recognize that adequate cross-examination is the essence of the right. *See also Bruton v. United States,* 391 U.S. 123 (1968); *Davis v. Alaska,* 415 U.S. 308, 315-17 (1974); *Lee v. Illinois,* 106 S. Ct. 2056, 2061-62 (1986); *Olden v. Kentucky,* 109 S. Ct. 480, 483 (1988) (per curiam); *Delaware v. Van Arsdall,* 106 S. Ct. 1431, 1435 (1986) (dictum). Even apart from the Sixth Amendment, fair opportunity for cross-examination is an indispensable element of due process in any hearing that may have significant adverse consequences for an individual. *Specht v. Patterson,* 386 U.S. 605, 610 (1967); *Jenkins v. McKeithen,* 395 U.S. 411, 428-29 (1969); *Goldberg v. Kelly,* subparagraph (B) *supra,* 397 U.S. at 268-70; *Morrissey v. Brewer,* 408 U.S. 471, 489 (1972); *Gagnon v. Scarpelli,* 411 U.S. 778, 785-87 (1973); *Vitek v. Jones,* subparagraph (B) *supra,* 445 U.S. at 494-96; *but see Baxter v. Palmigiano,* 425 U.S. 308, 321-23 (1976). "'[C]ross-examination . . . is beyond any doubt the greatest legal engine ever invented for the discovery of truth.'"

Ford v. Wainwright, 106 S. Ct. 2595, 2605 (1986), quoting 5 WIGMORE, EVIDENCE §1367 (Chadbourn rev. 1974). *Accord, Kentucky v. Stincer,* 107 S. Ct. 2658, 2662 (1987). And substantial impairment of cross-examination, no less than its "complete denial," violates these rights. *Smith v. Illinois,* 390 U.S. 129, 131 (1968). *See also Davis v. Alaska, supra,* 415 U.S. at 318. Since, as any experienced trial lawyer knows, uninformed cross-examination is worse than no cross-examination at all—a point that seems to underlie the decision in *United States v. Wade,* 388 U.S. 218, 227, 229-32, 235 (1967)—a refusal to the defense of pretrial discovery necessary to investigate and meet the prosecution's testimony at trial may unconstitutionally abridge the defendant's right of confrontation. Four Justices of the Supreme Court rejected this last proposition in *Pennsylvania v. Ritchie,* 107 S. Ct. 989 (1987), taking the view that "the right of confrontation is a *trial* right . . . [and that t]he ability to question adverse witnesses . . . does not include the power to require the pretrial disclosure of any and all information that might be useful in contradicting unfavorable testimony," *id.* at 999 (emphasis in original). Three Justices disagreed, concluding that "there might well be a confrontation violation if . . . a defendant is denied pretrial access to information that would make possible effective cross-examination of a crucial prosecution witness." *Id.* at 1004 (opinion of Justice Blackmun); *see also id.* at 1006-9 (opinion of Justice Brennan, joined by Justice Marshall). The issue therefore remains unsettled.

(D) *The right to present defensive evidence.* The Sixth Amendment guarantees a criminal defendant the right "to have compulsory process for obtaining witnesses in his favor." The Clause was incorporated into the Fourteenth Amendment in *Washington v. Texas,* 388 U.S. 14 (1967), and—coupled with the Due Process Clause—now supports assertion of a general right to present defensive evidence. *See Webb v. Texas,* 409 U.S. 95 (1972); *Crane v. Kentucky,* 106 S. Ct. 2142 (1986); *cf. Rock v. Arkansas,* 107 S. Ct. 2704 (1987). Indeed, the Supreme Court has recognized that "[f]ew rights are more fundamental than that of an accused to present witnesses in his own defense." *Chambers v. Mississippi,* 410 U.S. 284, 302 (1973). *See also*

Specht v. Patterson, subparagraph (C) *supra,* 386 U.S. at 610; *Jenkins v. McKeithen,* subparagraph (C) *supra,* 395 U.S. at 429; *Goldberg v. Kelly,* subparagraph (B) *supra,* 397 U.S. at 268-69; *Morrissey v. Brewer,* subparagraph (C) *supra,* 408 U.S. at 489; *Gagnon v. Scarpelli,* subparagraph (C) *supra,* 411 U.S. at 785-87; *Cool v. United States,* 409 U.S. 100 (1972); *cf. Ferguson v. Georgia,* 365 U.S. 570 (1961); *Townsend v. Burke,* 334 U.S. 736 (1948); *Wolff v. McDonnell,* subparagraph (B) *supra,* 418 U.S. at 566-67; *Green v. Georgia,* 442 U.S. 95, 97 (1979) (per curiam); *Vitek v. Jones,* subparagraph (B) *supra,* 445 U.S. at 494-96; *Ford v. Wainwright,* subparagraph (C) *supra,* 106 S. Ct. at 2604-5. "[O]rdinarily the right to present evidence is basic to a fair hearing . . . ." *Ponte v. Real,* 471 U.S. 491, 495 (1985) (dictum). An accompanying right to information in the possession of the prosecution that might lead to defensive evidence may be inferred. *Cf. Roviaro v. United States,* 353 U.S. 53 (1957); *United States v. Augenblick,* 393 U.S. 348, 356 (1969) (dictum). "The defendant's right to compulsory process is . . . designed to vindicate the principle that the 'ends of criminal justice would be defeated if judgments were to be founded on a partial or speculative presentation of the facts.' . . . Rules that provide for pretrial discovery of an opponent's witnesses serve the same high purpose. Discovery, like cross-examination, minimizes the risk that a judgment will be predicated on incomplete, misleading, or even deliberately fabricated testimony." *Taylor v. Illinois,* 108 S. Ct. 646, 653-54 (1988). In *Pennsylvania v. Ritchie,* subparagraph (C) *supra,* a five-Justice majority of the Supreme Court spoke inconclusively about the extent to which the Sixth Amendment Compulsory Process Clause supports a criminal defendant's claim of pretrial discovery rights. It noted that "the Court traditionally has evaluated claims such as those raised by Ritchie under the broader protections of the Due Process Clause"—referring specifically to the principles described in subsections (E) and (F) *infra*—and "conclude[d] that compulsory process provides no *greater* protections in this area than those afforded by due process." 107 S. Ct. at 1001 (emphasis in original). But it left unclear what it meant by "claims such as those raised by Ritchie" or "this area," and so did not foreclose defense reliance on the Compulsory Process Clause to undergird discovery rights in cases in which the purpose of the Clause to guard against criminal "'judgments . . . founded on a partial or speculative presentation of the facts,'" *Taylor v. Illinois, supra,* is particularly implicated.

(E) *The right against concealment of evidence that impeaches prosecution testimony.* A line of decisions from *Mooney v. Holohan,* 294 U.S. 103 (1935), to *Miller v. Pate,* 386 U.S. 1 (1967), condemns the prosecutive presentation of perjured testimony. *See generally United States v. Agurs,* subparagraph (B) *supra,* 427 U.S. at 103-4 (dictum). Specifically, the Court has held that the Due Process Clause invalidates a state conviction obtained after a trial at which the prosecutor has knowingly elicited false testimony from a witness, even on a matter relating to the witness's credibility rather than directly to the defendant's guilt, *Alcorta v. Texas,* 355 U.S. 28 (1957), or at which the prosecutor has knowingly permitted a witness to testify falsely on such a matter, *Napue v. Illinois,* 360 U.S. 264 (1959). Under *Napue,* if the prosecution knows of evidence inconsistent with the testimony of one of its material witnesses and "relevant to his [or her] credibility," the defense and "the jury [are] . . . entitled to know of it." *Giglio v. United States,* 405 U.S. 150, 155 (1972). *Cf. Moore v. Illinois,* 408 U.S. 786, 797-98 (1972) (dictum). It is but a short step to hold that since the whole of every witness's testimony impliedly asserts its veracity, nondisclosure of any material known to the prosecution that is legally admissible to impeach the witness would also violate due process. *Cf. Giles v. Maryland,* 386 U.S. 66 (1967); *Delaware v. Van Arsdall,* subparagraph (C) *supra,* 106 S. Ct. at 1435-36. The California Supreme Court, for example, has required disclosure of the felony record of a prosecution witness (see paragraph [381] *infra*) on this theory. *In re Ferguson,* 5 Cal. 3d 525, 487 P.2d 1234, 96 Cal. Rptr. 594 (1971). And in *United States v. Bagley,* 473 U.S. 667 (1985), the Supreme Court of the United States seems to have assimilated the doctrine of *Alcorta, Napue,* and *Giglio* into that of *Brady v. Maryland,* subparagraph (G) *infra,* saying generally that "[i]mpeachment evidence . . . as well as exculpatory evidence" must be disclosed under *Brady.* 473 U.S. at 676.

(F) *The right against prosecutorial suppression of evidence favorable to the defense.* This right was recognized as an alternative ground of decision in *Pyle v. Kansas,* 317 U.S. 213 (1942), and *Wylde v. Wyoming,* 362 U.S. 607 (1960). It is best expounded in *United States ex rel. Almeida v. Baldi,* 195 F.2d 815 (3d Cir. 1952). Its implications for the right of defense counsel to interview witnesses without prosecutorial interference are suggested in paragraph [116] *supra.* It would also seem to imply a right of defense access to any exculpatory or favorable materials that are within the exclusive control of the prosecutor, such as impounded physical objects. The Supreme Court has recognized that if the police or the prosecutor, acting in "bad faith," destroy evidence "potentially useful" to the defense, its destruction violates the defendant's due process rights, *Arizona v. Youngblood,* 109 S. Ct. 333, 337 (1988) (dictum), at least when the defendant is left with no equally effective "alternative means of demonstrating . . . innocence," *Trombetta v. California,* 467 U.S. 479, 490 (1984) (dictum). And as long as the evidence has not been destroyed but is still in the state's possession, the language and logic of *Youngblood* are clear that "the good or bad faith of the State [is] irrelevant" and that the prosecution must "disclose to the defendant material exculpatory evidence." 109 S. Ct. at 337.

(G) *The right to prosecutorial disclosure of evidence helpful to the defense.* The line is thin between the suppression cases, involving affirmative prosecutorial action that impedes access by the defense to information potentially useful to it, and cases in which the prosecutor, knowing of such information and knowing that it is not readily available to the defense, fails to disclose it. In *Brady v. Maryland,* 373 U.S. 83 (1963), the Court crossed that line and held that prosecutorial nondisclosure of evidence peculiarly in state control and potentially helpful to the defense (there, a codefendant's confession that identified the codefendant as the lone triggerman in a robbery-murder) violates the Due Process Clause "irrespective of the good faith or bad faith of the prosecution," *id.* at 87.

(1) *Brady* is now treated as establishing the "well-settled [rule] that the Government has the obligation to turn over evidence in its possession that is both favorable to the ac-

cused and material to guilt or punishment." *Pennsylvania v. Ritchie*, subparagraph (C) *supra*, 107 S. Ct. at 1001. In *Ritchie*, the Court held that this obligation extended to exculpatory information contained in the confidential files of a public child-protection agency and required a state trial court to examine those files *in camera* to determine whether anything in them would have been material to the defense of a rape/incest charge. Neither the fact that the material was in the possession of a state agency other than the prosecutor nor the fact that the agency's records were made confidential (with some exceptions) by statute prevented the application of the *Brady* disclosure duty.

(2) *United States v. Agurs*, 427 U.S. 97 (1976), holds that *Brady* applies only to information favorable to the defense; it does not require disclosure of the prosecution's evidence of guilt. But the subsequent decision in *United States v. Bagley*, 473 U.S. 667 (1985), makes it plain that the concept of "'evidence favorable to an accused'" (*id.* at 676) is a practical one: "Impeachment evidence . . . as well as exculpatory evidence, falls within the *Brady* rule." *Ibid.*

(3) Defense counsel in *Brady* had asked for disclosure of the sort of evidence that the prosecutor withheld. Lower courts subsequently found *Brady* violations in cases in which no request was made, *United States ex rel. Thompson v. Dye*, 221 F.2d 763 (3d Cir. 1955); *Ashley v. Texas*, 319 F.2d 80 (5th Cir. 1963), and even when diligent independent investigation by defense counsel might have uncovered the evidence, *United States ex rel. Meers v. Wilkins*, 326 F.2d 135 (2d Cir. 1964); *Barbee v. Warden*, 331 F.2d 842 (4th Cir. 1964). But *cf. Moore v. Illinois*, 408 U.S. 786, 794-95 (1972) (dictum). In the *Meers* case and in *Levin v. Katzenbach*, 363 F.2d 287 (D.C. Cir. 1966), it should be noted that the evidence in question could hardly be said to have been peculiarly available to the prosecution, except in the sense that evidence is always peculiarly available to a person who knows of its existence while others do not.

(4) In the *Agurs* case, subparagraph (G)(2) *supra*, the Supreme Court undertook to define the prosecutor's *Brady* obligations in three situations. *Agurs* held that when "there has

been no [defense discovery] request at all" or "merely a
general request" (such as a request "for 'all *Brady* material'
or for 'anything exculpatory'"), 427 U.S. at 106-7, a prosecutorial failure to disclose any evidence which "creates a
reasonable doubt that did not otherwise exist" violates the
Due Process Clauses of the Fifth and Fourteenth Amendments, *id.* at 112, and requires the allowance of a new trial
if the evidence comes to light after verdict. On the other
hand, when a "specific" defense request gives "the prosecutor notice of exactly what the defense desire[s]," *id.* at 106,
and "if the subject matter of such a request is material, or
indeed if a substantial basis for claiming materiality exists,
it is reasonable to require the prosecutor to respond either
by furnishing the information or by submitting the problem
to the trial judge. When the prosecutor receives a specific
and relevant request, the failure to make any response is
seldom, if ever, excusable," *ibid.* But in *United States v. Bagley, supra,* the Court revisited *Agurs* and blurred the distinction between its "no-request-or-general-request" and "specific request" categories. Justice Blackmun, speaking only
for himself and Justice O'Connor in *Bagley,* rejected the application of different standards of materiality to the two
categories of cases, saying that a single standard should
apply to both: "The [undisclosed] evidence is material only
if there is a reasonable probability that, had the evidence
been disclosed to the defense, the result of the proceeding
would have been different. A 'reasonable probability' is a
probability sufficient to undermine confidence in the outcome." 473 U.S. at 682. However, Justice Blackmun's opinion does not make the fact and specificity of pretrial defense
requests for disclosure entirely irrelevant to the consequences of prosecutorial nondisclosure. Justice Blackmun
notes that "the more specifically the defense requests certain evidence, thus putting the prosecutor on notice of its
value, the more reasonable it is for the defense to assume
from the nondisclosure that the evidence does not exist,
and to make pretrial and trial decisions on the basis of this
assumption." *Id.* at 682-83. This may cause the defense to
"abandon lines of independent investigation, defenses, or

trial strategies that it otherwise would have pursued," *id.* at 682; and "any adverse effect that the prosecutor's failure to respond might have had on the preparation or presentation of the defendant's case" is to be taken into account in applying the reasonable-probability-of-a-different-result standard. *Id.* at 683. Chief Justice Burger, Justice White, and Justice Rehnquist, in a concurring opinion, agreed that the applicable materiality standard in *Bagley* was Justice Blackmun's reasonable-probability-of-a-different-result standard, *id.* at 685, but they saw "no reason to attempt to elaborate on the relevance to the inquiry of the specificity of the defense's request for disclosure, either generally or with respect to this case," *ibid.* Yet in a subsequent majority opinion, *Pennsylvania v. Ritchie,* subparagraph (C) *supra,* the Court cited Justice Blackmun's *Bagley* opinion with apparent approval for the proposition that "the degree of specificity of Ritchie's request may have a bearing on the . . . assessment . . . of the materiality of the nondisclosure," 107 S. Ct. at 1002 n.15. With the law in this muddle, defense counsel are advised to make their discovery requests as specific as possible. See paragraph [268](B) *supra.* When counsel lacks sufficient information to fine-tune a request, s/he should explain that problem explicitly in his or her motions papers. Speaking in an analogous context, the Supreme Court has recognized that the degree of specificity required of a defense request depends upon the amount of information which defense counsel already has and can bring to bear in framing the request. *United States v. Valenzuela-Bernal,* 458 U.S. 858, 870-71, 873 & n.8 (1982).

(5) Neither the *Brady* doctrine discussed in this subpararaph (G) nor the related caselaw discussed in subparagraphs (E) and (F) *supra* announces a right to pretrial discovery as such. All of the Due Process cases deal with the situation in which a prosecutor has allowed the trial to go through to conviction without disclosure. But the assumption of the cases appears to be that when disclosure is constitutionally required, it is required at a sufficiently early stage of the proceedings so that the defense can make effective use of whatever is disclosed. *See United States ex rel. Drew*

v. Myers, 327 F.2d 174 (3d Cir. 1964); *cf. United States v. White,* 324 F.2d 814 (2d Cir. 1963). And, in any event, both prosecutors and judges should be sensitive to the argument that pretrial discovery is a better way to run a system than disclosure at trial, with a constitutionally compelled mistrial and continuance or postconviction litigation of questions of nondisclosure. "[T]he aim of due process 'is not punishment of society for the misdeeds of the prosecutor but avoidance of an unfair trial to the accused.'" *Smith v. Phillips,* 455 U.S. 209, 219 (1982). This is why, as the Supreme Court noted pointedly in *Agurs,* subparagraph (G)(3) *supra,* "the prudent prosecutor will resolve doubtful questions in favor of disclosure." 427 U.S. at 108.

(H) *The right against an unfair balance of advantage favoring the prosecution.* The decision in *Wardius v. Oregon,* 412 U.S. 470 (1973), described in paragraph [274] *infra,* appears to be seminal inasmuch as it recognizes that the Due Process Clause "does speak to the balance of forces between the accused and his accuser." 412 U.S. at 474. *See also United States v. Ash,* 413 U.S. 300, 309 (1973), paragraph [233](B)(2) *supra,* noting the Sixth Amendment's concern against "the imbalance in the adversary system that otherwise [that is, without defense counsel] resulted with the creation of a professional prosecuting official." These decisions suggest that Justice Cardozo's famous phrase about keeping "the balance true," *Snyder v. Massachusetts,* 291 U.S. 97, 122 (1934), may be more than just a jurisprudential attitude: It may be a constitutionally enforceable right of the defendant. Although this notion is still embryonic, two obvious implications of *Wardius* deserve note.

(1) Any criminal procedures that provide "nonreciprocal benefits to the State" in regard to the investigation, preservation, and presentation of its evidentiary case should be constitutionally assailable "when the lack of reciprocity interferes with the defendant's ability to secure a fair trial." 412 U.S. at 474 n.6. For example, if procedures are available by which the prosecution can detain witnesses, or collect and secure other evidence, favorable to its case, then either the prosecution should be obliged equally to collect, secure, and make available witnesses and evidence favor-

able to the defense, or at least the defense should be given equal use of the procedures. *Cf. People ex rel. Gallagher v. District Court,* 656 P.2d 1287 (Colo. 1983) (defendant was denied due process when police refused to perform forensic test requested by defense counsel before testing was rendered impossible by preparation of homicide victim's body for burial); compare the cases holding that the unnecessary destruction of material evidence in the course of forensic testing by the prosecution, so as to preclude independent testing by defense experts, constitutes a violation of due process, *People v. Hitch,* 12 Cal. 3d 641, 527 P.2d 361, 117 Cal. Rptr. 9 (1974); *People v. Nation,* 26 Cal. 3d 169, 604 P.2d 1051, 161 Cal. Rptr. 299 (1980) (dictum); *People v. Gomez,* 198 Colo. 105, 596 P.2d 1192 (1979); *People v. Garries,* 645 P.2d 1306 (Colo. 1982); *People v. Taylor,* 54 Ill. App. 3d 454, 369 N.E.2d 573 (1977); *People v. Dodsworth,* 60 Ill. App. 3d 207, 376 N.E.2d 449 (1978); *cf. California v. Trombetta,* 467 U.S. 479 (1984) (limiting this doctrine to evidence that "both possess[es] an exculpatory value that was apparent before the evidence was destroyed, and [is] . . . of such a nature that the defendant would be unable to obtain comparable evidence by other reasonably available means," *id.* at 489), *and Arizona v. Youngblood,* 109 S. Ct. 333, 337 (1988), limiting the doctrine to destruction in "bad faith"). If court orders or compulsory process can be issued to assist the prosecution in conducting lineups, fingerprint, handwriting, or voice comparisons, or other scientific tests (see paragraph [163](B) *supra*), the results of those investigations must be disclosed to the defense; and judicial process must be made available for the conduct of similar investigations at the instance of the defense. *Evans v. Superior Court,* 11 Cal. 3d 617, 522 P.2d 681, 114 Cal. Rptr. 121 (1974); *cf. United States v. Ash,* 461 F.2d 92, 104 (D.C. Cir. 1972) (en banc) (dictum), *rev'd on other grounds,* 413 U.S. 300 (1973). Indeed, in view of the wide-ranging subpoena power available to the grand jury to compel the testimony of witnesses in the service of the prosecution (*see Branzburg v. Hayes,* 408 U.S. 665, 701-2 (1972); paragraphs [161](B), [163] *supra*), it is not evident why the defense should not be constitutionally entitled to conduct equally wide-ranging depositions of potential witnesses prior to trial. At the least, the prosecutor's traditional one-sided use of the grand jury transcript to aid in the preparation of the prosecutive case (see paragraph [160] *supra; e.g.,* FED. R. CRIM. P. 6(e)) should be challengeable under *Wardius. Cf. McMahon v. Office of the City and County of Honolulu,* 51 Haw. 589, 465 P.2d 549, 550-51 n.3 (1970).

(2) *Wardius* raises the question to what extent "the State's inherent information-gathering advantages suggest that if there is to be any imbalance in discovery rights, it should work in the defendant's favor." 412 U.S. at 475 n.9. In a case in which a strong record has been made in the fashion sketched out by paragraph [271](B) *infra,* it may be possible to persuade a court that the traditional plight of the impecunious criminal defendant — going into trial blind in the face of a well-prepared adversary — itself requires the allowance of corrective discovery measures under *Wardius.*

(I) *The obligation of the Equal Protection Clause that a state not permit an indigent defendant to be deprived of "the basic tools of an adequate defense" by reason of poverty. Britt v. North Carolina,* 404 U.S. 226, 227 (1971) (dictum). This Equal Protection doctrine is discussed in paragraph [299] *infra.* One method of compensating for the investigative disadvantage suffered by indigent defendants, compared to defendants who have money, is to give the indigent defendant access to the results of the prosecution's investigations through discovery. Because some of these constitutional theories may have more immediate applicability than others to the specific form of discovery sought by the defense in the context of a particular prosecution (see paragraph [271](A) (*infra*), it has seemed best to enumerate them separately. They are not, however, unconnected. More than one of them may support any given discovery request; and in some instances (especially when the approach described in paragraph [271](B) *infra* is followed), counsel may want to emphasize their interrelationship. Two ways of stating this interrelationship follow:

(J) Speaking of the criminal-trial rights guaranteed by the Sixth Amendment (subparagraphs (A) through (D) *supra*), the

Supreme Court has noted that its "decisions . . . have not given to these constitutional provisions a narrowly literalistic construction." *Herring v. New York,* subparagraph (A) *supra,* 422 U.S. at 857. "The rights to notice, confrontation, and compulsory process, when taken together, guarantee that a criminal charge may be answered in a manner now considered fundamental to the fair administration of American justice—through the calling and interrogation of favorable witnesses, the cross-examination of adverse witnesses, and the orderly introduction of evidence. In short, the Amendment constitutionalizes the right in an adversary criminal trial to make a defense as we know it." *Faretta v. California,* subparagraph (B) *supra,* 422 U.S. at 818 (dictum). And "[t]he right to the assistance of counsel . . . ensures to the defense in a criminal trial the opportunity to participate fully and fairly in the adversary factfinding process." *Herring v. New York,* subparagraph (A) *supra,* 422 U.S. at 858; *cf. Kimmelman v. Morrison,* subparagraph (A) *supra,* 106 S. Ct. at 2588, quoting *Strickland v. Washington,* subparagraph (A) *supra,* 466 U.S. at 690 ("'counsel's function . . . is to make the adversarial testing process work in the particular case'"). Full and fair defense participation in an adversary factfinding process depends upon adequate defense discovery. *Kimmelman v. Morrison,* subparagraph (A) *supra,* 106 S. Ct. at 2588-89.

(K) All of the Bill of Rights guarantees mentioned in the preceding subparagraphs have been extended to state criminal defendants on the ground that "they are part of the 'due process of law' that is guaranteed by the Fourteenth Amendment to defendants in the criminal courts of the States." *Faretta v. California,* subparagraph (B) *supra,* 422 U.S. at 818. See authorities collected in paragraph [57-A](B)(1) *supra.* Put another way, they have been recognized as the measure of "the 'process that is due,'" *Gerstein v. Pugh,* 420 U.S. 103, 125 n.27 (1975), in criminal trials in order to assure that these trials are "fundamentally fair," *Murphy v. Florida,* 421 U.S. 794, 799 (1975). Denials of discovery requests that implicate these several Bill of Rights guarantees operate cumulatively to impair the fairness of the trial; and their cumulation may, on the facts of a particular case, make the trial so unfair as to violate

Due Process. *Cf. Chambers v. Mississippi,* subparagraph (D) *supra.*

[271] Specific discovery procedures; formal discovery and informal discovery. (A) Counsel should consider attempting to use some or all of the following procedures:

(1) *Interrogatories to the prosecutor,* seeking the names of witnesses, specific details of the alleged offense, and other investigative leads.

(2) *Depositions of witnesses* (complainants, police, and so forth), orally or on written interrogatories; *and motions for leave to take these depositions.*

(3) *Motions for production or inspection* of—

(a) *Physical objects.* (Counsel should ask that these be released for testing by defense experts, if advised; or the court should be requested to order that defense experts be allowed to attend testing by prosecution experts. *Cf.* paragraph [270](H) *supra.*)

(b) *Medical and scientific reports and records* made by the prosecution's investigators or collected in its investigation of the crime or preparation for trial.

(c) *Police and other investigative reports.* (These are particularly valuable sources of information for the defense. Usually made shortly after the date of the events giving rise to the criminal charge, they offer contemporaneous accounts of those events by prosecution witnesses that are persuasive for impeachment when, as often happens, the witnesses later change their stories. The reports also reveal investigative failings and ineptitudes on the part of the police that may persuade a judge or jury to discredit the prosecution's case, and they can often provide leads to claims of unconstitutional police conduct that will support a suppression motion or the exclusion of prosecution evidence. Police departments vary widely in the reports they make, and local practitioners should be consulted for a list of those that are ordinarily made in any particular kind of case. The following are common:)

(i) *Complaint reports* (also known as "incident reports" or "event reports"). These are written up by the investigating officer when a complainant first reports, or the police first observe, possibly criminal conduct (hereafter, "the crime"). The report usually contains information identifying the complainant (name, aliases, address, phone number, sometimes occupation and place of employment); a note of the time and location of the crime; the complainant's and eyewitnesses' descriptions of the crime, the perpetrator and the perpetrator's clothing, and any weapons observed; a description of any property involved (in theft crimes) and any injuries suffered by the victim (in crimes of violence), often together with a notation of the hospital to which the complainant was taken, if s/he was taken to a hospital for treatment.

(ii) *Arrest reports*. These are filled out by an arresting officer. The report usually contains a notation of the exact time of arrest; a description of all property taken from the defendant at the time of arrest (but not necessarily of property later taken from the defendant at the lockup); a summary or verbatim record of any incriminating statements made by the defendant and of statements made to the defendant, together with his or her responses or failure to respond; a physical description of the defendant (which may prove useful in cases in which identification is in issue, when the defendant's appearance changes between the time of the offense and the time of a suppression motion or of trial) and of any injuries observed on the defendant; background information on the defendant obtained from him or her; any significant conduct by the defendant when approached by the arresting officers (for example, attempted flight or resistance); and sometimes a narrative account of the crime, particularly in cases in which it was observed in whole or in part by the arresting officers.

(iii) *Police phone and radio communication tapes,* including any emergency phone call to the police by a complainant, reporting the crime (also known as "911 calls"). The tapes contain verbatim records of the original communications, often disclosing police movements prior to an arrest, search, or seizure of the defendant and, in the case of 911 calls, the complainant's earliest description of the crime and the perpetrator in the complainant's own words. Discovery of the tapes should be sought by the defense at the earliest possible time, since many police departments preserve the tapes only for a brief period of time before erasing or re-using them.

(iv) *Precinct or lockup logs and booking cards or booking sheets* (also known as "charge cards" or "charge sheets"). These are entries made at the stationhouse or lockup to which the defendant is taken after arrest. They usually contain a notation of the charge or charges; the defendant's name and some identifying information (age, address, phone); a note of the exact time when the defendant is "logged in" at the stationhouse or lockup; and, in the case of booking cards and particularly of booking sheets, a note of the time of arrest; a description of all property taken from the defendant at the stationhouse or lockup (and sometimes also of property taken from the defendant at the time of arrest); a summary or verbatim record of any incriminating statements made by the defendant during the booking process, and sometimes of incriminating statements made by the defendant at the time of arrest and *en route* to the stationhouse or lockup; a physical description of the defendant and of any injuries observed on the defendant at the time of his or her arrival at the stationhouse or lockup; background information on the defendant obtained from him or her by the booking officer; and any significant conduct by the defendant during the booking process.

(v) *Arrest photographs and booking photographs* (also known as "mug shots").

(vi) *Audiotapes and videotapes of incriminating statements made by the defendant to the police during postarrest interrogation.*

(vii) *Eyewitness identification reports.* These reports (which some departments make on standard "lineup report" forms) describe any identification confrontations staged with the defendant and the complainant or eyewitnesses. They usually contain a description of the identification procedure; names and identifying information for the witnesses; a description of the defendant and of any other persons exhibited with the defendant in a lineup (sometimes with names and indentifying information for these persons); and a description of the words used by the witnesses in identifying the defendant.

(viii) *Records of confessions and admissions* (also known as "statement reports"). These are reports handwritten or typed by investigating officers, recording incriminating statements made by the defendant during the postarrest period. They usually contain a description of the *Miranda* warnings given to the defendant and of the defendant's responses, with a note of the time when these were administered or made; a verbatim recitation of any oral statement by the defendant; a summary or verbatim recitation of any written statement made by the defendant; and sometimes a description of the defendant's conduct or demeanor at the time of the statement.

(ix) *Property inventories.* These are of two general types: logs of property obtained by the police during their investigation and held for possible use as evidence, and logs of property taken from the defendant at the time of his or her arrest and at the time of his or her arrival at the stationhouse or lockup, which are held for him or her in an "inmate's property envelope." Both sorts of inventories may be kept in any given case. Some departments record the inventories on tags affixed to the containers in which the property is preserved. *Evidence tags* usually note when, where, and by what officer each item was obtained; any marks made on the item by the officer for purposes of subsequent authentication testimony; and sometimes dates, times, and places of any police testing of the item, with notations of the name and badge number of the officer who took the item from the evidence storage locker for testing and returned it after testing, and sometimes of the agency or name of the forensic expert to whom it was taken for testing.

(x) *Crime scene reports.* Some departments have a standard form in which investigating officers are required to describe the crime scene and their investigation of it in detail. These are most common in homicide cases and other serious crimes. They usually include a diagram of the crime scene as well as a narrative description of it. Photographs may be attached to the report.

(xi) *Forensic expert's reports.* These are reports of examinations and tests conducted at the scene of the crime or upon physical objects and substances taken from the defendant or from the defendant's property at or after arrest, found by the police at the scene of the crime, or otherwise known or believed connected with the crime. The reports usually describe the object or substance in detail; they indicate the testing procedure and materials used and any positive results; sometimes they also note negative results or can be used to prove negative results because they indicate that a particular test was made but do not indicate its results. Forensic expert's reports are particularly common in cases in which the evidence gathered by the police includes fingerprints, footprints, tire prints, hair, blood, semen, clothing or other fabric pieces or threads, physical objects requiring analysis to connect them with the crime or the defendant, poisons, and drugs.

(xii) [In drug cases] *Narcotics reports* (also known as "buy reports") describing the nature and amount of the drugs involved and the transaction in which an undercover officer purchased the drug from the defendant, if that is the basis for the charge; *chemist's reports* reporting the exact weight of the drug and its identification and characteristics under chemical analysis; and *narcotics offender reports* containing detailed background information about the defendant and his or her drug usage habits and history obtained by questioning him or her before or during booking.

(xiii) [In cases involving firearms] *Firearms reports* describing any gun involved in the crime or taken from the defendant, reporting its serial number, noting the number of bullets found in and with the weapon, and describing them; *ballistics reports* describing the results of test-firing of the gun, including its operating characteristics and a comparison of the slugs fired from it with those known or believed to be connected with the crime; and *reports of paraffin tests* made on the defendant after arrest, indicating whether s/he had recently fired a gun.

(xiv) [In cases of physical injury to the complainant] *Reports of victim's injuries.* Some police departments require that a form report be filled out in cases of physically injured victims, describing the injury and any treatment administered at the scene. The reports usually also identify any hospital or physician that the police arrange to treat the complainant.

(xv) [In cases of rape, sexual assault, child molesting and incest] *Reports of the physical examination of the complainant,* which ordinarily indicate any bodily evidence of recent intercourse and of force or violence used on the complainant, and note the blood type of any semen recovered from the complainant's body; and *serology reports* comparing the defendant's blood type with that of semen recovered from the complainant's body.

(xvi) [In homicide cases] *Coroner's reports or medical examiner's reports.* See paragraph [123-A] *supra.*

(xvii) [In cases involving physical descriptions of otherwise unidentified perpetrators who are to be sought by the police] *Composite drawings and police artists' sketches* made from descriptions by complainants and eyewitnesses.

(d) *Police regulations, policy manuals, operations manuals, and police academy training materials.* These may describe how the police investigation *should* have been conducted in a particular sort of case. When the actual investigation deviated from police regulations governing arrests, searches and seizures, interrogation, or identification confrontations or when the applicable regulations confer undue discretion on investigating officers, that may give the defense an asset on a motion to suppress or an objection to prosecution evidence as illegally obtained. See particularly paragraphs [223], [236](A)(3) and (C)(1) and (D), [238](A)(2), [246](D)(2), [251](A)(3), and [253](E) *supra.* When the actual investigation deviated from prescribed procedures for the examination or handling of evidence, the deviation may be used to persuade a trier of fact at trial that the reliablility of the resulting evidence is questionable; or the unreliability of the evidence — together with the prospect of embarrassment of the police when a claim of its unreliability is aired at trial — may persuade the police or the prosecutor to drop charges or persuade the prosecutor to accept a plea bargain favorable to the defendant (see paragraph [100] *supra.*

(e) *Written and oral statements of the defendant and of any codefendants and alleged accomplices.*

(f) *Statements of witnesses.* (It should be noted that these are not now available before trial in federal practice under Federal Criminal Rules 16(a)(2), 17(h), 26.2, and 18 U.S.C. §3500(a).)

(g) *Official records* (prison records, jail records, hospital records, parole records, probation records, social-work agency records, employment records, and so forth) *of the defendant, codefendants, alleged accomplices, prosecution and defense witnesses,* including materials relevant to credibility in the personnel files of police witnesses, investigative reports relating to previous complaints by the present complainant, and records of all police and prosecutorial transactions with any undercover agents involved.

(h) *Criminal records of the defendant, codefendants, and prosecution and defense witnesses.*

(i) *The grand jury transcript.* (A special shibboleth of secrecy has traditionally surrounded grand jury proceedings and made courts reluctant to disclose grand jury records. There has been some erosion of this protectionistic attitude, "consonant with the growing realization that disclosure, rather than suppression, of relevant materials ordinarily promotes the proper administration of criminal justice." *Dennis v. United States,* 384 U.S. 855, 870 (1966). *Compare id.* at 868-75 *with Pittsburgh Plate Glass Co. v. United States,* 360 U.S. 395 (1959), both dealing with the disclosure of the prior grand jury testimony of a government trial witness, after s/he has testified at trial, for purposes of impeachment — a subject discussed in paragraph [380] *infra* and now governed, in federal practice, by Federal Rule of Criminal Procedure 26.2(f)(3). Nevertheless, the notion is still rife that "the proper functioning of our grand jury system depends upon the secrecy of grand jury proceedings," *Douglas Oil Co. v. Petrol Stops Northwest,* 441 U.S. 211, 218 (1979); *see also United States v. Sells Engineering, Inc.,* 463 U.S. 418, 424 (1983), and *pretrial* discovery of the grand jury transcript remains difficult to obtain. In the federal courts, it is controlled by Federal Rule of Criminal Procedure (6)(e), and "[p]arties seeking grand jury transcripts under Rule 6(e) [which is made virtually the exclusive vehicle of pretrial disclosure by Federal Rule of Criminal Procedure 16(a)(3)] must show that the material they seek is needed to avoid a possible injustice in another judicial proceeding, that the need for disclosure is greater than the need for continued secrecy, and that their request is structured to cover only material so needed." *Douglas Oil Co. v. Petrol Stops Northwest, supra,* 441 U.S. at 222; *United States v. Sells Engineering, Inc., supra,* 463 U.S. at 443. [This "standard for determining when the traditional secrecy of the grand jury may be broken," 441 U.S. at 222, applies to Rule 6(e)(3)(C)(i), allowing disclosure when "directed by a court preliminarily to or in connection with a judicial proceeding" (*see United States v. Baggot,* 463 U.S. 476 (1983)). In addition, Rule 6(e)(3)(C)(ii) authorizes federal courts to permit disclosure "at the request of the defendant, upon a showing that grounds may exist for a motion to dismiss the indictment because of matters occurring before the grand jury," see paragraph [161](A), (B) *supra.*] Most state courts also continue to deny or severely restrict pretrial disclosure of grand jury materials to the defense, *e.g., Proskin v. County Court,* 30 N.Y.2d 15, 280 N.E.2d 875, 330 N.Y.S.2d 44 (1972), although a few states allow it more freely, *see, e.g., State v. Faux,* 9 Utah 2d 350, 345 P.2d 186 (1959). *Cf.* paragraph [270](H) *supra.*

(j) *Photographs and other visual aids shown to witnesses by investigating officers for purposes of identification.* (*See Simmons v. United States,* 390 U.S. 377, 388 (1968) (dictum).)

(4) *Motions for medical or psychiatric examination of complainants and prosecution witnesses.*

(5) *Motions for disclosure of the names and whereabouts of complainants, prosecution witnesses, and undercover agents; motions for*

orders that such persons who are in the custody or control of the prosecution be made available for interviewing by the defense (cf. United States v. Valenzuela-Bernal, 458 U.S. 858, 870 (1982); *motions for the detention of such persons as material witnesses* (see paragraphs [273], [284] *infra*); *motions for orders that police witnesses talk to the defense* (see paragraph [116] *supra*).

(6) *Motions for transcription of any untranscribed prior proceedings in the case.* (See paragraph [266] *supra.*)

(7) *Motions for disclosure of records kept, or investigations conducted, by the prosecution relating to prospective jurors.* (See paragraph [325] *infra.*)

If the defendant is indigent, it will often be appropriate to couple these discovery procedures with a motion for state-paid investigative assistance. See the following subparagraph and paragraphs [298]-[301] *infra.*

(B) Obviously, counsel should choose among the foregoing discovery devices those best suited to the needs of the particular case that are recognized by the local law or practice of the jurisdiction. In view of the increasing liberality of the common law of criminal discovery in recent years (see paragraph [265] *supra*), counsel should not hesitate to request previously unrecognized forms of discovery insofar as s/he needs them, couching such requests in the forms suggested by paragraph [268] *supra* and supporting them with the argument sketched in paragraph [269] *supra.* If local law is unduly regressive, counsel may invoke any of the federal constitutional rights described in paragraph [270] *supra* that appear relevant to particular discovery requests. But counsel should not be overly optimistic about prevailing on constitutional grounds. No general federal constitutional rights to pretrial discovery, as such, have yet been authoritatively recognized; and it seems that very strong factual showings of need in particular cases are going to be required before the courts will compel criminal discovery on constitutional grounds. *See United States v. Augenblick,* 393 U.S. 348 (1969); *Wardius v. Oregon,* 412 U.S. 470, 474 (1973) ("the Due Process Clause has little to say regarding the amount of discovery which the parties must be afforded, but cf. *Brady v. Maryland,* 373 U.S. 83 (1963) . . ."); *United States v. Agurs,* 427 U.S. 97, 103-12 (1976); *Weatherford v. Bursey,* 429 U.S. 545, 559-60 (1977); *United States v. Bagley,* 473

U.S. 667, 675 (1985) ("the prosecutor is not required to deliver his [or her] entire file to defense counsel, but only to disclose evidence favorable to the accused that, if suppressed, would deprive the defendant of a fair trial"); *Pennsylvania v. Ritchie,* 107 S. Ct. 989, 1002-3 (1987). Nevertheless, when counsel is hurting badly for want of discovery and when litigation of discovery issues is not otherwise ill-advised (because, for example, of the pretrial delay or the irritation of the prosecutor or the judge that it may entail), a powerful constitutional case for discovery can be mounted in the following fashion:

> Prior to trial, counsel should file requests or motions for *all* the forms of discovery enumerated in subparagraph (A) *supra* that are related to any evidence that the prosecution might have, basing each motion upon the federal constitutional grounds relevant to it (and if the defendant is indigent, adding a motion for state-paid assistance). If these motions are denied, counsel should renew them all at the beginning of the trial, basing them upon all of the previously asserted constitutional grounds and representing to the court that—because the defense has been denied any opportunity for investigation and preparation to meet the prosecution's charges—counsel feels that s/he is not adequately prepared to conduct the defense. Assuming that these motions are also overruled, counsel should, at the close of testimony of each critical prosecution witness, move for a mistrial or, in the alternative, a continuance, on the ground that the witness's testimony comes as a surprise to counsel and that s/he needs time (and whatever further discovery seems appropriate) to investigate and prepare to meet it. These motions, in turn, should be renewed at the close of the prosecution's entire case, on the ground that counsel and the defendant have been totally deprived of a fair opportunity to defend, in violation of all the constitutional guarantees enumerated in paragraph [270] *supra.* At this juncture counsel has the best possible record on which to obtain a mistrial, or the reversal of an ensuing conviction on appeal, by reason of federal constitutional rights to discovery. See also paragraph [300] *infra.*

(C) In many localities where the law authorizes criminal defendants to apply for court-ordered discovery through one or more of the devices mentioned in subparagraph (A) *supra,* a practice of "informal discovery" has grown up to supplement the formal motions procedure. Defense counsel writes the prosecutor a letter — or, in some localities, phones the prosecutor's office or meets with the prosecuting attorney at an informal "discovery conference" — and requests disclosure or production of whatever defense counsel wants. The prosecutor hands over as much as s/he is willing to deliver without a court order; then, if this does not satisfy defense counsel, defense counsel files a motion requesting the court to order additional items produced.

(1) Where this practice exists, counsel should ordinarily use it before resorting to the court. Informal discovery is relatively fast and effortless; in addition, its use is advisable for the reason noted in paragraph [268](A) *supra* and because prosecutors are sometimes willing, in particular cases, to turn over voluntarily materials that a court would not order them to produce.

(2) Counsel can avoid duplication of effort by writing the "informal discovery" letter so that it describes the items sought in the same form in which s/he would describe them in a formal motion. (See paragraph [268](B) *supra.*) Then, if a motion proves to be necessary, s/he can make it a simple, one-page document, attaching the informal discovery letter (or, if the prosecutor has voluntarily produced some of the items listed in it, a modified version which omits those items), alleging that the prosecutor has been asked to produce the items listed in the exhibit and has refused to do so, and requesting that the court order him or her to produce the listed items. This technique should not be used if the prosecutor is known or reputed to be more liberal in responding to informal discovery requests made in a casual or apparently off-the-cuff style than in responding to meticulously detailed, imposing-looking requests. Counsel should ask knowledgeable local defense attorneys the prosecutor's attitude in this regard.

(3) In localities where there is a public defender office, private defense counsel will also find it useful to ask someone in that office whether it uses a standard-form inter-office memo to the prosecutor's office for the purpose of requesting informal discovery and, if

so, to get a copy of the form to use as a starting point in drafting his or her own informal discovery letter. Public defender's office forms often have exhaustive checklists of the major categories of items that the defense will want to discover. They should not be slavishly copied without regard to the needs of counsel's particular case, but the use of their language where it does fit counsel's needs can strike a responsive chord in a busy prosecuting attorney who is accustomed to granting discovery requests couched in that language.

[272] Defensive discovery at trial. Defensive discovery at trial principally seeks material, not previously made available, that would be useful in the impeachment of prosecution witnesses. Counsel should request:

(A) *All prior statements made by the witness to the police, prosecutor, or other government agents.* [Paragraph [380] *infra.*]

(B) *The grand jury minutes of the witness's testimony.* [Paragraph [380] *infra.*]

(C) *The witness's criminal record and any other material known to the prosecutor that would be admissible under local practice to impeach the witness.* [Paragraph [270](E) *supra.*]

(D) *All photographs and other visual aids shown by investigating officers, at any time, to a witness who has purported to identify the defendant.* (The denial of discovery of such materials in the *Simmons* case, paragraph [271](A)(3)(j) *supra,* was rested upon exceedingly narrow grounds that careful planning by defense counsel can avoid.)

[273] Disclosure of the identity of government informers. (A) The courts have recognized an "informer's privilege" which empowers the government to conceal the name of a confidential source of information, upon a claim of the privilege by government counsel and a representation that disclosure would endanger the government's interests. In *Rovario v. United States,* 353 U.S. 53 (1957), the Supreme Court discussed the applicability of the privilege to block a criminal defendant's request for the name of an informer who appeared, from the trial testimony, to have been a central figure in the narcotics transactions with which the defendant was charged. The Court there required disclosure of the name, concluding "that no fixed rule with respect to disclosure is justifiable. The problem is one that calls for balancing the public interest in protecting the flow of information against the individual's right to prepare his defense. Whether a proper balance renders nondisclosure erroneous must depend on the particular circumstances of each case, taking into consideration the crime charged, the possible defenses, the possible significance of the informer's testimony, and other relevant factors." *Id.* at 62. *See also United States v. Valenzuela-Bernal,* 458 U.S. 858, 870-71 (1982) (dictum). Following *dicta* in *Rovario,* the lower federal courts and some state courts allowed *pretrial* disclosure of the informer's name, in connection with a motion to suppress evidence challenged as the product of an unconstitutional search and seizure, whenever the information provided by the informer was necessary to make out the probable cause upon which the prosecution relied (see paragraph [241] *supra*) to validate a search and seizure without a warrant. *E.g., United States v. Robinson,* 325 F.2d 391 (2d Cir. 1963). (In warrant cases, the informer's name was denied, apparently on the ground that review of the issuance of a warrant was limited to the record before the magistrate, and if the magistrate had not seen fit to demand the informer's name, a reviewing court need not. This notion predated *Franks v. Delaware,* 438 U.S. 154 (1978), described in paragraph [241](B)(2)(b) *supra,* and must now be adjusted to *Frank's* rules governing the impeachment of warrant affidavits. See particularly 438 U.S. at 170.) However, the refusal of a state court, at a pretrial hearing on a motion to suppress, to disclose the name of an informer whose information was used to support a warrantless arrest and an incidental seizure was sustained by the Supreme Court in *McCray v. Illinois,* 386 U.S. 300 (1967). *See also United States v. Raddatz,* 447 U.S. 667, 679 (1980) (dictum). *McCray,* a somewhat diffuse opinion, does not make clear exactly how much of *Rovario* it retracts. The cases are distinguishable in that (a) *McCray* was a state case, *Roviaro* a federal one (*but see United States v. Matlock,* 415 U.S. 164, 174-75 (1974) (dictum); *Franks v. Delaware, supra,* 438 U.S. at 167 (dictum)); (b) *McCray* involved a pretrial request for disclosure of the informer's name, *Rovario* a request at trial; (c) *McCray* involved an informer whose information was pertinent only to a search-and-seizure issue, *Rovario* an informer who had information bearing on guilt or innocence. Whether some or all of these factors are dispositive of *McCray* remains uncertain. Moreover, it is arguable that *McCray* would not bar the disclosure of an informer's name, at least in the discretion of the court, even at a federal suppression hearing when the informer's tip appears from the testimony of the officers who relied upon it to have been equivocal or marginally credible or when the officers' own credibility is called into serious question: "*McCray* . . . concluded only that the Due Process Clause of the Fourteenth Amendment did not require the State to expose an informant's identity routinely, upon a defendant's mere demand, when there was ample evidence in the probable-cause hearing to show that the informant was reliable and his information credible." *Franks v. Delaware, supra,* 438 U.S. at 170. So, for the present, defense counsel would be warranted in continuing to press for the disclosure of informers' names, both before and at trial, as defensive needs dictate. Of course, the attempt should be made to assimilate the case as much to *Rovario,* and to distance it as far from *McCray,* as possible. If an informer's identity is needed both to challenge a search and seizure, for example, and to defend on the guilt issue, a pretrial discovery motion should be rested principally on the latter need.

(B) Note that the informer's privilege is not a blanket prohibition of inquiry regarding informants' identities: it *is* an evidentiary privilege, which must be claimed and justified by the government. The privilege does not protect "the contents of a communication [when these] will not tend to reveal the identity of an informer"; nor does it protect the informer at all "once . . . [his or her] identity . . . has been [otherwise] disclosed to those who would have cause to resent the communication." *Rovario v. United States,* subparagraph (A) *supra,* 353 U.S. at 60 (dictum). Its purpose is to prevent the improvident unmasking of government undercover agents. *Cf. Weatherford v. Bursey,* 429 U.S. 545, 557-60 (1977). Nothing in the privilege, therefore, precludes inquiry into such matters as a confidential informant's batting average (see paragraph [241](B)(4)(d) *supra*) or the terms of the informant's compensation by the government or the informant's own guilt of criminal offenses or the promises of immunity made to the informant to induce him or her to inform. Nor, once an informant is known, does the privilege authorize the government to shield that informant from being interviewed by the defense. When counsel ascertains an informant's identity and finds that s/he is evading efforts by the defense to contact or to interview him or her or when it otherwise appears that s/he may vanish before trial, counsel should not hesitate to seek his or her arrest as a material witness. See paragraph [284] *infra*. Police spies, "special agents," and undercover informers often are criminals cooperating with the government in return for nonprosecution; in drug cases they are usually addicts; they are exceedingly unstable and likely to disappear without a trace; and the government cannot be relied upon to keep track of their whereabouts. If defense counsel wants to be assured that they will be around at the time of trial, s/he may have no option but to use material-witness procedures to have them jailed. *Cf.* paragraph [289] *infra*. In federal practice the deposition procedure authorized by Federal Rule of Criminal Procedure 15(a) is a useful alternative or adjunct to a motion to detain a slippery informer as a material witness.

[273-A] **Work product.** *Dictum* in *United States v. Nobles*, 422 U.S. 225, 236 (1975), indicates that the "work product" doctrine recognized as a limitation upon civil discovery in *Hickman v. Taylor*, 329 U.S. 495 (1947), also applies to both the pretrial and trial stages of federal criminal cases and protects materials that reveal "the mental processes of the attorney," 422 U.S. at 238, for the prosecution as well as the defense, *see id.* at 238 & n.12; *cf. United States v. Valenzuela-Bernal*, 458 U.S. 858, 862 n.3 (1982). (However, *Goldberg v. United States*, 425 U.S. 94, 101-8 (1976), establishes that "work product" protection does not bar production at trial of prior statements of government witnesses which are "otherwise producible under the Jencks Act" (*id.* at 108) mentioned in paragraph [380] *infra*.) The contours of the "work product" doctrine are explored in the *Hickman* opinion and in *Upjohn Co. v. United States*, 449 U.S. 383, 397-402 (1981). Whether such a limitation of defense discovery is recognized in state criminal cases is, of course, in the first instance a matter of local law. But local law cannot extend "work product" protection to materials that are constitutionally required to be disclosed to the defense under the any of the principles catalogued in paragraph [270] *supra, see Davis v. Alaska,* 415 U.S. 308 (1974); and the passing reference to prosecutorial "work product" protection in *Nobles* does not purport to qualify, for example, the consistent line of Due Process holdings that the prosecution must disclose exculpatory materials (see paragraph [270](G) *supra*) and such impeaching information as the existence of promises made by the prosecutor to prosecution witnesses (see paragraph [270](E) *supra;* paragraph [372] *infra*), whether or not those items could be considered "work product."

[273-B] Other claims of governmental privilege. It is not uncommon for prosecutors to "stonewall" defense discovery requests by broad claims of some unspecified privilege to protect "governmental secrets" or "government operations" or the "confidential relations" of government employees. If any privilege of this sort is recognized beyond the scope of the informer's privilege (paragraph [273] *supra*) and the attorney's work product doctrine (paragraph [273-A] *supra*), it is extremely narrow, *see, e.g., United States v. Nixon,* 418 U.S. 683 (1974); *Kerr v. United States District Court,* 426 U.S. 394 (1976), and is arguably altogether inapplicable in criminal prosecutions because "it is unconscionable to allow [a government] . . . to undertake prosecution and then invoke its governmental privileges to deprive the accused of anything which might be material to his defense." *United States v. Reynolds,* 345 U.S. 1, 12 (1953) (dictum).

[274] Discovery by the prosecution against the defense. (A) Except for statutes requiring notice of the defenses of alibi and insanity (paragraph [193](G), (H) *supra*), many jurisdictions make no provision for discovery in favor of the prosecution. Indeed, it has been traditionally supposed that discovery by a prosecutor in a criminal case would constitute a plain violation of the privilege against self-incrimination. In *Jones v. Superior Court,* 58 Cal. 2d 56, 372 P.2d 919, 22 Cal. Rptr. 879 (1962), the California Supreme Court overrode the claim of privilege concerning matters that the defendant was planning to introduce at trial (although sustaining it as to other matters) and compelled a defendant to produce to the prosecutor certain medical reports, X-rays, and the names of medical witnesses, to the extent that the defendant was going to use them in evidence. The theory of the decision was that the defendant would produce these matters at the trial in any event and the privilege is not violated by merely advancing the *time* of the production. The Supreme Court of the United States employed essentially the same theory to sustain an alibi-notice requirement in *Williams v. Florida,* 399 U.S. 78 (1970), paragraph [193](H) *supra;* and, in the wake of *Williams,* quite a number of states have begun to provide new forms of prosecutorial discovery by statute or court rule.

(B) In the absence of an applicable statute or rule, defense counsel should oppose any discovery motions by the prosecution, on the ground that such a radical change in criminal procedure is a matter for the legislature and should not be ordered by a court without express legislative authorization. It is one thing for the judiciary to institute criminal discovery procedures in favor of the defendant, inasmuch as these procedures tend to promote constitutional values that are particularly committed to the care of courts (see paragraph [270] *supra; and see Jencks v. United States,* 353 U.S. 657 (1957)); it is quite another thing to institute unprecedented procedures in favor of the prosecution — procedures that often raise close constitutional questions (*see* Mosteller, *Discovery Against the Defense: Tilting the Adversarial Balance,* 74 CALIF. L. REV. 1567 (1986)) and that prosecutors (unlike criminal defendants) surely have the power to obtain from the legislature if the legislature deems those procedures advisable. *Cf. United States v. LaSalle National Bank,* 437 U.S. 298, 312-13 (1978) (dictum); paragraph [163](D) *supra.*

(C) Even when discovery by the prosecutor is legislatively authorized, it is "limited . . . by . . . constitutional privileges." *Standefer v. United States,* 447 U.S. 10, 22 (1980) (dictum).

(1) Under the theory of *Jones* and *Williams,* subparagraph (A) *supra,* prosecutorial discovery is limited specifically to material that the defendant intends to produce at trial. Compelled disclosure of any matter that the defendant does not intend to produce at trial arguably violates the Fifth Amendment. *See Prudhomme v. Superior Court,* 2 Cal. 3d 320, 466 P.2d 673, 85 Cal. Rptr. 129 (1970).

(a) This is clearly established with regard to any information or material of a "testimonial" character (see paragraph

[232](B)(3), (C) *supra*) that is obtained from the defendant personally. *Boyd v. United States,* 116 U.S. 616 (1886); *cf. New Jersey v. Portash,* 440 U.S. 450, 459 (1979); *Estelle v. Smith,* 451 U.S. 454, 463-66 (1981).

(b) However, with regard to preexisting writings the *Boyd* decision was severely limited by *Fisher v. United States,* 425 U.S. 391 (1976), holding that the Fifth Amendment does not forbid compulsory process ordering the production of documents written by a third party that incriminate the person ordered to produce them. *Fisher* further says in *dictum* (*id.* at 410 n.11) that the Fifth Amendment would not forbid compulsion of an individual to produce his or her own previously made, incriminating writings, unless either (1) the writings are the individual's "private papers," or (2) the act of producing them (as distinguished from their contents) is incriminating. In *United States v. Doe,* 465 U.S. 605 (1984), the Court extended *Fisher* to deny Fifth Amendment protection to "the contents of an individual's tax records in his [or her] possession," 465 U.S. at 610, but reiterated that even though "the contents of a document may not be privileged, the act of producing the document may be," *id.* at 612. The effect of these decisions is:

(i) generally to foreclose Fifth Amendment objections to the compelled production of existing documents and other physical objects on the sole ground that their content or nature is incriminating;

(ii) to leave open the possibility of Fifth Amendment objections to the compelled production of some sorts of "private papers" that are more intensely personal than tax or other "business records," *id.* at 609, on the ground that their content or nature is incriminating; and

(iii) to support Fifth Amendment objections to the compelled production of documents or objects whenever the act of production itself could be incriminating because it would provide the prosecution with evidence of the defendant's possession of documents or objects, or of their existence, or of their authenticity (or identity), unless "possession, existence, and authentication [are] . . . a 'foregone conclusion,'" *id.* at 614 n.13; see paragraph [163](B) *supra,* or would in any other way furnish a link in the chain of evidence, or investigative leads to evidence, that could be used against the defendant, see paragraphs [161](E), [232](B) *supra.*

(c) Similarly, the compulsory disclosure to the prosecution of information obtained by defense counsel from third parties whose identities or connections with the case could lead the prosecution to incriminating evidence should be forbidden. Whatever the original source of that information may have been, it is now being sought from the defendant through legal process addressed to the defendant (*compare United States v. Miller,* 425 U.S. 435 (1976), and *Andresen v. Maryland,* 427 U.S. 463 (1976), discussed in paragraph [163](B); and see paragraph [232](B)(2) *supra*), for possible use by the prosecutor in prosecuting the defendant, and it thus satisfies all of the requisites for Fifth Amendment protection. See paragraph [232] *supra.*

(d) Admittedly, *United States v. Nobles,* 422 U.S. 225 (1975), described in paragraph [408-A] *infra,* appears to hold that the Fifth Amendment privilege does not cover records of defense interviews with persons other than the defendant, at least when those persons are independently available to the prosecution. But *Nobles* was a case involving the prosecution's power to get discovery of portions of a defense investigator's report after (i) the prosecution had concluded its case in chief at trial and (ii) the defendant had called the investigator to testify concerning interviews with prosecution witnesses. *See Corbitt v. New Jersey,* 439 U.S. 212, 219 n.8 (1978). In this situation, the defense has voluntarily presented evidence about a set of facts; its evidence indicates that the underlying facts are not only already known to the prosecution but also have already been the subject of testimony by prosecution witnesses; disclosure of the evidence would not lead the prosecution to any additional witnesses or independent evidence bearing upon the underlying facts; and the defendant's Fifth Amendment claim is therefore necessarily limited to a contention that a particular recorded version of those facts is privileged merely because it was made by an agent of the defense other than the defendant. *Nobles'* rejection of that contention does not imply that a defendant can be compelled by court order to come forward with information collected by his or her agents from third parties and useful by the prosecutor to incriminate the defendant, *unless and until* s/he has voluntarily elected to produce that evidence at trial. This compulsion would affront the basic policy of the Self-Incrimination Clause that requires the prosecution "'to shoulder the entire load,'" *Miranda v. Arizona,* 384 U.S. 436, 460 (1966); *compare Andresen v. Maryland, supra,* 427 U.S. at 475-76 & n.8.

(2) Counsel should therefore resist, on Fifth Amendment grounds, the obligation to disclose anything at all before s/he has had an opportunity to investigate and prepare the defense case. S/he should insist upon the right to defer decision concerning what s/he will present at trial until s/he has been given sufficient prior disclosure of the prosecutor's case (see paragraphs [256]-[271] *supra*) to enable counsel to make that decision intelligently. *Williams'* allowance of discovery by the prosecutor is qualified by *Wardius v. Oregon,* 412 U.S. 470 (1973), which holds specifically that Due Process "forbids enforcement of alibi [notice] rules unless reciprocal discovery rights are given to criminal defendants," *id.* at 472, and says more generally that "[t]he State may not insist that trials be run as a 'search for truth' so far as defense witnesses are concerned, while maintaining 'poker game' secrecy for its own witnesses," *id.* at 475. *Wardius* does not determine how much discovery must be made available to a defendant in order to justify any particular amount of discovery against that defendant. But the implications of *Brooks v. Tennessee,* 406 U.S. 605 (1972), are plain that no disclosure may be required of a defendant unless

(a) *prior* to the time when the defendant is asked to disclose,

(b) s/he is given enough of a preview of the prosecutor's case to make an advised and intelligent decision what, if any, defensive evidence s/he will present at trial.

Brooks invalidated a statute requiring that if a defendant was going to testify, s/he must testify before any other defense evidence was presented. That requirement was held to violate the Fifth Amendment on the ground that the constitutional privilege against self-incrimination forbids forcing the defense to decide whether or not to present the defendant's testimony before "its value can be realistically assessed," *id.* at 610. But surely, if a defendant cannot be compelled to decide whether to testify and to "subject himself [or herself] to impeachment and cross-examination at a time when the strength of *his [or her]* other evidence is not yet clear," *id.* at 612 (emphasis added), a defendant cannot be compelled to furnish the prosecution with information that may be used in any fashion to incriminate him or her—even merely by "focusing investigation on [the defendant] . . . as a result of his [or her] compelled disclosures," *Kastigar v. United States,* 406 U.S. 441, 460 (1972)—before the defendant has been sufficiently informed about the *prosecutor's* evidence to decide what defensive evidence will be "necessary or even helpful to his case," *Lakeside v. Oregon,* 435 U.S. 333, 339 n.9 (1978) (dictum). Under *Brooks,* such a requirement violates not merely the Fifth Amendment but also the Sixth Amendment right to counsel, "[b]y requiring the accused and his [or her] lawyer to make [an important tactical decision regarding the presentation of defensive evidence] . . . without an opportunity to evaluate the actual worth of their evidence." *Brooks v. Tennessee, supra,* 406 U.S. at 612. *See also Cuyler v. Sullivan,* 446 U.S. 335, 344 (1980) (dictum).

(D) Reference is made to the "work product" doctrine in paragraph [273-A] *supra.*

(1) As that paragraph notes, the question whether "work product" protection should or should not be extended to shield prosecutorial files from defensive discovery is initially a matter of state law. "Work product" protection of defense files against prosecutorial discovery, on the other hand, is arguably a federal constitutional requirement. This is so because the function of the "work product" doctrine is to provide "a privileged area within which [the attorney] . . . can analyze and prepare his [or her] client's case," *United States v. Nobles,* 422 U.S. 225, 238 (1975), in order to "assure the thorough preparation and presentation of . . . the case," *ibid.;* and the Sixth Amendment countenances "no restrictions upon the function of counsel in defending a criminal prosecution in accord with the traditions of the adversary factfinding process," *Herring v. New York,* 422 U.S. 853, 857 (1975). The *Nobles* case, subparagraph (C)(1)(d) *supra,* holds nothing to the contrary, although it does permit limited prosecutorial discovery of a defense investigator's report *after* the defendant has presented the investigator's testimony at trial and

thereby waived both the "work product" and Sixth Amendment protections. *See* 422 U.S. at 240 n.15; paragraph [408-A] *infra*.

(2) The "work product" doctrine is primarily designed to shield materials that reveal an attorney's analyses and assessments of the case, including evaluations of potential witnesses. For this reason, it is particularly protective of counsel's own notes of oral statements of witnesses, as distinguished from written or transcribed statements of witnesses or even defense investigator's reports reflecting the oral statements of witnesses. *See Upjohn Co. v. United States,* 449 U.S. 383, 399-402 (1981). Thus counsel may wish to increase the likelihood of avoiding prosecutorial discovery by taking oral instead of written statements from witnesses and by including appropriate evaluative matter in his or her notes of those statements. See paragraphs [81], [110] *supra*. Anything that discloses counsel's "litigating strategies [is not] . . . the subject of permissible inquiry by his [or her] opponent. . . ." *United States v. Valenzuela-Bernal,* 458 U.S. 858, 862 n.3 (1982) (dictum).

(E) It is a difficult question whether the Fifth Amendment forbids conditioning defense discovery upon reciprocal disclosures that, if ordered directly, would violate the privilege. (*See, e.g.,* the counterdiscovery provisions of FED. R. CRIM. P. 16(b).) Certainly, when the defendant has a constitutional right to discovery under any of the doctrines discussed in paragraph [270] *supra,* the defendant's enforcement of that right cannot be conditioned upon the waiver of another constitutional right, and the reciprocal disclosure requirement would seem to be invalid. *Cf. Simmons v. United States,* 390 U.S. 377, 389-94 (1968), and cases cited following *Simmons* in paragraph [180](E)(2)(a) *supra*. In other cases, however, it is likely that a requirement of reciprocation can be imposed and that the defense can be forced to choose between both giving and getting or neither.

(F) When discovery by the prosecution is allowed, defense counsel's failure to disclose items of evidence covered by a discovery request or order may result in the exclusion of those items at trial, at least in cases in which the failure is found to be willful. *Taylor v. Illinois,* 108 S. Ct. 646 (1988). However, the *Taylor* opinion suggests that the application of the exclusionary sanction can be challenged as "unnecessarily harsh" (*id.* at 656) and thereby violative of the defendant's Sixth Amendment right to compulsory process (see paragraph [270](D) *supra*) on the facts of any particular case. *See* 108 S. Ct. at 657 n.23. Unnecessarily rigid or sweeping preclusions of defense evidence are assailable under the Sixth Amendment because its guarantees of the right to present a defense to criminal charges are fundamental. *Rock v. Arkansas,* 107 S. Ct. 2704 (1987).

(G) If the prosecution's requests for pretrial discovery are granted or cannot be successfully opposed and if the defendant or the case is a subject of media attention or potential public interest, counsel should ask the court for a protective order forbidding the prosecutor to reveal to anyone before trial the contents or the nature of the information that the defense is disclosing in discovery. The order can be written with provisions (1) allowing the prosecution to reveal the information only to its investigators and prospective witnesses, to the extent necessary in preparing its case for trial; (2) requiring the prosecuting attorney to deliver a copy of the protective order to each investigator or witness to whom s/he reveals the information, and (3) forbidding each such investigator or prospective witness from revealing the information to anyone else. (If the court can be persuaded to make it, an even better form of order would require the prosecuting attorney to obtain specific authorization from the court, at a hearing with notice to defense counsel, before disclosing the information to any particular investigator or prospective witness.) Protective orders limiting the prosecutor's dissemination of information received from the defense by discovery are more likely to be granted than general "gag" orders prohibiting the prosecutor from publicly revealing information about the case that s/he has received from nondefense sources, because the narrower sort of order invokes "the duty and discretion of [the] . . . trial court to oversee the discovery process." *Seattle Times Co. v. Rhinehart,* 467 U.S. 20, 31 (1984). Defense counsel can, of course, simultaneously oppose prosecutorial discovery requests and move in the alternative for a protective order. But it is preferable to oppose the requests first and to seek a protective order only if and when the court overrules counsel's objections to prosecutorial discovery, unless local practice or the judge's temperament makes it predictable that this two-step process will strain the judge's patience.

[275] The pretrial conference. (A) In most cases, it is customary for the court, the prosecutor, and the defense lawyer to confer briefly at sidebar immediately prior to the commencement of trial, to review the status of pretrial matters (for example, to assure that all the necessary procedural steps required to bring the defendant to trial have been taken; to assure that all pending motions that should be disposed of before trial have been disposed of); to estimate the probable length of trial and to plan convenient recesses; to make special arrangements for the appearance of particular witnesses when appropriate (for example, to schedule an expert witness's appearance to accommodate his or her other commitments); to discuss any problems occasioned by the failure of witnesses to appear; and sometimes to attempt to expedite matters by stipulations.

(B) In protracted cases in some jurisdictions, an earlier and more formal pretrial conference is held, ordinarily in chambers, to define issues, stipulate to the qualifications of experts, stipulate to the admission of certain items of evidence or to some of the technical predicates for their admissibility in order to dispense with time-wasting foundation testimony, and generally for the same purposes as a pretrial conference in a civil case (not excluding, with some judges, settlement negotiations, see paragraphs [206]-[219] *supra*)—that is, to look for means to make the presentation and disposition of the case more efficient by agreement of the parties upon matters of procedure. At the close of the conference the judge may enter a pretrial order embodying the agreements reached. (In federal practice *see* FED. R. CRIM. P. 17.1. Several states have similar rules.)

(C) Counsel may be well advised to request such a pretrial conference if one is not routinely held. Its utility should be considered for the following purposes, among others:

(1) *To attempt to enlist some judicial support if counsel feels that the prosecutor is taking an unreasonable position in pressing certain charges which should be dropped* (see paragraphs [99]-[103], [150] *supra*); *or that the prosecutor is taking an unreasonable position in plea negotiations* (see paragraphs [206]-[219] *supra*); *or to "try out" an agreed sentenc-*

ing recommendation on the judge (see paragraph[211] *supra*). Judges differ considerably on whether they will involve themselves in plea negotiation and what they regard as a reasonable disposition of particular kinds of cases. Counsel must therefore know or inquire about the attitudes of the presiding judge before deciding whether to bring up these subjects.

(2) *To arrange informally to speed up or slow down the pace of pretrial proceedings and advance or delay the trial date.* [See paragraphs [302]-[311] *infra*]

(3) *To anticipate evidentiary problems that will arise at trial and attempt to resolve them.* Particularly important may be the opportunity to alert the judge and prosecutor to defense objections to expected lines or items of prosecutive evidence at trial and to arrange (1) that the prosecutor not mention these items in his or her opening statement (see paragraph [350] *infra*) and (2) that the prosecutor's examination be conducted in a fashion that will permit both a defense objection and a ruling on it prior to the time when matters have been disclosed to the jury that may cause prejudice and may therefore require a mistrial if the defense objection is sustained (see paragraphs [359], [414] *infra*). Counsel may want to suggest that the prosecutor forgo offering items of evidence that will create problems of admissibility or prejudice at a joint trial, so that, if the prosecutor insists on presenting these items, counsel can request a severance (see paragraphs [259]-[264] *infra*). Counsel may want to propose, in a jurisdiction where the normal procedure for litigating the admissibility of a defendant's confession is upon objection at the time of trial (see paragraphs [224] *supra* and [363]-[367] *infra*), that a pretrial hearing be conducted on the issue instead, in order to prevent prolonged interruption of a jury trial and avert the risk that the jury will learn of a confession that is ultimately excluded. *Cf.* paragraph [222](D) *supra*.

(4) *To arrange to stipulate certain matters, in the interest of trial convenience* (for example, see paragraphs [357], [398] *infra*), *and to put certain sorts of exhibits into safe and unexceptionable form* (for example, see paragraph [369] *infra*).

(5) *To obtain agreement that certain witnesses need not be subpoenaed by either party and that neither will request or be entitled to a missing witness charge as a result.* (See paragraphs [288]-[289] *infra*.) Coun-

sel may also want to seek other agreements or advance judicial rulings regarding matters that will determine whether s/he is going to call particular witnesses: for example, rulings on whether certain convictions or arrests may be used by the prosecutor in cross-examining character witnesses (see paragraph [222](D) *supra;* paragraphs [403]-[405] *infra*).

(6) *To discover what can be discovered of the prosecutor's case through discussion of the foregoing and similar matters.*

(7) *To impress the judge.* A pretrial conference offers an excellent opportunity for defense counsel to become known to the judge, who ordinarily will already be familiar with the prosecutor. If counsel's learning, preparation, and reasoned judgment make a good impression, the judge may be more receptive to counsel's positions on questions that arise at trial than if counsel were entirely unknown.

(8) *To get a sense of the judge's attitude toward the case.* Counsel will want to learn, if s/he can, both how the judge is likely to react to certain kinds of evidentiary issues at trial (for example, whether the judge is disposed to exercise liberally or sparingly the court's discretion to exclude prejudicial matter, see paragraph [356] *infra;* whether the judge is likely to respond favorably to a highly technical hearsay argument) and how the judge is likely to react to the case and to the defendant at sentencing in the event of conviction. The answer to the latter questions may well cause counsel to decide that a jury waiver or even a guilty plea is advised rather than a trial before this judge. (See paragraphs [217]-[218] *supra.*)

[276] Memorializing the pretrial conference. If the judge who conducts the pretrial conference drafts an order purporting to record agreements and dispositions reached at the conference, counsel should give it careful study upon its receipt and immediately call to the judge's attention any point on which counsel's recollection differs from the judge's or anything to which counsel objects. If the judge does not draft an order, counsel should make his or her own file memorandum memorializing the conference. If agreements reached there include important matters on which s/he intends to rely, s/he may want to embody them in a proposed pretrial order for the judge's signature; or s/he may want to embody them in a letter of "understanding" to the judge, of which a copy should be sent to the prosecutor and another filed. In this fashion, counsel will be able to document the legitimacy of any complaints s/he may have in the unhappily common event that the court or the prosecution breaches an agreed course of conduct at trial.

XIX. DEFENSE TRIAL PREPARATION

[277] **Preparation and organization.** Defense trial preparation culminates in the selection of witnesses and evidence that will be presented at trial. Counsel must be wide ranging in the search for sources of proof but must be highly selective in what s/he actually puts on at the trial. It is vital that s/he have an integrated theory of defense and that the evidence be tightly organized so that the defense theory will come across clearly in a cohesive trial presentation.

[278] **Selection of witnesses.** Obviously, the principal criterion in selecting or rejecting witnesses for trial is whether a witness has something to say that materially supports the theory of the defense. But a second criterion, only slightly less important, is whether the witness will improve or depreciate the *atmosphere* of the defense. To some extent, a defendant is identified with his or her witnesses by jurors and judges. The witness is testifying *for* the defendant, and jurors especially tend to interpret that fact as signifying that in some manner the witness is vouching for the defendant. This makes the demeanor of defense witness critical — their apparent honesty, sound judgement, equanimity, and likeableness. A personable witness might be called to testify cumulatively on a minor point, whereas a shifty or abrasive witness would not be similarly used. Counsel should never put a witness on the stand without knowing whether the witness has a criminal record and without having evaluated the possible prejudice to the defense if it is used to impeach the witness. See paragraphs [381]-[382], [390](F) *infra*. Every prospective witness must therefore be asked whether s/he has ever been charged with any criminal offense and what was the disposition of the charge. To make the investigation complete and the inquiry as little embarrassing as possible, counsel should ask about "any sort of criminal charge, big or little, including traffic violations and that sort of thing"; s/he can further ease the witness's embarrassment by explaining that s/he always asks this question "because lots of people have some sort of criminal charge made against them at some time." *After* counsel has ob-

243

tained the witness's complete record, s/he can explain (if this is the case under local practice) that traffic offenses and other minor convictions cannot be used in court to impeach the witness.

[279] Preparing witnesses to testify. The technique of preparing a witness to testify is different from that of interviewing a witness to discover facts. Whereas investigative interviews involve striking up a congenial relationship and encouraging expansiveness that produces free-roaming narration by the witness, trial preparation focuses on what specific pertinent testimony the witness has to offer and on how to present it most effectively.

(A) Counsel should review the facts previously ascertained from this witness and others, point out any discrepancies or unclarities, and have the witness resolve them to the extent that they are truthfully resolvable. (It is not necessary, or even desirable, that all defense witnesses come into trial with the same "pat" story; but no defense witness should be permitted to testify without awareness of the points at which his or her testimony diverges from that of other known witnesses or without a plausible explanation for the divergence.) Counsel should explain the general theory of the defense to each witness and demonstrate the witness's role and exact place in this defense. Trial procedures, including the purpose and method of direct, cross and redirect examination, and objections, should also be explained. The atmosphere of court must be made as familiar as possible so that the witness will be at ease when s/he arrives for the trial. Indeed, with a particularly important and nervous defense witness, it may be wise for counsel to take the witness to observe the examinations of witnesses in another trial.

(B) The witness should be instructed (1) not to answer any question unless s/he understands it but simply to say that s/he does not understand the question if s/he does not (many witnesses do not realize that this is appropriate or even permissible behavior in court) and (2) to give answers that are true to the best of the witness's knowledge rather than trying to guess and say what would be a favorable answer from the defense standpoint. The importance of the overall impression created by the witness's conduct in the courtroom (both on the stand and off) should be mentioned, and counsel should discuss with the witness how the witness can make the best impression. (This may be different for different witnesses. In some cases, it is desirable for the witness to appear serious and businesslike; in some cases, relaxed and easy-going; in some cases, nervous or upset. Counsel cannot ethically or practically teach a witness to act in ways that dissimulate but can and should assist the witness to perceive and control aspects of the witness's demeanor that may convey undesired messages.) It is ordinarily wise for counsel to suggest to the witness how s/he should dress for court and, if practicable, to ask the witness to come to a pretrial interview dressed as s/he will dress when s/he testifies. (Admonitions to some witnesses to "dress well" or "dress casually" will produce results that will amaze — and horrify — counsel; it is best for counsel to see in advance what the witness thinks these admonitions mean.)

(C) Counsel should ordinarily engage every witness in a thorough "dry run" of direct, cross, and redirect examination, asking every question that counsel intends to ask in court and foresees that the cross-examiner may ask. If counsel's questions are not bringing out the desired answers, they should be changed and that portion of the examination should be rerun until both counsel and the witness are satisfied with it. Counsel will often find it useful to ask for the witness's help in framing questions best suited to elicit the witness's story or particular details of it that counsel has noted in earlier investigative interviewing:

Last time we talked you said _____. That seemed to me to be something that the court will want to hear. Now I am trying to get the right question to ask you, so that in your answer you will say it pretty much the same way you said it in our last interview. Would it be better if I asked _____ [suggesting one form of question] or if I asked _____ [suggesting another form of question]? Or maybe you can suggest a way to ask it that will be sure to bring out the information we want.

In this process, counsel may have to explain to the witness — without confusing technicalities and legal jargon — some of the constraints imposed by the rules of evidence upon counsel's questioning.

I can't just call you to the witness stand and say, "Okay, go ahead and tell your story." It's got to be a back-and-forth thing, in which I ask you particular questions, and you give the answers.

There are certain legal rules about the questions I can ask. For example, I can't do what lawyers call "leading a witness," which means putting words into the witness's mouth by stating in my question the exact thing that I know from talking with you is going to be your answer. You've told me that it was very dark out that evening. I can't ask you in court, "Was it very dark out?" and simply have you say "Yes." I've got to ask you something like, "Would you please describe the lighting conditions," and then *you* have to say, "It was very dark out," if it was.

You see what I mean? My questions can direct you to the subject that I am asking about, but you have to be the one who fills in the details by your answer. So, if there are important details, you must be the one who remembers them and says them, and I must find the right questions.

Also I have to ask the questions in a certain logical order. I can't ask, "What time did Joe arrive at the drive-in?" before you have first testified that Joe *did* come to the drive-in that evening. Lawyers would call that question "assuming a fact not in evidence," and the judge would not let it be asked until I had first asked some question that caused you to tell the court that Joe did come to the drive-in.

Now, going back to the beginning of the evening, let me try out a line of questions. After you have answered them we can go over the answers and see if everything has been brought out, and maybe we can improve the questions so as to be sure that they will bring everything out completely.

(D) Optimal predictability in getting the answers that counsel wants is usually obtained by making the conditions in the "dry run" as similar as possible to those that will exist in the courtroom.

(1) The sequence of the questioning should be the same; and once counsel has worked out questions that produce the desired result, s/he should stick closely to them in form and language. If alternative possible forms have been tried out, both counsel and the witness should be clear at the end of the "dry run" which questions will be asked in court and which will not.

(2) In important areas of the witness's testimony, single questions should not be asked in isolation; sizeable blocks of questions and answers should be run—and rerun as often as necessary—so that each question will be asked in the "dry run" against the same background that will frame it when it is later asked in court.

(3) To avoid confusion and to maximize the similarity between the "dry run" and the courtroom examination, counsel will find it useful to conduct the "dry run" itself with counsel standing and facing the witness, or at least sitting face-to-face with the witness some distance apart. When breaks are made in the "dry run" to discuss the questions and answers, to work on reformulations of questions, or to conduct follow-up investigative questioning that will not be used in court, counsel should change his or her physical position—for example, by coming over and sitting down beside the witness—so that the demarcation between the questioning that will occur in court and all the other conversation in the preparatory interview will be sharp and clear.

If the witness is left confused and thinks that counsel intends to ask in court certain questions that counsel actually meant to ask in the preparatory interview only for his or her information, or as try-outs that counsel then rejects as unsatisfactory, trouble is likely to follow. When the witness finds in court that the questions s/he expects are not being asked, s/he may begin to worry and think that s/he has done something wrong to cause counsel to deviate from the prepared line of questioning. Consequently, s/he may begin to look apprehensive or insecure or may blurt out the answer to the question that counsel "forgot" to ask, instead of responding to the question actually asked, or s/he may do both. Conversely, if questions that the witness does not expect to have asked in court *are* asked, the witness may feel that s/he has been misled or even betrayed by counsel; s/he is likely to lose his or her bearings and become visibly rattled. The key to effective witness preparation is a clear, common understanding by counsel and the witness concerning exactly what will happen in the courtroom.

(E) A witness should be instructed that if s/he is asked on cross-examination whether s/he has previously discussed his or her testimony with defense counsel, s/he should reply that s/he has — and should do so in a manner that communicates a tone of "why, of course!" or "certainly! doesn't everybody?" If s/he is asked whether s/he has rehearsed his or her testimony with counsel, s/he should answer something along the lines of "[Mr.][Ms.] _____ asked me all of the questions that were asked in court today, and I told [him][her] exactly what my answers would be." If asked whether defense counsel did not tell the witness how to answer the questions — or what answers were expected to the questions — the witness should reply in the vein of "No, first I told [Mr.][Ms.] _____ exactly what I knew about the case, and then we went through all of these questions and answers because [Mr.][Ms.] _____ told me that [he][she] wanted to prepare the best questions to bring out in court the facts that I had told [him][her]." (If the prosecutor impugns the witness's integrity by asking any of these questions in a derisive manner, counsel may find it advisable at trial, *after letting the witness answer the question,* to demand in the jury's presence that the prosecutor produce the basis for the innuendo or discontinue that line of questioning.) It is important for counsel to assure the witness that the "dry run" and other preparation of the witness's testimony which they are doing is perfectly proper — "I wouldn't ask you to do it if it weren't" — so that the witness will not feel or appear guilty when s/he is asked about it on cross-examination. And, in order to permit counsel to prepare the witness to answer questions on cross-examination in the manner just described both truthfully and comfortably, counsel should tell the witness, *before beginning the first rehearsal or "dry run,"* that, of course, counsel wants the witness to tell the truth in court; that counsel now wants to review the witness's testimony in order to assure that all of counsel's questions will be clear and understandable and to assure that counsel will be asking the best questions, in the best order, to bring out the witness's story. Counsel also wants to try out the sorts of questions that the prosecutor might ask on cross-examination, so that counsel can determine whether any redirect examination is likely to be necessary and can prepare questions for the redirect examination. (If the witness is one whom counsel wishes to invite to assist counsel in the formulation of questions, this is also the time for an explanation of that process, as suggested in sub-paragraph (C) *supra.*)

(F) In doing the dry run of cross-examination, counsel should spare the witness nothing that the prosecutor may possibly use against the witness at trial. Counsel may want to introduce delicate or embarrassing subjects in a friendly way by interrupting the dry run to explain why the prosecutor will probably question the witness on such-and-such a subject and why it is important that the witness should answer the questions satisfactorily. But eventually the questions must be put to the witness on the "dry run" in the toughest form in which the prosecutor could put them. Rehabilitation can follow. See paragraph [115](B) *supra.* There is a natural human tendency for defense counsel to go easy on a witness who, after all, is doing the defendant the favor of testifying in support of the defense case. That tendency should be avoided like the plague, since it can prove equally deadly.

(G) A witness who has prior convictions that can be used for impeachment (see paragraph [278] *supra*) should be told of the way in which s/he may be questioned about them at trial. See paragraphs [381]-[382], [390](F) *infra.* S/he should be instructed that when s/he is asked whether s/he is the person who was convicted of such-and-such a crime on such-and-such a date, s/he should listen carefully to the description of the crime and, if it is correct, s/he should answer the question by a simple yes, without attempting to explain the conviction away. Any explanatory matter allowed by local practice can best be developed on redirect examination, and this aspect of the redirect should be rehearsed with care. Poor explanations of prior convictions are worse than none.

(H) Concerning the desirability of taking written statements from witnesses, see paragraph [119] *supra.*

[280] **Preparing the defendant.** Preparing the defendant to testify requires special care. The defendant's testimony is more carefully scrutinized than that of any other witness. That a criminal defendant is presumed to be innocent until proved guilty is a canard. In reality, most criminal defendants must prove their innocence — and often their likeableness as well.

(A) The defendant ordinarily testifies last so that s/he can have heard all the other testimony given in the case. It has been held unconstitutional to require a defendant to testify first in a case in which the defense intends to present the testimony of the defendant and other defense evidence. *Brooks v. Tennessee,* 406 U.S. 605 (1972); *see also Cuyler v. Sullivan,* 446 U.S. 335, 344 (1980) (dictum). Because the defendant has a right to be present throughout the trial (see paragraph [341] *infra*), s/he cannot be excluded during the testimony of earlier witnesses by the prosecutor's invocation of the rule on witnesses (paragraph [348] *infra*), *Perry v. Leeke,* 109 S. Ct. 594, 600 (1989) (dictum); and the court's power to forbid consultation between the defendant and defense counsel during the course of the trial is significantly limited by the Sixth Amendment, *compare Geders v. United States,* 425 U.S. 80 (1976), *with Perry v. Leeke, supra.* Thus a defendant who is reasonably bright and articulate usually makes the best clean-up hitter. There are bound to be some inconsistencies even in the most well-planned defense testimony, but if the defendant testifies last s/he is given the opportunity to reconcile any contradictions that have been left by earlier defense witnesses. This role must be explained to the defendant if counsel wants the defendant to play it.

(B) The theory of the defensive case should be thoroughly described to the defendant. Counsel should explain what s/he is attempting to show by each witness, including the defendant, and how it all hangs together. To the best of counsel's ability, s/he should foresee and tell the defendant exactly what will happen at trial. It is important that the defendant be put at ease as much as possible, and the device of taking an unsophisticated defendant to observe other trials (*cf.* paragraph [279](A) *supra*) is often advised.

(C) As with other witnesses, the defendant's testimony should be subjected to "dry runs" to assure against omissions and inadvertent inconsistencies and to organize it in the most comprehensible and persuasive manner. See paragraph [393] *infra*. Direct, cross, and redirect examination should be role-played; and in role-playing the cross-examination, counsel should press the defendant with the toughest questions that the prosecutor could conceivably ask at trial. See paragraph [394] *infra*. Particularly, the defendant must have a plausible explanation for any confessions, admissions to police, or other prior inconsistent statements with which counsel can expect the defendant to be impeached. A serious problem in preparing the defendant's testimony is that there may be some prior statements of which counsel is unaware. (These may not surface before the defendant testifies. When a defendant has made multiple statements to the police, a canny prosecutor will often withhold some of them in the prosecution's case-in-chief, so as to leave fresh material for impeachment of the defendant or for rebuttal.) Discovery and investigation must be as complete as possible when the defendant's testimony is prepared, to minimize this hazard.

(D) Counsel should help the defendant to see ways in which the defendant can present himself or herself to the jury as a responsible and likeable person, both in the defendant's demeanor on the witness stand and in the defendant's deportment at counsel table throughout the trial. It is important that the defendant come across as someone the jurors can identify with and will want to acquit. But counsel should not ordinarily attempt to have the defendant dress, behave, or talk in a manner to which s/he is substantially unaccustomed or use vocabulary that is out of keeping with his or her character or situation in life. This sort of acting is seldom convincing. Whether "street talk" should be laundered depends upon counsel's appraisal of how it will go over with the judge or jury; common profanities may not be punished by contempt, at least in the absence of prior warning by the judge that they are out of order. *Eaton v. City of Tulsa,* 415 U.S. 697 (1974) (per curiam).

[281] Defendant's dress for trial. If a defendant is in custody, counsel should arrange for him or her to have civilian clothes to wear during the trial. A defendant is entitled to appear at trial in a dignified manner and, upon timely request, s/he has a federal constitutional right to be garbed in civilian clothes. *Estelle v. Williams,* 425 U.S. 501 (1976) (considered dictum); *see, e.g., Bentley v. Crist,* 469 F.2d 854 (9th Cir. 1972), and cases cited. Counsel should also insist that the defendant be permitted a haircut, if needed, and adequate opportunity to shave daily during the trial. Clients not in custody should be advised to dress and groom neatly. The more "respectably" or "well" dressed they can appear without looking costumed for the occasion, the better. Counsel should ask the client to dress for one of their pretrial interviews as the client will dress at trial, so that counsel can look over the client's outfit and suggest any necessary improvements. See paragraph [279](B) *supra*.

[282] **Codefendants and accomplices.** Codefendants and alleged accomplices must also be interviewed with special care and their stories probed in detail. If there is even a slight possibility of conflict between the testimony of a codefendant and that of the defendant or the defendant's other witnesses, counsel should not represent the codefendant, should ordinarily undertake to obtain a severance of trials (see paragraphs [259]-[260], [264] *supra*), and should ordinarily not call the codefendant as a witness. The same is true if the codefendant is unappetizing. Frequently a jury tends to identify the defendant with his or her codefendants, and the defendant can be convicted because of the bad reputation or appearance of a codefendant. Except in unusual cases it is not wise to call a codefendant or any alleged accomplice to testify for the defense. If s/he disagrees with the defendant, both, to the jury's way of thinking, are liars; if s/he agrees, both are calculated liars. (Counsel appointed to represent codefendants in cases in which a conflict of interest appears can, of course, secure relief from conflicting appointments. *Holloway v. Arkansas,* 435 U.S. 475 (1978). *Cf. Cuyler v. Sullivan,* 446 U.S. 335 (1980); *and see Wheat v. United States,* 108 S. Ct. 1692, 1697-98 (1988).)

[283] **Expert witness.** (A) In interviewing potential expert witnesses for the defense, counsel must both prepare them and learn from them. Counsel has to become familiar with the area of their expertise so that s/he can intelligently determine how best to present the experts' testimony at trial. Considerable familiarity will also be necessary to cross-examine prosecution experts in the field. Although counsel cannot afford to rely on the defense expert alone for education and should do independent reading on the subject, s/he will ordinarily have to draw heavily on the expert to explain technical matters that counsel inevitably

will find difficult. Counsel should describe the entire legal theory of the defense to the expert and should ask the expert to suggest ways in which his or her testimony might best be presented to support the defensive theory.

(B) Once the expert's presentation has been worked out, it should ordinarily be committed to writing in the form of a report from the expert to counsel and should be dated and signed by the expert. Such a report will be useful to the expert in reviewing the case prior to trial, it will be useful to counsel in examining the expert at trial, and it may be admissible in evidence to illuminate and clarify the witness's testimony. So used, it provides an easy way of assuring that all points are presented and cohesively connected. A report of this sort will probably be subject to discovery by the prosecution after the expert has testified at trial, whether or not it has been used in direct examination or reviewed by the expert in preparing to testify (see paragraph [408-A] *infra*), and it may become discoverable before trial under the circumstances and within the limitations described in paragraph [274] *supra*. Counsel should therefore not ask the expert to make an *initial* report in writing. The risks are altogether too great that a legally untutored person — or even a person with considerable forensic experience who has not been thoroughly advised about the defense to be presented in a particular case — may expose himself or herself to impeachment by unconsidered or incautious phrasing. After the expert has made an initial oral report (or perhaps more than one, in complex matters), counsel should decide whether s/he is going to use that expert in the defendant's defense. If so, the expert's testimony should be hammered out, with attention to details of phrasing, in a series of interviews and dry-run examinations in which counsel advises the expert completely of the needs and pitfalls of the case and of the expert's role in it. Counsel should also inform the expert that his or her report will be available to the prosecutor for cross-examination and should instruct the expert, with specific examples, of the ways in which an adept cross-examiner can turn ambiguous language into inconsistencies. *Then* the expert should be asked to prepare a *draft* report, which can be finalized after it has been reviewed by counsel. See paragraph [401] *infra*. Because any notes made by the expert in the course of his or her examinations, researches, or preparations may also be discoverable, counsel should tell the expert *before the expert begins any work on the case* that notes or memoranda must be made with extreme caution.

(C) An expert's testimony should be keyed to the level of understanding of the factfinder. Use of commonly intelligible, dramatic illustrations and examples is one of the best methods of clarifying expert testimony. Concepts of mathematical probability, for example, may be expressed in terms of the likelihood that a coin which is flipped fairly will come up heads 5,000 times in a row. Or the level of probability that the expert's test results are not due to chance may be favorably compared with the level of probability used in testing potentially dangerous medical drugs before they can be marketed. For additional suggestions concerning expert testimony, see paragraphs [397]-[402] *infra*.

[284] **Keeping in touch with witnesses for trial; depositions.** (A) Counsel should keep records of all witnesses s/he has interviewed who know anything about the case, containing their addresses, their telephone numbers, any expected plans to move, and the names of persons through whom they can be contacted. See paragraph [114] *supra*. Once counsel has decided to use a witness at trial, it is particularly important to keep in close touch with the witness. The witness should be given counsel's telephone number and be told to call in the event of a change in residence or a trip out of town. If the witness is crucial and appears geographically unstable, it may be wise for counsel to call the witness at reasonable intervals during the pretrial period. This assures that s/he will not be gone long before s/he is missed by counsel and that counsel can take up pursuit while the trail is fresh. The witness should, of course, be advised as far in advance as possible of any trial date at which s/he may have to appear — except in the case of uncooperative witnesses who may react by flight.

(B) If a witness is leaving the jurisdiction, if the witness's health is bad, or if s/he may be unavailable at trial for any other reason, counsel should take the witness's deposition. Local statutory procedures for the taking of depositions to preserve testimony must be consulted. (Frequently these will be codified only in codes of civil procedure, but an examination of their terminology will disclose that they are applicable in criminal cases as well.) In the case of hostile witnesses whom counsel has reason to believe may flee, hide out, or avoid service of a subpoena, an application to the court for their arrest as material witnesses may be advised. Most jurisdictions have statutes authorizing the detention of material witnesses that can be invoked by the defense as well as the prosecution. When material-witness procedures are limited by law or practice to the prosecutor's use, defense counsel should invoke them anyway and argue that such a limitation is unconstitutional within the principles of paragraph [270](H) *supra.*

[285] **Compulsory process — subpoenas for witnesses; habeas corpus ad testificandum.** (A) If counsel wants a witness to appear at trial, s/he should always subpoena that witness. Counsel should never rely on the witness's voluntary appearance or on the hope that the prosecutor will bring the witness in. If possible, service of a subpoena should be made by a private process server rather than by the marshal, a sheriff, a police officer, or other law enforcement personnel, for they will likely tell the prosecutor the identity of witnesses to whom defense subpoenas have been directed.

(B) If counsel needs a witness who is involuntarily confined in a prison or hospital, counsel must apply to the court for a writ of *habeas corpus ad testificandum.* The writ directs the custodian of the confining institution to produce the witness for trial. In some cases a judge will also issue the writ to bring a witness to a place where counsel can conveniently interview him or her. Issuance of the writ is ordinarily discretionary, and courts require some showing of the materiality of the witness's testimony. But see paragraph [286] *infra.*

[286] **Rights to compulsory process.** A criminal defendant has constitutional and statutory rights to compulsory process to obtain the attendance of witnesses at trial. In some jurisdictions the process issues routinely at public expense. When the defendant is an indigent, the Equal Protection Clause of the Fourteenth Amendment doubtless requires the issuance of subpoenas

for material defense witnesses at public expense. See paragraph [299] *infra; cf.* paragraph [132] *supra*. If counsel is confronted with the prevalent statutory requirement that the applicant for *forma pauperis* subpoenas show "good cause" or "materiality" of the witness or "what the witness will testify" or that the witness is "necessary to an adequate defense," counsel should ascertain from the clerk of court or from experienced defense attorneys in the locality whether it is customary — as it is in many courts — to issue subpoenas on the basis of conclusionary affidavits by defense counsel, merely tracking the language of the statute (that is, averring that the witness "is necessary to an adequate defense," or whatever the statutory formula may be). If this is the case, counsel should file such an affidavit. If factually detailed documentation is demanded instead, counsel should prepare an affidavit making the requisitely detailed showing (*see United States v. Valenzuela-Bernal,* 458 U.S. 858, 867 n.7 (1982) (dictum); *Caldwell v. Mississippi,* 472 U.S. 320, 323-24 n.1 (1985)), seal the affidavit, and file it with a motion asking that the court receive it in sealed form and consider it *in camera,* without disclosure to the prosecutor, on the ground that it reveals an aspect of defense trial strategy. If this motion is denied, counsel should move to dismiss all charges on the ground that its denial has rendered a fair trial impossible, and then either refuse to make the required factual averments or make them under objection (depending on whether s/he can practicably afford to go to trial without the witness) on the ground that the defendant's rights under the Compulsory Process Clause of the Sixth Amendment to the federal Constitution, under the Equal Protection Clause of the Fourteenth Amendment, and under the parallel state constitutional guarantees are infringed if an indigent is obliged to disclose his or her defensive case in a way that a defendant with money is not, as the precondition of obtaining compulsory process. See paragraph [301] *infra.* (In this connection, counsel should note *Washington v. Texas,* 388 U.S. 14 (1967), and the subsequent decisions of the Supreme Court collected in paragraph [270](D) *supra,* incorporating the Compulsory Process Clause of the Sixth Amendment into the Fourteenth. The contours of the federal constitutional right to compulsory process thereby given are largely undeveloped, but the implications of the right for attack upon state-law restrictions and obstructions of defensive subpoenas, *habeas corpus ad testificandum,* and so forth, are considerable.) Of course, this tactic will not be necessary if local practice provides some satisfactory procedure for the *ex parte* submission of confidential requests for *forma pauperis* subpoenas and supporting affidavits to the judge or the clerk; but counsel should be sure, before following the local practice, that it actually preserves the confidentiality it promises. In some courthouses the prosecutor can and does obtain access to the supposedly confidential documents filed by the defense. Once again, therefore, inquiries should be made among locally knowledgeable defense lawyers to determine whether the *ex parte* procedure is safe to use.

[287] **Persons subject to subpoena.** Any person in a jurisdiction who has relevant testimony may be subpoenaed. Under local practice an expert witness may be immune from subpoena to testify solely *as* an expert witness, but s/he is not immune from process when s/he has factual information that is pertinent to a proceeeding. For this reason counsel may ordinarily subpoena government doctors and psychiatrists, for example, when they have examined the defendant in jail, in prisons, or in state hospitals. Counsel may also subpoena police laboratory personnel, coroner's personnel (see paragraph [123-A] *supra*), the complainant's physician (subject to the claim of any applicable doctor-patient privilege), and the like.

[288] **Subpoenas to avoid a missing-witness instruction against the defense.** The missing-witness instruction tells the jury that when a witness who is shown to have some knowledge of the facts in issue is peculiarly available to one of the parties but is not called by that party, the jury may draw an inference that the witness's testimony would not have been favorable to the party. The charge may be given in a criminal case on request of either the prosecution or the defense if the judge is satisfied that a factual basis for it exists in the failure of the other party to call a particular witness. If counsel's request for the charge is successful, s/he can make effective use of it in closing argument, identifying the witness or witnesses available to the

other side who were not called. Local practice varies concerning whether, if an adequate basis for the missing-witness charge is not laid, counsel is permitted to argue from the failure of the other side to call a witness. To avoid the use of the charge against the defense, counsel should review his or her evidence prior to trial, noting whether there are witnesses (a) whom s/he has been unable to locate or does not plan to call and (b) who will appear from the trial testimony either (1) to have material evidence helpful to the defense if the defense version of the facts is true (for example, a person who, defendant will testify, was with the defendant at some other place at the time of the offense) or (2) to have witnessed events relating to the offense and to be allied in interest with the defense (for example, defendant's brother who was with the defendant at the time of the episode giving rise to the charge). Counsel should subpoena these persons. If they are served and appear, s/he can tender them to the prosecutor. If they cannot be served or if they are served and do not appear, s/he can inform the court and the prosecutor that s/he has attempted to serve the witness or has served the witness, as the case may be. Counsel should have the process server prepared to testify that service was made or that diligent unsuccessful efforts to find the witness were made, and counsel should proffer the process server's testimony to this effect. The defense is now virtually immune against the possibility of a missing-witness charge. In some cases, when the prosecutor is denying the existence of a person whom the defendant claims was with the defendant at the time of the offense and when the process server has found verification of the existence of such a person in the course of unsuccessful efforts to locate him or her, defense counsel may want to call the process server to testify before the jury. In this situation the avowed purpose of the testimony is to show vigorous efforts to locate the missing person in order to rebut any negative inference from that person's absence, and hearsay reports about the person that the process server attempted to follow up are admissible to prove the extent of the process server's efforts. Incidentally, these reports tell the jury that the person does exist. Of course, if bringing a particular witness into the case is going to give the prosecutor something s/he can use advantageously and does not yet have, counsel may well prefer to risk a missing-witness instruction rather than to issue a subpeona.

[289] **Laying a foundation for the missing-witness instruction against the prosecution.** A missing-witness charge is often refused if the party requesting it appears to have had ample opportunity to subpoena the witness. (The theory seems to be that such a witness is not uniquely available to the opposing side.) Therefore, if counsel's investigation identifies an individual who would appear able to help the prosecution's case but whom counsel cannot locate or whom counsel knows the prosecution is not going to call, counsel will often want to have that person subpoenaed and to be prepared to prove the unsuccessful diligent efforts of a process server to find the person. This will lay the basis for a defense request that the missing-witness charge be given against the prosecution. In connection with police spies, informers, "special agents," and other similar marginal and transitory police characters, counsel should both issue subpoenas and write the prosecutor at an early stage of the investigation, asking the prosecutor to make certain that the police keep tabs on the whereabouts of the witness, so that s/he can be available for trial. Frequently s/he will disappear, and counsel is then in a position to request a missing-witness instruction (even if the prosecutor can show unsuccessful present efforts to locate the person), based on the prosecutor's failure, after notice, to keep in touch with the witness when s/he had an opportunity to do so. *Cf.* paragraphs [273](B), [284] *supra*.

[290] **Procedure for obtaining subpoenas.** Subpoenas are ordinarily obtained from the office of the clerk of the court. Although issued in the name of the judge or the court, they customarily are filled out—or handed out in blank for completion by counsel—by the clerk or a deputy clerk, without action of the judge. *Forma pauperis* subpoenas often may issue only by leave of court, granted upon motion. The prosecution may resist such a motion by the defense. In the case of paid subpoenas any objections are ordinarily raised by a motion to quash the subpoenas, made by the person subpoenaed or by the party adverse to the litigant who has procured issuance of the subpoena, after the

subpoena has been served. Subpoenas may be quashed on various grounds covered by local practice, including improper service, ignorance on the part of the subpoenaed person of any matter relevant to the proceedings, lack of jurisdiction or statutory authority of the court to issue the subpoena, and privilege. The subpoena may also be resisted by having the subpoenaed person appear and refuse to be sworn. Prosecutors will occasionally move *ex parte* for the quashing of defense subpoenas directed to government officers or employees, and courts have been known to grant the motion, leaving defense counsel uninformed until the time of trial that it has been granted. If counsel suspects that the prosecutor may resist a subpoena directed to a witness allied in interest with the prosecution, counsel should inform the prosecutor a few days before trial that the witness has been subpoenaed (a fact which the prosecutor doubtless already knows) and that the witness's presence at the trial is particularly wanted by defense counsel. In this fashion, if the witness does not appear by reason of some secret or last-minute maneuvering by the prosecutor, counsel is in a position to be righteously indignant over the prosecution's lack of candor when, at trial, the defense makes its motion for a bench warrant (paragraph [292] *infra*), continuance (paragraph [304] *infra*), or mistrial (paragraphs [420]-[422] *infra*), as may seem appropriate.

[291] **Subpoenas duces tecum.** In addition to subpoenas *ad testificandum,* subpoenas may be directed to the custodians of records and documents to appear in court with their papers. These subpoenas, called subpoenas *duces tecum,* are ordinarily required to specify with considerable particularity the documents or records sought. In theory, the subpoenas *duces tecum* are not to be employed for discovery but only to procure evidentiary matter for use at trial. However, as a practical matter counsel may be able to persuade the custodian to permit counsel to examine the subpoenaed record or document outside of court or may be able to persuade the judge to order the custodian to allow counsel to inspect it before trial, during preliminary proceedings, or during a recess, in the interest of saving time at trial. (In federal practice, pretrial production orders are expressly authorized by Federal Rule of Criminal Procedure

17(c).) Some documents, including hospital records, juvenile court records, police personnel records, and, in some jurisdictions, police investigative reports cannot be obtained by counsel except through subpoena. It is wise to serve subpoenas *duces tecum* long before trial, since some agencies require weeks or even months to find the subpoenaed records in their files and arrange to have them brought to court by a representative qualified to authenticate them.

[292] **Enforcing subpoenas.** The mere service of a subpoena does not guarantee the appearance of the subpoenaed person at trial. If a defense subpoena has been served and the witness fails to appear, counsel should call the process server to testify that service was made. Counsel should then state for the record that the defense needs the witness, and counsel can request the court to issue a *capias,* attachment, or bench warrant to have the witness arrested and brought into court. A continuance will be required unless counsel has other witnesses ready to testify. When the reluctant witness appears under arrest, the judge will order him or her to testify or be held in contempt of court. Of course, having a witness arrested is harsh business and is not likely to make the witness friendly. Except in the case of witnesses who are already irretrievably hostile, it is therefore best for counsel to advise the court, when a witness first fails to apear, that counsel will personally attempt to locate the witness and would like a continuance to do so, before requesting the issuance of body process.

[293] **Review of decisions relating to compulsory process.** A refusal by the court to direct the issuance of process or an attachment or to grant a defense continuance requested because of the failure of a properly subpoenaed witness to appear ordinarily is not appealable. Should this refusal occur in the course of a protracted trial, counsel may have time to apply to an appellate court for a writ of mandamus to compel the trial judge to act. See paragraphs [312]-[314] *infra.* The ordinary method of review, however, is upon appeal from a final judgment of conviction. To establish a record for that appeal, counsel should make a proffer at the time s/he requests the process or attachment or continuance, relating the

general purport of the nonappearing witness's testimony. Counsel should make a considerably more detailed proffer in the course of renewing the request at the close of defense testimony, reciting specifically what the witness would have testified had s/he appeared. The detailed proffer should ordinarily not be made earlier than at this time, because if the witness subsequently appears or is found, the proffer may have given the prosecutor useful material for impeachment.

[294] **Preparing real evidence.** (A) When relevant, physical evidence is ordinarily highly persuasive. Counsel should collect and preserve for trial any objects or items that s/he may want to present. S/he should have them retained in the custody of some person (an investigator or counsel's secretary will do) under lock and key. The person who has had custody of the item can then be called at trial to identify it and to testify that there has been no change in its condition since the time it was first received. If the physical condition of any object is important and is subject to change, counsel should have the custodian inspect the object and make a written, signed description of it at the time of its receipt, one copy of which should be retained with the object and another in counsel's files. The custodian should also photograph the object if photography will capture the condition that is subject to change. When the custodian is likely to have more than one object of a kind, each should be tagged with the date of its receipt, the name of the person from whom the custodian received it, and the name of the case to which it relates. (Of course, at trial, counsel will also have to present witnesses who can trace the chain of custody of the object from the time of its acquisition or its involvement in relevant events until it reached the custodian's hands. For this reason, if possible, counsel should have the object collected in the first instance by counsel's investigator or secretary rather than by counsel personally, since it is undesirable — and, in some courts, forbidden — for counsel to testify.) If counsel wishes to have tests made on the object or to show it to anyone, counsel should have the custodian deliver the object personally to the tester or individual in question, and the custodian should then recover it personally when the test or inspection has been completed. This simplifies problems of

proving the identity of the object and the lack of change in its condition at the time of trial.

(B) Real objects in the possession of law enforcement or government officers or third parties can be reached by subpoenas *duces tecum*. If counsel wishes to inspect them or to have them tested by defense experts before trial, a motion for production and inspection should be made. See paragraphs [268]-[271] *supra.*

[295] Tests on physical objects. If counsel has defense experts inspect or test physical objects, counsel should instruct the expert to make some mark on the object that, although not affecting its probative quality, will allow the expert to identify it at trial as the object that s/he examined. The expert's written report to counsel should describe the object and indicate what mark the expert made on it.

[296] Photographs and other visual aids. Whenever a description of the physical characteristics of a site or of an object not capable of being presented in court is important, counsel should arrange to have appropriate photographs taken. Photographs are ordinarily quite convincing, particularly if they are taken from several angles and at several distances, so that all spatial relations involved are fully depicted. Counsel should remember that photographs are not admissible until a foundation has been laid by a person who testifies that they are an accurate reproduction of the scene which s/he observed. A photographer should therefore be selected who will be available at the time of the trial and who will make a good and personable witness. S/he should be informed that s/he will be asked at trial, as a basis for testifying that the photographs are accurate, whether s/he has a present recollection of the scene that s/he photographed. Other useful visual aids include slides prepared by fingerprint or ballistics experts, anatomical charts in cases involving injury, and maps and diagrams drawn by witnesses to exemplify their testimony. When possible, maps and diagrams that are drawn in court for display to the court or jury should be drawn with a marking pen on large sheets of graph paper. This procedure is more satisfactory than that of using a blackboard, since the chart or diagram can be preserved in its original form for appeal.

[297] **Preparation of a trial folder or "trial brief" and an exhibit file.** Orderly presentation of examination and quick citation of relevant authority impress judges and jurors. In addition, a well-presented case is easier for the trier of fact to grasp. Counsel will ordinarily find that an indispensible aid to the orderly presentation of a case at trial is a trial folder or, as it is sometimes called, a trial brief. This folder is for counsel's own use in the courtroom. Arranged to suit counsel's taste, it may helpfully contain (1) all papers filed of record; (2) reproductions of relevant statutes and cases; (3) a checklist of questions for *voir dire*; (4) a checklist of questions for each witness; (5) a checklist of exhibits, indicating through which witness each will be introduced; (6) proposed jury instructions with supporting citations; (7) statements taken from prosecution witnesses; (8) statements taken from defense witnesses; (9) any reports prepared by defense experts; (10) reproductions of all documentary exhibits; (11) copies of defense subpoenas and their returns; and (12) any other documents and all materials gathered by investigators. A separate file should be maintained of the original documents that counsel will put into evidence, in their proper order. Counsel should ascertain before trial whether it is the court's custom to have counsel mark (that is, number) their own exhibits or whether this is done by the clerk. If the former, counsel should save possible trial fumbling by marking the exhibits in advance. Each should be designated "Defendant's Exhibit No. _____" or by some similar form, so that they can be numbered before trial without reference to the possible number of prosecution exhibits.

XX. STATE-PAID ASSISTANCE FOR THE DEFENSE

[298] Availability of state-paid assistance under local practice. (A) In capital cases most jurisdictions authorize the provision of expert consultants and investigative assistance to indigent defendants at public expense. In noncapital cases there is great variation from state to state and sometimes from locality to locality, with some courts furnishing little or no aid to indigents beyond the appointment of counsel. (Federal practice, under the Criminal Justice Act of 1964, 18 U.S.C. §3006 (A)(e), is relatively liberal.) Even where state or county payment for defense support services is authorized, it is frequently limited by statutorily specified ceilings that render it inadequate or is doled out by budget-conscious judges in amounts that are insufficient to meet the real needs of defense. Procedures for drawing down whatever funds are available may also be unsatisfactory. In some localities the court must approve each specific defense expenditure in advance, upon a showing of need in a form that discloses the nature of defense trial preparation to the prosecutor. In other localities defense counsel is reimbursed, after a *post facto* audit, for expenditures that the judge finds were reasonable. The latter system puts the defendant in the unconscionable posture of having to rely on the ability and willingness of the defense attorney to advance sums that may not be repaid. *Cf. State v. Robinson,* 123 N.H. 665, 465 A.2d 1214 (1983).

(B) When counsel is appointed to represent an indigent client, s/he should ascertain from the clerk of court what expenses and services, if any, will be provided out of public funds and how to apply for them. Whether counsel is appointed or retained, if the client cannot afford fees and costs for court process, expert witnesses, consultative services, or investigative aids that counsel believes are legitimately needed, counsel should ascertain the local practice for requesting funds and should comply with it insofar as possible. To the extent that local practice fails to authorize public payment for services that counsel needs or when it unreasonably restricts the sums allowed—either by limiting the amount available or by imposing crippling procedural preconditions — counsel may have to challenge the practice as unconstitutional. In this situation counsel should move the court to authorize the necessary expenditures without requiring the defendant to comply with the objectionable preconditions or else dismiss the prosecution, on the ground that failure to provide an impecunious defendant with adequate financial resources for a fair defense denies the defendant the equal protection of the laws and the due process of law guaranteed by the Fourteenth Amendment. See paragraphs [299]-[301] *infra*.

(C) Reasonable recoupment provisions (that is, requirements that an indigent defendant who has been provided state-paid defensive assets repay the state if and when s/he becomes financially able to do so) are not *per se* unconstitutional, *Fuller v. Oregon*, 417 U.S. 40 (1974); but the terms of any recoupment statute should be carefully reviewed in the light of *Rinaldi v. Yeager*, 384 U.S. 305 (1966), and *James v. Strange*, 407 U.S. 128 (1972).

[299] Rights under the Equal Protection Clause. (A) In *Griffin v. Illinois*, 351 U.S. 12 (1956), the Supreme Court held that the Equal Protection Clause compelled a state to furnish a state-paid transcript of a criminal trial to a convicted defendant who needed the transcript for presentation of an appeal and who could not afford to pay for it. Noting that a nonindigent defendant could purchase a transcript and that under Illinois practice convicted defendants "needed a transcript in order to get adequate appellate review of their alleged trial errors," *id.* at 16, the Court decided the case on the broad ground that "[t]here can be no equal justice where the kind of trial a man gets depends on the amount of money he has." *Id.* at 19. *See also Williams v. Illinois*, 399 U.S. 235, 241 (1970); *Bearden v. Georgia*, 461 U.S. 660, 664 (1983); *Estelle v. Williams*, 425 U.S. 501, 505-6 (1976) (dictum); *Black v. Romano*, 471 U.S. 606, 614-15 (1985) (dictum).

(B) Following *Griffin*, the Court has required the provision of free transcripts to indigents on both direct and collateral criminal appeals, *e.g., Draper v. Washington*, 372 U.S. 487 (1963); *Long v. District Court*, 385 U.S. 192 (1966); *Gardner v. California*, 393 U.S. 367 (1969); *Williams v. Oklahoma City*, 395 U.S. 458 (1969); *Mayer v. City of Chicago*, 404 U.S. 189 (1971); *compare United States v. MacCollom*, 426 U.S. 317 (1976); the waiver of filing fees for both appeals and collateral-attack proceedings, *Burns v. Ohio,* 360 U.S. 252 (1959); *Smith v. Bennett,* 365 U.S. 708 (1961); and the provision of appointed counsel on at least a criminal defendant's first appeal as of right from conviction, *Douglas v. California,* 372 U.S. 353 (1963); *Swenson v. Bosler,* 386 U.S. 258 (1967); *compare Ross v. Moffitt,* 417 U.S. 600 (1974); *Wainwright v. Torna,* 455 U.S. 586 (1982) (per curiam); *Pennsylvania v. Finley,* 107 S. Ct. 1990 (1987). The full purport of the *Griffin* line of cases remains to be developed. But it is possible to state its principle comprehensively as a command that the state which prosecutes an indigent must furnish him or her with every defensive resource that a nonindigent defendant could purchase and that is necessary "to assure . . . an adequate opportunity to present his [or her] claims fairly in the context of the State's [criminal] . . . process," *Ross v. Moffitt, supra,* 417 U.S. at 616 (dictum).

(C)The cases such as *Roberts v. LaVallee,* 389 U.S. 40 (1967), cited in paragraph [266](B) *supra* establish that this command extends to matters needed for trial preparation. *Britt v. North Carolina,* 404 U.S. 226 (1971), in particular, describes the command as a requirement "that the State . . . provide indigent prisoners with the basic tools of an adequate defense or appeal, when those tools are available for a price to other prisoners," *id.* at 227; and although a free transcript was not required "in the narrow circumstances of [the *Britt*] . . . case" itself, *ibid.,* the Court detailed those circumstances in a manner which leaves no doubt that generally an indigent defendant must be given free transcription of all relevant prior judicial proceedings "as a discovery device in preparation for trial, and as a tool at the trial itself for the impeachment of prosecution witnesses," *id.* at 228. *See id.* at 229-30.

(D) *Mayer v. City of Chicago,* subparagraph (B) *supra,* phrases the Equal Protection requirement in terms of assuring "the indigent as effective [a trial] . . . as would be available to the defendant with resources to pay his own way." 404 U.S. at 195. In addition, *Mayer* firmly resists the notion that an indigent defendant's needs are to be "balanced" against the cost to the state of providing them or denied if they are too expensive. "*Griffin* does not represent a balance between the needs of the accused and the interests of society; its principle is a flat prohibition against pricing indigent defendants out of as effective [a defense] . . . as would be available to others able to pay their own way. . . . The State's fiscal interest is, therefore, irrelevant." 404 U.S. at 196-97. (*See also Bounds v. Smith,* 430 U.S. 817, 825 (1977) ("the cost of protecting a constitutional right cannot justify its total denial").)

(E) Certainly, the most immediate implications of the *Griffin-Roberts-Britt-Mayer* line of decisions require that the state record and transcribe, at public expense, all court proceedings in an indigent case and that prior to trial, upon motion of the defendant, s/he be furnished free transcripts of all earlier proceedings in the case (and perhaps in related cases) in adequate time to make use of them for trial preparation. See paragraphs [132], [144], [266](B) *supra.* The indigent defendant's right to compulsory process *in forma pauperis* to secure the attendance of material defense witnesses (see paragraphs [132], [286] *supra*) also seems obvious. *See Greenwell v. United States,* 317 F.2d 108 (D.C. Cir. 1963); *Welsh v. United States,* 404 F.2d 414, 417 (5th Cir. 1968); *compare United States v. Pitts,* 569 F.2d 343, 348-49 & n.10 (5th Cir. 1978); *United States v. Valenzuela-Bernal,* 458 U.S. 858, 867 n.7 (1982) (dictum). Under *Ake v. Oklahoma,* 470 U.S. 68 (1985), an indigent defendant who "demonstrates to the trial judge that his [or her] sanity at the time of the offense is to be a significant factor at trial . . . must [be given free] . . . access to a competent psychiatrist who will conduct an appropriate examination and assist in evaluation, preparation, and presentation of the defense." *Id.* at 83. *See also Bush v. McCollum,* 231 F. Supp. 560 (N.D. Tex. 1964), *aff'd,* 344 F.2d 672 (5th Cir. 1965). And *Williams v. Martin,* 618 F.2d 1021 (4th Cir. 1980), requires the provision of a state-paid independent pathologist to an indigent defendant charged with homicide when the cause of death is debatable and medically complicated. *See also Cherry v. Estelle,* 507 F.2d 242, 243 (5th Cir. 1975) (impliedly recognizing the right to provision of a state-paid independent ballistics expert under certain circumstances, *see Hoback v. Alabama,* 607 F.2d 680, 682 n.1 (5th Cir. 1979)), *subsequent history in* 424 F. Supp. 548 (N.D. Tex. 1976); *Bowen v. Eyman,* 324 F. Supp. 339 (D. Ariz. 1970) (requiring provision of a state-paid defense expert when the prosecution has failed to conduct potentially exonerating chemical tests); *People v. Watson,* 36 Ill. 2d 228, 221 N.E.2d

645 (1966) (requiring provision of a state-paid examiner of questioned documents). From these authorities, the argument for state-paid investigative services, when reasonably needed, seems plain. *See Corenevsky v. Superior Court,* 36 Cal. 3d 307, 682 P.2d 360, 204 Cal. Rptr. 165 (1984); *State v. Second Judicial District Court,* 85 Nev. 241, 453 P.2d 421 (1969); *Mason v. Arizona,* 504 F.2d 1345, 1351-52 (9th Cir. 1974) (dictum); *Smith v. Enomoto,* 615 F.2d 1251, 1252 (9th Cir. 1980) (dictum).

[300] Rights under the Due Process Clause. (A) The denial of free experts and investigative services to the defense in indigent cases touches Due Process Clause concerns as well as Equal Protection Clause concerns. *See Evitts v. Lucey,* 469 U.S. 387, 403-5 (1985); *cf. Little v. Streater,* 452 U.S. 1, 16 (1981). A criminal defendant's inability to marshal the information necessary to present his or her version of the facts, in the context of a litigation process that is essentially adversary, smacks of fundamental unfairness. It was just this consideration that led the Supreme Court in *Gideon v. Wainwright,* 372 U.S. 335 (1963), to hold that the right to counsel is a component of due process, *see Argersinger v. Hamlin,* 407 U.S. 25, 31-33 (1972); *Ross v. Moffitt,* 417 U.S. 600, 610 (1974) (dictum); *Middendorf v. Henry,* 425 U.S. 25, 41 (1976) (dictum); *McCoy v. Court of Appeals,* 108 S. Ct. 1895, 1900 (1988) (dictum); and counsel unaided in a case in which counsel needs aid to provide an adequate defense hardly satisfies the *Gideon* command. *Williams v. Martin,* 618 F.2d 1021, 1025, 1027 (4th Cir. 1980). In *McCoy v. Court of Appeals, supra,* the Supreme Court considered the obligations of court-appointed counsel on appeal and concluded that the constitutional "principle of substantial equality [between defendants who can and those who cannot afford to retain counsel] . . . require[s] that appointed counsel make the same diligent and thorough evaluation of the case as a retained lawyer. . . ." *Id.* at 1902. Appointed counsel at the trial level have obligations that are at least as demanding, *see id.* at 1900, and "thorough evaluation of the case" cannot be performed without adequate investigative resources. "Because the right to counsel [announced in *Gideon*] is so fundamental to a fair trial, the Constitution cannot tolerate trials in which counsel, though present in name, is unable to assist the defendant to obtain a fair decision on the merits." *Evitts v. Lucey, supra,* 469 U.S. at 395; *see also Rogers v. Israel,* 746 F.2d 1288 (7th Cir. 1984). The federal caselaw cited in paragraphs [53] and [270](A) *supra,* to the effect that defense counsel must be given adequate time to prepare, also suggests that s/he must be given adequate resources with which to prepare. A like command may be implied in the Sixth and Fourteenth Amendment rights to compulsory process, see paragraphs [270](D), [286] *supra,* and in the Due Process requirement of a fair adversarial balance in criminal procedures, see paragraph [270](H) *supra.*

(B) Perhaps timely disclosure to the defense of the prosecutor's case and such exculpatory or mitigating materials as diligent police investigation has unearthed may fufill these due process requirements. That, however, is subject to considerable doubt, since the police are not likely to be as vigorous in their researches for a defendant as in those against the defendant. In any event, the denial to an indigent defendant both of disclosure of the products of the state's investigation (see paragraphs [265]-[273-B] *supra*) and of resources to conduct his or her own investigation clearly invites attack under the Due Process Clause. For this reason counsel is advised to couple a full range of discovery requests with applications for state-paid investigative and expert assistance. See paragraph [271](A), (B) *supra.*

[301] **Procedures.** (A) Whatever local procedures are available for requesting state-paid assistance should be employed unless their use is unduly burdensome or dangerous. When it is, counsel may attempt some reasonable modification. For example, when applicable rules require that expenditures be approved in advance by the court, on the filing of an affidavit describing in detail the services for which each expenditure is required, counsel may reasonably take the position that the defendant should not have to disclose the theory and strategy of the defense to the prosecutor — and should certainly not be compelled to disclose potentially self-incriminating information (see paragraphs [161](E), [232], [274] *supra*) — as the precondition of state financial assistance. *Cf. Simmons v. United States,* 390 U.S. 377, 384-94 (1968), and cases cited following *Simmons* in paragraph [180](E)(2) *supra.* The double-bind problem is recognized

in *United States v. Branker,* 418 F.2d 378, 380-81 (2d Cir. 1969) (dictum); *cf. United States v. Kahan,* 415 U.S. 239 (1974) (per curiam); but *Branker's* proposed solution to it — precluding prosecutorial use at trial of any evidence disclosed by the defendant in proceedings seeking *forma pauperis* assistance — is probably insufficiently protective to justify compelling the disclosure in the first place, at least in the absence of a formal grant of use and derivative-use immunity, *see Maness v. Meyers,* 419 U.S. 449, 461-63, 468-70 (1975); *Pillsbury Co. v. Conboy,* 459 U.S. 248, 256-57 & n.13 (1983). In any event, *Ake v. Oklahoma,* 470 U.S. 68, 82-83 (1985), paragraph [299] *supra,* explicitly states that the federal constitutional right to state-paid expert assistance which *Ake* recognizes is triggered when "the defendant is able to make an *ex parte* threshold showing to the trial court" of the facts which support that right.

(B) Therefore, counsel confronted with a local requirement that s/he detail defense investigative needs or proposed expenditures as the precondition of allowance of funds may be advised to file an affidavit

- Asserting the needs of the defense in unrevealing, conclusory form (see paragraph [286] *supra*);
- Averring that a more particularized description would reveal counsel's "litigating strategies" (*United States v. Valenzuela-Bernal,* 458 U.S. 858, 862 n.3 (1982), paragraph [274](D) *supra*) or would reveal leads to potentially incriminating matter (see paragraph [274](C)(1) *supra*) or both and would thus unconstitutionally subject the defendant to a burden to which defendants with money are not subjected;
- Citing *Ake;* and
- Offering to make the detailed showing *ex parte* in chambers.

Cf. Greenwell v. United States, paragraph [299] *supra.* The fourth item is crucial: A merely conclusory assertion of need will not protect the record. *See Caldwell v. Mississippi,* 472 U.S. 320, 323-24 n.1 (1985).

(C) When no state procedure is applicable, a simple motion to the court for provision of state-paid assistance or, in the alternative, for dismissal of the prosecution by reason of deprivation of the opportunity to prepare a defense, is probably most appropriate. The motion may be supported by counsel's affidavit (1) describing defense investigative and preparatory needs insofar as they can be described without making any harmful disclosures, and (2) offering to make a fuller showing *in camera* or by sealed affidavits to be considered by the court *ex parte*. The motion should also be supported, of course, by the defendant's detailed affidavit of poverty. The latter affidavit can be prepared from the information furnished by the client in response to the questions in the bail-information questionnaire set out in paragraph [60] *supra*.

XXI. THE TIMING OF PRETRIAL AND TRIAL PROCEEDINGS

[302] **Terms of court.** Statutes or court rules establish criminal terms of court, at which the principal criminal business is done. Local practice may or may not allow the handling of particular phases of criminal cases out of term, such as the hearing and disposition of pretrial motions or the entry of a guilty plea and reference of the defendant for presentence investigation. Of course, magistrates and justices of the peace ordinarily sit continually throughout the year; and in the courts of record, matters that are handled by ancillary procedures such as *habeas corpus* are never confined to the criminal terms. The criminal terms themselves may be infrequent or frequent. In rural areas there may be only two or three criminal terms a year. A grand jury term will ordinarily precede the criminal term, and all defendants charged will be arraigned either on an arraignment date following the final return of the grand jury or on the first day of the criminal term. In urban centers there will ordinarily be monthly grand jury terms and criminal terms. Both the grand jury and the criminal courts will be in session continually, and arraignments will be held throughout each term.

[303] **Calendar control.** The time of presentation of a bill to the grand jury or of filing of an information is usually determined solely by the prosecutor. Once the charging paper has been filed, the prosecutor may retain or may lose practical control over the timing of the case in its subsequent stages — arraignment, pretrial, trial. In some courts the criminal calendar is controlled exclusively by the prosecutor at all stages. The prosecutor unilaterally decides when to list a case for arraignment and, at arraignment or thereafter, selects the trial date. In other courts a judge, clerk, or court functionary controls the calendar and notifies both the prosecution and the defense of listings. Court control is more usual in metropolitan areas, which may have an assignment judge or clerk or a court administrator. In some jurisdictions, as in federal practice (*see* 18 U.S.C. §§3161-3174; FED. R. CRIM. P. 50 (b)), criminal calen-

daring is strictly supervised by the court pursuant to a set of published rules, often called a "speedy trial plan." The extent to which the prosecutor can "backdoor" the court personnel who are in charge of the calendar and can thus control the scheduling of a case with no need for formal motions for continuances or advancements, varies. Usually, no matter who formally sets the calendar, the prosecutor has some influence that s/he can apply informally to speed up or slow down the progress of a case.

[304] **Continuances.** (A) For the reason just stated, defense counsel who wants a continuance will usually do best to talk to the prosecutor first. If the prosecutor cannot arrange the matter by rescheduling the case on his or her own authority or by a phone call to the court officials who manage the calendar, s/he should be asked to join or acquiesce in a motion addressed to the appropriate judge (the calendar judge, the presiding judge, a motions judge, or the judge to whom the particular case has been assigned). Joint continuance motions and defense motions marked "no opposition" by the prosecutor are granted routinely in many courts, although this is less likely where a "speedy trial plan" is in effect (see the preceding paragraph).

(B) Practice varies with regard to whether applications for continuances of pretrial hearings and of trial are required to be made in writing, on notice, in advance of the proceeding sought to be continued or whether they may be made orally on the date when the matter is listed. Ordinarily, if an evidentiary hearing or a trial is involved, counsel should either move in writing in advance or inform the prosecutor in advance of counsel's intention to request a continuance when the case is called. Whether or not the prosecutor is going to accede to the request, s/he is thus put on notice and can notify prosecution witnesses that the case may be rescheduled. A defense motion for a continuance made in court without this prior notice will, in all likelihood, be vigorously opposed by the prosecutor and received with irritation by the judge. Each will be suspicious that defense counsel is attempting to use a last-minute plea of "not prepared" as a tactic to discourage prosecution witnesses who, having been dragged needlessly into court on one occasion, will be less enthusiastic about appearing the next time that the case is called.

(C) The trial judge ordinarily has exceedingly broad discretion to grant or to deny continuances. *See, e.g., Morris v. Slappy,* 461 U.S. 1, 11-12 (1983); *United States v. Cronic,* 466 U.S. 648, 661 & n.31 (1984). The discretion is not absolute, however, and defense counsel who seeks a continuance without a prior assurance of cooperation by the prosecutor should protect the record by a detailed statement of the reasons for postponement, reciting, for example, the date of counsel's recent appointment to represent the defendant and the other commitments that have made it impossible for counsel to prepare the case adequately since that date; or the specifics of counsel's conflicting obligation to appear in another courtroom; or the exigency of the circumstances that have made a defense witness unavailable and the importance of that particular witness to the defense. These recitations should be made by affidavit unless clearly established local practice permits oral representations in open court. If the reasons for the requested continuance would reveal defense strategy or would disclose the identity or the contents of the testimony of defense witnesses that the prosecutor does not already know about, they should be stated in a sealed affidavit and filed with a motion requesting their consideration by the court *ex parte. Cf.* paragraphs [286], [301] *supra.*

(D) If counsel is being rushed so quickly at any stage that s/he has inadequate opportunity to prepare, s/he should support an application for a continuance by reference not only to the general equities of the situation but also to the defendant's federal and state constitutional rights to counsel and to a fair trial. Denials of ample time for defense preparation have been held to violate these guarantees. See paragraphs [53], [270](A) *supra.*

(E) Prejudicial publicity or public hostility that threatens to impair a defendant's constitutional right to trial by an impartial jury may also be urged in support of a motion for "postponement of the trial to allow public attention to subside." *Nebraska Press Ass'n v. Stuart,* 427 U.S. 539, 563-64 (1976). "That time soothes and erases [public prejudice] is a perfectly natural phenomenon, familiar to all." *Patton v. Yount,* 467 U.S. 1025, 1034 (1984). See paragraphs [255](A), [256] *supra;* paragraphs [315](C), [334] *infra.*

[305] Speeding up the proceeding by waivers. The defend-ant can ordinarily speed up the disposition of the case considera-bly by one or more of the following procedures: by waiving preliminary hearing (see paragraph [137] *supra*); by waiving in-dictment (see paragraph [157] *supra*); by pleading guilty (see paragraph [202] *supra*); by waiving jury trial (see paragraph [317] *infra*); and by stipulating to submit the case to the court on a case-stated basis or on the police report (see paragraph [355] *infra*). Occasionally prosecutors in urban centers will have a reg-ularized method of telescoping procedures and bringing on mi-nor cases for disposition in a few hours on a showing of special urgency: for example, cases of seamen arrested on shore leave and due to sail the next day. Counsel handling these cases should ask the prosecutor how to wrap them up quickly.

[306] Speedy trial rights — generally. In a more ordinary case, when no waivers are contemplated but counsel wants to speed the process up, again s/he should consult the prosecutor. If the prosecutor is uncooperative, a defendant whose case is proceeding to trial more slowly than s/he wishes may move to advance it, ask the court for an immediate listing, request re-lease on his or her own recognizance during the period of the delay, move for dismissal, or seek other appropriate relief. The sources of law that may support these motions are identified in the following paragraph. They reflect the general recognition that, in legal contemplation, a defendant may be hurt by trial delay in each of three distinct ways: (1) by unduly prolonged pretrial incarceration; (2) by the inconvenience, indignity, and anxiety of having unresolved charges pending for a protracted period; and (3) by prejudice to the defendant's ability to present defensive evidence at trial. Each of these three harms is the product of differing circumstances in addition to the fact and duration of the delay — whether the defendant is jailed or bailed; whether, if bailed, the pendency of charges affects the defend-ant's eligibility for military service, for public assistance, or for other benefits; whether the evidence in support of the charge and of the defenses to it is largely testimonial or documentary, and, if it is testimonial, whether the witnesses disappear or grow forgetful. Each harm is appropriately remedied by a different relief: (1) prolonged incarceration alone, by release from custody; (2) "pendency" problems alone, by dismissal of the charges without prejudice; (3) evidence loss and similar fair trial problems, by dismissal with prejudice. The various sources of "speedy trial" rights listed in the next paragraph may respond to concern for only one of these harms, or more than one, and may therefore offer relief that is appropriate or inappropriate to remedy undue delay under the circumstances of a given case. It is important to keep this in mind in reading the applicable statutes and judicial decisions, which are often confusingly written. An example will make the point. A defendant is arrested, jailed, indicted, and held six months without trial because of docket congestion and a prosecutor whose trial staff is overloaded. At the end of six months the defendant moves for dismissal of the indictment, citing the constitutional right to a speedy trial. The motion is denied. Two months later the defendant is tried and convicted. An appellate court affirms in an opinion stating broadly that six months' delay (or eight) did not violate the speedy trial right. What this means is only that the defendant's right to be tried within a period when s/he could fairly defend against the charges or else to have the prosecution dismissed with prejudice was not here violated. It does not mean that if an identical defendant, after four months, moved for an immediate trial listing, the Constitution would not entitle that defendant to it. Cf. *Braden v. 30th Judicial Circuit Court,* 410 U.S. 484, 489-90 (1973). And it does not mean that if the defendant moved for release from custody by reason of the delay, the Constitution would not require his or her release on recognizance within considerably less than eight months — or six, or four. (These conclusions are not inconsistent with the apparently monolithic view taken of the remedy for denial of a speedy trial in *Strunk v. United States,* 412 U.S. 434 (1973), since that case holds only that when delay *has* been determined to be sufficient to warrant dismissal with prejudice, *id.* at 435-37, then "dismissal must remain . . . 'the only possible remedy,'" *id.* at 440. Similarly, the discussion in *United States v. MacDonald,* 435 U.S. 850, 858-61 & n.8 (1978), occurs in the context of "[t]he issue . . . whether a defendant could appeal, prior to trial, a District Court's order denying his motion *to dismiss the indictment* because of an alleged violation of his Sixth Amendment right to a speedy trial." *United States v. Hollywood Motor Car Co.*, 458 U.S. 263, 266-67 (1982) (per curiam) (emphasis added).)

[307] Sources of speedy trial rights. Defense counsel may invoke one or more of the following sources of authority in support of a complaint of undue trial delay:

(A) *Court rules or the inherent power of the court authorizing the court to control its calendar and, if necessary, to dismiss for want of prosecution.* [Paragraph [308] *infra*]

(B) *Statutes delimiting the periods within which a charging paper must be filed following commitment or within which a trial must be had following commitment or the filing of the charging paper.* [Paragraph [309] *infra*]

(C) *Statutes requiring that prisoners be brought to trial within a specified time following their demand for trial.* [Paragraph [310] *infra*]

(D) *The Interstate Agreement on Detainers.* [Paragraph [310] *infra*]

(E) *State constitutional guarantees of speedy trial.* [Paragraph [311] *infra*]

(F) The Sixth Amendment guarantee of speedy trial. [Paragraph [311] *infra*]

(G) *The Due Process right of fair trial.* [Paragraph [311] *infra*]

[308] The court's docket control; dismissal for want of prosecution. All courts have power to control their dockets and the calendaring of pending cases. They may entertain motions to advance or requests for an immediate trial listing. They may also dismiss for want of prosecution. These powers may be expressly recognized by statute or court rule, such as 18 U.S.C. §3162(a) and Federal Criminal Rule 48(b). But, whether or not expressly conferred, they are an inherent attribute of every court. A motion to advance or to dismiss grounded on this power invokes the court's discretion, reviewable for abuse, and raises no particularly vexing technical problems. The question presented is simply whether, in light of all the circumstances of the case, the harm shown to have occurred or that will occur to the defendant by reason of trial delay, and the general policies of speedy criminal trial (a policy that has a constitutional base, see paragraph [311] *infra*) and docket preference for criminal cases (a policy frequently explicit in court rules, such as Federal Criminal Rule 50), the case should be advanced or dismissed as requested. "The longer the delay, the greater the presumptive or actual prejudice to the defendant, in terms of his [or her] ability to prepare for trial or the restrictions on his [or her] liberty." *United States v. Taylor*, 108 S. Ct. 2413, 2421 (1988). Dismissal may be with or without prejudice, depending on the sort of harm to the defendant that appears (see paragraph [306] *supra*) and on the general equities of the situation. Counsel who secures an order of dismissal should be sure that it specifies dismissal with prejudice if this is what it means. The form of the motion and the judge to whom it is addressed (presiding judge, assignment judge, trial judge) are dictated by local practice. Counsel will find that s/he increases the defendant's equities and the probability of a favorable ruling if s/he moves to advance as soon as s/he is ready for trial and thereafter renews that motion or moves to dismiss. Judges will not be sympathetic to a case in which the defense allows several months to go by without asking for a trial and then moves for dismissal on the ground that the defendant has not been tried. If counsel does not claim that the prosecution should be dismissed and is not anxious to precipitate trial but *is* concerned about the defendant's having to remain in jail throughout a protracted pretrial period, an application for release on recognizance is in order. This may ordinarily be entertained by the court at any time (see paragraphs [70]-[72] *supra*), and the duration of past and anticipated future confinement is a pertinent consideration on the merits.

[309] Statutes delimiting time periods in the pretrial stages. (A) Most states have statutes (often called "two-term statutes" because of the prevalence of that period as a time restriction) which make one or more of the following requirements: (1) that indictment or information be filed within a specified time (in days or months or terms of court) following bind-over (or "commitment"); (2) that the case be brought to trial within a specified time after filing of indictment or information; (3) that, irrespective of the time of filing of the indictment or information, the case be tried within a specified time following bind-over (or "commitment").

(B) The statutes are generally very badly drafted and raise vexing problems of construction. Among the question on which the jurisdictions split, for example, are (a) under statutes requiring that a defendant "committed" on a charge be indicted or tried within x period, (i) whether the statute applies only to jailed defendants or to both jailed defendants and bailed defendants; (ii) whether "commitment" means arrest or bind-over or something else (such as receipt within the county of a defendant arrested elsewhere); (b) under statutes which require that a defendant not timely indicted or tried be "discharged by the court," (i) whether "discharge" means release from custody or dismissal of the charges; (ii) if the former, release on what terms; (iii) if the latter, whether the dismissal is with or without prejudice; and (c) under statutes that excuse delay beyond the specified period if it happens "upon the application of the defendant," (i) whether defense application merely tolls the statutory period or entirely deprives the defendant of the statute's benefit after one "application," and (ii) whether "application" means an express request for continuance or may be supplied constructively if the defendant files a time-consuming motion of another sort (a motion to suppress, for example) or if the defendant merely acquiesces in the delay.

(C) This last issue is the point of entry of the so-called *demand rule* adopted under the statutes by a number of jurisdictions. The "demand rule" holds that a defendant waives the benefit of the statutory periods unless, by formal motion to the court, s/he expressly invokes them and demands a trial. The effect of the demand rule ordinarily is that the statutory periods, which appear on the statute books to run from "commitment," "indictment," and so forth, actually run from demand. The early defense demand suggested as advisable in paragraph [308] *supra* is accordingly an absolute essential under the statutes if counsel wants to hold the prosecution to anything approaching the statutory timetables. (The Supreme Court's rejection of the "demand rule" under the Sixth Amendment (see paragraph [311](C)(2) *infra*) does not, of course, oblige the state courts to abandon it insofar as speedy trial rights are claimed under state law rather than the federal Constitution. However, the reasoning of the decision, *Barker v. Wingo,* 407 U.S. 514 (1972), can be cited to the state courts in support of an argument for a similar ruling as a matter of state law.)

(D) Another point of trouble under the statutes has been the question of their application to persons imprisoned on other convictions or awaiting trial on other charges, within or without the jurisdiction. Traditionally, the "two-term statutes" were held inapplicable to these persons, with the result that special statutory provisions were enacted to deal with them in some states. See paragraph [310] *infra.* Where there is no statute of the latter sort, the courts are increasingly coming to hold that the general "two-term statutes" do apply to defendants incarcerated under other convictions or charges and that they require the prosecuting authority to make diligent efforts, at the least, to borrow the defendant temporarily from his or her custodians so that s/he may be tried within the statutory period if s/he wishes. And see paragraph [311](C)(1) *infra.*

(E) The local statutes and their construction are the starting place for research when counsel has a speedy-trial problem. On issues that are not resolved by the caselaw in counsel's jurisdiction, research in other jurisdictions will often produce persuasive authority for favorable constructions of the local law, since many jurisdictions have statutes that use similar terminology.

[310] Statutes requiring that prisoners be brought to trial on demand; the Interstate Agreement. (A) In a number of states, statutes authorize persons serving terms of imprisonment to demand that other outstanding charges against them be tried expeditiously. These statutes commonly provide for dismissal of the outstanding charges (usually with prejudice) if the prisoner is not brought to trial within a specified time after his or her demand.

(B) The statutes are ordinarily construed to apply only to state prisoners within the state. The problem of outstate prisoners is the subject of the Interstate Agreement on Detainers. This interstate compact, in force in most states, provides essentially (1) that a prisoner in any contracting state (state *A*) against whom there are pending charges in another contracting state

(state *B*) which have been lodged against the prisoner as detainers may request trial by written notice to the prosecutor and court where the charges are pending; (2) that the notice serves as a waiver of extradition and a request for trial on all charges which have been lodged as detainers against the prisoner in state *B;* (3) that the prisoner's custodians shall thereupon notify all other prosecutors and courts in state *B* where there are pending charges lodged as detainers against the prisoner and shall deliver the prisoner to state *B;* (4) that the prisoner must be tried within 180 days of his or her request for trial and within 120 days of his or her receipt in state *B,* or the charges upon which s/he demanded trial shall be dismissed with prejudice; and (5) that the prisoner may be tried on other pending charges in state *B,* which were lodged as detainers against him or her, but if s/he is not tried on those charges before s/he is returned to state *A,* the charges must be dismissed with prejudice. The Interstate Agreement is a complicated document and must be consulted for details. *See generally United States v. Mauro,* 436 U.S. 340 (1978); *Cuyler v. Adams,* 449 U.S. 433 (1981); *Carchman v. Nash,* 473 U.S. 716 (1985).

[311] State and federal guarantees of speedy trial; the federal Due Process guarantee. (A) Backstopping the common-law and statutory protections against undue trial delay are the constitutional Speedy Trial Clauses, state and federal. These are significant not only in their own right but also as expressions of a policy in light of which the often ambiguous statutes must be read (paragraph [309] *supra*) and the common-law judicial discretion exercised (paragraph [308] *supra*).

(B) The caselaw in a jurisdiction must be consulted to determine whether the applicable state constitutional provision is construed to protect all three of the "speedy trial" concerns identified in paragraph [306] *supra.* The federal Sixth Amendment Speedy Trial Clause, incorporated into the Fourteenth Amendment and hence made binding on the states by *Klopfer v. North Carolina,* 386 U.S. 213 (1967), is so construed. "This guarantee is an important safeguard to prevent undue and oppressive incarceration prior to trial, to minimize anxiety and concern accompanying public accusation and to limit the possibilities that long delay will impair the ability of an accused to defend himself [or herself]." *United States v. Ewell,* 383 U.S. 116, 120 (1966). *See also Barker v. Wingo,* 407 U.S. 514, 532 (1972); *Dillingham v. United States,* 423 U.S. 64, 65 (1975) (per curiam); *United States v. MacDonald,* 435 U.S. 850, 858 (1978); *United States v. MacDonald,* 456 U.S. 1, 7-9 (1982). The Speedy Trial Clause may thus be invoked to support a demand for trial or for release from confinement or for dismissal of pending charges or for outright dismissal of the prosecution with prejudice, as the circumstances make appropriate. *See Klopfer v. North Carolina, supra* (demand for trial); *Braden v. 30th Judicial Circuit Court,* 410 U.S. 484 (1973) (demand for trial); *Smith v. Hooey,* 393 U.S. 374 (1969) (demand for trial or dismissal); *Dickey v. Florida,* 398 U.S. 30 (1970) (dismissal); *Strunk v. United States,* 412 U.S. 434 (1973) (dismissal). The standards that must be met in order to justify each of these four sorts of relief are obviously different. Each considers, however, both the duration of the delay (measured from the starting point described in paragraph (D) *infra*) and its "oppressive" quality, in terms of willful vexatiousness or avoidable negligence of the prosecution on the one hand and harm to the relevant interests of the defendant on the other. *See, e.g., Petition of Provoo,* 17 F.R.D. 183 (D.Md. 1955), *aff'd per curiam,* 350 U.S. 857 (1955). *Compare Dickey v. Florida, supra, with Harrison v. United States,* 392 U.S. 219, 221-22 n.4 (1968). The major factors to be considered in determining whether pretrial delay violates the Sixth Amendment have been described as the "[l]ength of delay, the reason for the delay, the defendant's assertion of his [or her] right, and prejudice to the defendant." *Barker v. Wingo, supra,* 407 U.S. at 530. *See also United States v. MacDonald,* 435 U.S. 850, 858 (1978); *United States v. Loud Hawk,* 106 S. Ct. 648, 655 (1986); *United States v. Eight Thousand Eight Hundred and Fifty Dollars,* 461 U.S. 555, 564 (1983); *United States v. Valenzuela-Bernal,* 458 U.S. 858, 868-69 (1982) (dictum). "[N]one of the four factors [is] . . . either a necessary or sufficient condition to the finding of a deprivation of the right of speedy trial. Rather, they are related factors and must be considered together with such other circumstances as may be relevant." *Barker v. Wingo, supra,* 407 U.S. at 533; *see Moore v. Arizona,* 414 U.S. 25, 26 (1973) (per curiam). Thus "an affirmative demonstration of prejudice" is not always necessary to sustain a speedy trial claim. *Ibid.* Nor is it any longer necessary (as implied in *Pollard v. United States,* 352 U.S. 354, 361 (1957)) that the delay be "purposeful or oppressive." "Unintentional delays caused by overcrowded court dockets or understaffed prosecutors are among the factors to be weighed less heavily than intentional delay, calculated to hamper the defense, in determining whether the Sixth Amendment has been violated but, as we noted in *Barker v. Wingo,* 407 U.S. 514, 531 (1972), they must

> 'nevertheless . . . be considered since the ultimate responsibility for such circumstances must rest with the government rather than with the defendant.'"

Strunk v. United States, supra, 412 U.S. at 436.

(C) In the ordinary criminal case the time within which the Sixth Amendment requires that the defendant be tried will seldom be shorter than the time limited for trial by the local "two-term statute," court rule, "speedy trial plan," or other state-law limitation. But the incorporation of the Sixth Amendment, so as to make it applicable to state criminal trials, is nevertheless important for several reasons.

(1) Whatever may be the law under the relevant local statutes (see paragraphs [309]-[310] *supra*), the *Smith v. Hooey, Dickey,* and *Braden* decisions, subparagraph (B) *supra,* firmly establish that the Sixth Amendment right to a speedy trial is not tolled during a period of the defendant's out-of-state incarceration. Rather, upon the defendant's demand for trial, the state must make all practicable efforts to obtain the defendant's return to the jurisdiction; and if it does not, the defendant is constitutionally entitled to appropriate relief (see paragraph [306] *supra*) from the ensuing harm.

(2) In *Barker v. Wingo,* 407 U.S. 514 (1972), the Supreme Court rejected the "demand rule" (paragraph [309](C) *supra*) in its usual categorical state-law form of a "rule that a defendant who fails to demand a speedy trial forever waives his [or her] right." 407 U.S. at 528. Under the Sixth Amendment, then, a demand for trial is not the necessary precondition of a claim of denial of a speedy trial, although "the defendant's assertion of or failure to assert his [or her] right to a speedy trial [by demand-

ing trial] is one of the factors to be considered in an inquiry into the deprivation of the right." *Ibid.*

(3) Because the Sixth Amendment responds to all three of the basic speedy-trial concerns, whereas a state statute or court rule may not (see paragraph [306] *supra;* subparagraph (B) *supra*), the Amendment may prohibit delays that are immune against correction under state law. Similarly, because it does not turn upon such technicalities as "commitment" (see paragraph [309](B) *supra*), it may reach cases that fall through loopholes in the state speedy-trial laws.

(4) Sixth Amendment claims seeking to expedite trial (*see Braden v. 30th Judicial Circuit Court,* subparagraph (B) *supra*) or complaining of failure to dismiss prosecutions for want of a speedy trial (*see Barker v. Wingo, supra*) may be raised in federal *habeas corpus* proceedings before or after trial respectively, following exhaustion of state remedies (see paragraph [71] *supra;* paragraph [472](D) *infra*). Federal *habeas* is now available to defendants who have been released on bail or recognizance as well as to those in custody. *Hensley v. Municipal Court,* 411 U.S. 345 (1973); *Justices of Boston Municipal Court v. Lydon,* 466 U.S. 294 (1984).

(D) When prolonged delay adversely affects an accused's ability to prepare, preserve, and present defensive evidence, the Due Process right to a fair trial may be violated. *E.g., United States v. Chase,* 135 F. Supp. 230 (N.D. Ill. 1955). The significance of this independent Fifth and Fourteenth Amendment right against trial delay arises principally from the limitation imposed upon the Speedy Trial Clause of the Sixth by *United States v. Marion,* 404 U.S. 307 (1971), holding that the Sixth Amendment right to speedy trial attaches only at the time of "indictment, information, or other formal charge" or of "arrest," *id.* at 321, whichever comes first (*see Dillingham v. United States,* subparagraph (B) *supra; United States v. MacDonald,* 456 U.S. 1, 6-7 (1982); *United States v. Gouveia,* 467 U.S. 180, 190 (1984) (dictum); *United States v. Loud Hawk,* subparagraph (B) *supra,* 106 S. Ct. at 653-54 & n.13 (dictum); *Baker v. McCollan,* 443 U.S. 137, 144 (1979) (dictum)). *Marion* involed a speedy-trial claim based entirely on prearrest, precharge delay (*see also United States v. MacDonald,* 456 U.S. 1, 11 (1982)); and so it does not foreclose the contention that protracted precharge delay may be a relevant or even controlling consideration in determining how speedily postcharge proceedings must move in order to satisfy the Sixth Amendment in cases in which a defendant complains of *both* precharge and postcharge delay. *Cf. Taylor v. United States,* 238 F.2d 259 (D.C. Cir. 1956). There is an unfortunate *dictum* in *United States v. Lovasco,* 431 U.S. 783, 788 (1977), to the effect that "as far as the Speedy Trial Clause of the Sixth Amendment is concerned, [precharge, prearrest] . . . delay is wholly irrelevant"; but *Lovasco,* like *Marion,* raised an issue only of "delay between the commission of an offense and the initiation of prosecution" in the case of an unarrested defendant, 431 U.S. at 784, and the *dictum* cannot properly be read as forbidding consideration of precharge delay insofar as it compounds the harms suffered by a defendant whose Sixth Amendment contention rests in part upon undue delay in bringing him or her to trial following the filing of the charging paper. Similarly, in *United States v. Loud Hawk,* subparagraph (B) *supra,* in which the Court held that after an indictment had been dismissed and the defendants were not "incarcerated or subjected to other substantial restrictions on their liberty, a court should not weigh that time towards a claim [that prosecution following reinstatement of the indictment was barred] under the Speedy Trial Clause," 106 S. Ct. at 654, the defendants do not appear to have made any assertion that the excluded time interacted in any way with delays during periods that *were* governed by the Sixth Amendment, so as to exacerbate any prejudice caused by the latter delays. In any event, both *Marion* (404 U.S. at 324-26) and *Lovasco* (431 U.S. at 789, 795-97 & n.17) recognize that the Due Process Clauses forbid delay at any stage of a criminal proceeding—including prearrest, precharge delay—that unfairly hampers the defendant's ability to make a defense. *See also United States v. MacDonald,* 456 U.S. 1, 7-8 (1982); *cf. Fontaine v. California,* 390 U.S. 593, 595-96 (1968); and see the cases collected in the *Marion* opinion, 404 U.S. at 316-17 n.8, 324 n.17. "[T]he due process inquiry must consider the reasons for the delay as well as the prejudice to the accused," *United States v. Lovasco, supra,* 431 U.S. at 790; and although "investigative delay" will not support a due process contention, at least in the absence of very substantial and well-documented prejudice to the accused's trial defenses, *id.* at 795-96, any sort of "delay undertaken by the [prosecution] . . . solely 'to gain tactical advantage over the accused,'" *id.* at 795, or perhaps "'prosecutorial delay incurred in reckless disregard of circumstances, known to the prosecution, suggesting that there existed an appreciable risk that delay would impair the ability to mount an effective defense,'" *id.* at 795 n.17, would present a stronger case for dismissal on due process grounds. *See United States v. Gouveia, supra,* 467 U.S. at 192 (dictum). Federal Due Process claims, like Sixth Amendment claims, are not confined by the technicalities of the "two-term statutes" or by the demand rule (*see United States v. Chase, supra*) and are raisable in federal *habeas corpus.*

XXII. INTERLOCUTORY REVIEW AND PREROGATIVE WRITS

[312] **Obtaining interlocutory review of pretrial orders by prerogative writ and similar proceedings.** In most jurisdictions pretrial rulings against a criminal defendant relating to such matters as discovery (see paragraphs [265]-[274] *supra*), trial delay (see paragraphs [302]-[311] *supra*), severance (see paragraphs [259]-[264] *supra*), and change of venue (see paragraphs [254]-[257] *supra*) are unappealable because they are interlocutory. The traditional manner of securing appellate review of claimed errors in these matters is upon an appeal from the final judgment of conviction. See paragraph [472] *infra*. Except in a few states—for example, California, where interlocutory review by prerogative writs is expressly authorized by statute in some situations and has been encouraged by judicial decision in others—there is no established practice of providing immediate review of interim orders in criminal proceedings even when, as a practical matter, they may be uncorrectable after verdict. (Concerning the restricted scope of pre-judgment appeals as of right in federal practice, *see Abney v. United States*, 431 U.S. 651 (1977) (denial of motion to dismiss indictment on grounds of double jeopardy is appealable); *Richardson v. United States*, 468 U.S. 317 (1984) (same); *Helstoski v. Meanor*, 442 U.S. 500 (1979) (denial of motion to dismiss indictment on grounds of violation of Speech or Debate Clause is appealable); *United States v. MacDonald*, 435 U.S. 850 (1978) (denial of motion to dismiss indictment on grounds of violation of the right to speedy trial is not appealable); *United States v. Hollywood Motor Car Co.*, 458 U.S. 263 (1982) (per curiam) (denial of motion to dismiss indictment on grounds of prosecutorial vindictiveness is not appealable); *Flanagan v. United States*, 465 U.S. 259 (1984) (order disqualifying defense counsel from representing multiple defendants is not appealable).)

[313] **Mandamus and prohibition.** Yet in virtually every state there are excellent doctrinal bases to support interlocutory review. Appellate courts are generally given by statute the power to issue the prerogative writs of mandamus and prohibi-

tion. Traditionally, the writs lie to compel (in the case of mandamus) or to prohibit (in the case of prohibition) action by an inferior court that is conducting any proceeding in a manner rendered unlawful by lack of jurisdiction or gross abuse of discretion. Many pretrial rulings in criminal cases would seem susceptible of being brought within the framework of these concepts. "Jurisdiction" is a flexible notion, as the evolution of the term in *habeas corpus* practice attests. *See Johnson v. Zerbst,* 304 U.S. 458 (1938); *Fay v. Noia,* 372 U.S. 391 (1963). "Lack of jurisdiction" needs not be used exclusively to connote the absence of any competence in a court to act at all in a proceeding; it may also signify that some fundamental principle of law disempowers the particular action which the court is taking in a matter otherwise within its competence to adjudicate. *See Pulliam v. Allen,* 466 U.S. 522, 532-36 (1984) (dictum). And "gross abuse of discretion" may mean almost anything an appellate court wants it to mean, as every lawyer knows. Moreover, it is not uncommon for appellate courts, when refusing to issue prerogative writs on the ground that no "abuse of discretion" appears, nevertheless to offer some gratuitous advice to the trial court regarding the appropriate exercise of its discretion or otherwise to express opinions on the merits that the trial court may thereafter take to heart. *See, e.g., Kerr v. United States District Court,* 426 U.S. 394, 405-6 (1976). Hence, particularly when defense counsel can urge that a pretrial order in a criminal matter (a) is plainly wrong or (b) is wrong by force of a constitutional guarantee and (c) has the effect of imposing adverse consequences upon the defendant that may be irremediable at a subsequent stage, the case for interlocutory relief by prerogative writ would seem to be strong. Two obvious instances will serve to exemplify the principle:

(A) A defendant who has been held for months without trial moves for the setting of a trial date forthwith, urging that his or her rights under the Speedy Trial Clauses of the federal and state constitutions will be violated by any further delay. The defendant does not contend that those constitutional guarantees require the dismissal of the prosecution with prejudice if s/he is not tried immediately, but s/he does assert that they require that s/he be tried immediately. In other words, s/he says that s/he has a right to speed up the proceedings, even if s/he has no right to absolution from criminal liability if they are not speeded up. See paragraphs [306], [311] *supra*. The trial court denies the motion. Clearly, if the defendant is now obliged to wait for trial and to raise his or her contention on appeal from conviction, the contention will be entirely defeated. It will be mooted by trial, and there will remain nothing for an appellate court to do except to lament the uncorrectable violation of a constitutional right. *Cf. Abney v. United States*, 431 U.S. 651, 660-62 (1977), paragraph [312] *supra*. Since the right that this defendant seeks to vindicate — unlike the right to *dismissal of the prosecution* for denial of a speedy trial (*see United States v. MacDonald*, 435 U.S. 850 (1978)) — is "one that must be upheld prior to trial if it is to be enjoyed at all," *United States v. Hollywood Motor Car Co.*, 458 U.S. 263, 270 (1982) (per curiam) (dictum), pretrial appellate review by way of prerogative writ is imperative. *Cf. Stack v. Boyle*, 342 U.S. 1, 4 (1951) (bail).

(B) A defendant moves for the appointment of a psychiatric expert, at state expense, to assist in the preparation of a defense of insanity. The defendant alleges that s/he is indigent, that s/he has a constitutional right to the assistance of a psychiatric consultant at public expense (see paragraphs [299]-[300] *supra*), and that it is crucial that the psychiatrist examine the defendant *now*, at a time relatively soon after the date of the offense, since the greater the lapse of time between the date on which the defendant seeks to prove s/he was insane and the date of the examination, the less persuasive proof the examination will provide. *Cf. Drope v. Missouri*, 420 U.S. 162, 183 (1975), and authorities cited. The motion is denied. If the defendant must wait for trial and appeal to raise the claim of error in this ruling, s/he may not be examined for years. Of course, unlike the contention in the preceding example, this contention needs not be irrevocably lost. A court on appeal after conviction could sustain the contention and hold that the denial of a mental examination before trial so prejudiced the defense that the Constitution now forbids the defendant's conviction and requires the charges to be dismissed. But an appellate court might well be persuaded of the unsatisfactory nature of that result as compared with giving the defendant a psychiatric examination when s/he asks for it. Here again, the argument for interlocutory review appears overwhelming.

[314] The advantages of interlocutory review. Counsel would be well advised to keep in mind the possibility of using the prerogative writs to secure relief against unfavorable pretrial orders. Issues such as speedy trial, double jeopardy, discovery, change of venue, and the right to state-paid expert consultants and investigative services seem particularly suited to interlocutory review by mandamus and prohibition. As a practical matter, defense claims relating to these subjects will frequently appear to an appellate court in a more favorable light before trial than after. After trial the result of sustaining the defendant's contention is the reversal of a conviction, making waste of a good deal of judicial and prosecutorial effort. After trial the case may come before appellate judges on a record that reeks of the defendant's guilt. Under these circumstances it is no surprise that the judges will resolve all doubts in favor of the prosecution. Furthermore, particular claims may be made more persuasive and their equities more visible at the pretrial stage. In reviewing the denial of a defendant's request for discovery after verdict, the appellate court will have the benefit of hindsight and may say that, in light of the developments at trial, the defendant does not seem to have been hurt by not knowing whatever s/he was denied the right to know in preparing his or her defense. On an application for a prerogative writ before trial, the appellate judges know no more about the case than does defense counsel. Sharing counsel's helplessness, they can better appreciate it. They may, therefore, rule in the defendant's favor before trial in a case in which they would be hard pressed to do so after conviction. Finally, interlocutory review proceedings may be a headache for the prosecutor. S/he is probably going to have to face an appeal after conviction in any event, so the prospect of such an appeal does not give the prosecutor any uncommonly strong reason to capitulate on close questions that the trial court can probably be persuaded to decide in the prosecution's favor. By contrast, the extra work of opposing an interlocutory petition for mandamus or prohibition may seem to the prosecutor to be incommensurate with the harm of giving the defendant what defense counsel wants.

TABLE OF CASES AND AUTHORITIES

(References are to section numbers)

CASES

A

Abel v. United States, 362 U.S. 217 (1960), 231, 248
Abney v. United States, 431 U.S. 651 (1977), 312, 313
Adams v. Illinois, 405 U.S. 278 (1972), 270
Adams v. Williams, 407 U.S. 143 (1972), 230, 236, 246
Aetna Life Ins. Co. v. Lavoie, 106 S. Ct. 1580 (1986), 258
Aguilar v. Texas, 378 U.S. 108 (1964), 230, 236, 240, 241
Air Pollution Variance Board v. Western Alfalfa Corp., 416 U.S. 861 (1974), 231, 244
Aiuppa v. United States, 338 F.2d 146 (10th Cir. 1964), 236
Ake v. Oklahoma, 470 U.S. 68 (1985), 299, 301
Albertson v. Subversive Activities Control Board, 382 U.S. 70 (1965), 232
Alcorta v. Texas, 355 U.S. 28 (1957), 270
Alderman v. United States, 394 U.S. 165 (1969), 230, 231, 243, 245, 251
Allen v. Illinois, 106 S. Ct. 2988 (1986), 232
Almeida-Sanchez v. United States, 413 U.S. 266 (1973), 230, 240, 246
Amadeo v. Zant, 108 S. Ct. 1771 (1988), 224
Amos v. United States, 255 U.S. 313 (1921), 240
Andresen v. Maryland, 427 U.S. 463 (1976), 230, 232, 240, 241, 253, 274
Anspach v. United States, 305 F.2d 48, 960 (10th Cir. 1962), 243
Argersinger v. Hamlin, 407 U.S. 25 (1972), 233, 300
Arizona v. Hicks, 107 S. Ct. 1149 (1987), 223, 230, 231, 240, 243, 248, 253
Arizona v. Mauro, 107 S. Ct. 1931 (1987), 232, 233, 237, 240
Arizona v. Manypenny, 451 U.S. 232 (1981), 222
Arizona v. Roberson, 108 S. Ct. 2093 (1988), 232, 233, 240
Arizona v. Youngblood, 109 S. Ct. 333 (1988), 237, 270
Arkansas v. Sanders, 442 U.S. 753 (1979), 246, 248
Arsenault v. Massachusetts, 393 U.S. 5 (1968) (per curiam), 233
Ashley v. Texas, 319 F.2d 80 (5th Cir. 1963), 270

B

Baker v. McCollan, 443 U.S. 137 (1979), 228, 230, 311
Baldasar v. Illinois, 446 U.S. 222 (1980), 233
Barbee v. Warden, 331 F.2d 842 (4th Cir. 1964), 270
Barker v. Wingo, 407 U.S. 514, (1972), 311
Baxter v. Palmigiano, 425 U.S. 308 (1976), 232, 270
Baxter v. United States, 188 F.2d 119 (6th Cir. 1951), 244
Baysden v. United States, 271 F.2d 325 (4th Cir. 1959), 240, 241
Bearden v. Georgia, 461 U.S. 660 (1983), 299

Beasley v. State, 81 Nev. 431, 404 P.2d 911 (1965), 266
Beatty v. United States, 389 U.S. 45 (1967) (per curiam), *rev'g* 377 F.2d 181 (5th Cir. 1967), 233, 249
Beck v. Ohio, 379 U.S. 89 (1964), 236, 246, 247
Beecher v. Alabama, 389 U.S. 35 (1967) (per curiam), 228
Bell v. Wolfish, 441 U.S. 520 (1979), 229, 231, 237, 242
Bellis v. United States, 417 U.S. 85 (1974), 232
Benanti v. United States, 355 U.S. 96 (1957), 245
Bentley v. Crist, 469 F.2d 854 (9th Cir. 1972), 281
Berger v. New York, 388 U.S. 41 (1967), 230, 240, 243
Berkemer v. McCarty, 468 U.S. 420 (1984), 232, 233, 236, 237, 240
Berry v. United States, 369 F.2d 386 (3d Cir. 1966), 246
Bielicki v. Superior Court, 57 Cal. 2d 602, 371 P.2d 288, 21 Cal. Rptr. 552 (1962), 242
Bivens v. Six Unknown Named Agents of Federal Bureau of Narcotics, 403 U.S. 388 (1971), 240
Black v. Romano, 471 U.S. 606 (1985), 299
Blackburn v Alabama, 361 U.S. 199 (1960), 228
Block v. Rutherford, 468 U.S. 576 (1984), 242
Bounds v. Smith, 430 U.S. 817 (1977), 266, 299
Bowen v. Eyman, 324 F. Supp. 339 (D. Ariz. 1970), 299
Bowen v. United States, 422 U.S. 916 (1975), 246
Boyd v. United States, 116 U.S. 616 (1886), 274
Braden v. 30th Judicial Circuit Court, 410 U.S. 484 (1973), 306, 311
Brady v. Maryland, 373 U.S. 83 (1963), 270, 271
Bram v. United States, 168 U.S. 532 (1897), 232
Branzburg v. Hayes, 408 U.S. 665 (1972), 270
Braswell v. United States, 108 S. Ct. 2284 (1988), 232
Brewer v. Williams, 430 U.S. 387 (1977), 233, 251
Brinegar v. United States, 338 U.S. 160 (1949), 241
Britt v. North Carolina, 404 U.S. 226 (1971), 270, 299
Brooks v. Florida, 389 U.S. 413 (1967) (per curiam), 228, 237
Brooks v. Tennessee, 406 U.S. 605 (1972), 270, 274, 280
Brower v. County of Inyo, 109 S. Ct. 1378 (1989), 236, 247
Brown v. Illinois, 422 U.S. 590 (1975), 232, 236, 251, 253
Brown v. Mississippi, 297 U.S. 278 (1936), 228
Brown v. Texas, 443 U.S. 47 (1979), 229, 230, 236, 243, 246
Brown v. United States, 411 U.S. 223 (1973), 242, 253
Bruton v. United States, 391 U.S. 123 (1968), 264, 270
Bumper v North Carolina, 391 U.S. 543 (1968), 240
Burdeau v. McDowell, 256 U.S. 465 (1921), 250
Burns v. Ohio, 360 U.S. 252 (1959), 299
Bush v. McCollum, 231 F. Supp. 560 (N.D. Tex. 1964), *aff'd*, 344 F.2d 672 (5th Cir. 1965), 299
Bynum v. United States, 262 F.2d 465 (D.C. Cir. 1959), 236

C

Cady v. Dombrowski, 413 U.S. 433 (1973), 229, 246

Caldwell v. Mississippi, 472 U.S. 320 (1985), 286, 301

California v. Beheler, 463 U.S. 1121 (1983) (per curiam), 232, 233, 236

California v. Byers, 402 U.S. 424 (1971), 232

California v. Carney, 471 U.S. 386 (1985), 230, 246

California v. Ciraolo, 106 S. Ct. 1809 (1986), 231, 242, 244

California v. Greenwood, 108 S. Ct. 1625 (1988), 223, 231, 243, 247, 248, 253

California v. Trombetta, 467 U.S. 479 (1984), 237, 268, 270

California Bankers Ass'n v. Shultz, 416 U.S. 21 (1974), 232

Camara v. Municipal Court, 387 U.S. 523 (1967), 229, 240, 246

Carchman v. Nash, 473 U.S. 716 (1985), 311

Cardwell v. Lewis, 417 U.S. 583 (1974), 230, 246, 248

Carroll v. United States, 267 U.S. 132 (1925), 230, 246, 247

Carter v. Kentucky, 450 U.S. 288 (1981), 232

Cash v. Williams, 455 F.2d 1227 (6th Cir. 1972), 246

Chambers v. Maroney, 399 U.S. 42 (1970), 230, 241, 246

Chambers v. Mississippi, 410 U.S. 284 (1973), 270

Chandler v. Florida, 449 U.S. 560 (1981), 255

Channel v. United States, 285 F.2d 217 (9th Cir. 1960), 240

Chapman v. United States, 365 U.S. 610 (1961), 229, 230, 240

Cherry v. Estelle, 507 F.2d 242 (5th Cir. 1975), *subsequent history in* 424 F. Supp. 548 (N.D. Tex. 1976), 299

Chimel v California, 395 U.S. 752 (1969), 229, 230, 232, 240

Christofferson v. Washington, 393 U.S. 1090 (1969), 241

City of Oklahoma City v. Tuttle, 471 U.S. 808 (1985), 228

City of Tacoma v. Heater, 67 Wash. 2d 733, 409 P.2d 867 (1966), 233, 237

Clewis v. Texas, 386 U.S. 707 (1967), 233

Clinton v. Virginia, 377 U.S. 158 (1964)(per curiam), *rev'g* 204 Va. 275, 130 S.E.2d 437 (1963), 243

Cole v. Arkansas, 333 U.S. 196 (1948), 270

Coleman v. Alabama, 399 U.S. 1 (1970), 270

Coleman v. Kemp, 778 F.2d 1487 (11th Cir. 1985), *rehearing en banc denied*, 782 F.2d 896 (11th Cir. 1986), 255

Coleman v. Zant, 708 F.2d 541 (11th Cir. 1983), 256

Collins v. Loisel, 262 U.S. 426 (1923), 222

Colonnade Catering Corp. v. United States, 397 U.S. 72 (1970), 236, 240

Colorado v. Bannister, 449 U.S. 1 (1980) (per curiam), 229, 230, 231, 246

Colorado v. Bertine, 107 S. Ct. 738 (1987), 229, 230, 238, 246

Colorado v. Connelly, 107 S. Ct. 515 (1986), 223, 228, 232, 233, 250, 251

Colorado v. Spring, 107 S. Ct. 851 (1987), 232, 233

Combs v. United States, 408 U.S. 244 (1972), 240, 243

Commonwealth v. Barnett, 484 Pa. 211, 398 A.2d 1019 (1979), 247

Commonwealth v. Borecky, 277 Pa. Super. 244, 419 A.2d 753 (1980), 250
Commonwealth v. Dembo, 451 Pa. 1, 301 A.2d 689 (1973), 250
Commonwealth v. Harris, 491 Pa. 402, 421 A.2d 199 (1980), 247
Commonwealth v. Smith, 470 Pa. 220, 368 A.2d 272 (1977), 240
Commonwealth v. Upton, 394 Mass. 363, 476 N.E.2d 548 (1985), 227
Connally v. Georgia, 429 U.S. 245 (1977) (per curiam), 240, 258
Connecticut v. Barrett, 107 S. Ct. 828 (1987), 233
Contee v. United States, 215 F.2d 324 (D.C. Cir. 1954), 241
Cool v. United States, 409 U.S. 100 (1972), 270
Coolidge v. New Hampshire, 403 U.S. 443 (1971), 229, 230, 231, 232, 240, 246
Cooper v. California, 386 U.S. 58 (1967), 229, 246
Corbitt v. New Jersey, 439 U.S. 212 (1978), 274
Corenevsky v. Superior Court, 36 Cal. 3d 307, 682 P.2d 360, 204 Cal. Rptr. 165 (1984), 299
Corbitt v. New Jersey, 439 U.S. 212 (1978), 274
Corngold v. United States, 367 F.2d 1 (9th Cir. 1966), 248, 250
Costello v. United States, 324 F.2d 260 (9th Cir. 1963), 241
Costello v. United States, 298 F.2d 99 (9th Cir. 1962), 241
Couch v. United States, 409 U.S. 322 (1973), 231, 232, 243, 248
Counselman v. Hitchcock, 142 U.S. 547 (1892), 232
Crane v. Kentucky, 106 S. Ct. 2142 (1986), 228, 270
Crist v. Bretz, 437 U.S. 28 (1978), 222
Cruz v. New York, 107 S. Ct. 1714 (1987), 264
Culombe v. Connecticut, 367 U.S. 568 (1961), 232
Cupp v. Murphy, 412 U.S. 291 (1973), 230, 236, 238, 247
Cuyler v. Adams, 449 U.S. 433 (1981), 310
Cuyler v. Sullivan, 446 U.S. 335 (1980), 233, 270, 274, 280, 282

D

Dalia v. United States, 441 U.S. 238 (1979), 240, 243, 249
Davis v. Alaska, 415 U.S. 308 (1974), 270, 273-A
Davis v. Mississippi, 394 U.S. 721 (1969), 231, 236
Davis v. North Carolina, 384 U.S. 737 (1966), 232
Davis v. United States, 328 U.S. 582 (1946), 230
Delaware v. Prouse, 440 U.S. 648 (1979), 229, 230, 231, 236, 238, 240, 246
Delaware v. Van Arsdall, 106 S. Ct. 1431 (1986), 270
DeLuna v. United States, 308 F.2d 140 (5th Cir. 1962), *rehearing denied*, 324 F.2d 375 (5th Cir. 1963), 232, 264
Dennis v. United States, 384 U.S. 855 (1966), 271
Desist v. United States, 394 U.S. 244 (1969), 243
Dickey v. Florida, 398 U.S. 30 (1970), 311
Dillingham v. United States, 423 U.S. 64 (1975) (per curiam), 311
Dobbert v. Florida, 432 U.S. 282 (1977), 255, 257

Doe v. United States, 108 S. Ct. 2341 (1988), 232, 250
Donovan v. Dewey, 452 U.S. 594 (1981), 229, 231, 236, 240, 243, 246
Donovan v. Lone Steer, Inc., 464 U.S. 408 (1984), 240
Douglas v. California, 372 U.S. 353 (1963), 299
Douglas Oil Co. v. Petrol Stops Northwest, 441 U.S. 211 (1979), 271
Dow Chemical Co. v. United States, 106 S. Ct. 1819 (1986), 231, 242, 243, 244
Doyle v. Ohio, 426 U.S. 610 (1976), 232, 233
Draper v. United States, 358 U.S. 307 (1959), 230, 236, 241
Draper v. Washington, 372 U.S. 487 (1963), 299
Drope v. Missouri, 420 U.S. 162 (1975), 313
Dukes v. Warden, 406 U.S. 250 (1972), 220
Dunaway v. New York, 442 U.S. 200 (1979), 230, 236, 241, 251
Dunn v. United States, 442 U.S. 100 (1979), 270
Durham v. United States, 403 F.2d 190 (9th Cir. 1968), 240
Dyke v. Taylor Implement Mfg. Co., 391 U.S. 216 (1968), 246

E

Eaton v. City of Tulsa, 415 U.S. 697 (1974) (per curiam), 280
Edwards v. Arizona, 451 U.S. 477 (1981), 232, 233, 240
Elkins v. United States, 364 U.S. 206 (1960), 251
Eng Fung Jem v. United States, 281 F.2d 803 (9th Cir. 1960), 240
Escobedo v. Illinois, 378 U.S. 478 (1964), 227, 233, 237
Estelle v. Smith, 451 U.S. 454 (1981), 232, 233, 237, 238, 274
Estelle v. Williams, 425 U.S. 501 (1976), 281, 299
Evans v. Superior Court, 11 Cal. 3d 617, 522 P.2d 681, 114 Cal. Rptr. 121 (1974), 270
Evitts v. Lucey, 469 U.S. 387 (1985), 233, 300
Exotic Coins, Inc. v. Beacom, 474 U.S. 892 (1985) (per curiam), *dismissing appeal from* 699 P.2d 930 (Colo. 1985), 240

F

Fare v. Michael C., 442 U.S. 707 (1979), 233
Faretta v. California, 422 U.S. 806 (1975), 270
Fay v. Noia, 372 U.S. 391 (1963), 313
Ferguson, *In re*, 5 Cal. 3d 525, 487 P.2d 1234, 96 Cal. Rptr. 594 (1971), 270
Ferguson v. Georgia, 365 U.S. 560 (1961), 270
Fields v. Wyrick, 706 F.2d 879 (8th Cir. 1983), 233
Finch v. United States, 433 U.S. 676 (1977) (per curiam), 222
Fisher v. United States, 425 U.S. 391 (1976), 231, 232, 253, 274
Flanagan v. United States, 465 U.S. 259 (1984), 312
Florida v. Meyers, 466 U.S. 380 (1984) (per curiam), 246
Florida v. Riley, 109 S. Ct. 693 (1989), 231, 242, 243, 244
Florida v. Rodriguez, 469 U.S. 1 (1984) (per curiam), 236, 240, 241, 247

Florida v. Royer, 460 U.S. 491 (1983), 230, 236, 240, 241, 247, 248, 253
Fong Foo v. United States, 369 U.S. 141 (1962) (per curiam), 222
Fontaine v. California, 390 U.S. 593 (1968), 311
Ford v. Wainwright, 106 S. Ct. 2595 (1968), 270
Fort Wayne Books, Inc. v. Indiana, 109 S. Ct. 916 (1989), 240
Foster v. California, 394 U.S. 440 (1969), 228
Frank v. Maryland, 359 U.S. 360 (1959), 240
Franks v. Delaware, 438 U.S. 154 (1978), 229, 230, 240, 240-A, 241, 273
Frazier v. Cupp, 394 U.S. 731 (1969), 230, 240
Frazier v. Roberts, 441 F.2d 1224 (8th Cir. 1971), 241
Fuller v. Alaska, 393 U.S. 80 (1968) (per curiam), 245
Fuller v. Oregon, 417 U.S. 40 (1974), 298

G

G.M. Leasing Corp. v. United States, 429 U.S. 338 (1977), 224, 229, 231, 240, 246
Gagnon v. Scarpelli, 411 U.S. 778 (1973), 270
Gannett Co. v. DePasquale, 443 U.S. 368 (1979), 255, 256
Gardner v. California, 393 U.S. 367 (1969), 299
Garner v. United States, 424 U.S. 648 (1976), 232, 233
Garrity v. New Jersey, 385 U.S. 493 (1967), 232
Gasaway v. State, 249 Ind. 241, 231 N.E.2d 513 (1967), 222
Gault, *In re*, 387 U.S. 1 (1967), 270
Geders v. United States, 425 U.S. 80 (1976), 233, 270, 280
Gerstein v. Pugh, 420 U.S. 103 (1975), 229, 233, 240, 241, 270
Gideon v. Wainwright, 372 U.S. 335 (1963), 227, 233, 270, 300
Giglio v. United States, 405 U.S. 150 (1972), 270
Gilbert v. California, 388 U.S. 263 (1967), 227, 232, 233, 237, 238, 240, 251
Gilbert v. United States, 291 F.2d 586 (9th Cir. 1961), *holding on other issues vacated*, 370 U.S. 650 (1962), 240
Giles v. Maryland, 386 U.S. 66 (1967), 270
Giordano v. United States, 394 U.S. 310 (1969), 251
Giordenello v. United States, 357 U.S. 480 (1958), 236
Goldberg v. Kelly, 397 U.S. 254 (1970), 270
Goldberg v. United States, 425 U.S. 94 (1976), 273-A
Goldman v. United States, 316 U.S. 129 (1942), 243
Gonzales v. United States, 348 U.S. 407 (1955), 270
Goss v. Lopez, 419 U.S. 565 (1975), 270
Gouled v. United States, 255 U.S. 298 (1921), 224, 249
Green v. Georgia, 442 U.S. 95 (1979) (per curiam), 270
Green v. Yeager, 223 F. Supp. 544 (D.N.J. 1963), *aff'd per curiam*, 332 F.2d 794 (3d Cir. 1964), 250
Greenholtz v. Inmates of the Nebraska Penal and Correctional Complex, 442 U.S. 1 (1979), 270

Greenwell v. United States, 317 F.2d 108 (D.C. Cir. 1963), 299, 301
Griffin v. California, 380 U.S. 609 (1965), 232
Griffin v. Illinois, 351 U.S. 12 (1956), 299
Griffin v. Wisconsin, 107 S. Ct. 3164 (1987), 229, 230, 231, 240, 241
Groppi v. Wisconsin, 400 U.S. 505 (1971), 255
Grosso v. United States, 390 U.S. 62 (1968), 232
Gustafson v. Florida, 414 U.S. 260 (1973), 238
Guzman v. State, 283 Ark. 112, 672 S.W.2d 656 (1984), 240

H

Hair v. United States, 289 F.2d 894 (D.C. Cir. 1961), 251
Hamilton v. Alabama, 368 U.S. 52 (1961), 220, 233
Harris v. New York, 401 U.S. 222 (1971), 251
Harris v. United States, 390 U.S. 234 (1968), 231, 240, 246
Harrison v. United States, 392 U.S. 219 (1968), 251, 253, 253-A, 311
Hayes v. Florida, 470 U.S. 811 (1985), 230, 236
Haynes v. United States, 390 U.S. 85 (1968), 232
Haynes v. Washington, 373 U.S. 503 (1963), 228, 237
Heike v. United States, 227 U.S. 131 (1913), 232
Heller v. New York, 413 U.S. 483 (1973), 240
Helstoski v. Meanor, 442 U.S. 500 (1979), 312
Henry v. United States, 361 U.S. 98 (1959), 230, 236
Hensley v. Municipal Court, 411 U.S. 345 (1973), 311
Hernandez v. United States, 353 F.2d 624 (9th Cir. 1965), 248
Herring v. New York, 422 U.S. 853 (1975), 270, 274
Hester v. United States, 265 U.S. 57 (1924), 231, 244
Hickman v. Taylor, 329 U.S. 495 (1947), 273-A
Higgins v. United States, 209 F.2d 819 (D.C. Cir. 1954), 240
Hill v. California, 401 U.S. 797 (1971), 222, 230, 236
Hoback v. Alabama, 607 F.2d 680 (5th Cir. 1979), 299
Hobson v. United States, 226 F.2d 890 (8th Cir. 1955), 244
Hoffa v. United States, 387 U.S. 231 (1967), 243, 249
Hoffa v. United States, 385 U.S. 293 (1966), 232, 249
Hoffman v. United States, 341 U.S. 479 (1951), 232
Holbrook v. Flynn, 106 S. Ct. 1340 (1986), 256
Holloway v. Arkansas, 435 U.S. 475 (1978), 233, 282
Holt v. Virginia, 381 U.S. 131 (1965), 258
Holzhey v. United States, 223 F.2d 823 (5th Cir. 1955), 248
Hudson v. Palmer, 468 U.S. 517 (1984), 231, 242
Hughes v. Johnson, 305 F.2d 67 (9th Cir. 1962), 240
Hutto v. Ross, 429 U.S. 28 (1976) (per curiam), 220

I

Illinois v. Andreas, 463 U.S. 765 (1983), 231, 242, 243, 248
Illinois v. Batchelder, 463 U.S. 1112 (1983) (per curiam), 246

Illinois v. Gates, 462 U.S. 213 (1983), 227, 240-A, 241, 253
Illinois v. Krull, 107 S. Ct. 1160 (1987), 223, 225, 253
Illinois v. LaFayette, 462 U.S. 640 (1983), 229, 230, 238, 240, 246, 247
Immigration and Naturalization Service v. Delgado, 466 U.S. 210 (1984), 231, 236
Immigration and Naturalization Service v. Lopez-Mendoza, 468 U.S. 1032 (1984), 251
Ingraham v. Wright, 430 U.S. 651 (1977), 236
Irvin v. Dowd, 366 U.S. 717 (1961), 256
Irwin v. Superior Court, 1 Cal. 3d 423, 462 P.2d 12, 82 Cal. Rptr. 484 (1969), 236

J

Jackson v. Denno, 378 U.S. 368 (1964), 228, 255
Jackson v. Superior Court, 13 Cal. App. 3d 440, 91 Cal. Rptr. 565 (1970), 254
Jackson v. Virginia, 443 U.S. 307 (1979), 270
James v. Louisiana, 382 U.S. 36 (1965) (per curiam), 230, 240
James v. Strange, 407 U.S. 128 (1972), 298
Jencks v. United States, 353 U.S. 657 (1957), 274
Jenkins v. McKeithen, 395 U.S. 411 (1969), 270
Jennings v. United States, 247 F.2d 784 (D.C. Cir. 1957), 240
Jernigan v. Louisiana, 446 U.S. 958 (1980), 236
Johnson v. Louisiana, 406 U.S. 356 (1972), 233, 251
Johnson v. Mississippi, 108 S. Ct. 1981 (1988), 224
Johnson v. Mississippi, 403 U.S. 212 (1971), 258
Johnson v. New Jersey, 384 U.S. 719 (1966), 251
Johnson v. United States, 333 U.S. 10 (1948), 229, 230, 231, 236, 240, 241, 246, 251
Johnson v. Zerbst, 304 U.S. 458 (1938), 313
Jones v. Cunningham, 313 F.2d 347 (4th Cir. 1963), 270
Jones v. Superior Court, 58 Cal. 2d 56, 372 P.2d 919, 22 Cal. Rptr. 879 (1962), 274
Jones v. United States, 362 U.S. 257 (1960), 231, 240, 241, 242
Jones v. United States, 357 U.S. 493 (1958), 229
Jones v. United States, 339 F.2d 419 (5th Cir. 1964), 231
Judd v. United States, 190 F.2d 649 (D.C. Cir. 1951), 240
Justices of Boston Municipal Court v. Lydon, 466 U.S. 294 (1984), 311

K

Kaiser v. New York, 394 U.S. 280 (1969), 243
Kastigar v. United States, 406 U.S. 441 (1972), 232, 251, 274
Katz v. United States, 389 U.S. 347 (1967), 229, 231, 242, 243, 245, 247, 248
Kehoe v. State, 521 So. 2d 1094 (Fla. 1988), 236

Kelley v. United States, 298 F.2d 310 (D.C. Cir. 1961), 236, 247
Kentucky v. Stincer, 107 S. Ct. 2658 (1987), 270
Ker v. California, 374 U.S. 23 (1963), 227, 240
Kercheval v. United States, 274 U.S. 220 (1927), 220
Kerr v. United States District Court, 426 U.S. 394 (1976), 273-B, 313
Kimmelman v. Morrison, 106 S. Ct. 2574 (1986), 223, 269, 270, 271
Kirby v. Illinois, 406 U.S. 682 (1972), 233, 238
Klopfer v. North Carolina, 386 U.S. 213 (1967), 311
Kolender v. Lawson, 461 U.S. 352 (1983), 232, 236
Kuhlmann v. Wilson, 106 S. Ct. 2616 (1986), 233, 249

L

Lakeside v. Oregon, 435 U.S. 333 (1978), 232, 274
Lankford v. Gelston, 364 F.2d 197 (4th Cir. 1966), 240, 241
Lanier v. South Carolina, 106 S. Ct. 297 (1985) (per curiam), 236
Lanza v. New York, 370 U.S. 139 (1962), 231, 242
Lee v. Florida, 392 U.S. 378 (1968), 245
Lee v. Illinois, 106 S. Ct. 2056 (1986), 264, 270
Lee v. United States, 221 F.2d 29 (D.C. Cir. 1954), 242, 247
Lefkowitz v. Cunningham, 431 U.S. 801 (1977), 232
Lefkowitz v. Turley, 414 U.S. 70 (1973), 232
Lego v. Twomey, 404 U.S. 477 (1972), 223
Levin v. Katzenbach, 363 F.2d 287 (D.C. Cir. 1966), 270
Lewis v. United States, 445 U.S. 55 (1980), 222
Lewis v. United States, 385 U.S. 206 (1966), 231, 249
Liljeberg v. Health Services Acquisition Corp., 108 S. Ct. 2194 (1988), 258
Linkletter v. Walker, 381 U.S. 618 (1965), 251
Lisenba v. California, 314 U.S. 219 (1941), 228
Little, *In re*, 404 U.S. 553 (1972), 258
Little v. Streater, 452 U.S. 1 (1981), 300
Lo-Ji Sales, Inc. v. New York, 442 U.S. 319 (1979), 230, 231, 240
Long v. District Court, 385 U.S. 192 (1966), 299
Lopez v. United States, 373 U.S. 427 (1963), 249
Lopez v. United States, 370 F.2d 8 (5th Cir. 1966), 241
Luce v. United States, 469 U.S. 38 (1984), 222, 224
Lucero v. Donovan, 354 F.2d 16 (9th Cir. 1965), 237

M

Maine v. Moulton, 474 U.S. 159 (1985), 233, 249
Malley v. Briggs, 106 S. Ct. 1092 (1986), 223, 240-A
Mallory v. United States, 354 U.S. 449 (1957), 223
Malloy v. Hogan, 378 U.S. 1 (1964), 227, 232
Mancusi v. DeForte, 392 U.S. 364 (1968), 229, 231, 240, 242, 243
Maness v. Meyers, 419 U.S. 449 (1975), 232, 301

Manson v. Brathwaite, 432 U.S. 98 (1977), 228, 233, 251

Mapp v. Ohio, 367 U.S. 643 (1961), 223, 227

Marchetti v. United States, 390 U.S. 39 (1968), 232

Marron v. United States, 275 U.S. 192 (1927), 230, 240

Marshall v. Barlow's Inc., 436 U.S. 307 (1978), 229, 231, 240, 242, 246, 249

Marshall v. Jerrico, Inc., 446 U.S. 238 (1980), 258

Martin, *In re*, 58 Cal. 2d 509, 374 P.2d 801, 24 Cal. Rptr. 833 (1962), 237

Martin v. Virginia, 365 F.2d 549 (4th Cir. 1966), 270

Marullo v. United States, 328 F.2d 361 (5th Cir. 1964), *rehearing denied*, 330 F.2d 609 (5th Cir. 1964), 231, 244

Maryland v. Garrison, 107 S. Ct. 1013 (1987), 230, 236, 240, 240-A

Maryland v. Macon, 472 U.S. 463 (1985), 230, 231, 236, 240, 248

Mason v. Arizona, 504 F.2d 1345 (9th Cir. 1974), 299

Mason v. United States, 244 U.S. 362 (1917), 232

Massachusetts v. Painten, 368 F.2d 142 (1st Cir. 1966), *cert. dismissed*, 389 U.S. 560 (1968), 236, 240

Massachusetts v. Sheppard, 468 U.S. 981 (1984), 223, 229, 230, 240, 240-A

Massachusetts v. Upton, 466 U.S. 727 (1984) (per curiam), 241

Massiah v. United States, 377 U.S. 201 (1964), 233, 249

Maxwell v. Stephens, 348 F.2d 325 (8th Cir. 1965), 240

Mayberry v. Pennsylvania, 400 U.S. 455 (1971), 258

Mayer v. City of Chicago, 404 U.S. 189 (1971), 299

McCoy v. Court of Appeals, 108 S. Ct. 1895 (1988), 233, 300

McCray v. Illinois, 386 U.S. 300 (1967), 273

McDaniel v. North Carolina, 392 U.S. 665 (1968) (per curiam), 251

McDonald v. United States 335 U.S. 451 (1948), 229, 240, 246, 253, 264

McGinnis v. United States, 227 F.2d 598 (1st Cir. 1955), 240

McKnight v. United States, 183 F.2d 977 (D.C. Cir. 1950), 240

McMahon v. Office of the City and County of Honolulu, 51 Haw. 589, 465 P.2d 549 (1970), 270

McNabb v. United States, 318 U.S. 332 (1943), 223

Michigan v. Chesternut, 108 S. Ct. 1975 (1988), 236

Michigan v. Clifford, 464 U.S. 287 (1984), 229, 231, 240

Michigan v. DeFillippo, 443 U.S. 31 (1979), 230, 236, 238, 240, 241, 251

Michigan v. Jackson, 106 S. Ct. 1404 (1986), 227, 233, 237

Michigan v. Long, 463 U.S. 1032 (1983), 227, 229, 230, 236, 238, 240, 246, 247

Michigan v. Mosley, 423 U.S. 96 (1975), 232, 233, 237

Michigan v. Summers, 452 U.S. 692 (1981), 229, 230, 236, 240, 241

Michigan v. Thomas, 458 U.S. 259 (1982) (per curiam), 246

Michigan v. Tucker, 417 U.S. 433 (1974), 232, 251

Michigan v. Tyler, 436 U.S. 499 (1978), 229, 230, 231, 240, 243

Middendorf v. Henry, 425 U.S. 25 (1976), 300

Miller v. Fenton, 106 S. Ct. 445 (1985), 228, 232
Miller v. Pate, 386 U.S. 1 (1967), 270
Miller v. United States, 357 U.S. 301 (1958), 240
Mincey v. Arizona, 437 U.S. 385 (1978), 229, 230, 231, 240, 246, 250
Minnesota v. Murphy, 465 U.S. 420 (1984), 232, 233, 240
Miranda v. Arizona, 384 U.S. 436 (1966), 227, 232, 233, 237, 240, 251, 253, 274
Mitchell v. United States, 316 F.2d 354 (D.C. Cir. 1963), 237
Montana v. Tomich, 332 F.2d 987 (9th Cir. 1964), 236, 246
Moody v. United States, 163 A.2d 337 (M.C.A.D.C. 1960), 250
Mooney v. Holohan, 294 U.S. 103 (1935), 270
Moore v. Arizona, 414 U.S. 25 (1973) (per curiam), 311
Moore v. Illinois, 434 U.S. 220 (1977), 233, 237, 238, 251
Moore v. Illinois, 408 U.S. 786 (1972), 270
Moran v. Burbine, 106 S. Ct. 1135 (1986), 228, 233, 237, 240
Morgan v. United States, 304 U.S. 1 (1938), 270
Morris v. Slappy, 461 U.S. 1 (1983), 304
Morrissey v. Brewer, 408 U.S. 471 (1972), 270
Mt. Healthy City School District Board of Education v. Doyle, 429 U.S. 274 (1977), 251
Munoz v. United States, 325 F.2d 23 (9th Cir. 1963), 240
Murphy v. Florida, 421 U.S. 794 (1975), 270
Murphy v. Waterfront Commission, 378 U.S. 52 (1964), 232, 269
Murray v. United States, 108 S. Ct. 2529 (1988), 251
Murray v. United States, 380 U.S. 527 (1965) (per curiam), *vacating* 333 F.2d 409 (10th Cir. 1964), 240, 242

N

Napue v. Illinois, 360 U.S. 264 (1959), 270
Nardone v. United States, 308 U.S. 338 (1939), 251
Nathanson v. United States, 290 U.S. 41 (1933), 240-A, 241
National Labor Relations Board v. Robbins Tire and Rubber Co., 437 U.S. 214 (1978), 269
National Treasury Employees Union v. Von Raab, 109 S. Ct. 1384 (1989), 250
Nebraska Press Ass'n v. Stuart, 427 U.S. 539 (1976), 255, 256, 304
Neely v. Pennsylvania, 411 U.S. 954 (1973), 220
Neil v. Biggers, 409 U.S. 188 (1972), 233
New Jersey v. Portash, 440 U.S. 450 (1979), 222, 232, 250, 274
New Jersey v. T.L.O., 469 U.S. 325 (1985), 229, 230, 231, 236, 238, 240, 242, 247, 248, 251
New York v. Belton, 453 U.S. 454 (1981), 229, 230, 237, 238, 240, 246, 247
New York v. Burger, 107 S. Ct. 2636 (1987), 230, 231, 238, 240, 242, 246
New York v. Class, 106 S. Ct. 960 (1986), 230, 231, 243, 246

New York v. P.J. Video, Inc., 106 S. Ct. 1610 (1986), 240

New York v. Quarles, 467 U.S. 649 (1984), 233

Nicaud v. State *ex rel.* Hendrix, 401 So. 2d 43 (Ala. 1981), 250

Niemotko v. Maryland, 340 U.S. 268 (1951), 246

Nix v. Williams, 467 U.S. 431 (1984), 223, 251

Nixon v. Administrator of General Services, 433 U.S. 425 (1977), 240, 243

North v. Russell, 427 U.S. 328 (1976), 240

North Carolina v. Butler, 441 U.S. 369 (1979), 233

O

O'Connor v. Ortega, 107 S. Ct. 1492 (1987), 229, 230, 231, 240, 242, 248, 251

Olden v. Kentucky, 109 S. Ct. 480 (1988) (per curiam), 270

Oliver v. United States, 466 U.S. 170 (1984), 231, 240, 242, 243, 244

Oliver v. United States, 239 F.2d 818 (8th Cir. 1957), 248

Olmstead v. United States, 277 U.S. 438 (1928), 243

On Lee v. United States, 343 U.S. 747 (1952), 249

One 1958 Plymouth Sedan v. Pennsylvania, 380 U.S. 693 (1965), 246

Oregon v. Elstad, 470 U.S. 298 (1985), 233, 236, 251

Oregon v. Mathiason, 429 U.S. 492 (1977) (per curiam), 232, 233, 236

Osborn v. United States, 385 U.S. 323 (1966), 243, 249

P

Palmer v. Peyton, 359 F.2d 199 (4th Cir. 1966), 228

Patterson v. Illinois, 108 S. Ct. 2389 (1988), 233, 249

Patton v. Yount, 467 U.S. 1025 (1984), 257, 305

Payton v. New York, 445 U.S. 573 (1980), 229, 230, 231, 240, 248

Pembaur v. City of Cincinnati, 106 S. Ct. 1292 (1986), 240

Pennsylvania v. Finley, 107 S. Ct. 1990 (1987), 299

Pennsylvania v. Mimms, 434 U.S. 106 (1977) (per curiam), 230, 231, 236, 246

Pennsylvania v. Ritchie, 107 S. Ct. 989 (1987), 268, 270

People v. Barber, 94 Ill. App. 3d 813, 419 N.E.2d 71, 50 Ill. Dec. 204 (1981), 250

People v. Beavers, 393 Mich. 554, 227 N.W.2d 511 (1975), 249

People v. Berv, 51 Cal. 2d 286, 332 P.2d 97 (1958), 250

People v. Collins, 1 Cal. 3d 658, 463 P.2d 403, 83 Cal. Rptr. 179 (1970), 236

People v. Ditson, 57 Cal. 2d 415, 369 P.2d 714, 20 Cal. Rptr. 165 (1962), 251

People v. Dodsworth, 60 Ill. App. 3d 207, 376 N.E.2d 449 (1978), 270

People v. Garries, 645 P.2d 1306 (Colo. 1982), 270

People v. Gomez, 198 Colo. 105, 596 P.2d 1192 (1979), 270

People v. Hitch, 12 Cal. 3d 641, 527 P.2d 361, 117 Cal. Rptr. 9 (1974), 270

People v. Houston, 42 Cal. 3d 595, 724 P.2d 1166, 230 Cal. Rptr. 141 (1986), 227, 233

People v. Nation, 26 Cal. 3d 169, 604 P.2d 1051, 161 Cal. Rptr. 299 (1980), 270

People v. P.J. Video, Inc., 68 N.Y.2d 296, 501 N.E.2d 556, 508 N.Y.S.2d 907 (1986), 227

People v. Shabaz, 424 Mich. 42, 378 N.W.2d 451 (1985), 247

People v. Taylor, 54 Ill. App. 3d 454, 369 N.E.2d 573 (1977), 270

People v. Watson, 36 Ill. 2d 228, 221 N.E.2d 645 (1966), 299

People ex rel. Gallagher v. District Court, 656 P.2d 1287 (Colo. 1983), 270

Perry v. Leeke, 109 S. Ct. 594 (1989), 270, 280

Peterson v. United States, 351 F.2d 606 (9th Cir. 1965), 266

Pillsbury Co. v. Conboy, 459 U.S. 248 (1983), 232, 251, 301

Pittsburgh Plate Glass Co. v. United States, 360 U.S. 395 (1959), 271

Polk v. United States, 291 F.2d 230 (9th Cir. 1961), aff'd after remand, 314 F.2d 837 (9th Cir. 1963), 243, 244

Pollard v. United States, 352 U.S. 354 (1957), 311

Ponte v. Real, 471 U.S. 491 (1985), 270

Powell v. Alabama, 287 U.S. 45 (1932), 270

Preston v. United States, 376 U.S. 364 (1964), 229, 231, 246

Proskin v. County Court, 30 N.Y.2d 15, 280 N.E.2d 875, 330 N.Y.S.2d 44 (1972), 271

Provoo, Petition of, 17 F.R.D. 183 (D. Md. 1955), aff'd per curiam, 350 U.S. 857 (1955), 311

Prudhomme v. Superior Court, 2 Cal. 3d 320, 466 P.2d 673, 85 Cal. Rptr. 129 (1970), 274

Public Utilities Commission v. Pollak, 343 U.S. 451 (1972), 258

Pulliam v. Allen, 466 U.S. 522 (1984), 313

Pyle v. Kansas, 317 U.S. 213 (1942), 270

Q

Quinn v. United States, 349 U.S. 155 (1955), 232

R

Rakas v. Illinois, 439 U.S. 128 (1978), 225, 231, 240, 242, 243, 245, 246, 248

Rathbun v. United States, 355 U.S. 107 (1957), 245

Rawlings v. Kentucky, 448 U.S. 98 (1980), 225, 230, 231, 236, 242, 243, 247, 248, 251, 253

Recznik v. City of Lorain, 393 U.S. 166 (1968) (per curiam), 231, 240, 241

Reeves v. Warden, 346 F.2d 915 (4th Cir. 1965), 240

Regalado v. California, 374 U.S. 497 (1963) (per curiam), 231, 243

Reid v. Georgia, 448 U.S. 438 (1980) (per curiam), 230, 236, 247
Rhode Island v. Innis, 446 U.S. 291 (1980), 233, 237
Richardson v. Marsh, 107 S. Ct. 1702 (1987), 264
Richardson v. United States, 468 U.S. 317 (1984), 312
Richmond Newspapers, Inc. v. Virginia, 448 U.S. 555 (1980), 255
Riggan v. Virginia, 384 U.S. 152 (1966) (per curiam), 241
Rinaldi v. Yeager, 384 U.S. 305 (1966), 298
Rios v. United States, 364 U.S 253 (1960), 229, 231, 236, 242, 247
Roaden v. Kentucky, 413 U.S. 496 (1973), 229, 240
Roberts v. LaVallee, 389 U.S. 40 (1967), 266, 299
Roberts v. United States, 445 U.S. 552 (1980), 232, 240
Roberts v. United States, 332 F.2d 892 (8th Cir. 1964), 240
Roberts v. United States, 325 F.2d 290 (5th Cir. 1963), 270
Rochin v. California, 342 U.S. 165 (1952), 228
Rock v. Arkansas, 107 S. Ct. 2704 (1987), 270, 274
Rogers v. Israel, 746 F.2d 1288 (7th Cir. 1984), 300
Rogers v. Richmond, 365 U.S. 534 (1961), 251
Romero v. United States, 318 F.2d 530 (5th Cir. 1963), 248
Rosencranz v. United States, 356 F.2d 310 (1st Cir. 1966), 240, 244
Ross v. Moffitt, 417 U.S. 600 (1974), 299, 300
Roviaro v. United States, 353 U.S. 53 (1957), 270, 273
Rugendorf v. United States, 376 U.S. 528 (1964), 230, 240, 241

S

Sabbath v. United States, 391 U.S. 585 (1968), 240
Sanabria v. United States, 437 U.S. 54 (1978), 222
Santana v. United States, 329 F.2d 854 (1st Cir. 1964), 248
Satterwhite v. Texas, 108 S. Ct. 1792 (1988), 233, 237, 238
Schmerber v. California, 384 U.S. 757 (1966), 232, 238, 242
Schneckloth v. Bustamonte, 412 U.S. 218 (1973), 228, 229, 230, 233, 240,
    253
Schwartz v. Texas, 344 U.S. 199 (1952), 245
Scott v. United States, 436 U.S. 128 (1978), 229, 236, 243, 251
Seals v. United States, 325 F.2d 1006 (D.C. Cir. 1963), 236
Seattle Times Co. v. Rhinehart, 467 U.S. 20 (1984), 274
Securities and Exchange Commission v. Jerry T. O'Brien, Inc., 467 U.S.
    735 (1984), 231, 232, 248
See v. City of Seattle, 387 U.S. 541 (1967), 240, 246
Segura v. United States, 468 U.S. 796 (1984), 223, 230, 240, 248, 251
Selective Service System v. Minnesota Public Interest Research Group,
    468 U.S. 841 (1984), 232
Serfass v. United States, 420 U.S. 377 (1975), 222
Sgro v. United States, 287 U.S. 206 (1932), 240
Shadwick v. City of Tampa, 407 U.S. 345 (1972), 230, 240
Shapiro v. United States, 335 U.S. 1 (1948), 232

Sheppard v. Maxwell, 384 U.S. 333 (1966), 255
Shipley v. California, 395 U.S. 818 (1969), 240
Shuttlesworth v. City of Birmingham, 394 U.S. 147 (1969), 246
Sibron v. New York, 392 U.S. 40 (1968), 230, 236, 247
Silverman v. United States, 365 U.S. 505 (1961), 231, 243
Silverthorne Lumber Co. v. United States, 251 U.S. 385 (1920), 251
Simmons v. United States, 390 U.S. 377 (1968), 253, 255, 271, 272, 274, 301
Sims v. Georgia, 389 U.S. 404 (1967) (per curiam), 228, 237
Skinner v. Railway Labor Executives' Ass'n, 109 S. Ct. 1402 (1989), 229, 231, 237, 238, 243, 246, 248, 250
Smayda v. United States, 352 F.2d 251 (9th Cir. 1965), 231
Smith v. Bennett, 365 U.S. 708 (1961), 299
Smith v. Enomoto, 615 F.2d 1251 (9th Cir. 1980), 299
Smith v. Hooey, 393 U.S. 374 (1969), 311
Smith v. Illinois, 469 U.S. 91 (1984) (per curiam), 233, 237
Smith v. Illinois, 390 U.S. 129 (1968), 270
Smith v. Maryland, 442 U.S. 735 (1979), 231, 245, 249
Smith v. Phillips, 455 U.S. 209 (1982), 270
Smith v. United States, 344 F.2d 545 (D.C. Cir. 1965), 251
Snyder v. Massachusetts, 291 U.S. 97 (1934), 270
South Dakota v. Neville, 459 U.S. 553 (1983), 232, 238
South Dakota v. Opperman, 428 U.S. 364 (1976), 229, 230, 246
Spano v. New York, 360 U.S. 315 (1959), 228
Specht v. Patterson, 386 U.S. 605 (1967), 270
Spinelli v. United States, 393 U.S. 410 (1969), 230, 231, 240, 241
Stack v. Boyle, 342 U.S. 1 (1951), 313
Standefer v. United States, 447 U.S. 10 (1980), 274
Stanford v. Texas, 379 U.S. 476 (1965), 230, 240
Staples v. United States, 320 F.2d 817 (5th Cir. 1963), 246
State v. Adkins, 346 S.E.2d 762 (W. Va. 1986), 241
State v. Blair, 691 S.W.2d 259 (Mo. 1985), 236
State v. Coyle, 95 Wash. 2d 1, 621 P.2d 1256 (1980), 240
State v. Chrisman, 100 Wash. 2d 814, 676 P.2d 419 (1984), 240
State v. Daniel, 589 P.2d 408 (Alaska 1979), 246
State v. Daugherty, 94 Wash. 2d 263, 616 P.2d 649 (1980), 244
State v. Dineen, 296 N.W.2d 421 (Minn. 1980), 247
State v. Faux, 9 Utah 2d 350, 345 P.2d 186 (1959), 271
State v. Glass, 583 P.2d 872 (Alaska, 1978), 227
State v. Hobart, 94 Wash. 2d 437, 617 P.2d 429 (1980), 236
State v. Latham, 30 Wash. App. 776, 638 P.2d 592 (1982), aff'd, 100 Wash. 2d 59, 667 P.2d 56 (1983), 222
State v. Moriarty, 39 N.J. 502, 189 A.2d 210 (1963), 241
State v. Naturile, 83 N.J. Super. 563, 200 A.2d 617 (1964), 240
State v. Novembrino, 105 N.J. 95, 519 A.2d 820 (1987), 227

State v. Opperman, 247 N.W.2d 673 (S.D. 1976), 246

State v. Robinson, 123 N.H. 665, 465 A.2d 1214 (1983), 298

State v. Scrotsky, 39 N.J. 410, 189 A.2d 23 (1963), 250

State v. Second Judicial District Court, 85 Nev. 241, 453 P.2d 421 (1969), 299

State v. Simpson, 95 Wash. 2d 170, 622 P.2d 1199 (1980), 227

State v Stoddard, 206 Conn. 157, 537 A.2d 446 (1988), 227, 233

State v. Sundel, 121 R.I. 638, 402 A.2d 585 (1979), 240

State *ex rel.* Marshall v. Eighth Judicial District Court, 80 Nev. 478, 396 P.2d 680 (1964), 266

Steagald v. United States, 451 U.S. 204, (1981), 229, 230, 236, 240, 241, 246, 251

Stevens v. Marks, 383 U.S. 234 (1966), 220

Stone v. Powell, 428 U.S. 465 (1976), 223, 241, 242, 251, 253

Stoner v. California, 376 U.S. 483 (1964), 229, 231, 240

Stovall v. Denno, 388 U.S. 293 (1967), 228, 233, 251

Strickland v. Washington, 466 U.S. 668 (1984), 233, 270

Strunk v. United States, 412 U.S. 434 (1973), 306, 311

Swenson v. Bosler, 386 U.S. 258 (1967), 299

T

Tabasko v. Barton, 472 F.2d 871 (6th Cir. 1972), 241

Taglavore v. United States, 291 F.2d 262 (9th Cir. 1961), 228

Taglianetti v. United States, 394 U.S. 316 (1969), 251

Tague v. Louisiana, 444 U.S. 469 (1980) (per curiam), 232, 233, 237

Taylor v. Alabama, 457 U.S. 687 (1982), 230, 236, 241, 251, 253

Taylor v. Hayes, 418 U.S. 488 (1974), 258

Taylor v. Illinois, 108 S. Ct. 646 (1988), 270, 274

Taylor v. United States, 286 U.S. 1 (1932), 244

Taylor v. United States, 238 F.2d 259 (D.C. Cir. 1956), 311

Tennessee v. Garner, 471 U.S. 1 (1985), 228, 229, 231, 237, 238, 240

Terry v. Ohio, 392 U.S. 1 (1968), 229, 230, 231, 236, 242, 246, 248

Texas v. Brown, 460 U.S. 730 (1983), 229, 230, 231, 240, 241, 243, 246, 248

Texas v. White, 423 U.S. 67 (1975), 246

Thompson v. Louisiana, 469 U.S. 17 (1984) (per curiam), 229, 230, 231, 240

Tomich, *Application of,* 221 F. Supp. 500 (D. Mont. 1963), *aff'd sub nom.* Montana v. Tomich, 332 F.2d 987 (9th Cir. 1964), 236

Tony C., *In re,* 21 Cal. 3d 888, 582 P.2d 957, 148 Cal. Rptr. 366 (1978), 236

Torres v. Puerto Rico, 442 U.S. 465 (1979), 229, 230, 240, 246, 247, 248

Townsend v. Bomar, 331 F.2d 19 (6th Cir. 1964), 270

Townsend v. Burke, 334 U.S. 736 (1984), 270

Travis v. United States, 362 F.2d 477 (9th Cir. 1966), 241

Tumey v. Ohio, 273 U.S. 510 (1927), 258

U

Ullmann v. United States, 350 U.S. 422 (1956), 232, 269
United States v. Agurs, 427 U.S. 97 (1976), 268, 270, 271
United States v. Anderson, 453 F.2d 174 (9th Cir. 1971), 241
United States v. Apfelbaum, 445 U.S. 115 (1980), 232
United States v. Ash, 413 U.S. 300 (1973), 233
United States v. Ash, 461 F.2d 92 (D.C. Cir. 1972) (en banc), *rev'd on other grounds*, 413 U.S. 300 (1973), 270
United States v. Augenblick, 393 U.S. 348 (1969), 270, 271
United States v. Baggot, 463 U.S. 476 (1983), 271
United States v. Bagley, 473 U.S. 667 (1985), 268, 270, 271
United States v. Barone, 330 F.2d 543 (2d Cir. 1964), 240
United States v. Beck, 602 F.2d 726 (5th Cir. 1979), 247
United States v. Berkus, 428 F.2d 1148 (8th Cir. 1970), 241
United States v. Biswell, 406 U. S. 311 (1972), 230, 240
United States v. Blok, 188 F.2d 1019 (D.C. Cir. 1951), 240, 242
United States v. Branker, 418 F.2d 378 (2d Cir. 1969), 301
United States v. Brignoni-Ponce, 422 U.S. 873 (1975), 230, 236, 246
United States v. Bugarin-Casas, 484 F.2d 853 (9th Cir. 1973), 246
United States v. Burr, 25 Fed. Cas. 30 (No. 14,692d) (C.C.D. Va. 1807), 265
United States v. Caceres, 440 U.S. 741 (1979), 223, 240, 245, 249, 251
United States v. Calandra, 414 U.S. 338 (1974), 223
United States v. Ceccolini, 435 U.S. 268 (1978), 222, 223, 236, 242, 251
United States v. Chadwick, 433 U.S. 1 (1977), 229, 230, 231, 238, 240, 242, 243, 246, 247, 248
United States v. Chase, 135 F. Supp. 230 (N.D. Ill. 1955), 311
United States v. Chavez, 416 U.S. 562 (1974), 223, 243
United States v. Chun, 503 F.2d 533 (9th Cir. 1974), 243
United States v. Cortez, 449 U.S. 411 (1981), 230, 236, 246
United States v. Crews, 445 U.S. 463 (1980), 237, 251, 253
United States v. Cronic, 466 U.S. 648 (1984), 233, 270, 305
United States v. Del Toro, 464 F.2d 520 (2d Cir. 1972), 236
United States v. Di Francesco, 449 U.S. 117 (1980), 222
United States v. Di Re, 332 U.S. 581 (1948), 236, 240
United States v. Dionisio, 410 U.S. 1 (1973), 231, 232
United States v. Doe, 465 U.S. 605 (1984), 232, 274
United States v. Donovan, 429 U.S. 413 (1977), 230, 243
United States v. Dunn, 107 S. Ct. 1134 (1987), 231, 242, 244
United States v. Edwards, 415 U.S. 800 (1974), 230, 237, 238
United States v. Eight Thousand Eight Hundred and Fifty Dollars, 461 U.S. 555 (1983), 311
United States v. Euge, 444 U.S. 707 (1980), 232, 233, 236

United States v. Ewell, 383 U.S. 116 (1966), 311
United States v. Francolino, 367 F.2d 1013 (2d Cir. 1966), 246
United States v. Giordano, 416 U.S. 505 (1974), 243, 251
United States v. Gouveia, 467 U.S. 180 (1984), 233, 311
United States v. Hall, 565 F.2d 917 (5th Cir. 1978), 240
United States v. Hallman, 365 F.2d 289 (3d Cir. 1966), 247
United States v. Harris, 403 U.S. 573 (1971), 241
United States v. Harris, 321 F.2d 739 (6th Cir. 1963), 236, 240
United States v. Hatcher, 473 F.2d 321 (6th Cir. 1973), 241
United States v. Havens, 446 U.S. 620 (1980), 251
United States v. Helstoski, 442 U.S. 477 (1979), 222
United States v. Henry, 447 U.S. 264 (1980), 233, 237, 249
United States v. Hensley, 469 U.S. 221 (1985), 229, 230, 231, 236, 241, 246
United States v. Hill, 500 F.2d 315 (5th Cir. 1974), 241
United States v. Hinton, 219 F.2d 324 (7th Cir. 1955), 240
United States v. Hittle, 575 F.2d 799 (10th Cir. 1978), 241
United States v. Hollywood Motor Car Co., 458 U.S. 263 (1982) (per curiam), 306, 312, 313
United States v. Jacobsen, 466 U.S. 109 (1984), 229, 230, 231, 236, 242, 248, 250
United States v. Janis, 428 U.S. 443 (1976), 242, 250, 253
United States v. Jeffers, 342 U.S. 48 (1951), 229, 240, 242, 253
United States v. Jenkins, 420 U.S. 358 (1975), 222
United States v. Johns, 469 U.S. 478 (1985), 230, 246, 248
United States v. Johnson, 457 U.S. 537 (1982), 229, 240, 251, 253
United States v. Kahan, 415 U.S. 239 (1974) (per curiam), 253, 301
United States v. Kahn, 415 U.S. 143 (1974) 240, 243
United States v. Karo, 468 U.S. 705 (1984), 225, 229, 231, 240-A, 241, 242, 243, 245, 249
United States v. Klapholz, 230 F.2d 494 (2d Cir. 1956), 236, 237
United States v. Knotts, 460 U.S. 276 (1983), 231, 243, 246
United States v. Kopp, 429 U.S. 121 (1976) (per curiam), 222
United States v. LaSalle National Bank, 437 U.S. 298 (1978), 274
United States v. Lee, 274 U.S. 559 (1927), 231
United States v. Lefkowitz, 285 U.S. 452 (1932), 240
United States v. Leon, 468 U.S. 897 (1984), 223, 225, 240, 240-A, 241, 253
United States v. Loud Hawk, 106 S. Ct. 648 (1986), 311
United States v. Lovasco, 431 U.S. 783 (1977), 311
United States v. MacCollom, 426 U.S. 317 (1976), 266, 299
United States v. MacDonald, 456 U.S. 1 (1982), 311
United States v. MacDonald, 435 U.S. 850 (1978), 306, 311, 312, 313
United States v. Mallides, 473 F.2d 859 (9th Cir. 1973), 236
United States v. Mandujano, 425 U.S. 564 (1976), 232, 233

United States v. Mara, 410 U.S. 19 (1973), 232

United States v. Marion, 404 U.S. 307 (1971), 311

United States v. Martin Linen Supply Co., 430 U.S. 564 (1977), 222

United States v. Martinez-Fuerte, 429 U.S. 543 (1976), 230, 231, 236, 246

United States v. Matlock, 415 U.S. 164 (1974), 230, 240, 253, 273

United States v. Mauro, 436 U.S. 340 (1978), 310

United States v. Mendenhall, 446 U.S. 544 (1980), 236, 240, 246

United States v. Merritt, 293 F.2d 742 (3d Cir. 1961), 240

United States v. Miller, 425 U.S. 435 (1976), 231, 243, 248, 274

United States v. Montoya De Hernandez, 473 U.S. 531 (1985), 229, 230, 236, 237, 246

United States v. Morrison, 449 U.S. 361 (1981), 233

United States v. Morrison, 429 U.S. 1 (1976) (per curiam), 222

United States v. Mullin, 329 F.2d 295 (4th Cir. 1964), 231, 244

United States v. New York Telephone Co., 434 U.S. 159 (1977), 245

United States v. Newman, 490 F.2d 993 (10th Cir. 1974), 247

United States v. Nixon, 418 U.S. 683 (1974), 269, 273-B

United States v. Nobles, 422 U.S. 225 (1975), 232, 253, 273-A, 274

United States v. Ortiz, 422 U.S. 891 (1975), 230, 231, 237, 246

United States v. Paroutian, 299 F.2d 486 (2d Cir. 1962), *aff'd after remand*, 319 F.2d 661 (2d Cir. 1963), 251

United States v. Payner, 447 U.S. 727 (1980), 225, 228, 231, 242, 248, 251

United States v. Peltier, 422 U.S. 531 (1975), 246, 251, 253

United States v. Pitts, 569 F.2d 343 (5th Cir. 1978), 299

United States v. Place, 462 U.S. 696 (1983), 229, 230, 231, 236, 242, 243, 246, 247, 248

United States v. Rabinowitz, 339 U.S. 56 (1950), 229, 240

United States v. Raddatz, 447 U.S. 667 (1980), 224, 232, 250, 253, 253-A, 273

United States v. Ramsey, 431 U. S. 606 (1977), 229, 230, 236, 237, 238, 246, 248

United States v. Reynolds, 345 U.S. 1 (1953), 273-B

United States v. Robinson, 414 U.S. 218 (1973), 230, 238, 246, 247

United States v. Robinson, 325 F.2d 391 (2d Cir. 1963), 273

United States v. Ross, 456 U.S. 798 (1982), 229, 230, 240, 241, 246, 247, 248

United States v. Rylander, 460 U.S. 752 (1983), 232

United States v. Salvucci, 448 U.S. 83 (1980), 225, 230, 231, 242, 248, 253

United States v. Santana, 427 U.S. 38 (1976), 230, 231, 236, 240, 243, 244

United States v. Sanford, 429 U.S. 14 (1976) (per curiam), 222

United States v. Scott, 437 U.S. 82 (1978), 222

United States v. Seale, 461 F.2d 345 (7th Cir. 1972), 233

United States v. Sells Engineering, Inc., 463 U.S. 418 (1983), 271

United States v. Sharpe, 470 U.S. 675 (1985), 230, 236, 240, 246

United States v. Sokolow, 109 S. Ct. 1581 (1989), 236

United States v. Sterling, 369 F.2d 799 (3d Cir. 1966), 241

United States v. Tane, 329 F.2d 848 (2d Cir. 1964), 251

United States v. Taylor, 108 S. Ct. 2413 (1988), 308

United States v. Townsend, 151 F. Supp. 378 (D.D.C. 1957), 228

United States v. United States District Court for the Eastern District of Michigan, 407 U.S. 297 (1972), 229, 240, 243, 246

United States v. Valenzuela-Bernal, 458 U.S. 858 (1982), 268, 270, 271, 273, 273-A, 274, 286, 299, 301, 311

United States v. Van Leeuwen, 397 U.S. 249 (1970), 231, 248

United States v. Ventresca, 380 U.S. 102 (1965), 240, 241

United States v. Villamonte-Marquez, 462 U.S. 579 (1983), 229, 246

United States v. Wade, 388 U.S. 218 (1967), 232, 233, 237, 238, 251, 270

United States v. Ward, 448 U.S. 242 (1980), 232

United States v. Ward, 488 F.2d 162 (9th Cir. 1973) (en banc), 236, 246

United States v. Washington, 431 U.S. 181 (1977), 232, 240

United States v. Watson, 423 U.S. 411 (1976), 230, 236, 240, 241

United States v. White, 401 U.S. 745 (1971), 231, 249

United States v. White, 324 F.2d 814 (2d Cir. 1963), 270

United States v. Williams, 328 F.2d 887 (2d Cir. 1964), 240

United States v. Wilson, 420 U.S. 332 (1975), 222

United States Department of Justice v. Julian, 108 S. Ct. 1606 (1988), 266

United States ex rel. Almeida v. Baldi, 195 F.2d 815 (3d Cir. 1952), 270

United States ex rel. Bloeth v. Denno, 313 F.2d 364 (2d Cir. 1963), 256

United States ex rel. Drew v. Meyers, 327 F.2d 174 (3d Cir. 1964), 270

United States ex rel. Gaugler v. Brierley, 477 F.2d 516 (3d Cir. 1973), 241

United States ex rel. Meers v. Wilkins, 326 F.2d 135 (2d Cir. 1964), 270

United States ex rel. Thompson v. Dye, 221 F.2d 763 (3d Cir. 1955), 270

United States ex rel. Wilson v. McMann, 408 F.2d 896 (2d Cir. 1969), 226

Upjohn Co. v. United States, 449 U.S. 383 (1981), 273-A, 274

V

Vale v. Louisiana, 399 U.S. 30 (1970), 229, 230, 240, 253

Villano v. United States, 310 F.2d 680 (10th Cir. 1962), 240, 242

Vitek v. Jones, 445 U.S. 480 (1980), 270

Von Cleef v. New Jersey, 395 U.S. 814 (1969), 240

W

Wainwright v. Sykes, 433 U.S. 72 (1977), 222, 224

Wainwright v. Torna, 455 U.S. 586 (1982) (per curiam), 299

Walker v. United States, 225 F.2d 447 (5th Cir. 1955), 244

Walter v. United States, 447 U.S. 649 (1980), 229, 231, 240, 248, 250

Ward v. Village of Monroeville, 409 U.S. 57 (1972), 258
Warden v. Hayden, 387 U.S. 294 (1967), 230, 240
Wardius v. Oregon, 412 U.S. 470 (1973), 233, 269, 270, 271, 274
Washington v. Chrisman, 455 U.S. 1 (1982), 231, 232, 240
Washington v. Texas, 388 U.S. 14 (1967), 270, 286
Watkins v. Sowders, 449 U.S. 341 (1981), 228
Watson v. United States, 249 F.2d 106 (D.C. Cir. 1957), 236, 237
Wayne v. United States, 318 F.2d 205 (D.C. Cir. 1963), 240
Weatherford v. Bursey, 429 U.S. 545 (1977), 233, 249, 251, 271, 273
Weaver v. United States, 295 F.2d 360 (5th Cir. 1961), 244
Webb v. Texas, 409 U.S. 95 (1972), 270
Welsh v. United States, 404 F.2d 414 (5th Cir. 1968), 299
Welsh v. Wisconsin, 466 U.S. 740 (1984), 229, 230, 236, 240, 241
Wheat v. United States, 108 S. Ct. 1692 (1988), 233, 270, 282
White v. Maryland, 373 U.S. 59 (1963) (per curiam), 233
White v. United States, 271 F.2d 829 (D.C. Cir. 1959), 247
Whitely v. Warden, 401 U.S. 560 (1971), 230, 236, 241
Williams v. Florida, 399 U.S. 78 (1970), 274
Williams v. Georgia, 349 U.S. 375 (1955), 224
Williams v. Illinois, 399 U.S. 235 (1970), 299
Williams v. Martin, 618 F.2d 1021 (4th Cir. 1980), 299, 300
Williams v. Oklahoma City, 395 U.S. 458 (1969), 299
Williams v. United States, 401 U.S. 646 (1971), 240
Williams v. United States, 237 F.2d 789 (D.C. Cir. 1956), 247
Winston v. Commonwealth, 188 Va. 386, 49 S.E.2d 611 (1948), 237
Winston v. Lee, 470 U.S. 753 (1985), 228, 229, 238
Withrow v. Larkin, 421 U.S. 35 (1975), 258
Wolff v. McDonnell, 418 U.S. 539 (1974), 270
Wong Sun v. United States, 371 U.S. 471 (1963), 236, 237, 241, 251
Work v. United States, 243 F.2d 660 (D.C. Cir. 1957), 240, 247
Wrightson v. United States, 222 F.2d 556 (D.C. Cir. 1955), 253
Wylde v. Wyoming, 362 U.S. 607 (1960), 270
Wyman v. James, 400 U.S. 309 (1971), 229, 240
Wyrick v. Fields, 459 U.S. 42 (1982) (per curiam), 233

Y

Ybarra v. Illinois, 444 U.S. 85 (1979), 230, 231, 236, 240, 241, 242, 243, 247
Yick Wo v. Hopkins, 118 U.S. 356 (1886), 246

Z

Zurcher v. Stanford Daily, 436 U.S. 547 (1978), 229, 232, 239, 240, 241

Statutes and Rules

United States Code

5 U.S.C. § 552 266	18 U.S.C. § 2518(8)-(10) 243
8 U.S.C. § 1357(a)(3) 246	18 U.S.C. § 2518(10)(a) .. 223, 251
18 U.S.C. §§ 2510-2520 .. 243, 245	18 U.S.C. § 3006 (A)(e) 298
18 U.S.C. § 2510(2) 242	18 U.S.C. § 3109 240
18 U.S.C. § 2511(1)(a) 242	18 U.S.C. §§ 3161-3174 303
18 U.S.C. § 2511(2)(c), (d) ... 245	18 U.S.C. § 3162(a) 308
18 U.S.C. §§ 2516-2519 243	18 U.S.C. § 3500 271
18 U.S.C. § 2518(1) 243	18 U.S.C. § 3502 237
18 U.S.C. § 2518(3) 243	18 U.S.C. § 3504 251
18 U.S.C. § 2518(4) 243	39 U.S.C. § 4057 248
18 U.S.C. § 2518(5) 243	47 U.S.C. § 605 245
18 U.S.C. § 2518(7) 243	50 U.S.C. §§ 1801-1811 243

D. C. Code

§ 23-591 240

Federal Rules of Criminal Procedure

5(a) 223	17.1 275
5.1(c) 266	20 255
6(e) 270, 271	26.2 271
6(e)(3)(C)(i) 271	26.2(f)(3) 271
6(e)(3)(C)(ii) 271	32(d) 220
11(e)(6) 220	41 241
12(b)(3) 224	41(c)(1) 241
12(d)(2) 222	41(c)(2) 241
15(a) 273	41(c)(2)(A) 241
16(a)(2) 271	41(e) 224
16(a)(3) 271	41(f) 224
16(b) 274	48(b) 308
17(c) 291	50 308
17(h) 271	50(b) 303

Federal Rules of Evidence

104(a) 253	410 220
104(d) 253	1101(d)(1) 253

Other Authorities

AMERICAN BAR ASSOCIATION PROJECT ON MINIMUM STANDARDS FOR CRIMINAL JUSTICE, STANDARDS RE- LATING TO DISCOVERY AND PROCEDURE BEFORE TRIAL (1970), 268

Amsterdam, *Perspectives on the Fourth*

Amendment, 58 Minn. L. Rev. 349 (1974), 249

Brennan, *State Constitutions and the Protection of Individual Rights,* 90 Harv. L. Rev. 489 (1977), 227

Brennan, *The Criminal Prosecution: Sporting Event or Quest for Truth?* 1963 Wash. U.L.Q. 279, 268

Bureau Draft, *A State Statute to Liberalize Criminal Discovery,* 4 Harv. J. on Legis. 105 (1966), 268

Calkins, *Criminal Justice for the Indigent,* 42 U. Det. L. J. 305 (1965), 268

Calkins, *Grand Jury Secrecy,* 63 Mich. L. Rev. 455 (1965), 268

Capra, *Access to Exculpatory Evidence: Avoiding the Agurs Problems of Prosecutorial Discretion and Retrospective Review,* 53 Fordham L. Rev. 391 (1984), 268

Carlson, *False or Suppressed Evidence: Why a Need for the Prosecutorial Tie,* 1969 Duke L.J. 1171, 268

Cook, Constitutional Rights of the Accused — Pretrial Rights (1972), 226

Cook, Constitutional Rights of the Accused — Trial Rights (1974), 226

Falk, *Foreword, The State Constitution: A More than "Adequate" Nonfederal Ground,* 61 Calif. L. Rev. 273 (1973), 227

Fletcher, *Pre-Trial Discovery in State Criminal Cases,* 12 Stan. L. Rev. 293 (1960), 268

George, Constitutional Limitations on Evidence in Criminal Cases (1973 printing), 226

Goldstein, *The State and the Accused: Balance of Advantage in Criminal Procedure,* 69 Yale L. J. 1149 (1960), 268

Hall, Search and Seizure (1982), 226

II Hawkins, Pleas of the Crown (8th ed. 1824), 232

Kamisar, Police Interrogation and Confessions: Essays in Law and Policy (1980), 226

Krantz, *Pretrial Discovery in Criminal Cases: A Necessity for Fair and Impartial Justice,* 42 Neb. L. Rev. 127 (1962), 268

LaFave, Search and Seizure (1978), 226

Levy, Origins of the Fifth Amendment (1968), 232

Linde, *First Things First: Rediscovering the States' Bills of Rights,* 9 U. Balt. L. Rev. 379 (1980), 227

Loftus, Eyewitness Testimony (1979), 226

Loftus and Doyle, Eyewitness Testimony: Civil and Criminal (1987), 226

Louisell, *Criminal Discovery: Dilemma Real or Apparent?* 49 Calif. L. Rev. 56 (1961), 268

Markle, Criminal Investigation and Presentation of Evidence (1976), 226

Markle, The Law of Arrest and Search and Seizure (1974), 226

Mosteller, *Discovery Against the Defense: Tilting the Adversarial Balance,* 74 Calif. L. Rev. 1567 (1986), 274

Nakell, *Criminal Discovery for the Defense and the Prosecution — The Developing Constitutional Considerations,* 50 N.C. L. Rev. 437 (1972), 268

Nakell, *The Effect of Due Process on Criminal Defense Discovery,* 62 Ky. L.J. 58 (1973-74), 268

Note, *Disclosure of Grand Jury Minutes to Challenge Indictments and Impeach Witnesses in Federal Criminal Cases,*

111 U. PA. L. REV. 1154 (1963), 268

Peskin, *Innovative Pre-Trial Motions in Criminal Defense,* 1 AM J. TRIAL ADVOCACY 35 (1977), 222

Peters, *State Constitutional Law: Federalism in the Common Law Tradition,* 84 MICH. L. REV. 583 (1986), 227

Rezneck, *The New Federal Rules of Criminal Procedure,* 54 GEO. L.J. 1276 (1966), 268

RINGEL, IDENTIFICATION AND POLICE LINEUPS (1968), 226

RINGEL, SEARCHES & SEIZURES, ARRESTS AND CONFESSIONS (2d ed. 1979/1980), 226

SOBEL, EYEWITNESS IDENTIFICATION — LEGAL AND PRACTICAL PROBLEMS (2d ed. 1981), 226

Traynor, *Ground Lost and Found in Criminal Discovery,* 39 N.Y.U. L. REV. 228 (1964), 268

Utter, *Freedom and Diversity in a Federal System: Perspectives on State Constitutions and the Washington Declaration of Rights,* 7 U. PUGET SOUND L. REV. 491 (1984), 227

VARON, SEARCHES, SEIZURES AND IMMUNITIES (2d ed., 1974), 226

WALL, EYEWITNESS IDENTIFICATION IN CRIMINAL CASES (1965), 226

Westen, *The Compulsory Process Clause,* 73 MICH L. REV. 71 (1974), 268

5 WIGMORE, EVIDENCE (Chadbourn rev. 1974), 270

Young, *Confessions and Interrogations,* in PUBLIC DEFENDER SOURCEBOOK, 327 (Singer ed. 1976), 226

ZAGEL, CONFESSIONS AND INTERROGATIONS AFTER MIRANDA: A COMPREHENSIVE OUTLINE OF THE LAW (1971), 226

INDEX OF SUBJECTS

(References are to section numbers)

A

Abuse of discretion, 313

Accomplices
criminal records of, 271
discovery of statements of, 271
official records pertaining to, 271
preparing to testify, 282

Accosting of defendant: evidence
obtained following
unconstitutional accosting,
235, 236

Acquittal
appeal by prosecution following,
222
refiling of charges following, 222

Admissions. *See also* Confessions
derivative evidence emanating
from, 251
impeachment of defendant with,
280
pretrial discovery of, 271, 280

Advance, motion to, 308

Affidavits
for arrest warrant, 241
of bias, 258
conclusory, 241
for continuances, 304
for discovery, 268
for disqualification of judge, 258
for *forma pauperis* subpoenas, 286
impeachment of representations in,
241
judicial review of sufficiency of
warrant affidavits, 230, 241
known criminal averment, 241
on motions, 222
oral testimony in lieu of, 241
of poverty, 301
for search warrant, 240, 241
for state-paid assistance, 301
for venue change, 256, 257

Alibi notice, 220

Anatomical charts: defense
preparation as evidence, 296

Announcement of authority and
purpose, requirement of,
before police enter building,
240

Appeal
of compulsory process issues, 293
counsel, right to, 299
of discovery issues, 314
guilty plea, denial of motion to
withdraw, 220
interlocutory review, 312-314
by prerogative writs, 312-314
of pretrial rulings, 222, 224
by prosecution, 222
of severance issues, 312
of suppression issues, 224

Argument, of pretrial motions, 221

Arraignment
counsel, right to, 220, 233
deadline for misjoinder motions,
259
postponing guilty pleas to some
charges when others will be
tried, 261

Arrest
of automobile driver or occupant,
246
challenge to legality of, 236
constitutionality of, 236
detention distinguished, 236
evidence obtained following
unlawful arrest, 236
good faith, 236
photographs, 271
postarrest custodial treatment, 237
postarrest interrogation. *See*
Interrogation
probable cause, 230, 236, 241
reports, 271

search without warrant incident to,
    230, 236, 240, 247
sham, 236
warrants. *See* Arrest warrant;
    Arrest without warrant
Arrest warrant
    affidavit for, 236, 241
    Fourth Amendment conditions for
        issuance of, 230, 236
    hearsay, use to support, 241
    home, entrance into, 230, 240
    judicial review of affidavit, 241
    known criminal averment, 241
    oral testimony as basis for, 241
    probable cause, 230, 236, 241
Arrest without warrant
    building entries and, 240
    constitutionality of, 230, 236
    hearsay, use to support, 241
    hot pursuit, 230, 240
    informer's privilege, 272
    probable cause, 230, 236, 241
    on view, 236
Attachment where witness fails to
    appear, 292, 293
Attorney's work product doctrine,
    273-A, 274
Automobiles
    arrest of driver or occupant, 246
    border search doctrine, 230, 246
    Carroll doctrine, 246
    containers found in, 236, 246, 247
    inspection of, 246
    inventory search, 246
    license-check stops, 246
    passenger compartment of vehicle,
        236, 246
    plain view doctrine, 231, 246
    privacy expectations, 246
    probable cause for search, 246
    reasonable suspicion permitting
        stop, 230, 246
    search of, 230, 236, 246
    spot-check procedures, 246
    stop of, 230, 246

surveillance of, 243
tire casts and paint scrapings from,
    248
traffic stops, 246
trunk, search of, 246
warrantless search of, 230, 236,
    246

B

Bail
    proceedings, discovery potential of,
        266
    unconstitutional denial of right to,
        as tainting evidence, 237
Ballistics tests
    reports pertaining to, 271
    slides prepared by experts, 296
    state-paid assistance, 299
Bank records: authorizing release to
    government as
    self-incrimination, 232
Beepers. *See* Electronic surveillance
Bench trial
    consolidation of bench trial and
        jury trial, 262
    defendant cannot be forced to elect
        between jury trial and fair
        trial, 255
Bench warrant, for witness arrest,
    292, 293
Bill of particulars, as discovery
    device, 267
Bind-over
    discovery potential of commitment
        and review proceedings, 266
    as triggering speedy trial rights,
        309
Body searches and extractions, 238,
    247
Body-test results, 236, 238
Booking cards or sheets, 271
Booking photographs, 271
Border searches, 230, 236, 238, 246
Breaking and entering
    announcement requirements, 240

search warrant authorizing, 240
Briefs
  on evidentiary hearing issues, 222
  trial brief, 297
Building entry. *See* Search and seizure
Business office
  Fourth Amendment protection of,
    231, 240
  rules governing search of, 240

C

Calendar control, 303
  continuances and, 304
  speedy trial plans, 303, 304
  speedy trial rights and, 306, 307,
    308
Challenges, peremptory
  disqualification of judge, 258
  number at joint trial, 264
Change of venue. *See* Venue, change
  of
Charge cards or sheets, 271
Charges
  dead-listed, as potential detainers,
    263
  dismissal of. *See* Dismissal of
    charges
  refiling of, 222
  right to counsel attaches when
    made, 233
  right to fair notice of, 270
Charging paper. *See also* Indictment;
  Information
  dismissal of, for improper venue,
    254
  joinder in, 259
  severance of charges, 260
  and speedy trial, 303, 306, 307,
    308, 309
  venue, 254
Chemical tests
  reports, 271
  self-incrimination when suspect
    forced to participate in, 232
  state-paid assistance, 299

Child molestation, physical
  examination reports of, 271
Codefendants
  confession of, admissibility against
    defendant, 260, 264
  conflict of interest as ground for
    relief from joint appointment,
    282
  criminal records of, 271
  discovery of statements of, 271
  impeachment of, 264
  interviewing, 282
  joinder. *See* Joinder
  juror reactions to, 264
  official records pertaining to, 271
  preparing to testify, 282
  relative blameworthiness of, 264
  severance. *See* Severance
  as witnesses
    for prosecution, 264
    for defense, 282
Coerced confessions, 228, 232
Commitment. *See* Bind-over
Common scheme, supporting joinder
  of charges, 259
Communications between defendant
  and counsel protected by Sixth
  Amendment, 233, 274
Complainants
  disclosure of names and
    whereabouts of, 271
  physical and psychiatric
    examinations of, 271
Complaint reports, 271
Composite drawings, 271
Compulsory process
  availability to defense and
    prosecution, 270
  constitutional rights to, 270, 286,
    299
  for defense witnesses, 285-293
  enforcing subpoenas, 292
  indigent's right to, 299
  obtaining subpoenas, 290
  and pretrial discovery rights, 270

Compulsory Process Clause, 270, 286
Conclusory affidavits, insufficient to
    support warrants, 240-A, 241
Conference
    discovery, 271
    pretrial, 220, 275-276
Confessions
    admissibility, 228, 232, 236, 237,
        251, 253
    Bruton rule, 264
    codefendant's, 260, 264
    coerced, 228, 232
    derivative evidence emanating
        from, 251
    discovery of records of, 271
    Due Process Clause and, 228
    exclusion of illegally obtained, 236,
        237, 251
    illegal detention, made during,
        236, 237
    pretrial discovery of, 271
    private party eliciting, 250
    voluntariness of, 228, 232
Confidential informant
    as source of probable cause, 241
    disclosure of name of, 273
Confinement
    conditions of, 237
    speedy trial rights and, 306, 311
Conflict of interest, and
        representation of
        codefendants, 282
Confrontation
    admissibility of codefendant's
        confession against defendant,
        264
    cross-examination as essence of
        right, 270
    and discovery, 270
    pretrial right, 270
Consolidation
    of charges, 261-263
    consent to, 261
    discovery potential of proceedings,
        266

    of jury-tried and bench-tried cases,
        262
    pretrial motion for, 220, 261-264
    of sentencing proceedings, 261
Contempt of court, when profanity
        used by witness, 280
Continuance
    application for, 304
    counsel, right to, 304
    court's discretion, 304
    fair trial rights and, 255, 304
    prejudicial publicity necessitating,
        255, 257, 304
    of pretrial hearings, 304
    of trial, 304
    pending warrant-quashing
        proceeding, 224
    when witness fails to appear, 292,
        293
Conviction
    appeal of. *See* Appeal
    impeachment use, 261, 278, 279
    prior conviction. *See* Prior
        convictions
    simultaneous convictions, 263
    successive convictions, 263
Coroner's inquest, discovery potential
        of, 266
Coroner's personnel, subpoena of,
    287
Coroner's reports, 271
Counsel, right to
    adequate time to prepare, 270
    on appeals by indigents, 299
    at arraignment, 220, 233
    body searches, 238
    and continuances, 304
    critical stages of prosecution, 233
    custody, persons in, 233
    and discovery, 270
    effective assistance of counsel, 270,
        300
    improper procedures producing
        incriminating evidence, 233
    indigents, 233, 299

initiation of adversary judicial
proceedings, 233, 237, 238
at interrogation, 232, 233, 237
investigative phase of prosecution,
233
guilty plea, 220, 233
at lineups, 233, 237
Miranda warning, 233
at physical examinations, 238
and plea withdrawal, 220
police activity, restrictions on, 227,
233, 237, 238
and police spies, 237, 249
pretrial preparation and, 270
in pretrial proceedings, 233
privacy of communications
between counsel and
defendant, 233
and protection of defendant in
investigative process, 233
and psychiatric examinations, 237,
238
Sixth Amendment, 227, 233, 237,
249, 270
state-paid assistance, 299, 300
timely appointment of counsel, 270
waiver of, 233
when right attaches, 233
and withdrawal of uncounseled
pleas, 220
Court calendars. *See* Calendar control
Crime scene reports, 271
Criminal record, discovery of, 271,
272
Cross-examination
and confrontation rights, 270
of defendant, 280
disallowance as cumulative in joint
trial, 264
dry run of, 279
of expert witnesses, 283
impeachment of witnesses. *See*
Impeachment
pretrial witness preparation for,
279, 280, 283

Sixth Amendment right, 270
Curtilage, 244
Custodial interrogation. *See*
Interrogation
Custody, and speedy trial rights, 306,
311

D

Defendant
codefendant. *See* Codefendants
criminal records of, discovery of,
271
dress for trial, 280, 281
indigent. *See* Indigents
official records pertaining to,
discovery of, 271
preparation for trial, 280
presence at trial, 280
statements, discovery of, 271
as witness. *See* Witnesses
writings by, and prosecutorial
discovery, 274
Defense
conflicting defensive theories at
joint trial, 264
evidence. *See* Evidence
investigation. *See* Defense
investigation
joint trials, effect of, 263, 264
pretrial motion raising, 222
trial preparation, 277–297
withdrawal of plea in order to
present, 220
Defense investigation
and defense discovery, 265–273-B
disclosure to prosecutor, 269, 274
equal access to prosecutor's
investigative processes, 270
state-paid, for indigent defendants,
271, 298–300
Defensive evidence. *See* Evidence
Delay. *See also* Speedy trial
appellate review of pretrial rulings
concerning, 312, 313

of arrested defendant's first
appearance before magistrate,
and exclusion of illegally
obtained evidence, 237
harm caused defendant, 306, 311
intentional versus unintentional,
311
of preliminary arraignment, 237
pretrial evidentiary hearings and,
222
pretrial procedures and, 220,
302-311
of trial date, obtaining, 275, 304
undue, remedies for, 302-311
Demand rule, in obtaining speedy
trial, 309, 311
Depositions
leave to take, 271
of material witnesses, 273
in pretrial discovery, 266, 270, 271,
273
unavailable witnesses, preserving
testimony of, 266, 273, 284
Destruction of exculpatory evidence
by prosecuting authorities, 270
Detainers, Interstate Agreement on,
310
Detention
arrest distinguished, 236
in border searches, 236, 246
evidence obtained following
unconstitutional detention,
236, 237, 247
investigative, constitutionality of,
236
of material witnesses, 271, 273,
284
of objects, 248
search warrant, incident to, 230,
236, 240
Diagrams
in suppression hearings, 253
as trial evidence, 296
Discovery
adversarial system and, 269

affidavits supporting requests, 268
appellate review of pretrial rulings,
312-314
argument for, 269-270
authorities discussing, 268
bail hearings, discovery potential
of, 266
balance of forces between accused
and accuser, 270
bill of particulars, 267
Brady doctrine, 270
checklist of self-help devices, 266
checklist of formal procedures, 271
classifying items in discovery
requests, 268
complainants, 271
concealment of evidence
impeaching prosecution
testimony, 270
conference, 271
confrontation right and, 270
consolidation motions, discovery
potential of, 266
constitutional concerns, 270, 300
coroner's inquest, discovery
potential of, 266
court-ordered, 265, 268, 271
danger of defendant's misbehavior
as argument for denying, 269
by defense, generally, 265-271
of defense experts' reports, 283
defense investigation information,
269
defensive evidence and, 270
depositions, 266, 268, 271, 284
discretion of court permitting, 265
discussions with prosecutor and
police, 266
double jeopardy pleas, discovery
potential of, 266
drafting discovery motions, 268
effective assistance of counsel and,
270
exclusionary sanction, 274
exculpatory evidence, 270

fingerprint evidence, 270
fishing expeditions, 268
freedom of information laws, 266
fundamental fairness and, 270
generic sorts of information, 268
government informer's identity, 273
governmental privilege, generally, 273-B
grand jury transcripts, 266, 270, 271, 272
habeas corpus, discovery potential of, 266
identification aids, 271
impeachment evidence, 270
indigent defendants, 266, 270, 271, 300
informal discovery, 271
of informer's identity, 273
informer's privilege, 273
interrogatories, 271
lineup materials, 270, 271
list of witnesses, 267
materiality requirement, 268, 270, 271
medical and scientific reports and records, 271
motions hearings, discovery potential of, 222, 266
notice of charges and, 270
physical objects, 270, 271
police and investigative reports, 271
preliminary hearing, discovery potential of, 266
pretrial motions for, 220, 265–271
by prosecution, 274
prosecutorial suppression of evidence favorable to defense, 270
protective orders, 274
reciprocal disclosure, 274
records of prosecution witnesses, 270, 271, 272
relevance of requested material, 268, 270, 271

requests sent to prosecutor, 268, 271
sample request for material, 268
self-incrimination privilege and prosecutorial, 269, 274
self-operating, 265
severance motions, discovery potential of, 260, 266
specificity of requests, 268, 269, 270, 271
strategy, 268, 269, 271
suppression motions, discovery potential of, 224, 266
at trial, 272
undercover agents, 271, 273
witnesses, 271
witness intimidation as argument against, 269
work product doctrine, 273-A, 274
Dismissal of charges, 222
Interstate Agreement on Detainers, 310
speedy trial rights and, 306, 308, 309, 310, 311
on venue grounds, 254
Dismissal of prosecution
speedy trial rights and, 306, 308, 309, 310, 311
when state-paid assistance unavailable, 301
Dismissal for want of prosecution, 308
Docket control, 308
Documents. See Writings
Double jeopardy
attachment of jeopardy, 222
discovery potential of motion, 266
prosecutorial appeals, 222
Due Process Clause
balance of forces between accused and accuser, 270
coerced confessions, 228
compulsory process, 286
and discovery by defense, 270, 300
fair trial right, 270, 300, 311

police activity, restrictions upon,
227, 228
police brutality, 228
speedy trial, 311
state-paid assistance, 300

E

Eavesdropping. *See* Electronic
surveillance
Electronic surveillance, 231, 243,
245, 249
bugged informers, 245, 249
derivative evidence, 251
Fourth Amendment restrictions on,
231, 243, 245
of intimate activities, 242, 243
nontrespassory, 243
probable cause, 243
as search, 231, 243
standing to complain of unlawful
surveillance, 240, 242, 245,
251
of temporary occupant of public
place, 242, 243
trespassory, 231, 240, 243
warrantless eavesdropping, 243
wiretapping. *See* Wiretapping
Employment records, discovery of,
271
Entry into building as Fourth
Amendment search, 231, 240
Equal Protection Clause
and compulsory process, 286
and discovery, 270
indigent defendants, 299
police activity, restrictions upon,
227
right to free transcripts, 266, 299
and state-paid assistance, 299
Evidence
anticipation of problems, 275
balance of forces between accused
and accuser, 270
chain of custody, 294

concealment of, by prosecuting
authorities, 270
cumulation of, at joint trial, 263
defensive
exclusion of, as discovery
sanction, 274
prosecutorial disclosure of
exculpatory, 270
prosecutorial discovery of, 274
rebutting illegally obtained
evidence, 253-A
right to present, 270
speedy trial rights and, 306
testimony by defendant, timing
of, 274, 280
derivative, 251
destruction of material evidence,
270
deviation from prescribed
procedures for handling or
examining, 271
exclusionary rule. *See* Exclusionary
rule
exculpatory, 270, 300
guilty plea as, 220
identification, 233, 251
illegally obtained, 223–253-A
arrest, accosting, or stopping
unlawful, 235, 236
authorities discussing, 226
body searches and extractions,
238
body-test results, 236
conditions giving rise to claim of
illegality, 234–250
confessions, 228, 232, 233, 236
connection of evidence to
substantive violation, 225
consent improperly obtained,
236, 240
defensive evidence rebutting,
253-A
derivative evidence, 251
detention, illegal, 236, 237

discovery potential of
suppression proceedings, 224,
266
electronic surveillance evidence,
231, 243, 245
exclusionary rule. *See*
Exclusionary rule
fingerprint exemplars, 236
flagrancy principle, 251
hearsay used in suppression
hearings, 253
impeachment use, 223, 251
indictment or information,
motion to quash, 224
infringement of defendant's own
interests, 225, 240, 242, 243,
245, 246, 248
invalid warrant, 240, 240-A, 241
issues raised by objection to, 225
joint trial, use of evidence at,
264
lineup identifications, 233, 236,
237, 251
methods of objection to, 224
motions for suppression of, 220,
223–253-A, 266
objection to admission of, 223,
224
observations following police
illegality, 236,240
physical evidence seized
at arrest, 230, 236
in search, 229–231, 236–238,
240–242, 246–248
physical examinations, 238
postarrest custodial treatment,
237
premises with more than
transitory connections, 240
pretrial motions to suppress and
for return of, 224, 252, 253,
266
probable cause determination
and, 241
quashing indictments, 224

quashing search warrants, 224
return of seized items, 224
search and seizure, 223–231,
234–253-A
standing, 225, 240, 242, 243,
245, 246, 248
subpoena-compelled testimony,
239
suppression of, 220, 223–253-A,
266
trial, objection to admission or
motion to exclude at, 224
unconstitutional arrest,
accosting, or stopping, 235,
236
immunity grants and derivative,
251
impeachment. *See* Impeachment
inadmissible
effect of joint trial, 264
motion *in limine* to forbid use of,
222, 224
news reports disclosing, 255, 256
pretrial conference, raising
evidentiary issues at, 275
notice of intention to present, 220
photographs, 296
physical
preparation of, 294
subpoena duces tecum, 294
tests on, 295
police activity. *See* Police
prejudicial, motions *in limine* to
forbid use of, 222
prescreening through discovery,
269
real, preparation of, 294–295
relevancy of, 222
search and seizure. *See* Search and
seizure
state's power to gather and
preserve, 269
suppression of exculpatory, right
against, 270
tags, 271

Evidentiary hearings
  of pretrial motions, 221, 222
  pretrial discovery and, 222
Exclusionary rule, 223–253-A
  arrest, accosting, or stopping
    unlawful, 235, 236
  Due Process Clause, 227, 228
  Equal Protection Clause, 227
  exceptions to, 223, 225, 240-A,
    251, 253
  Fifth Amendment rights, 227,
    232–233, 250, 251
  Fourth Amendment rights,
    227–231, 234–250
  invalid warrant as grounds, 223,
    240-A
  postarrest custodial treatment and,
    237–238
  search and seizure, 223–253-A
  Sixth Amendment rights, 227, 233,
    251
  standing, 225, 240, 242, 243, 245,
    246, 248
  state and federal constitutional
    guarantees as basis of claims,
    227
Exculpatory evidence
  prosecutor's duty to disclose, 270
  state-paid assistance, 300
Exhibit file, 297
Exhibits, pretrial conference and, 275
Expert witnesses. *See* Witnesses
Extradition, 310
Eyewitness
  discovery of photographs shown to,
    271, 272
  drawings and sketches from
    descriptions of, 271
  identification reports, 271

F

Fair trial
  as basis for continuance request,
    304
  Due Process Clause, 270, 300, 311
reciprocity in preparation of
    evidentiary case and, 270
  speedy trial rights and, 311
  venue change for inability to
    obtain, 255–257
Federal habeas corpus
  to enforce speedy trial rights, 311
  waiver, by failure to specify claims
    of error, 222
Fees, right of indigent to proceed
    without paying, 298–301
Fifth Amendment. *See* Double
    jeopardy; Self-incrimination
Fingerprint tests
  availability of results to defense
    and prosecution, 270
  illegally obtained exemplars, 236
  slides of prints, defense preparation
    as evidence, 296
Firefighting officials, warrantless
    building entries by, 240
Fourteenth Amendment. *See* Due
    Process Clause; Equal
    Protection Clause
Fourth Amendment, 229–231,
    234–253
  arrest, 230, 236, 240
  automobile searches and stops,
    230, 236, 246
  building searches and entries, 229,
    230, 240, 242
  body searches, 236, 237, 238, 247
  curtilage, 244
  derivative evidence, 251
  effects, search and seizure of, 247,
    248
  electronic surveillance, 243, 245
  general reasonableness theory, 229
  index of fact situations raising
    issues, 234
  index of issues, 225
  informers and police spies, 249
  open fields, 244
  personal property, search and
    seizure of, 247, 248

plain view, 231, 240, 246, 248
police activity, restriction upon, 227
preference for warrant, 229, 240, 241, 246
privacy issues, 231
stop and frisk, 236
summary of doctrine, 230–231
taint, 251, 253
warrant theory, 229
wiretapping, 243, 245
Freedom of information laws, 266

G

Gag orders, 274
Governmental privilege, 273-B
Government offices, search of, 230, 240, 242
Grand jury proceedings
impeachment of trial witness with grand jury testimony, 271
secrecy of, 271
transcript of. *See* Grand jury transcript
Grand jury transcript, defense discovery of
at trial, 271, 272
before trial, 266, 271
Grounds, search of, 244

H

Habeas corpus
challenging arrest, 266
challenging bindover, 266
discovery potential, 266
federal. *See* Federal habeas corpus
Habeas corpus ad testificandum, 285
Handwriting tests
availability of results to defense and prosecution, 270
right to counsel when exemplars taken, 233
self-incrimination, exemplars as, 232

Hearings, evidentiary, of pretrial motions, 221, 222
Hearsay
admissibility of codefendant's confession against defendant, 264
as probable cause for warrant, 241
at suppression hearings, 253
Helicopter surveillance, 231, 243, 244
Homicide cases, discovery in, 271
Hospital records, discovery of, 271

I

Identification procedures, counsel's presence at, 233, 237
Illegally obtained evidence. *See* Evidence
Immunity grant, derivative evidence issues, 251
Immunity statutes, 232
Impeachment
of affidavit for warrant, 241
of the defendant, 253, 280
defensive discovery at trial, 272
delaying guilty plea to prevent conviction being used for, 261
discovery of prior convictions useful for, 270, 272
discovery of prior statements useful for, 272
evidence, concealment of, 270
expert witness's report used for, 283
grand jury testimony used for, 271, 272
illegally obtained evidence used for, 223
photographs used for, 272
preliminary hearing transcript used for, 222
pretrial evidentiary hearings and, 222
preparation of witnesses to avoid, 278–280, 283

prior convictions used for, 264, 278, 279

prior testimony used for, 266, 272

of prosecution testimony, 270

prosecutorial duty to disclose evidence useful for, 270

In limine motions, 222, 224

Incest cases, physical examination reports in, 271

Indictment

discovery potential of motions to quash, 266

dismissal for misjoinder, 259

dismissal for wrong venue, 254

motion to dismiss, disclosure of grand jury minutes to support, 271

motion to quash, 224, 266

time of presenting bill to grand jury, 303

time for filing, 309

waiver of, 305

witnesses' names endorsed on, 266

Indigents

compulsory process, right to, 286, 301

counsel, right to, 233, 299, 300

defense psychiatric expert, right to, 299

discovery rights of, 266, 270, 271, 300

expert consultants, right to, 299

investigative assistance, right to, 271, 298–300

state-paid assistance availability of, 298

Due Process Clause, 300

Equal Protection Clause, 299

investigative assistance, 271, 298-301

motion for dismissal where not available, 301

procedures for requesting, 301

recoupment provisions, 298

transcriptions at public expense, 266, 299

Information

motion to quash, 224

time for filing, 303, 309

Informers and police spies

bugged, 245, 249

disclosure of names and whereabouts of, 271, 273

discovery of records of police and prosecutorial transactions with, 271

entries by, 249

Fourth Amendment restrictions on, 249

incriminating statements elicited by, 233, 237, 249

informer's privilege, 273

missing-witness instruction, 289

probable cause provided by, 241

right to counsel violated by 233, 237, 249

Insanity notice, 220

Instructions to jury. *See* Jury instructions

Interlocutory review

of pretrial orders, 222, 312–314

pretrial suppression motion, 224

Interrogation

counsel, right to, 233, 237

detention for, 236

discovery of audiotapes and videotapes of, 271

discovery of records of, 271

Due Process limitations on, 227, 228

right to counsel during, 233, 237

Interrogatories, to prosecutor, 271

Interstate Agreement on Detainers, 310

Intimate activities, surveillance of, 242

Investigation, defense. *See* Defense investigation

J

Jail records, discovery of, 271
Jails, searches in, 230, 231, 238, 242, 247
Joinder, 259–264
  of jury-tried and bench-tried cases, 262
  misjoinder, 259, 260
  of more than one defendant, 259, 264
  of more than one offense, 259, 263
  motion for mistrial when allegations supporting joinder are not proved, 259
  prejudicial, 259, 260
  severance, 260
Joint trials, 260–264
Judges
  bench trial. *See* Bench trial
  disqualification of, 220, 258
  peremptory challenge to, 258
  pretrial conference and, 275–276
  pretrial motions listing and, 222
  recusal, 258
  selection of, 220, 222
Jurisdiction, lack of, 313
Jurors
  bias, 255–257
  boring or irritating, dangers of, 222
  challenge to venire of, 220, 257
  cumulation of evidence, effect of, 263
  discovery of prosecutor's records of investigations relating to, 271
  homogeneity of, 255
  hostility of, as ground for venue change, 255–257
  inflammatory publicity, 255–257
  investigation of, 220
  overcharging, effect on, 263
  panel, challenge to, 257
  prejudicial publicity, 255–257
  racial and social classes of, 255
  sentencing by. *See* Sentencing
  sequestration of, prejudicial publicity and, 255, 257
  venire of, challenges to, 220, 257
  venue change for inability to empanel impartial, 255–257
  voir dire examination. *See* Voir dire examination of jurors
Jury instructions
  admissibility of codefendant's confession against defendant, 264
  proposed, in trial brief, 297
Jury trial
  consolidation of bench-tried and jury-tried cases, 262
  election of, 220
  preparation for, 277–297
  waiver of right to, 305
  prejudicial publicity and, 255
  severance of charges and, 262

L

Laboratory personnel, subpoena of, 287
Lesser included offense verdict and jury's assessment of relative blameworthiness of codefendants, 264
Lie detector tests, 238
Lineups
  availability to defense as well as prosecution, 270
  discovery of materials relating to, 270, 271
  during illegal arrest or detention, 236
  right to counsel at, 233, 237
Lockup
  logs, discovery of, 271
  search in, 230, 231, 238, 242, 247

M

Magistrate's finding of probable cause. *See* Probable cause
Mail, search of, 230, 248

Mandamus, writ of, 313, 314
Maps, defense preparation as
    evidence, 296
Material witnesses, 271, 273, 284
Medical examinations. *See* Medical
    records and reports; Physical
    examinations; Psychiatric
    examinations
Medical examiner's reports, discovery
    of, 271
Medical records and reports
    motions for production or
        inspection of, 271
    physical examination reports,
        discovery of, 271
    victim injury reports, discovery of,
        271
Mental examination. *See* Psychiatric
    examination
Misdemeanor procedure: warrantless
    arrests, 236
Misjoinder. *See* Joinder
Mistrial
    when allegations supporting joinder
        are not proved, 259
    for unpreparedness because of
        denial of adequate discovery,
        271
Motions
    affidavits in support of, 222
    for consolidation, 220, 261–264
    for a continuance, 304
    for discovery, 220, 265–273
    evidentiary hearing of, 222
    in limine, 222, 224
    oral, 222
    pretrial, generally, 220–222
    for recusation of a judge, 258
    for severance, 220, 259–264
    for speedy trial, 306–311
    for state-paid assistance, 298–301
    for suppression of illegally obtained
        evidence, 220, 223–253-A,
        266
    for venue change, 255–257

written, 221, 222
Mug shots, discovery of, 271

N

Narcotics cases
    dogs trained to detect drugs, 248
    illegally obtained evidence in, 224
    investigation reports, discovery of,
        271
    police barbarism in extracting
        evidence, 228
News conferences, supporting change
    of venue, 256
News reporting
    supporting change of venue, 255,
        256
    subpoena of news media, 256
911 calls, discovery of, 271
No-knock statutes, 240
Notice
    of alibi, 220
    of charges, 270
    of insanity, 220
    of pretrial motions, 220, 221
    right to fair, 270

O

Objections
    to admission of illegally obtained
        evidence, 223, 224
    anticipatory, to prosecution
        evidence, 275
    to misjoinder, 259
    pretrial conference and, 275
    pretrial motion compared to, 222
    to venue, 254
Obscene materials, seizure of, 240
Obscenity cases, illegally obtained
    evidence in, 224
Opinion polls, prejudicial publicity
    and, 256
Outbuildings, search of, 244

P

Panel, challenge to, 257

Papers. *See* Writings

Paraffin test reports, discovery of, 271

Parole records, discovery of, 271

Passersby, summoning of, to prove local bias supporting change of venue, 256

Pat-downs, 229, 230, 236

Pathologist's tests, state-paid assistance and, 299

Perjury
right against prosecutive presentation of, 270
in warrant affidavit, as invalidating warrant, 240-A, 241

Petitions, proof of, supporting change of venue, 256

Photographs
admissibility of, 296
arrest, discovery of, 271
booking, discovery of, 271
defense preparation as evidence, 296
discovery at trial, 272
of physical evidence, 294
right to counsel at photographic identification, 233
shown to witnesses, discovery of, 271

Physical examinations
of complainants, 271
illegally obtained evidence derived from, 236, 238
of prosecution witnesses, 271
reports, discovery of, 271
right to counsel, at, 233, 238

Physical objects
defense preparation as evidence, 294–295
derived from illegally obtained confession, 251
derived from illegal search and seizure, 251, 253

forensic testing of, 271
motions for production or inspection of, 271
search and seizure of, 230, 231, 236, 237, 238, 240, 247, 248, 250

Physicians, subpoena of, 287

"Plain view" doctrine, 231, 243, 246, 247

Plea negotiations
discovery potential of, 266
police embarrassment forcing acceptance of, 223
pretrial conference and, 275
pretrial motion forum, use of, 222

Pleas
bargaining. *See* Plea negotiations
denial of counsel at plea, 220, 233
discovery potential of plea negotiations, 266
guilty
consolidation of charges for disposition following, 261
motion for leave to withdraw, 220
motion to vacate, 220
speeding up disposition by, 305
vacation of, 220
venue change and, 255
withdrawal of, 220
ineffective assistance of counsel as invalidating, 220
involuntariness of, 220
lack of understanding, 220
negotiations. *See* Plea negotiations
not guilty, motion for leave to withdraw, 220
prearraignment motions waived by, 220
special, motion for leave to file, 220
validity of, 220
withdrawal of, 220

Police
  academy training materials,
      discovery of, 271
  brutality, 228, 237, 238
  discovery, discussions in aid of, 266
  dispatch bootstrap, 241
  evidence gathering by, 269
  hearsay information used by, 241
  manuals, discovery of, 271
  on-the-street detentions by, 230,
      236
  operations manuals, discovery of,
      271
  phone and radio communication
      tapes, discovery of, 271
  private party's aid solicited by, 250
  regulations, discovery of, 271
  reports, discovery of, 271
  restrictions upon activity
      connection of challengeable
          evidence to substantive
          violation, 225, 236, 237, 241,
          251
      Due Process Clause, 227, 228
      Equal Protection Clause, 227
      exclusionary sanctions, 223, 225,
          227, 251, 253
      Fifth Amendment, 227, 232–233
      Fourth Amendment, 227,
          228–231, 234–250
      infringement of defendant's own
          interests, 225, 240, 242, 243,
          245, 246, 248
      Sixth Amendment, 227, 233,
          249
  spies. *See* Informers and police
      spies
  witnesses, at suppression hearing,
      253
Police artists' sketches, discovery of,
    271
Polygraph tests, 238
Postarraignment procedures: checklist
    of defensive procedures, 220

Prearraignment motions, waived by
    plea, 220
Precinct logs, discovery of, 271
Prejudicial joinder, 259, 260
Prejudicial material, pretrial motions
    to keep from jury, 222
Prejudicial publicity, 255, 256, 257
  continuance due to, 255, 257, 304
Preliminary arraignment, undue
    delay of, 237
Preliminary hearing
  counsel, right to, 233
  discovery potential of, 266
  waiver of, 305
Prerogative writs, 222, 312, 313, 314
Pretrial conference, 275–276
Pretrial orders, interlocutory review
    of, 312–314
Pretrial procedure
  appellate review of adverse rulings,
      222, 312–314
  change of venue, motion for, 220,
      254–257
  conference, 220, 275–276
  consolidation, motion for, 220,
      261–264
  continuances of hearings, 304
  counsel, right to, 233, 270
  defenses raised by pretrial motion,
      222
  delay issues, 220, 302–311
  discovery proceedings, 220,
      265–274
  effective assistance of counsel
      during, 233, 270
  judge, disqualification of, motion
      for, 220, 258
  jury trial, election of, 220
  motions
      checklist of, 220
      generally, 221–222
      oral, 222
      written, 221, 222
  notices required, 220

plea, withdrawal of, motion for, 220

prospective jurors, investigation of, 220

severance, motion for, 220, 259–264

speedy trial rights and, 309, 311

subpoenas duces tecum, 291

suppression motions, 220, 223–253-A

venire of petit jurors, challenge to, 220

Prior convictions
impeachment of codefendant, 264
impeachment of defense witness, 278, 279

Prior statements, discovery at trial, 272

Prison
records, discovery of, 271
searches in, 231, 242, 247
witness confined in, 285

Privacy
abandoned objects, 248
automobiles, 246
communications between counsel and defendant, 233
property in possession of arrested person, 238, 240, 247
search and seizure, 231, 242, 243, 244, 246, 247, 248
surveillance of intimate activities, 242

Private individuals, investigative activity by, 250

Privilege against self-incrimination. *See* Self-incrimination

Probable cause
for arrest, 230, 236, 241
for electronic surveillance, 241, 243
generally, 241
hearsay and, 241
informers, 241
for search and seizure, 230, 240, 241, 243, 246

tainted evidence as, 241
for wiretapping, 243

Probationer's homes, warrantless search of, 240

Probation records, discovery of, 271

Production, pretrial motion for, 220

Prohibition, writ of, 313, 314

Proof, failure of on joinder issues, 259

Property inventories, discovery of, 271

Prosecutor
discovery potential of discussions with, 266
discovery requests to, 268, 271
evidence gathering by, 269
notice of pretrial motion served on, 221
venue choice, 254

Protective orders, in discovery practice, 274

Psychiatric examinations
of complainants, discovery of, 271
for indigent defendants, 299
interlocutory review of pretrial orders connected with, 313
of prosecution witnesses, discovery of, 271
right to counsel, 233, 238
self-incrimination, 232
state-paid, for indigent defendants, 299

Psychiatrist, subpoena of, 287

Public expense. *See* Indigents

Public opinion
prejudicial publicity and, 255–257
venue change and, 255–257

Publicity, prejudicial, 255, 256, 257, 304

R

Rape cases, discovery of physical examination reports in, 271

Reasonable cause, as ground for opening mail, 248

Reasonable suspicion
  permitting automobile stop, 230,
    246
  permitting stop and frisk, 230,
    236, 246
Recidivist statutes, applicability to
    simultaneous convictions, 263
Recoupment, 298
Recusation motion, 258
Review, interlocutory. *See*
    Interlocutory review
Reporters. *See* News conferences;
    News reporting
Right to counsel. *See* Counsel, right
    to
Rule on witnesses, 253, 280

S

Sanity of defendant. *See* Insanity
    notice; Psychiatric
    examinations
Schoolchildren, searches of, 230, 231,
    240, 247
Scientific tests
  availability to defense as well as
    prosecution, 270
  ballistics tests. *See* Ballistics tests
  body searches and extractions, 236,
    237, 238, 247
  body tests, 236, 238
  chemical tests. *See* Chemical tests
  destruction of material evidence by
    prosecuting authorities, 270
  forensic expert's reports, discovery
    of, 271
  motions for production or
    inspection of, 270, 271
  paraffin tests, discovery of, 271
  right to counsel in connection with,
    233, 237, 238
  self-incrimination when defendant
    forced to participate in, 232
  serology reports, discovery of, 271
  state-paid assistance, 299–300

Search and seizure, 233–253-A
  abandoned objects, 231, 248
  administrative search, 230, 240,
    246
  arrest, accosting, or stopping, 230,
    235, 236
  arrest, search incident to, 230, 240,
    246, 247
  automobiles, 230, 236, 246
  body searches and extractions, 236,
    237, 238, 247
  border cases, 230, 236, 238, 246
  building searches and entries, 229,
    230, 240, 242
  business offices, 231, 240
  closed containers, 230, 248
  clothing searches, 237, 238, 247
  consent, 230, 236, 240, 247
  curtilage, 244
  definition of search, 231
  definition of seizure
    of effects, 248
    of persons, 236
  derivative evidence, 251
  detention, 236
  "dropsie" problem, 247
  due process restrictions on, 227,
    228
  effects, 247, 248
  electronic surveillance. *See*
    Electronic surveillance
  exclusionary rule. *See* Exclusionary
    rule
  Fourth Amendment restrictions,
    227, 228–231, 234–250
  grounds, 244
  hot pursuit, 230, 240
  illegally obtained evidence. *See*
    Evidence
  index of fact situations raising
    issues, 234
  index of issues, 225
  informers, 241, 245, 248, 249, 273
  inventory search, 230, 238, 246,
    247

jails and prisons, 231, 242, 247
luggage in transit, 230, 231, 247, 248
mail, 230, 248
manner of building entry, 240
mobile containers, 230, 248
narcotics detection dogs, 248
objects, 230, 231, 236, 238, 240, 247, 248
obscene materials, 240
open fields, 244
outbuildings, 244
pat-downs, 229, 230, 236
personal property, 247, 248
personal security, liberty and dignity, 231
persons, 230, 231, 240, 242
plain view doctrine, 231, 240, 243, 246, 248
police discretion, 238, 240, 246
preference for warrant, 229, 240, 241, 246
premises, 230, 240, 242
privacy issues, 231, 242, 243, 247
private individuals, 250
probable cause, 230, 236, 240, 241, 246
public places, 242
record subpoenas, 239
regulated industries, 230, 240
schoolchildren, 230, 231, 240, 247
searchlights and binoculars, 231
Sixth Amendment restrictions, 227, 233, 249
stop and frisk, 229, 230, 236, 246
subpoena-compelled testimony, 239
surveillance, 231, 243, 245, 249
surface inspections of objects, 248
trespass on vacant lands, 231, 244
visual observation, 231, 243
warrants. See Search warrant; Search without warrant
wiretapping. See Wiretapping
yards, 244

Search warrant
administrative searches, 230, 240, 246
affidavits, 240, 240-A, 241
detention of occupants of premises, 230, 236, 240
exceptions to requirement, 229, 230, 240
Fourth Amendment conditions for issuance of, 229, 230, 240
hearsay, use of, 241
houses, 230, 240
invalid warrant, 223, 240, 240-A
judicial review of affidavit, 240-A, 241
known criminal averment, 241
manner of building entry, 240
no-knock warrant, 240
oral testimony in issuance of, 241
person issuing, 240
probable cause, 230, 240, 241
proceedings to quash, 224
specificity of, 230, 240
validity of, 240
Search without warrant
arrest and, 230, 236, 238, 240, 246, 247
automobiles, 230, 246
border cases, 230, 246, 248
buildings, 230, 240, 248
closed containers, 247, 248
consent, 230, 240, 247
evanescent evidence, 230, 236, 238
exceptional circumstances justifying building entry, 230, 240
exigent circumstances, 230, 240
government employees' offices, 230, 240, 242
hot pursuit, 230, 240
inventory search, 230, 238, 246
probable cause, 230, 240, 241
regulated industries cases, 230, 240
schoolchildren, 230, 231, 240, 247
stipulation as to warrantless search, 253

Self-incrimination, 227, 232, 233, 238, 239, 251, 274
communications or testimony, 232
compelled production of documents, 274
compulsion, presence of, 232, 250, 274
discovery, lack of reciprocity as argument against, 269, 274
Miranda warnings, 232–233
natural persons, privilege limited to, 232
person against whom compulsion directed, 232
private party, coercive conduct by, 250
prosecutorial discovery and, 269, 274
and psychiatric examination of the defendant, 232, 238
real or physical evidence, 232
realistic threat of incrimination, 232
state-paid assistance, disclosures necessary to obtain, 301
summary of doctrine, 232
testimonial and nontestimonial compulsion, 232
Sentencing
of codefendants who turn state's evidence, 264
consolidation of cases for, 261
on multiple charges, 263
plea withdrawal, different standards before and after, 220
recidivist statutes, applicability to simultaneous convictions, 263
relative blameworthiness of codefendants and, 264
simultaneous convictions, 263
successive convictions, 263
Sequestration of jurors, prejudicial publicity and, 255, 257
Serology reports, discovery of, 271

Severance
appellate review of decisions relating to, 312–314
discovery potential of proceedings, 260, 266
jury trial waiver and, 262
prejudicial joinder as grounds, 260
pretrial motion for, 220, 259–264
time-saving considerations, 260
trial, motion made during, 260
Sexual assault cases, discovery of physical examination reports in, 271
Showup, counsel present at, 233, 237, 238
Sidebar proceedings, pretrial motions and, 222
Sixth Amendment. *See* Confrontation; Counsel, right to; Jury trial; Speedy trial
Social work agency records, discovery of, 271
Speedy trial
calendar control and, 307, 308
demand rule, 308, 309, 311
Due Process Clause and, 311
fair trial rights and, 311
habeas corpus proceedings and, 311
inherent power of the court to assure, 308
interlocutory review of pretrial orders relating to, 313–314
Interstate Agreement on Detainers, 310
joint trial and, 263
prejudicial publicity and, 255
pretrial stages, time allotted for, 309
remedies for violation, 306, 308, 309, 311
rights, generally, 306–311
Sixth Amendment right to, 311
sources of rights, 307
statutes, 309, 310

time right attaches, 309, 311
tolling of right, 309, 311
two-term statutes, 309, 311
waiver of right to, 255
Speedy Trial Clause, 311
Speedy trial plan, 303
Standing to object to illegally
    obtained evidence, 225, 240,
    242, 243, 245, 246, 248
State-paid assistance. *See* Indigents
Stenographer, pretrial motions and
    presence of, 222
Stipulation
    authenticity of news clippings,
        tapes or scripts, 256
    consolidation ordered on, 261
    joinder permitted by, 259
    pretrial conference and, 275
    warrantless search, 253
Stop and frisk, 229, 230, 236, 246
Stopping defendant. *See* Detention
Subpoenas
    copies of, in trial brief, 297
    for defense witnesses, 266, 285–293
    duces tecum, 239, 291
    to news media to prove prejudicial
        publicity, 256
    for physical evidence, 294
    enforcement of, 292
    exclusion of illegally compelled
        testimony, 239
    in forma pauperis, 286
    missing-witness charge and,
        288–289
    persons subject to, 287
    procedure for obtaining, 290
    quashing, 290
    refusal of court to issue, 293
    right to compulsory process, 286
    self-incrimination and
        subpoena-compelled testimony,
        239
    service of, 288
Summoning passersby, 256

Suppress, motion to. *See* Electronic
    surveillance; Evidence,
    illegally obtained;
    Exclusionary rule; Fourth
    Amendment; Search and
    seizure; Search warrant;
    Search without warrant
Suppression hearing, 253–253-A
Supreme Court review, written
    motions and, 222
Surveillance. *See* Electronic
    surveillance

T

Telephone wiretapping. *See*
    Wiretapping
Terms of court, 302
Transcripts
    grand jury proceedings, 266, 270,
        271, 272
    magistrate's, motion to quash, 224
    motions for transcription of any
        untranscribed prior
        proceedings, 271
    state-paid, 266, 299
    trial, state-paid, 299
Trespass to conduct search, 231
Trial
    bench trial. *See* Bench trial
    continuance of, 304
    date, 303
    delay. *See* Delay
    demand rule, 308, 309, 311
    fair. *See* Fair trial
    joint trials, 260, 263, 264
    jury. *See* Jury trial
    speedy. *See* Speedy trial
    transcripts, 299
Trial folder or brief, preparation of,
    297
Trial preparation, 277–297
    indigent defendants, 299
Truth serums, 238

U

Undercover agents. *See* Informers and police spies

V

Venire of jurors, challenge to, 220, 257
Venue
    allegation in charging paper, 254
    change of. *See* Venue, change of
    initial, 254
Venue, change of
    appellate review of decisions relating to, 312–314
    for convenience of parties and witnesses, 255
    fair trial rights and, 255–257
    grounds for, 255
    motion for, 220, 254–257
    new location at court's discretion, 255
    objections by defendant to, 254
    pretrial motion for, 256
    prosecution seeking, 254
    voir dire examination and, 255–257
Victim injury reports, discovery of, 271
Visual aids shown to witnesses, discovery of, 271
Voice tests
    availability of results to defense as well as prosecution, 270
    compulsion to speak as self-incrimination, 232
Voir dire examination of jurors: prejudicial publicity and, 255–257

W

Waivers, to speed up disposition, 305
Warrantless arrest. *See* Arrest without warrant
Warrantless search. *See* Search without warrant

Weapons pat-downs. *See* Stop and frisk
Wiretapping
    bugged informers, 245, 249
    derivative evidence, 251
    Fourth Amendment restrictions, 243, 245
    pen register, 245
    probable cause, 243
    standing to complain of unlawful wiretap, 245
    warrantless tapping, 243, 245
Witnesses
    accomplices as, 282
    adverse
        pretrial discovery of, 270
        right to confront, 270
    arrest for failure to appear when subpoenaed, 292
    compulsory process. *See* Compulsory process
    criminal records, discovery of, 271, 272
    cross-examination of. *See* Cross-examination
    defendant as
        dress for trial, 280, 281
        dry run of testimony, 279–280
        language used by defendant, 280
        multiple charges and, 263
        preparing to testify, 279–281
        at suppression hearing, 253
        timing of testimony, 274, 280
    defense
        compulsory process to obtain, 285–293
        dry run of examination, 279
        explanation of role to, 279
        flight of, 284
        interview of, 278
        keeping track of, 284
        missing-witness charge, 288
        preparing to testify, 279
        with prior convictions, 279

right to compulsory process to obtain, 270, 286

right to present, 270

selection of, 278

subpoena of, 285–293

unavailable, 284

depositions. *See* Depositions

detention of material witnesses, 271, 273, 284

discovery of names and whereabouts of, 271

expert

education of counsel by, 283

preparing to testify, 283

public opinion experts, 256

report prepared by, 283

subpoena of, 287

grand jury, identification of, 266

hostile, 253, 284

impeachment of. *See* Impeachment

intimidation of, as argument against discovery, 269

Jencks Act statements, 272

list of, 267

material witnesses, detention of, 271, 273, 284

missing-witness charge, 275, 288–289

official records pertaining to, 271

orders that witnesses talk to defense, 271

perjured testimony. *See* Perjury

physical or psychiatric examination of, 271

police witnesses, credibility of, 271

prior statements made by, 272

prosecution, and missing-witness charge, 289

statements of, discovery of, 271

subponeas. *See* Subpoenas

suppression hearings, 253

unavailable, depositions to preserve testimony of, 266, 284

venue change and, 255

Work product doctrine, 273-A, 274

Writings

expert's report, 283

preexisting, denied Self-Incrimination Clause protection, 232

prosecutorial discovery of, 274

questioned documents, 299

subpoenas duces tecum for, 291

subpoenas seeking records from the defendant, 239

taking from defendant, 247

Y

Yards, search of, 244